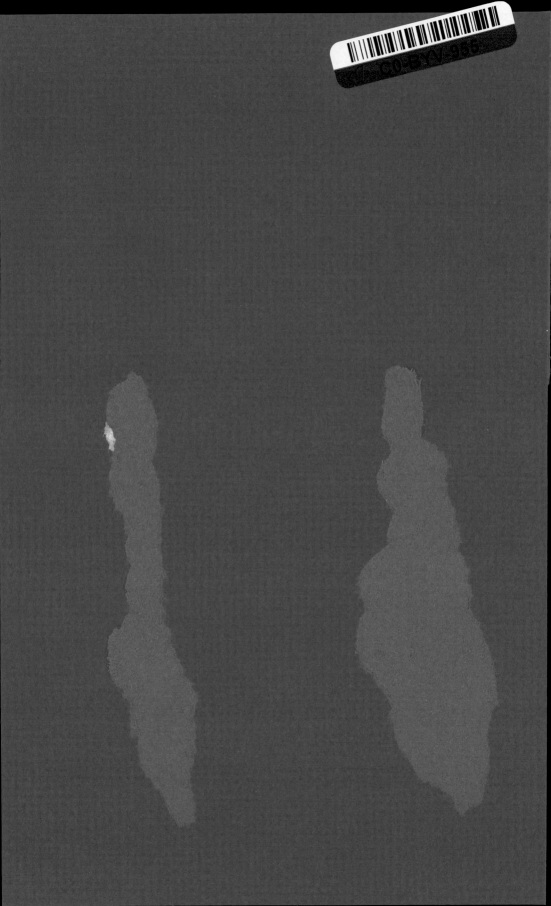

CYRUS ADLER
SELECTED LETTERS

THE   PUBLICATION   OF   THIS   BOOK   WAS   MADE

POSSIBLE   BY   A   GIFT   IN   MEMORY   OF

ADELE   SINGER   RIFKIND   1901   –   1984

קָמוּ בָנֶיהָ וַיְאַשְּׁרוּהָ
בַּעְלָהּ וַיְהַלְלָהּ:

Proverbs 31:28

CYRUS ADLER

SELECTED LETTERS

VOLUME TWO

EDITED BY IRA ROBINSON

PREFACE BY LOUIS FINKELSTEIN
INTRODUCTION BY NAOMI W. COHEN

THE JEWISH PUBLICATION SOCIETY OF AMERICA
THE JEWISH THEOLOGICAL SEMINARY OF AMERICA

Philadelphia/New York   *5745/1985*

Copyright © 1985 by The Jewish Publication Society of America
and the Jewish Theological Seminary of America
First edition   All rights reserved

Library of Congress Cataloging in Publication Data
Adler, Cyrus, 1863–1940.
    Cyrus Adler, selected letters.
    Includes bibliographical references and index.
    Contents: v. 1. 1883–1919—v. 2. 1920–1940.
    1. Adler, Cyrus, 1863–1940.   2. Jews—United States—
Correspondence.   3. Scholars, Jewish—United States—
Correspondence.   4. Jews—United States—Politics and
government—Addresses, essays, lectures.   5. United
States—Ethnic relations—Addresses, essays, lectures.
I. Robinson, Ira.   II. Title.
E184.J5A17   1985   973.91'092'4   83–316 ✓
ISBN 0–8276–0224–3 (set)

Manufactured in the United States of America

Designed by A D R I A N N E   O N D E R D O N K   D U D D E N

CONTENTS

VOLUME II

PART FIVE · **1920–1925**

PART SIX · 1926–1932

PART SEVEN · 1933–1940

PART FIVE
1920-1925

As the hopes kindled at Versailles faded, America attempted to ignore the problems of the world in a wave of isolationist sentiment. This new atmosphere brought new problems and challenges to American Jewry. In a letter to Herbert Hoover, who was being urged to run for the presidency in 1920, Adler paused to reflect on the post-war role of the United States

TO HERBERT C. HOOVER, NEW YORK CITY

Philadelphia, February 24, 1920

I have for some time been wanting to write to you but was deterred by the fact that with all your work, honorary degrees and medals and the accompanying speeches, plus the correspondence, you must be over-whelmed. And yet as this is but a few minutes of your time and comes from one whom you have been good enough to consider a person of sane judgment, maybe you will forgive it, even if it is a burden.

I can well imagine that the suggestion of the Presidency is a fearful thought to any man who is selfless and has some idea of the magnitude of the obligation. And yet I do hope that you will not overlook the genuineness of the call to you from the country.

What you said at Johns Hopkins—what you have been saying lately—does in my opinion represent that for which the sober thought of the country is looking. We are not to play the role of saviors of the earth, but to take our decent part in upbuilding a shattered world; we are to recover our own equilibrium at home, neither through reaction nor radicalism, and to accomplish this it may be necessary for the sober people of both political parties to combine. There is no living American who could lead such a movement with the authority that you can and since you are doing the right thing you are young enough and strong enough, even to lose on such an issue—for in such a cause even defeat may prove a victory. Not that I look for defeat. The cause which embraces our proper share in the Society of Nations, the defeat of the profiteer and the curbing of the radical socialist embraces the sound view of the great issues before us. May I enroll myself as humble follower under your banner? [W]

TO CHARLES H. SHAPIRO,[1] NEW YORK CITY

March 16, 1920

Replying to your letter of March 12 asking me for a statement in connection with the proposed "Back to the Synagogue" campaign, let me say that there is no campaign more urgently needed by and for the Jews of the United States than this one. Of recent years the attempt has been made from various points of view to emphasize one or another interest of the Jewish people; its national aspirations, its so-called cultural work, or its philanthropic activities. The belief in and practice of the Torah is the only mark which properly distinguishes the Jewish people from other peoples, and the shrine of this Torah is in the Synagogue and its practice is in the lives of those who belong to the Synagogue—in the house of worship itself, in the home, and in the market place. In order to perpetuate a true Judaism we must have a Judaism of knowledge and so the house of learning and the schools for children must also be supported as integral parts of the Synagogue which should become a Bet ha Keneset[2] for all the people. No Jew has the right to call himself or think himself a Jew in the fullest sense of the term without membership in the Synagogue. I believe the need so imperative that I should like to see the entire Synagogue united in this effort, though my own adherence is to the Traditional Synagogue. This traditional Synagogue, in order to hold the American youth, must with the fullest loyalty to Jewish tradition bring itself into harmony with the spirit of America. The Jewish Theological Seminary and later the United Synagogue and other religious and education agencies have been working to this end for some years patiently and steadily and I believe with success in view of the moderate support accorded them. If a real understanding of the issue is combined with genuine sincerity, I am confident that Traditional Judaism will find an abiding home in America. [W]

1. Charles H. Shapiro (1880–1922), New York lawyer and communal worker.
2. Synagogue—literally "House of Assembly."

American Jewry, which had given so much for the relief and rehabilitation of European Jewry during and after the First World War, was beginning to realize that the recipients of its largesse in Europe tended to resent their dependence on America and the Joint Distribution Committee.

Memorandum

March 19, 1920

. . . There is already a considerable hostility to American Jewry and in fact to America growing up in Europe, due to their belief that we have the desire to run everything. Europe wants from us money, not advice. The attitude of Doctor Salkind[1] in endeavoring to insinuate that because America has contributed money for the relief of European Jewry, we desire to impose our views upon them, is in the highest degree unfair. We have probably erred in the other direction and permitted the dictation of European methods to us to a degree which would not be countenanced by many of the donors to the Fund if they were aware of it. Since the future work of magnitude and importance will be the reconstruction work of the business corporation and since representatives of all the Eastern European countries fully expressed their views on this subject in writing and orally and since they really suggested the foundation of the plan, the only result of the conference on this point would be the opening up of great lines of discussion which would unduly delay a plan which in my opinion should be set in motion at once.

The Joint Distribution Committee has always been and is willing to receive advice and suggestions from anybody, but the plans for one country will no doubt differ from another and there is no particular reason why the Jews of Roumania should have a voice in the affairs of the Jews of Poland.

If it should appear that a majority of the Joint Distribution Committee favor a conference,[2] to which I am opposed, I think that only the Joint Distribution Committee should be represented and that if any individual committee, constituent of the Joint Distribution Committee, is represented directly, the Joint Distribution Committee should not be represented. The place of the conference should be neither Paris nor Switzerland, but New York, London or The Hague. The Joint Distribution Committee should itself lay out a program of the subjects on which it is prepared to confer and stipulate that the conference had no binding authority, but even with these restrictions, I deem a conference unwise. . . . [M]

1. Jacob M. Salkind (1875–1937), editor of the *Yiddishe Shtimme und Arbeiter Freund* (London).
2. A conference of the European directors of the Joint Distribution Committee would be held in November 1920 in Vienna.

Adler had learned through bitter experience that American involvement in Jewish organizations based overseas was an invitation to frustration. Moreover, such involvement gave fuel to the anti-Semites' accusations of an international Jewish conspiracy. On the other hand, it was clear that, given the position of America in the world, such involvement might well become necessary.

TO LOUIS MARSHALL, NEW YORK CITY

April 30, 1920

I have your letter of April 27 in which you tell me that M. Bigart[1] has asked you to inquire whether I would be willing to accept election as a member of the Central Committee of the Alliance Israélite Universelle. I greatly appreciate the confidence. I have a high opinion of the organization which has been created by the Alliance and of its work and consider that, in spite of the criticism of recent years from some quarters, it has been a great benefactor of Jewry.

I have however difficulties which I must lay before you. Membership by an American in the governing body of an organization which has its headquarters across the water imposes responsibility without the opportunity to take part in the shaping of the policies. My experience as a member of the governing body of the Haifa Technicum and of the Jewish Agricultural Experiment Station, taught me this.[2] Now the Alliance has important judgments to make both on political and educational matters. Let me assume for the moment that the gentlemen in Europe are much better acquainted with the political affairs than we are and that their judgments would be invariably correct. Would they always agree with our American point of view?

How about the educational policy? I know the schools of the Alliance and that they do much good, but even a quarter of a century or more ago when I saw them in the East they were not the kind of schools for which I should have been willing to hold myself responsible. That feeling is probably more acute now than it was then, unless there has been a change in their policy, which there may well have been.

There is yet another difficulty in my mind. The Alliance sets out to be an international Jewish Organization. I, and I believe you also, doubt the wisdom of giving any support to our unfriends' theory as to the existence of an international Jewry. I opposed the formation of an international bureau in Paris on this ground and partially, though not wholly, on this ground, the relief conference.[3] Does not the same argument apply to the Alliance? These are my difficulties.

On the other hand you say that it may be well for us to keep in touch with the Alliance because nobody can foretell when cooperation with the French group may become desirable. Cooperation with the French group, with the English group or with any others has always seemed to me very important. My theory has been that in each country, Jews should form a strong and effective organization for the protection of their own rights and those of their brethren. It is this and this only which interested me in the formation of the American Jewish Committee and in its continuance, but there appears to be a possibility of the Jews of America being in the future much less effective in aiding their brethren abroad than in the past. Should America continue in its isolation, should it decline to take part in the League of Nations, its prerogative to take action on behalf of peoples elsewhere or in support of the minority rights, which have been written into the treaties, will be challenged at every turn. Our voice could therefore only be heard through European organizations and it is this latter point only which makes me hesitate about declining. Now that you see my difficulties, maybe you can aid me in solving them. [W]

1. Jacques Bigart (1856–1934), secretary general of the Alliance Israélite Universelle.
2. See letter to Louis Marshall, January 22, 1914.
3. See Memorandum, March 19, 1920.

To the Editors, American Journal of Theology, *Chicago*

June 3, 1920

My attention has been attracted to an article which appeared in the *American Journal of Theology* for April, 1920, entitled "NISAN 14th and 15th in Gospel and Talmud" with the subheading "A Study in Jewish Camouflage."[1] It is not my intention to discuss the subject matter of the article, but rather its highly improper tone. I find that throughout it employs language which is intended to intimate that the Jewish scholars have deliberately for nearly 2000 years endeavored to deceive both the Jewish and Christian worlds, more particularly the latter, with regard to the question discussed. Such an allegation is false and ridiculous. The animus of the article is shown by the fact that it uses phrases like "nonsense word" for a technical term, speaks of its use as a "dodge," as an "ingenuous, tricky, and occult rule" of the wise men of Israel who could "chuckle over the gullibility of the goyim," indicates that the occurrence of Passover on Friday was prevented to avoid the "financial calamity" of the two-day holiday, etc. It speaks of great men like Maimonides and Bertinoro[2] as "throwing dust in the eye of the reader" and in general it is written in a tone which is so far removed from that which one is accustomed to in the *American Journal of Theology* or indeed in any scientific journal, published in any English-speaking land, that I am strongly moved to express the hope that a style like this is not to become fashionable in any other responsible American Journal, whether devoted to theology or to any other less exalted subject.

The question discussed by the writer is one which will no doubt lend itself to examination, but there are certain men who put themselves out of the pale of discussion. I am astonished that your *Journal* should have admitted any article on any subject written in such an indecent style and with such an evident intention of stirring up passionate hatred. I think that you owe an apology to your readers. [AJC]

1. The article was published in volume 24 of the journal, pp. 252–76, by Matthew A. Power, an English Jesuit. In the August 1920 issue, Solomon Zeitlin published a refutation entitled, "The Secret of Badhu, a Specimen of 'Jewish Camouflage,'" pp. 502–12.
2. Obadiah Bertinoro (c. 1450–d. before 1516), Italian rabbi, author of a standard commentary on the Mishna.

The Protocols of the Elders of Zion *was given its greatest publicity in the United States by Henry Ford, whose newspaper, the* Dearborn Independent, *became a focus for the dissemination of anti-Jewish propaganda. The support of the widely respected industrialist for this movement was the cause of grave alarm among the American Jewish leadership.*

TO JACOB H. SCHIFF, NEW YORK CITY

New York City, June 15, 1920

I have your letter with regard to the articles in Henry Ford's paper. Mr. [Louis] Marshall showed me his telegraphic exchange with Ford and his representatives some days ago and expressed the opinion that if Ford with his large means had determined upon an anti-Jewish campaign, the matter was very serious. It was agreed between us that it might be advisable to call a meeting of the Executive Committee of the American Jewish Committee to consider what action should be taken. At that time I had not seen the articles. Mr. [Harry] Schneiderman procured copies for me and I have read them. I confess that I had not made up my mind as to whether it was advisable to do anything or not and was just a little troubled by the exchange of telegrams which if not followed up placed us for the moment at a disadvantage.[1] Meanwhile as you probably know the Jewish press all over the United States has itself taken up this subject. In both East and West I see editorials and the chances are that Mr. Ford will get a form of publicity which will not be particularly helpful to him.

That there are attempts in various quarters to create the anti-Semitic agitation in America, is shown by a curious article in such an out of way place as the *American Journal of Theology*. I am sending you a copy of a letter which I wrote to the Editors some days ago and to which I have received no reply.[2] It was my thought if I received no reply to this at all, to bring it to the attention of the President of the University of Chicago[3] and also to Mr. [Julius] Rosenwald who is a Trustee of that Institution, but I am giving the editors a reasonable opportunity to make reparation.

Yesterday I received from Doctor Reuben Blank in London, a rather lengthy letter on the anti-Jewish agitation now prevailing in England and he sent me clippings from the secular press that shows the scope of this agitation. [Israel] Zangwill has written to me on the same subject also. I gather that it is the belief in England among our people that these attacks are due to Russian reactionaries and Polish imperialists, who have found their way either as exiles or as propagandists in considerable numbers to England and have succeeded in getting the ear of the press and of influential persons. I do not know whether there is anything in this or not. Lord Northcliffe[4] I know was formerly charged with being a direct supporter and agent of the Czarist regime. . . .

While I hate to "lay down" under the attack, I think that there is this in your view—that such a controversy in the American press would exaggerate what is already too much exaggerated there—Jewish affairs. The Jewish people, my dear Mr. Schiff, are somewhat to blame, in my opinion, for the attacks. We have made a noise in the world of recent years in America and England and probably elsewhere, far out of proportion to our numbers. We have demonstrated and shouted and paraded and congressed and waved flags to an extent which was bound to focus upon the Jew the attention of the world and having got this attention, we could hardly expect that it would all be favorable. Now it may be that many persons think that this was a wise policy. I do not. Of this I am personally convinced—the nationalist agitation is bound to bring about hatred of the Jew in any country in which he has settled. He cannot have two nationalities without proclaiming himself an alien. While he may explain all kinds of things to himself, the explanation does not satisfy the public. I believe that if the American Jewish Committee is to take any real step to ward off such attacks in the future, it must give some constructive advice to the Jews of the United States which will help to obviate these attacks rather than to simply meet them on the defensive when they occur.

Probably the best thing that could be done at the moment would be to have some influential newspapers not owned by Jews, deprecate this anti-Jewish agitation whether in the English or American press and indicate that it means a relapse from civilization into barbarism. [AJA]

1. For the text of these telegrams, see Reznikoff, *Louis Marshall,* 1:329.
2. See letter to the editors, *American Journal of Theology,* June 3, 1920.
3. Harry Pratt Judson (1849–1927), president of the University of Chicago, 1906–23. The journal was published by the university.
4. Alfred C. W. Harmsworth, Viscount Northcliffe (1865–1922), English newspaper publisher.

TO HARRY SCHNEIDERMAN, NEW YORK CITY

June 25, 1920

I have your letter of June 24 enclosing the draft of the [AJC] Minutes. I do not agree with you as to the form of the record . . . after Mr. [Louis] Marshall's statement, I think something like the following ought to come:

The matter was then discussed by those present. Judge Lehman[1] was of the opinion that the articles were not getting any wide publicity except in the Jewish press. Dr. Adler stated Mr. [Jacob H.] Schiff's view expressed to him in writing,[2] that a public defense at the present time might be undesirable and only lend further publicity to an unpleasant situation.

The gentlemen present were of the opinion that the Ford articles themselves were not so serious except as evidence of a worldwide movement.

Mr. Marshall stated that he had heard that the *Jewish Peril* was to be published in America. A clipping was presented from the *Chicago Tribune* containing a dispatch from Paris with a decidedly anti-Jewish character.

It was the opinion of the three gentlemen present that earnest preparation must be made with the possible view of having to meet the larger and more widespread attack in the future, and to this end, that the article of Ford and other similar attacks should be carefully analyzed under headings, and this material brought together, to make reply in case of necessity; that all the available literature bearing upon the present aspects of the anti-Semitic movement should be collected pro and con, so that this should be in readiness.

. . . It was stated that various persons had approached Mr. Ford and found him entirely immovable in his plans, that he had a large library of anti-Semitic literature and was a regular reader of the Jewish press. While it was considered perfectly natural that the Jewish press should be indignant on the subject and should make editorial reply, the suggestion which had been made in one Jewish newspaper of a boycott against Mr. Ford was deemed inadvisable, since any proposed boycott might act as a boomerang and produce a counter-boycott in which the Jews would greatly suffer. It was therefore deemed desirable that Mr. Marshall should issue a confidential letter, not for publication, to the editors of the Jewish press, cautioning them against advising a boycott, informing them that the whole subject was being carefully watched by our Committee. [AJC]

1. Irving Lehman (1876–1945), Justice of the New York Supreme Court, (1908–23); subsequently of the State Court of Appeals; president of the Jewish Welfare Board, 1921–40; active in the American Jewish Committee and the Union of American Hebrew Congregations.
2. See letter to Jacob H. Schiff, June 15, 1920.

Returning to America meant that Adler once more plunged into the affairs of the educational institutions he controlled, especially those of the Jewish Theological Seminary.

TO LOUIS GINZBERG, NEW YORK CITY

New York City, July 1, 1920

. . . The subject that you raise with regard to the whole subject of theology in the [Jewish Theological] Seminary is one which cannot be settled in the course of correspondence nor even at a Faculty meeting. The present program of the Seminary was, I have no doubt, made up after careful consideration of the curricula of the Seminaries in Europe. As far as I know, systematic theology was not taught in any of them—possibly is not. The theory was that our entire curricula would, as it were, naturally lead to a knowledge of what is called theology; that the students would secure it from the course in the Bible and the Talmud; that Philosophy meant in the main

Religious Philosophy—in other words that we were not concerned with the medieval views of physics or even of metaphysics, but rather with the way in which our thinkers have from time to time handled all the great categories of religion. These subjects too would appear in the courses in the Codes and I am inclined to think that there ought to be special attention paid to our Ethical literature. I have no recent catalogues of Jewish Seminaries in Europe, but I would be interested to know and I shall take the opportunity to find out how they deal with this subject. I have made a little study of the handling of this subject in the Christian Seminaries. They give a good deal of attention to what is called pastoral theology which we have tried to provide for in our course of communal work. Harvard Divinity School devotes a good deal of attention to the History of Religions, as you know, treating Judaism, the religions of the Roman Empire, Christianity, even China, Japan, India, the Germanic and Celtic religions, etc. They include under theology the study of the Prayer Book which of course we call liturgy and beside their own dogmatic theology they do include philosophy of religion and the psychology of religion beside many minor headings. For these subjects they draw upon their regular College Faculty who supplement the work of the Divinity School proper. I am inclined to think that you will find an Institution like the Union [Theological Seminary] does the same, using Columbia for this purpose. Now your desire that practically this whole ground shall be covered in the Seminary and shall all be given by one person, seems to me to be proposing a physical impossibility and I am not yet convinced of its desirability. I do not say that I cannot be convinced, but at all events, we must have some long talks.

Now that you should seriously throw yourself into this subject also seems to me to be a matter the advisability of which is open to considerable discussion. You are master of Talmudic learning. There is ample work on this subject to be done in the Seminary. There are many contributions to this learning that you can make. Your attention to theology after all is accidental. Why practically change your scholarly career because of an accident?

I know that it is the view of the Directors and also of the Alumni of the Seminary that the chair of theology shall be a distinct chair and that a man should be secured, or if he does not exist, should be developed, who is minded to devote himself exclusively to Jewish theology.

These are roughly the considerations which, floating about in my mind, made me delay replying to your letter and which give you this rather inconclusive reply at the moment.

I am sure that you will gather my guiding thought that sometime after we have had our summer's rest, we will meet and talk the entire subject over with the welfare of the Seminary and of Judaism in mind. I have no set opinion on a subject which cannot be altered and I dare say you are in a similar frame of mind. [W]

TO ABRAM SAMUEL ISAACS,[1] PATERSON, NEW JERSEY

July 13, 1920

. . . At the Seminary now, the young men are mostly either American-born or have come over when they were children and had their entire upbringing here. There are exceptions, of course, but the rule now is as I have stated.

Alas, the son of the old family does not wish to enter the Rabbinate. The family influence is generally against it. I spoke strongly on this subject at the last Commencement of the Seminary.

What I do object to is the attempt on the part of the immigrant population to dictate the affairs of Jews in connection with America and international subjects, when they misunderstand the former and have a distorted view of the latter. But old American Jews like [Louis D.] Brandeis, [Stephen S.] Wise, and [Richard] Gottheil have been the sinners in this—in that they have followed the undigested mass rather than led them.

I am not sure that the President of the Central Conference[2] was wise in his reference to Anti-Semitism, and have always thought that the agitation of the General Conference and the I.O.B.B.[3] with regard to the Merchant of Venice was puerile.[4]

The trouble is that we have shouted, and congressed, and paraded, and waved flags too much, and for this others than the immigrants are to blame. [W]

1. Abram Samuel Isaacs (1852–1920), rabbi and professor of Semitics at New York University.
2. Leo Morris Franklin (1870–1948), rabbi of Temple Beth El, Detroit; president of the Central Conference of American Rabbis, 1919–21.
3. International Order B'nai B'rith.
4. These groups campaigned to eliminate *The Merchant of Venice* from high-school curricula because of inadequate presentation of the Jewish aspects of the play by teachers.

In writing to a leader of the Cleveland Jewish community, Adler expressed his concern regarding the factors that militated against young men choosing a career in the rabbinate or in Jewish education.

TO M. B. FRIEDMAN, CLEVELAND

July 16, 1920

. . . The scarcity of rabbis is part of the general scarcity of teachers and professors. Men have drifted away from these professions because they feared they would not have the chance to live in them. The tenure of the rabbi is also very uncertain. Of course, you in Cleveland have large congregations who pay good salaries and are glad to keep your men. In fact, sometimes keep them possibly longer than they are serviceable, but when it comes to the smaller towns where men are offered $1800 or $2000 a year, are asked to preach in English and Yiddish, to superintend and teach a school and in some cases to even act as hazzan, you can readily see that the men get discouraged. I do not blame these small towns because the congregations are new and the membership limited. But what we really ought to have is a central fund by which to supplement for a period of years the salaries of men who go to the little towns. [JTS]

Writing to Edward Nathan, who had been posted to a consular position in Spain, Adler gave his views on American foreign policy.

TO EDWARD I. NATHAN, VIGO, SPAIN

August 20, 1920

. . . Since you wrote Poland has been on the verge of destruction, and if it is really destroyed, I have an idea that that will put an end to the League of Nations, or at least seriously shatter it, but the French military tactics may save it.[1] It is not at all certain in my opinion that America will keep out of the League. In the first place we do not know how the next election will turn out. The Republicans are not at all going to have the walk-over that they expected, and I have much reason to believe that except in rock-ribbed quarters the women are going to vote for the League and for the party that they believe supports it. . . .

. . . We have had a fairly cool but extremely sticky summer. I have had two vacations of about ten days each, the last one devoted exclusively to golf and detective stories. You will of course have heard of the terrible death of Professor [Israel] Friedlaender and his colleagues in the Ukraine.[2] He leaves a wife and six little children and his loss to the Seminary and the scholarly world is very great. . . .

The new Secretary of State, Colby,[3] is very much of a man. He takes things up with vigor, and, I may say in passing, is showing a very deep interest in everything in behalf of the Jews that is presented to him. The President evidently trusts him and lets him go ahead much on his own initiative. We are decidedly better off than we were under the colorless regime of [Robert] Lansing. I understand that the new Undersecretary, Norman Davis,[4] is a good man, but Mr. Colby is keeping Hugh Gibson at his side to advise on Polish affairs and Roland Morris, who came here at the beginning of June, is also in Washington as an adviser on the Japanese and Siberian questions. I had a long talk with Roland Morris before he went to the San Francisco Convention. If he would ever write down his experiences in Siberia—not to speak of Japan—it would make one of the most interesting of post-War books. [D]

1. In response to Polish claims on Russian territory, the Red Army invaded Poland in the summer of 1920. The Poles checked the Bolsheviks at the battle of the Vistula and invaded the Soviet Union. The war ended in March 1921 with the Poles in possession of large portions of White Russia and the Ukraine.
2. Friedlaender died in the Ukraine in 1919. On his mission, see Adler's letter to Fried-laender, March 4, 1918.
3. Bainbridge Colby (1869–1950), U.S. secretary of state, February 1920–March 1921.
4. Norman Davis (1878–1944), U.S. undersecretary of state, 1920–21.

TO LOUIS MARSHALL, SARANAC LAKE, NEW YORK

September 10, 1920

I am not going to intrude on your Rosh Hashanah with business, but politics is pleasure. You allude to the fact that Tom Watson[1] is to be elected Senator from Georgia and say that there is something fundamentally wrong in a political party that will choose such a representative. An important Democratic daily like the *New York World* of this date, September 10, prints an editorial which practically repudiates Watson as a Democratic candidate. I am enclosing it for your reading. I wonder whether in the midst of a presidential campaign a leading Republican paper would have been as outspoken had what purports to be the Republican party in a given state taken similar action. I have seen no violent marks of contrition at the way in which Newberry[2] was elected and am under the impression that LaFollette[3] has been for some years a representative of the Republican party. These men as individuals may not be quite as debased as is Watson, but their admission into the councils of a great party is, I think, even more debasing. I am sure that President [Woodrow] Wilson is at least as much grieved at the nomination of Watson as you are. So let us all be tolerant of each other's parties, admit that there may be flies in both the cups of ointment, and recognize at least that a great party like the Democratic party cannot be fundamentally wrong although here and there in spots it may occasionally wander off into error. . . . [W]

1. Tom Watson (1856–1922), Georgia Populist politician. During the agitations of the Leo Frank case (1914)—a virulent outbreak of anti-Semitism in Atlanta culminating in the lynching of a Jewish factory superintendent who had been wrongly convicted of murdering a gentile girl—he wrote vituperatively against Leo Frank and his supporters.
2. Truman Hardy Newberry (1864–1945), U.S. senator from Michigan, 1919–22.
3. Robert LaFollette (1885–1925), U.S. senator from Wisconsin, 1906–25. A leading figure in the Progressive movement, he was presidential nominee of the Progressive party in 1924.

The spread of anti-Semitic propaganda based upon the Protocols *forgeries caused great concern not only to Adler and his associates but also to concerned non-Jews, such as the journalist Louis Dabo.*

TO LOUIS MARSHALL, NEW YORK CITY

September 21, 1920
Last evening, September 20, I had an interview with Mr. Louis Scott Dabo. . . .
. . . Though a Louisiana man, his principal American hero is [Abraham] Lincoln and he seems to have a sort of feeling that it is an American's business to pattern himself after Lincoln as much as possible, and fight for and if need be, sacrifice one's self for a principle and for the ideal of a perfect union among all Americans for a righteous America. It is from the latter point of view that he feels impelled to take up the question of the anti-Jewish propaganda now going on in the United States. He is not so particularly concerned about seeing justice done to the Jews. He thinks that they are or ought to be able to take care of themselves and fight for their own rights and position and cannot

16 · CYRUS ADLER

understand why they have been so silent under the brutal attacks that are being made upon them.

What he is concerned about is that an ancient or medieval principle of hate is being imported into America thereby lowering the standard of American civilization and it is for the sake of America that he and one or two other friends of his, feel that they ought to do something. He said that he had plenty of other work to do and had no desire to mix into this matter if others would take it up, but kept on repeating the statement that somebody ought to do it.

As to the question of the anti-Jewish propaganda in this country, he told me that since 1917 at least on twenty occasions, different individuals had approached him either verbally or with typewritten documents to prove the dangers of the *Jewish Peril* and to urge him, as a journalist, to take steps to counteract it; that he had received no less than five typewritten copies of the *Protocols* before they had been printed and that there was no especial reason why he should be approached. He is of the opinion that hundreds and maybe thousands of journalists had been similarly approached. He stated that he believed that so far as the Russian end of this movement is concerned, it is probably with the view of creating such an excited public opinion in the United States as might result in pogroms.

Mr. Dabo told me very clearly that he desired and would accept no pecuniary help for any counter-propaganda that he might undertake and that whatever he did, would be done with his own means. He says that he has the names of all the people who have approached him on the subject and some letters; that he was not going to go into details with me at the first interview, at least until he got to know me better, but he did say, that of the persons who are interested in this project, three were persons of such prominence, that if their names were given, it would astonish me.

One of the angles which was rather new to me was his statement that a report was being circulated that the Jews in America had made a deal with the Catholics; that President [Woodrow] Wilson was in some way connected with this and had profited by it and that Mr. [Joseph P.] Tumulty was the agent in this enterprise. This is but one of the stories. He also said that to his knowledge, some of the College fraternities were being used as a means to spread this anti-Jewish propaganda.

In answer to his questions why the Jews of America had remained silent, I told him that naturally these things were highly unpleasant to us, but that so far as we were concerned, the *Protocols* were forgeries, the so-called conspiracy was a lie and that we had not up to this time, and in view of the fact that the Press had not taken up the subject, felt disposed to demean ourselves by entering into a controversy, but that what action we would take in the future, I do not know.

My own impression of Mr. Dabo is that he is an honest man; that the matter is very serious to him as an American. I think he is a man of high strung nervous temperament and may be a little inclined to see things very subjectively. He considers social and political affairs to be amenable to the same kind of treatment as a problem in mathematics. Given certain information he thinks that it can be predicted how a certain Government will act and given a certain amount of anti-Jewish propaganda, he thinks if allowed to go on for a certain length of time unchecked, certain definite things will happen in America, as for instance, a pogrom. It is this that he is fearful about.

I hope that I have given you some kind of a picture of this rather interesting and curious man. I believe that it would be very desirable now that you should have an interview with him—probably with me, because if I am present, he may take for granted what he said in the first interview and go a step further, giving us the names of people, whom he either knows, or believes to be at the back of this propaganda in America. He knows of you, has a very high opinion of you, and would be glad to talk with you. I am inclined to think that we ought to arrange for some place where we can talk without being in the earshot of other people. I met him last night at the Pennsylvania Hotel [in New York] and asked him to dine with me and of course we were pretty much surrounded by people. He talked in a rather low tone of voice for that reason no doubt, and maybe did not go as far as he would have, had we been in a private room. [W]

TO JACOB HEILPRIN,[1] NEW YORK CITY

October 3, 1920

. . . I have no hesitation in stating to you that it is not my intention to support Senator Harding.[2] I consider that the present campaign presents one of the most important moral issues with which America has ever been confronted. There is nothing comparable to it since the issue of the destruction of human slavery. That issue is the substitution of the covenant of the League of Nations for the older form of special alliance and secret treaties with all the misery and ills which attended them. It is a serious effort to bring about more open diplomacy, a greater sense of justice in the world, and is a long step toward preventing war. This effort has up to the present time so far as America has been concerned, been throttled by the Republican majority in the United States Senate. As far as I can make out from a reasonably careful reading of the speeches and statements of the Republican candidate, he is not satisfied with the throttling process, but is bent upon the absolute strangulation of all humane elements of the treaty and the covenant. Every hope of the small nations of Europe and of the minorities in central and Eastern Europe and Asia is centered in this Treaty and its failure and the failure of the League of Nations, or even partial failure due to the absence of so great a nation as the United States from this League, would be a blow at humanity. I can imagine no policy more humiliating to America than that which has been pursued in the past year by the Republican Party in the United States Senate, in which a Republican candidate promises to continue and improve upon if he should be elected. [AJC]

1. Director of the Jewish publicity department, Republican National Committee.
2. Warren Gamaliel Harding (1885–1923), Ohio Republican; twenty-ninth president of the United States, 1921–23.

TO RACIE ADLER

October 13, 1920

I have a copy of the new anti-Jewish book "The Cause of World Unrest" just issued by the Putnams.[1] It is as bad if not worse than the protocols.

I am afraid we have lost a lot of time by following the advice of Mr. [Jacob H.] Schiff who I am sure did not realize the extent of the propaganda.

I am awfully sorry to be away, dear, but it is really necessary now for decent Jews (of whom I hope I am one) to show themselves among men. I am sure I lost no friends for our cause to-night. [W]

1. The book, anonymously written, with an introduction by the editor of the *Morning Post* (London), describes a hidden conspiracy, mainly Jewish, which for centuries has striven to produce revolution, communism, and anarchy.

Ever since the convening of the American Jewish Congress at the end of the First World War, there were elements within the Jewish community which desired to create a World Jewish Congress, representing Jews in all countries. The World

Jewish Congress, which was finally created in 1936, was opposed by Adler on the same principles that caused him to oppose the American Jewish Congress with such fervor.

TO ABRAHAM S. SCHOMER,[1] NEW YORK CITY

October 17, 1920

I am in receipt of your invitation addressed to me in my capacity as Editor of the *Jewish Quarterly Review,* to become a member of the Executive Committee of the World Jewish Congress and to become one of the signers of a call for such a Congress. I enclose you my declination of the invitation and under ordinary circumstances would consider that sufficient. I am well aware of the fact that you have for many years been engaged in an agitation to bring about such a Congress and you may be aware of the fact that during all those years I have opposed such a Congress. The conditions at present to my mind justify this opposition in a very much stronger way than I have ever put it before. The very dangers which I foresaw have come to pass. The Jews of the entire world are today faced by an international conspiracy which threatens their standing and even their life throughout the entire world. At no time, in my opinion, even in the darkest days of the Middle Ages, has the danger been so great or the enemy so powerful and united. It may be very likely that this movement will fail in time as such movements have, and that it is only a passing phase of world reaction following the war, and that it is but the last gasp of the reactionary forces of Russia, of Poland, of Rumania, joined up with reactionary forces which always exist in Western Europe, to use the Jews in their effort to regain their lost power and to destroy liberal thought.

But whatever the main cause, I have no hesitation in saying that the Jews of the world have to a considerable extent contributed to furnishing an excuse, at least for the present attacks, and that this excuse largely lies in the agitation which would make the Jews throughout the world a separate nationality, thus stamping them as aliens and foreigners in every land. Nothing would furnish a better text for this charge than this call which you have issued. You propose a Congress which would exercise, among other things, right of taxation of the members of Israel throughout the world, the creation of an Executive, the restoration of something like the Exilarch[2] and you denounce any Israelite—Hebrew or Jew, whatever you call him—who attempts to oppose, interfere with, or obstruct your proposed Congress, in a language which is worthy of the Middle Ages.

I do not know you, sir, but from everything I know of you, I fully believe that you are sincere and selfless in your efforts. You must be aware of the fact that the same cannot be said for many of those who in the past have engaged in the creation of Congresses in America and in other lands, and that these organizations claiming to represent the majority of the Jews in their respective lands and in every case representing the minority, have fallen into the hands of people without vision or statesmanship and they have done infinite harm to the Jews of the world. Your present circular, if it fell into the hands of Mr. [Henry] Ford and of the publishers of the *Protocols* or of the scandalous book recently published by the Putnams in New York,[3] would be by them considered ample justification of the charges that they have put forward against Israel. If you would not have the blood of your brethren in Europe and of the destruction of your people everywhere upon your soul, you will desist in the effort in which you are now making, for I say to you again that I am fully convinced of the uprightness of your motives. [AJC]

1. Abraham S. Schomer (1891–1946), lawyer, author, and communal worker.
2. Lay head of the Babylonian Jewish community; claimed his extensive powers by virtue of his descent from the House of David.
3. See letter to Racie Adler, October 13, 1920.

Jacob Schiff died on September 25, 1920. In 1914 he had approached Adler for advice on publishing a Jewish classics series,[1] which Adler now felt would be a proper memorial. This series of texts and translations of classic Hebrew works of ancient and medieval times—known as the Schiff Library of Jewish Classics—was ultimately published by the Jewish Publication Society and contained nine titles.

TO MAYER SULZBERGER

Philadelphia, October 27, 1920
. . . I have had a little talk with Mortimer Schiff[2] and only the other day with Mrs. Felix Warburg,[3] about some form of memorial or memorials to their father.

Mrs. Schiff[4] is being overburdened with requests for permission to name halls, pavilions, clubs, lodges, etc., after Mr. Schiff and she seems particularly averse to having any buildings named after him. I myself thought of proposing to the Classics' Committee the idea of naming this Library the Schiff Library or Series, because undoubtedly Mr. Schiff got his idea from James Loeb's[5] Classical Series. In this particular case, as a matter of fact, I believe the idea was really Mrs. Schiff's and that it originated in a chance conversation. She was proudly showing me the first few volumes of James Loeb's Library and turned to her husband and said, "Why don't you do for Jewish literature what Jimmy is doing for Greek and Latin." He made no answer at the time and his announcement of his intention to make such a gift at the Bible dinner was probably the result of thinking over this suggestion. Under these circumstances probably the family would be delighted and I am very anxious to retain their interest in the Series.

I am going to propose next Sunday at the meeting of the Board of Directors of the Seminary to name a Professorship—probably the Professorship of History—after Mr. Schiff. This would be very sympathetic to the family as I have ascertained. [D]

1. See letter to Jacob Schiff, April 29, 1914.
2. Mortimer L. Schiff (1877–1931), banker and civic worker; son of Jacob Schiff.
3. Frieda Warburg (1876–1958), daughter of Jacob Schiff; philanthropist and Jewish communal leader.
4. Therese Loeb [Mrs. Jacob] Schiff (1854–1933).
5. James Loeb (1867–1933), banker and patron of the arts; founder of the Loeb Classical Library, Harvard University Press.

TO FELIX M. WARBURG, NEW YORK CITY

November 12, 1920

The last time I saw you, you made some inquiry about Rabbi Doctor Chaim Heller[1] concerning whom I think you said you received a letter from your brother in Hamburg.[2] Doctor Heller arrived in this country on the 4th of November. A great deal has been made of him in the Jewish press. . . .

. . . My own impressions were these. He is a squat man of not very attractive features, but evidently a man of great energy and what the journalists would call dynamic personality. I have little doubt that he is the great Talmudist that he is described to be. The one scientific work of his which I have seen published about nine years ago was on the Syriac version of the Bible and did not make a profound impression on me. I understand he has published a text of Maimonides which is very well edited.

Now my object in going into these particulars is this: Doctor Heller comes to America only secondarily to secure support for his scientific publications. His real purpose, the one which he has at heart, is to raise the sum of one million dollars to endow an institution of learning to be located preferably at Danzig. He says that the institution of the kind that he has in mind, was in contemplation six or seven years ago and that he had received large gifts for it running into some millions of rubles, before the days of the Bolshevik or even the Kerenski ruble; that this money was deposited in trust in the bank at Moscow and has all been confiscated. The institution that he has in mind is one which he claims will entirely appeal to Orthodox Jews and yet will contain a progressive note which he thinks spells salvation of East European Jewry. He says that Lithuania and Poland—indeed other parts of Russia—have hundreds of Rabbis well trained in the various Yeshibot, who, because of the lack of any secular knowledge or even organization of their Hebrew knowledge, would be practically useless in the tremendous problems now before East European Jewry; that if left to themselves, the Jewry in these lands will be spiritually leaderless. He proposes to take these men, ranging in ages from twenty-five to thirty-five and to some extent make them over, to support them and their families during the process; in general to make a central school which will entirely from within give East European Jewry the combination of leadership which it needs. The plan, I think, has force in it. He proposes to see you, Mr. [Louis] Marshall, Judge [Mayer] Sulzberger and Judge [Irving] Lehman about it. I told him that practically every Jewish organization and institution of higher learning or science, that I know anything about in this country, was broke. This was true of the Seminary, of the Gratz College in Philadelphia, of the Jewish Publication Society, of the Jewish Historical Society. I understood that great collections were being made for the Hebrew Union College which needed them and that I could not imagine that it was possible to secure the endowment of which he spoke or anything at all like it.

On the other hand, I told him that there was a strong feeling on the part of some men in the Joint Distribution Committee, that if this work could be kept up at all, some appropriation of funds should be devoted to religious and educational work with the very view that he had in mind of providing for the future and spiritual leadership of East European Jewry. You know that I have this feeling myself and I hope it will receive serious and adequate consideration soon.[3]

On the other hand, in view of the needs of the Seminary and of the other institutions, that I have referred to (I did not mention the Dropsie College which is not broke, but which could not move one step forward), I feel that any slight energy that I have left belongs to them and I feel bound to ask my friends to keep it in mind that our own position here is, to use a very mild term, precarious. The Seminary is costing me and I know it is Mr. Marshall, the deepest anxiety. Proportionately, although not to the same extent, our Publication Society is even in worse financial state. While I do not know exactly what the position of your institutions in the New York Federation is, there is not an institution in Philadelphia which is not facing an ever-increasing deficit. On top of this comes the new plan for the economic reconstruction of Palestine. I do not know where we in America are going to land. . . . [W]

1. Chaim Heller (1878–1960), rabbinical and biblical scholar. His major works include a critical edition of Maimonides' *Sefer ha-Mitzvot* and studies on the Samaritan version of the Pentateuch and the Palestinian Targum.
2. Max Warburg (1867–1946), banker and Jewish communal leader; a member of the German delegation to the Paris Peace Conference.
3. Adler was chairman of the Cultural Committee of the Joint Distribution Committee, which supported educational institutions in Eastern Europe.

TO OSCAR S. STRAUS, NEW YORK CITY

November 24, 1920

. . . An incident like this[1] makes me think of how much we have neglected our opportunities and I count myself one of the sinners. That in the 27 years which have elapsed [since the founding of the American Jewish Historical Society] no one thought it worth while to follow such a lead, shows that we have all considered American Jewish History a mere amusement not to be followed up seriously. Unless I am very much mistaken, both for scientific and practical purposes, the need for serious work in American Jewish History will be evident for a good many years, but I do not think it will be done unless we are put in position to have at least one or more people to devote all their time to this department of Jewish History. It is really pitiful to think of the small scale on which our work has been carried out. I am also convinced that the President of the American Jewish Historical Society should be a person who has many fewer offices and boards and committees to look after than I have and I have therefore determined to carry out my intention announced several years ago, to withdraw from the presidency at the end of my present term. My own view is that among our group, the one who would be best fitted for the office is Doctor A. S. W. Rosenbach,[2] whose knowledge of American Jewish History and whose collections on the subject far exceed those of any of us.

This change will not accomplish the purpose that I have in mind. In some of our institutions, I naturally lean to the Seminary, though maybe the Dropsie College would be better, there ought to be established a chair for American Jewish History, not so much because of the lectures that would be given to students, although this too has its value, as because it is only in this way that there will always be at least one man who can give all his time to the subject. [W]

1. In a letter published in the *Philadelphia Public Ledger* of November 24, 1920, it was asserted that a Jew, one Moses Simonsohn, had come over on one of the Pilgrim ships in 1621, contrary to the accepted belief that the first Jews in North America arrived in New York in 1654.

2. Abraham Simon Wolf Rosenbach (1876–1952), bibliophile and book dealer; president of Gratz College; became president of the American Jewish Historical Society.

Throughout Adler's tenure as president of the Jewish Theological Seminary, Mordecai Kaplan was one of the most important and influential members of the seminary faculty. Kaplan's controversial views on the form American Judaism should assume differed significantly from those of Adler and a number of supporters of the Seminary. Adler was concerned about Kaplan's influence on the students in the Seminary on the one hand, and about defending his academic freedom on the other. See Adler's letters to Kaplan, February 14, 1921 and September 21, 1923.

TO EDWIN KAUFMAN, NEW YORK CITY

December 31, 1920

Now I have your letter of December 27, and my attention has also been called this week to an editorial in the *Hebrew Standard* of December 24, touching upon the two articles written by Professor [Mordecai M.] Kaplan, to which you refer.[1]

I had read the articles casually and have heard something about the movement which has resulted in the formation of the society known as the Society for the Jewish Renaissance.[2] I did not take the matter very seriously because I thought that it was part of the unrest in the world which follows the war, when everybody felt that they must talk about reconstruction, and thought that when the remainder of the world settled down, some of the uneasy spirits whose minds had been shaken by the great catastrophe and misery of the world would also settle down.

Part of this unrest in Jewish circles is, I feel convinced, due to Zionism, which, as I pointed out at the last Seminary commencement, has the tendency in its nationalistic aspect, to remove the center of gravity of Judaism from the Torah to the land or the people.

Of course, if we are to take Professor Kaplan literally, he makes a charge against Orthodox Judaism which is not justified. You quote his statement that orthodoxy believes that tradition is infallible. I do not know the word "infallible" in connection with Judaism, and I do not recall that any orthodox authority has ever set up such a claim; many have deplored the lack of living authority among the rabbis of our day and hope for its revival.

A great deal of mischief has arisen from Jews using words that have a special and peculiar meaning in connection with the Christian church. It is largely for this reason that I have never liked to use the word orthodox because orthodox means "holding the right *opinions*" and Judaism, while it has doctrines and a creed (though there has never been a complete agreement upon the articles of the creed) has, as you know, laid much more stress upon what men *did* than upon what they *thought*. We Jews have held that there is no *doctrine* from which salvation can come. It is what we *do* in the practice of both the moral and ceremonial law, and not what we *think,* which to my understanding stamps us as good Jews or bad Jews.

It is needless for me to tell you, I presume, that I am not in sympathy with the views which Professor Kaplan seems to have expressed. I say seems, because I am not certain what they are and think they are expressed rather clumsily. As for the Society of the Renaissance, I consider its platform not so much dangerous as childish.

On the other hand I am very much opposed to an inquisition or to heresy-hunting. The *Hebrew Standard* is not quite above-board in endeavoring to make an issue of these articles. It has, for the past thirty years, attacked the Seminary. It did so during the lifetime of Dr. [Sabato] Morais, it did so during the lifetime of Dr. [Solomon] Schechter, and it has never lost an opportunity to continue this policy.

To raise such an issue of heresy with regard to these articles or this society, would in my opinion do traditional Judaism a great deal more harm than the articles or the Society can. Excommunication has gone out of fashion. I think it is generally recognized that the synagogue in Amsterdam made a great mistake when it excommunicated Spinoza.[3] If an issue is now made with Dr. Kaplan, he will become a martyr. He may be able, as he has an attractive personality, to rally to himself a goodly number of young men. The men of his synagogue who like him, may support him. We should then be forcing another new division. As it is, we have our own Seminary and the Hebrew Union College, and the Yeshibah, and Rabbi Stephen Wise and various downtown rabbis giving Semicha [ordination] indiscriminately, and thus I am sure, sufficient confusion without bringing about the establishment of a new school.

You may say that all this is better than permitting the minds of the Seminary students to be poisoned. Professor Kaplan's position in the Seminary is that of Professor of Homiletics. His work is to teach them the art of constructing a sermon, not the knowledge of Judaism which goes into the construction of the sermon. If he were a professor of theology, the matter might be more serious, at least from the Seminary's point of view. I do admit this Teacher's Institute does present a greater difficulty.

You see, however, my dear Mr. Kaufman, Jewish tradition does not sanction the views that an opinion constitutes a heresy, or as I prefer to call it, a sect. As long as a man *observes* the Jewish law, which Dr. Kaplan says he does, and I am convinced he does, he may speculate about philosophical matters. The great Maimonides wrote at least two kinds of books. The Moreh[4] was burned by some of his contemporaries, and the Yad ha-Chazakah,[5] with many, took the place of the Talmud. We have had many rabbis who are also philosophers and speculated more or less wisely on the nature of God and His attributes, on whether science should be studied or not, and exactly what was meant by the Revelation, and these men still remained leaders of the people. They were not forced into the actual position of becoming schismatics, which apparently they did not wish to become.

I am going to continue to think over the matter very carefully and with the help of God, I hope I may arrive at a wise conclusion. Meanwhile, I want to thank you for writing to me so frankly, to assure you that I am troubled as you are, and that being in doubt as to the best course to pursue (and I do not mean best from the point of view of policy, but I mean the best course for Judaism and for our institution) I think in so grave a matter, there should at least be no haste. [JTS]

1. The articles referred to are: "A Program for the Reconstruction of Judaism," *Menorah Journal* 6 (1920) and "The Society for the Jewish Renascence," *Maccabaean* 34 (1920). In these articles, Kaplan was severely critical of both Orthodox and Reform Judaism.
2. The Society for the Jewish Renascence was the forerunner of the synagogue-based Society for the Advancement of Judaism.
3. Baruch Spinoza (1632–77); philosopher, of Jewish descent; best known for his critique of revealed religion and his advocacy of reason.
4. *Guide of the Perplexed.*
5. Maimonides' Code of Jewish law.

TO SOLOMON SOLIS-COHEN, PHILADELPHIA

January 11, 1921

I thank you for the letter you wrote to the *Menorah Journal* and for the public expression of your confidence in me.[1]

It had become the fashion in "Congress" and Zionist circles to doubt my word and impugn my motives. This was done on a number of occasions in *The Maccabean,* the *American Jewish Chronicle* of unsavory memory, and the *Boston Jewish Advocate* while [Jacob] De Haas was Editor. [Julian W.] Mack himself told me once that it was currently stated that my convictions were democratic and Zionist, but that I had been "bought by [Jacob H.] Schiff." Of course, when Mr. Schiff became pro-Congress that myth was dispelled.

When the Essay appeared in the *Menorah Journal* I had fully intended to reply, but refrained because of the anti-Jewish attack in the country. I would not have done so in the objective way you did, but by opening up the whole subject. I had not meant to discuss the essay itself which is to my mind a combination of the results of propaganda and of a species of ingratitude not uncommon in mankind. The fault seems to me to lie in the method of the Menorah Society which chooses judges for its essays who can pass only upon the style and not upon the correctness of the subject matter.

The Editor's[2] apology prefixed to your letter I do not accept. An Editor should respect difference of opinion, but he has no right to circulate falsehood. Mr. Hurwitz uses the identical argument employed by George Haven Putnam in defense of their firm in proposing to circulate the Protocols.[3] [D]

1. The letter referred to was published in the *Menorah Journal* of December 1920 in response to an article appearing in the June 1920 issue entitled "The Passing of the Shtadlan," by John J. Smertenko, which was critical of the American Jewish Committee and of Adler personally.
2. Henry Hurwitz (1886–1961), founder of the Menorah Association and editor of the *Menorah Journal.*
3. See letter to Racie Adler, October 13, 1920.

TO BORIS D. BOGEN, PARIS

Philadelphia, February 1, 1921

Your letter of December 7 came into my hands through the Joint Distribution Committee about ten days ago and I have given it the careful consideration which any letter from you commands.

I am glad that you approve of the report of the Committee on Cultural Activities. I hope that it will be something more than a mere report, but whether anything comes out of it of course depends on whether we shall continue to get funds.

Theoretically, you are no doubt right that the administrative work should be carried on in Europe and the American end be devoted to the securing of funds, but knowing our constituency as I do, I do not believe that your plan can ever be carried into effect.

I appreciate the compliment involved in your desire to have me abroad and indeed a similar suggestion was made to me by Mr. [Felix M.] Warburg sometime since, but after consideration with him and with others, he himself withdrew the suggestion. The administrative end of the relief work is something for which I am not better fitted than a number of others and there are highly important educational interests in this country to which I am committed and which I am certain would suffer if I left them at this time, so that it was simply a question of where one can be most useful.

You are quite right in your estimate of [James H.] Becker who is one of the most remarkable men I have ever come across. I think all of his plans were adopted. We shall meet very shortly to see how to get the funds to carry out even the very limited program which the Vienna Conference adopted.

You probably know that America is going through a business depression naturally enough and that we are facing all kinds of deficits everywhere. With the exception of the Dropsie College which I have always kept rigidly within the income, I am not at this present date connected with a single Jewish institution of any kind whatsoever that is not facing considerable deficits.

What is to become of the Jews of Europe and of the Jews of America under these circumstances, I confess that I do not know. Maybe in a few months things will look better.

I know that politics is not your forte, but I have an abiding belief in keeping my agreements. I think that all the talk of *national* minority should be frowned down upon in Poland and elsewhere and on the other hand I think that all the rights accorded by the treaties should be striven for and that we should not take any back water on that point. [AJA]

TO MORDECAI M. KAPLAN, NEW YORK CITY

Philadelphia, February 14, 1921

I have your letter of February 10 and gladly comply with your request to make comments on your paper: "The Function and Organization of the Synagogue."[1]

In order that I may not repeat phrases, I have marked certain of them with a pencil on the margin which you can easily erase.

On page 1, the latter part of the opening paragraph was, in my opinion, an unjust and offensive attack upon persons whom you were addressing. I do not believe they wanted oratorical jazz. I am quite certain that the people did come together for the purpose of working out difficult problems and that they did not want to have a rousing time. It seems to me that it is not becoming in a teacher in Israel to begin his address to the people by insulting them.

The second phrase that I have marked, the attack upon the Reform congregations engaged in what they call back-to-the-Synagogue-movement, was also in my opinion in bad taste and not at all to the point.

These two passages, taken together, indicate the frame of mind that you are in—in general, that of attack. If you really want to bring about a renaissance, you ought to do so by actual positive work and not by attacking others.

I want to say in passing that you cannot be so certain as to just what the word "schul" did mean. It seems to me not impossible that it indicated something like incorporation, very much like the word college. Doctor [David S.] Blondheim has a very interesting investigation on this subject.

I think that your paradox about placing the Synagogue in the same class with houses of amusement, is unfortunate and unfair. If you use the word re-creation in its etymological sense, you come nearer to the truth.

I think the passages which I have marked on page 4, cry aloud for themselves as to their bad taste, if not impropriety. Your charges against the cantor abuse are undoubtedly true, but you speak of it as if it were a very general evil, while as I understand, it is only confined to a few congregations and certainly it is difficult to get anything from this whole matter except a discouragement of public worship.

On page 8, I take issue with you and I am inclined to think that the whole of Jewish tradition and law would take issue with you on the question as to whether a person is a Jew by birth or not. The whole Jewish world and the whole non-Jewish world, does now and has through all time, practically held that a Jew is a Jew by birth. If the Jew wills to leave Judaism, he ceases to be a Jew according to my understanding, but I am not so sure that he would cease to be a Jew according to the nationalist understanding. I agree with you, of course, that Judaism is not a biological fact. I proclaimed this on many occasions.

Later, on page 8 (and this is the part of the address that troubled me most), it seems to me that you have whittled down Judaism to what you call social inheritance. In other words, to a culture or civilization and I find no reference to what we commonly call religion in the part of the address where one would certainly expect it. Although you proclaim earlier that a man is not a Jew by birth, you assert that we had no alternative and that the Reform conception of Judaism is for this reason fundamentally wrong. Here there seems to me to be a confusion of thought which I confess I am unable to follow. In general, as far as I can see, while you set out to discuss the function and organization of the Synagogue, your paper is in effect destructive and not constructive.

Speaking for myself as one of the delegates to the United Synagogue, I consider the paper offensive and not helpful and a re-reading of it has rather emphasized that feeling. I should be very sorry to think that the younger men who are entering the Rabbinate, come with such a point of view. The great body of Jewry is sick. The Rabbis are the Doctors. The sickness is in the main mental and nervous. You know as well as anyone that this is not a case for heroic surgery, but for infinite patience. If our men are to be sent out with a lack of belief in the past and antagonism to the only surroundings in which they can be useful, then indeed I see little hope for the future. It is undoubtedly alright to object to the evangelic methods of the shouting exhorter or to the theatrical pose of the more polished of our leaders, be they Rabbinical or Lay, but the shock method can also become a pose.

I have put down very frankly the thoughts that have come to my mind upon the re-reading of your paper, they may look a little more coldly in type than they might sound, but I know you wanted my frank impression, so I am giving it to you. [AJA]

1. Presented at the 1921 Convention of the United Synagogue.

TO CLAUDE G. MONTEFIORE, LONDON

March 18, 1921

I would like to bring to your attention a situation which has arisen in this country which may cause much injury to individual Jews and a scandal to the Jewish name.

You are no doubt aware that in spite of the several Bills that have passed in the Houses of Congress, no change has yet been made in our immigration legislation. On the other hand the passport regulations of the war period are still in force and in order to overcome these there has arisen a regular trade, either in the forging of the passports or in the forging of visas of American Consuls to the passports or both. It has been reliably reported to the American Jewish Committee that during the last few months about forty Jews have been smuggled into the United States through Mexico by means of forged passports. In nine cases the forgeries were discovered and the holders of these passports are now in prison. We have further been informed (this is based upon the statements of the men in prison) that these forged passports were furnished them by a Jewish agency in Amsterdam and that another batch of Jewish immigrants, about 150 in number, will shortly arrive in the same way.

You can readily understand how damaging this will be to legitimate immigration.

My object in writing you is with the thought that through your connection with the International Colonization Association,[1] you may be able to have the reports which have reached us as to this agency in Amsterdam investigated and if they be found correct, to have steps taken to put an end to this unlawful and dangerous practice.

In this connection, I would say that impending immigrants who cannot secure passports and visas which would entitle them to come into the United States, ought to be advised to remain in Mexico. Mexico makes no requirements, as I understand, with regard to visas, and what would be a lawful entry into Mexico, is an unlawful entry into the United States.

The period of war and depression is now over in Mexico and I believe that many thousands of Jewish immigrants could be accommodated there. There is already a community of about 1,000 Jewish people in Mexico City and the small Jewish Communities on the border towns have already found employment for a number of men who came into Mexico.

The American Jewish Committee has asked the Industrial Removal Office[2] to establish an agency at Vera Cruz to distribute in Mexico and Central America the incoming Jewish Immigrants.

Whether our immigration laws are changed or not, and the sentiment for some further restriction is I believe very strong, the opportunities for a livelihood in America for a stranger are by no means good at the moment, and I have reason to believe that Mexico and South America at the present time offer very much better opportunities.

However, I have wandered just a little from my subject. I am sure you will see the urgency of having any underground and illegal agency for sending Jewish immigrants into this country stopped at once, and since we cannot undertake from this end without hue and cry, I thought that the Commissioner of the ICA would be the best to employ for the purpose. [AJC]

1. Jewish Colonization Association (ICA), founded in 1891 by Baron de Hirsch to encourage the emigration of impoverished Jews and aid in their resettlement. It established Jewish agricultural colonies in Russia, North and South America, and Palestine.
2. Industrial Removal Office, American Jewish agency founded in 1900 to disperse Jewish immigrants throughout the United States and away from the large cities of the East Coast.

Adler continued to express his disapproval of the nationalist thrust of the Zionist movement. He was thus wary of even a formal connection with those elements on the Jewish scene whose loyalty to the Jewish people did not extend to Judaism.

TO JULIAN W. MACK, NEW YORK CITY

March 21, 1921

I have your letter of March 18 inviting me to accept membership on the general reception committee in honor of Doctor [Chaim] Weizmann and his associates.[1] It would be easiest to follow the line of least resistance and accept membership on the committee which you are so gracious as to tender to me, but somewhere in my composition, there seems to be a strain which does not make it possible for me to follow the line of least resistance.

You gentlemen have already decided that a great public meeting shall be held in honor of Doctor Weizmann and his associates, to express the interest that all Jews have in the up-building of Palestine. What will be said at that meeting, no person can prejudge, but I am fairly familiar with the nationalist views of some of the gentlemen, that the Jews throughout the world are a nation in the fullest sense of that term; that it is only those who believe this who are really emancipated and that it was not the Jews of Eastern Europe, but we Jews of the West who require emancipation. Whether all the gentlemen hold this view I do not know, but the committee which you propose, which is not merely a social one having to do with the entertainment of these gentlemen but also as to their work, will in the last analysis be identified with the visitors.

Leaving aside the actual purpose of the meeting at the moment and speaking only of entertainment, I do not find myself in agreement even with this. The mass meeting has never appealed to me as a mode of entertainment and the arrangement of one or of a series of such meetings in the nature of demonstrations, is in my opinion not for the welfare of Jewry at the present time—nor even for the up-building of Palestine.

On two occasions in the last year or so, when we have been present together at meetings, I have indicated my opinion that the Jews, at least in America, ought to come to some understanding with regard both to their own life in America and their relationship to the up-building of Palestine and to the organization which has especially charged itself with this task. I had the same thought in mind in 1915. I have seen no real willingness for such an understanding and I regard the revival of the [American Jewish] Congress movement as a distinct threat against it. I am not anxious, moreover, to join in a movement which is representative "of all elements." There are "elements" among the Jews at the present time with whom I am not only not anxious to affiliate but even unwilling. I did so in our relief work under the compelling needs of great human suffering, but even there I have slowly arrived at the conviction that it was an error. I do not take, as you know, the view of some Jews that we are a church and nothing else, but I do take the view that our sole justification for existence is that of a religious people. While I know that there are different degrees of religiosity and some indifference to it here and there, I do not wish to be associated with Jewish "elements" who have gone beyond the stage even of indifference and are hostile to Judaism.

I am hoping that the presence of Sir Herbert Samuel,[2] the High Commissioner, will influence the Jewish settlement in Palestine in the direction which I believe is right. For myself I think that the first step toward the up-building of Palestine would be in subscription and over-subscription to the Palestine Loan when it is announced. This step seems to me of such supreme importance, that I regard any other movements at the present time which may divert money from it as being in the wrong direction. When the Palestinian Loan is announced, I shall be glad, if I have any influence with people, to urge subscription toward it and in my own humble opinion, all other funds for Palestine should wait upon this.

Since I regarded your invitation as purely personal to me, I am making a personal reply which may not represent the view of any one but myself and which I make without consultation. . . . [AJA]

1. Weizmann was to visit the United States in April 1921.
2. Herbert Louis, Viscount Samuel (1870–1963), British statesman; first professing Jew to hold a position in the British cabinet; the first high commissioner for Palestine, 1920–25.

TO LOUIS MARSHALL, NEW YORK CITY

Philadelphia, April 20, 1921

I am wondering what you think about the present widely advertised quarrel between Judge [Julian W.] Mack and Doctor [Chaim] Weizmann.[1]

For my part—though you know I have never held with any section of the Zionist organization—it seems to me a real misfortune for Palestine and for the Jewish people.

The mystery to me is why is should be so widely and so precipitately advertised. Do both sides want to draw a red-herring trail over the path of anticipated failure? The £25,000,000 will not be raised in one year or in five. Does each want to create a situation whereby the other can be blamed?

Judge Mack and his cohorts went to Paris with the claim that they represented (through the American Jewish Congress of evil memory) three million Jews. In the sworn statement to which I recently called your attention the Zionist organization of America claims but 58,000 members.

Dr. Weizmann I suppose claimed to the British government that he represented all the Jews including Judge Mack's three million—just as Mr. [Leo] Motzkin does. Now there is to be a showdown in cold cash. Naturally both gentlemen shrink from it and hence the smoke screen.

But it appears that the new American Jewish Congress is to be Dr. Weizmann's reliance and so the Frankenstein which Mr. Justice [Louis D.] Brandeis created is not to be so easily disposed of. Back of it all there is probably the real difference of opinion on the nationalist theory—substantially a difference between the attitude of Western and Eastern Jewry.

Here in Philadelphia rumor declares that you belong to the Weizmann party and that when Judge Mack and his organization are scrapped you are to take up the leadership!

Seriously speaking, do you not think that some of us should try to do something real at this juncture? I am satisfied that the Zionist organization has outlived its usefulness if it ever had any and that at all events Jews should now get together on some basis for common work. Do you not think that those of us who do not belong to the party and hence to none of its factions or fractions (as they call them) but yet are sincerely interested in Palestine might be of service in stopping this unseemly row or, better still, of bringing together a conference of all Jewish organizations who are willing to confer? Think what a figure we must be cutting in the eyes of the British and other governments.

I have as you know been pleading for understanding for the last six years. Can we have it or must we go on having nothing but misunderstandings?

I should be very much interested in your views so that I might say לשנה הבאה בירושלים [2] (which I was once accused of omitting) with a reasonably dear hope.

With kindest regards and best wishes for a pleasant Pesach. [AJA]

1. When he visited Palestine in 1919, Louis D. Brandeis was distressed by rampant disease and the poor management of Zionist funds. He therefore proposed the establishment of a company to oversee the funds on a businesslike, nonideological basis that would not include

Eastern European Zionist leaders. Weizmann rejected this proposal and a dispute arose between the two which mirrored the distrust and lack of understanding between the European and American Zionists. This dispute came to a head when Weizmann arrived in the United States, and at the convention of the Zionist Organization of America in Cleveland in June 1921, the Brandeis/Mack group lost the confrontation and abdicated the leadership of American Zionism, causing a schism in Zionist ranks which took nearly two decades to heal.

2. "Next year in Jerusalem."

TO LOUIS MARSHALL, NEW YORK CITY

Philadelphia, May 2, 1921

. . . Meanwhile, the Weizmann organization is engaged in very strong politics here. They are holding meetings and are industriously spreading the report that you are entirely with them and that the moment Judge [Julian W.] Mack steps out, you will take charge of the Zionist Organization of America.

As far as I can judge, apart from any side issues, the real question is Nationalism versus Zionism. This seems to be the tack that the speakers here are taking. As a matter of fact, I am inclined to think that Weizmann has been overawed by Shmarya Levin and Ussischkin.[1] There is also a very strong desire to get rid of nearly everybody in the Organization except Russian Jews. All others are called goyim. You understand of course that the differentiation is not based upon religiosity.

I have been approached by a certain Mr. Slonim[2] of New York to join the [Hebrew] University Committee. He sent me a pamphlet about the University. The University is to be a branch of the Keren Hayesod, but in view of the special character of the University, donors to the fund are to be allowed to pledge for the University. There is not a word as to how this Institution is to be managed, who are to be its trustees, who are to choose its Faculty or anything of the sort. The document constantly appeals to the "Jewish Nation." A Philadelphia Committee of professional men and a few Professors is proposing to give a dinner to Professor Einstein[3] for a consideration of the University problem and I am being badgered on the subject from all sides.

Meanwhile, I shall pay my respects to Professor Einstein by going to hear him lecture at Princeton on Monday, May 9, and join in an academic procession in his honor.

I hope you don't mind my bothering you about these affairs. Both wings come to me for advice and sympathy. [W]

1. Menahem Ussishkin (1863–1941), Russian Zionist leader; head of the Zionist Commission in Palestine, 1919–23; subsequently headed the Jewish National Fund, 1923–41.
2. Joel Slonim (1874–1944), Yiddish journalist.
3. Albert Einstein (1879–1955), physicist. An active Zionist, Einstein accompanied Weizmann on a fund-raising tour of the United States in 1921.

The problems of American Jewish education and particularly the position of the Yiddish language within that education concerned Adler deeply. He felt that Yiddish, as an expression of Jewish ethnicity, was a liability to the full acceptance of the Jews into American society.

TO BERNARD HARRIS, PHILADELPHIA

May 20, 1921

. . . My main difficulties in the matter are both on the question of general policy as well as education. The energy that goes in one direction cannot very well be brought forth in any other. The children must learn English. We want them to learn Hebrew and we are proposing to teach them Yiddish. Nearly everybody in this world is uni-lingual and to make any portion of the general population bi-lingual is a good deal of an effort, and to make them tri-lingual, almost an impossibility.

As for the matter of public policy, that is one which I think is bound very much to effect the whole Jewish position in this country. We teach Hebrew because it is a sacred language and the language of our prayers, but to endeavor to foster another language, if it is consciously and publicly done and to a great extent, will, I think, react unfavorably upon the position of the Jews in this country.

The hostility toward immigration, in my opinion, comes from two sources: First, from the Labor Unions, in order to restrict competition. I am quite certain that with the passage of the restricting immigration bill, there will be more strikes. The hostility to immigration, aside from this, is largely based upon the idea which was so tersely expressed by President [Theodore] Roosevelt, that it was the desire of the American people to be a nation and not a polyglot boarding house. We may satisfy some of the parents, but in the long run we will be taking a step which aids in preventing Jews from having the opportunity of migrating to the United States. . . . [W]

Adler had undertaken the task of writing Jacob Schiff's biography. The work ultimately appeared in 1928 in two volumes, Jacob H. Schiff, His Life and Letters *(Doubleday, Doran and Company).*

TO MORTIMER L. SCHIFF, NEW YORK CITY

July 14, 1921

. . . I very well recall an incident. I was at your father's house on Saturday evening, the 6th of February, 1904, and was discussing with Oscar Straus and Adolph Ochs the threatening reports in the newspapers as to the possibility of an outbreak of war between Japan and Russia. They both thought the war would be averted. I do not think your father heard the conversation. A little later in the evening he rapped on the table for silence and then astounded us by the following statement:

> Gentlemen:
>
> I have something very serious to say to you. Within 72 hours war will break out between Japan and Russia. The question has been presented to me of undertaking a loan for Japan. I would like to get your views as to what effect my undertaking this would have upon the fortunes of the Jewish people in Russia.

We then sat down and talked the matter over at great length. Mr. [Louis] Marshall, Isaac Seligman,[1] Morris Loeb, Cyrus L. Sulzberger and Nathan Bijur were some of those present. Of course I did not tell this story, but it was this that fixed the matter so firmly in my mind. If, however, as I said above, a loan was made to Japan prior to the outbreak of the war, then my conclusions are undoubtedly incorrect. As the incident I speak of happened in February 1904, the loan therefore would have to go back to at least earlier in 1904 than February or 1903.

Even if my facts are correct, of course, it is a question of policy whether they should be narrated. I had not consulted with anybody on that subject and had meant to do so in proof with Judge [Mayer] Sulzberger and Mr. Marshall. My own point of view, however, is this:

There is constant lying on this subject with regard to the attitude of the Jews to Russia. Your own firms are at the moment the targets. I do not know whether you keep up with Mr. [Henry] Ford, but you are the only favorite in the family upon whom the vials of his wrath do not descend. Paul Warburg is at the moment the principal victim. That your father aided the revolutionary cause in Russia is in my mind certain. He was apparently closely associated with the friends of Russian freedom and supplied them with funds, and part of these funds were used in propaganda among the Russian prisoners in Japan. It was part of his settled purpose to liberalize the Czaristic government. The Ford papers are constantly charging that he did this in Japan and his own private papers show that it is true. I have not thought it wise or necessary to mention this incident either, but I personally think it is a glory for any man to have done anything that helped to overthrow the Romanoffs or the Holhenzollerns or the Hapsburgs. I am willing to lump all these three together. My method of presentation was intended to show that he had no hostility to the Russian people or to a proper government in Russia, but that he was willing to aid in the overthrow of the government of the Czar. I believe, moreover, that if I do not in some way mention this, it will lead to much more severe attacks. I would be charged with being one of the conspirators with others to suppress the actual facts of his life and falsify history. I am not concerned about myself in the matter, but I do feel that to omit reference to this will only prove a boomerang.

What you have suggested as to his favorable feeling toward the Kerensky government[2] and his anti-Bolshevist attitude, I will add and thus help to mitigate the possible attacks of the anti-Semites, but I do not feel that we have to alter our lives or our writings simply because these mad beasts are about. Let us rather go ahead unafraid and take our chances. . . . [W]

1. Isaac Newton Seligman (1855–1917), New York banker, philanthropist, and Jewish communal worker.
2. Alexander Fedorovitch Kerensky (1881–1970) headed the provisional government in Russia after the February 1917 revolution, holding this office until overthrown by the Bolshevist Revolution in October 1917.

TO LOUIS MARSHALL, SARANAC LAKE, NEW YORK

August 4, 1921

I want to thank you most profoundly for your two letters of August 1. I am gratified to think that you found my sketch of Mr. [Jacob H.] Schiff[1] worthy of the subject.

I have stricken out entirely any reference to the reasons for Mr. Schiff's leaving home. I had originally placed this upon the ground of his rebellion against the rigorous religious atmosphere and the fact that the boys were obliged to rise at five o'clock in the morning and go to the synagogue in the coldest weather beside afternoons and evenings. I am rather certain that he told me this once and that the seeds of his revolt against orthodoxy were laid in Germany and not in America. Mrs. Schiff, however, thought it unwise to state this although she considered it true. In any event it is not of the highest importance and I am glad to follow your advice and eliminate it.

With regard to the passport question I am certain that my recollection is correct and that the history of this effort is not fully described in Mr. Wolf's book.[2] You will doubtless recall that there were many efforts made during Mr. [Theodore] Roosevelt's administration and all these were through purely diplomatic means.

When Mr. [William H.] Taft was nominated the American Jewish Committee determined to take the matter up with him at once. . . .

. . . It was then the understanding of the Committee that we would give Mr. Taft at least a year in his endeavor to do something. I recall that Mr. Schiff got extremely impatient and I have a letter from him in which he asked me if the Committee was still alive. At a meeting of the Executive Committee which I think took place in November, 1910 (it may have been December but I remember distinctly that the meeting was held in the library of the Temple Emanuel), Mr. Schiff complained of our non-action and I think that I was one of those who used the phrase "that we ought to lay our cards on the table." He asked what we meant and then the idea was suggested of going over the head of the Department of State to Congress and the public. The notion that this appeal should take the particular form of the abrogation of the Treaty was proposed a few weeks later by Judge [Mayer] Sulzberger.

Some time in December, 1910, the interview which I have described took place. Mr. Schiff, Judge Sulzberger and I represented the American Jewish Committee. President Taft received us in the Cabinet Room and Secretary Knox[3] and Rockhill[4] were present. I even remember the request of the President that Mr. Schiff should sit at his right and Judge Sulzberger at his left. Mr. Schiff demurred, saying that Secretary Knox should take the place. Secretary Knox made way for Mr. Schiff and the President insisted. The interview lasted two hours. Then and there it was that Secretary Knox brought up the question of our trade with Russia. Mr. Rockhill at the time spoke of his desire to leave Russia, alleging that the cost of living was very high and his inability to meet it. I remember very well Mr. Taft making the statement that he knew something about that, because on his way back from the Philippines he had come across Siberia and had stayed in St. Petersburg a short time and that his hotel bill was so large that he thought it would have been cheaper if he had bought the entire hotel.

The interview ended with Mr. Taft saying that the entire discussion would be carefully weighed by Secretary Knox, who would prepare a memorandum on the subject. . . . [W]

1. "Jacob Henry Schiff, a biographical sketch," *American Jewish Yearbook*, 23.
2. *Presidents I Have Known* (1918), autobiography of Simon Wolf.
3. Philander Chase Knox (1853–1921), U.S. secretary of state in Taft's cabinet, 1909–15.
4. William W. Rockhill (1854–1914), U.S. ambassador to Russia, 1900–11.

The refusal of the United States Senate to ratify the Treaty of Versailles was for Adler a bitter source of disappointment.

TO LOUIS MARSHALL, NEW YORK CITY

Philadelphia, September 16, 1921

It is awfully good of you to have taken the time when you were so busy to read the letter which I sent to the *New York World*[1] and to make your comments upon it.

I suppose that this is one of the subjects upon which we will have to agree to disagree and indeed I had not any thought of converting you.

Let me however restate to you my point of view as to the German Treaty.[2]

The whole American people was concerned in this War and in the outcome. Whatever the side lines, our War was with Germany. We have made a treaty which only the smallest fraction of the people of the United States can have the opportunity to understand. It would not have taken twenty lines more to apprise the people of the United States in general of what the treaty meant and these twenty lines could have gone into the treaty. Since we have to consider realities in this practical world of to-day, the reality is that ninety-nine percent of the people of the United States on reading the treaty, would not and could not understand what it means and while I do not charge an intention to deceive, the omission of the kind of summary which I gave at least looks as though there was not a strong disposition to inform. It would not have burdened the treaty very much if the numbers had been accompanied by the headings of the respective parts of the section. Compare this with the very detailed summary of the Treaty of Versailles which was given out officially.

My raising the question of morality has to do with claiming all the rights under the treaty which we refuse to ratify, and refusing to accept any of the obligations. I particularly had in mind our attitude toward France. Unless we make a separate treaty with France, in effect we take no cognizance of the settlement by which Alsace Lorraine is returned to France. Now I can understand this upon the strictly American theory, but the exceptions that I have pointed out with regard to Belgium, Switzerland (Monaco of all places) and missionary societies were so surprising to me that when I had after about three hours study made an analysis of the treaty, I could not believe my own eyes and doubted whether I was correct. I therefore submitted this analysis to Mr. Roland Morris and asked that he check it up to find whether I had misunderstood the Treaty or was in error. He checked it up and told me that as far as his knowledge of the Treaty went, my analysis was correct.

I had read carefully the statement given out by the Washington correspondents; I have read editorials in a good many papers and in not one, not even the *New York Times,* which after I had written my article did not publish an editorial referring to the Treaty as an "index"—in not one did I find a clear statement of what the Treaty was and therefore thought I would contribute the results of my humble studies to the press.

I hope your expectations about the Conference for the limitations of armaments will prove justified.[3] To me it seems that this Conference is called entirely in our own interest because if it were not, the subject of the Pacific alone would not have been coupled with it. As I see it, the intention is to limit naval armament and since for the United States there is no apprehension on the Atlantic, we couple the question of the limitation of armament with the question of the Pacific and are in effect endeavoring to make a combination against Japan. What has China to do at the Conference for the limitation of armaments?

I am glad that you have hope that in some way the moral sanction of the United States may be given to the minority treaties. Upon what theory our simon pure Americans are going to have such a treaty ratified, I do not know. I shall be very much interested to know how the minority treaties as such can even be got before the Senate. I have not seen the treaty with Austria but newspapers say it follows along the lines of the German Treaty exactly, which means of course that we take no cognizance of the protection of the rights of minorities in Hungary, Czecho-Slovakia, etc., nor any of the portion of territory that was added to Roumania. Then there will come next, I presume, the Polish Treaty and so on. What are we going to do about all these?

I am not pessimistic because I always expect that the right will prevail, but I am humiliated as an American at the present conduct of the United States.

Put whatever face upon it you will, the separate treaty with Germany was a blow to our associates in the World War and a heartening to Germany, and the moving force was the blind hatred of the "obstinate" man and the desire to manoeuvre for political advantage. For these two reasons we have forfeited our position in the world, temporarily, from the best beloved nation and have become, to put it mildly, the least liked. Germany will sign the Treaty with us and ratify it and of course five nations will come to a conference at Washington, but they do so only because of the fact that they owe us money, they need us and they are not in position to withstand any of our requests or whims for the time being. We have taken the attitude of the bully. I do not see how in his heart of hearts, any American can be proud of the situation.

Just one little point. We never went to war with Turkey. We claim, however, without assuming any obligation, a voice in the distribution of the remains of the Turkish Empire, including the mandates over Palestine and Mesopotamia. We claim that we contributed to the general result of the War and therefore are entitled to participate in all the results when we please and not to do so when it does not please us. I think that if our contribution to the conquest of Palestine were carefully looked into, the claim would not be well substantiated. I doubt very much whether any direct claim could be established with regard to Mesopotamia. The real solution of the question is probably to be found in the intimate relationship between the great Oil Company of America and the American Society of Foreign Missions. The miracle of the mixture of oil and holy water has been effected to make a hundred percent American foreign policy. I agree with you that we should be looking for matters of substance and not matters of mere form and I therefore see with dismay an American administration groping its way to matters of substance which were at hand because they had acquired a rooted objection for the mere form, also ready to hand, by which these matters of substance could have been secured.

I am sure that you yourself felt that the clauses of the Versailles Treaties relating to reparations and some of the economic clauses were extremely severe and yet these we swallow whole.

We could have accomplished the same purpose and avoided making a separate treaty with Germany had our Government recommended the ratification of the Versailles Treaty with all the clauses excepted which are excepted in the new treaty. This would at least have kept us within the family of which we were a member and not exposed us to the feeling which I am sure the separate treaty has aroused in France where it has been openly expressed and in England and where it will smoulder. [W]

1. This letter was published September 13, 1921.
2. Having rejected the Versailles Treaty in 1920, the United States ratified in October 1921 separate peace treaties with Germany, Austria, and Hungary.
3. Washington conference on naval disarmament, November 1921–February 1922, which resulted in an agreement limiting navies and political treaties on China and the Pacific Ocean.

TO JUDAH L. MAGNES

Philadelphia, December 22, 1921

. . . With regard to the long strike in the waist industry in Philadelphia,[1] I have made an attempt at the beginning to secure some form of arbitration through the Mayor of Philadelphia,[2] but the Mayor told me that he himself had already tried it and failed and did not think that he could usefully try again.

I also had several talks with Doctor [Abraham A.] Neuman on the subject in whose congregation a number of manufacturers are members and he has had talks with them and made the topic the subject for his Yom Kippur address, urging peace and harmony.

More recently, or I should say probably three or four weeks ago, a Mr. Reisberg, I believe one of the representatives of the local union, called to see me and asked me if I would undertake settlement. I told him I would if I thought I could do it usefully. I had a second interview with him at which he made the proposition that I should invite three of the representatives of the manufacturers' union whom he named and three of their own representatives to a meeting, not letting the manufacturers know that there was to be such a meeting, but simply asking them to come to my office. Mr. Reisberg said that he felt sure that if I could get these six men in a room together, they would agree.

I did not agree with this plan for reasons which I suppose would be obvious to you, but if they are not, I do not want to lure people into my office for any purpose, nor am I sure that Mr. Reisberg's theory was correct. The manufacturers might just as well turn upon their heels and walk out of my office as not. I do not think that anything is to be gained by what seems to me to be a trick and at least I do not care to be a part of it. Mr. Reisberg then told me that he would communicate with their people and let me know whether they wished me to undertake a meeting on the basis I have suggested, namely that both sides should be informed of the purpose of the meeting. I have not heard from him since. [M]

1. In November 1921 a major garment strike over the issue of piecework started in New York and spread to other garment centers, including Philadelphia.
2. John Moore (1864–1950), mayor of Philadelphia, 1920–23, 1932–35.

During the era of Prohibition, a dispute arose as to whether fermented wine was a necessity for such Jewish rites as kiddush *and* havdalah. *In 1925, the Internal Revenue Service would rule that wine for sacramental purposes was permissible to a limit of one gallon a year per adult, to be distributed by ministers and rabbis.*

TO LOUIS FINKELSTEIN,[1] NEW YORK CITY

December 28, 1921

I have your letter of December 27 in which you enclose me the proposed programme of the Convention of the Rabbinical Assembly. As for the morning session I shall be very glad to take the part in it that you indicate.

I do not know what Professor [Louis] Ginzberg's opinion is but in any event I do not like the way in which the title of his paper is phrased. You have it "The *Need* of Fermented Wines in Jewish Religious Ceremonies." Does not this title prejudge the case? Should it not be "The *Question* of Fermented Wines in Jewish Religious Ceremonies"? I want to suggest that the wine question be discussed in executive session and not to be open to representatives of the press or to the public. My reason for this suggestion is that this is now a subject for active newspaper discussion and it might very well be that sensational reports would appear in the news papers.

I do not know how active a question "The Courts of Arbitration" is. I think there is a good deal of danger in the question of Jewish Courts of Arbitration. If ordinary civic matters are settled in such courts we would undoubtedly have to face the cry of the attempt to create an imperium in imperio.

What I miss in the programme is something that would have to do with discussion as to the methods by which a greater observance of the Sabbath could be secured and in general a deepening of Jewish religious life. It is several years since a meeting has been held by the Seminary men and I think they ought seriously talk over that subject. [W]

1. Louis Finkelstein (b.1895), Conservative rabbi and scholar; at the time instructor at the Jewish Theological Seminary; later succeeded Adler as president of the institution.

TO SAMUEL COHEN,[1] NEW YORK CITY

January 3, 1922

. . . It seems to me that you as the Executive Director of the United Synagogue and I as one of the Council have to put in the forefront of our minds the effect of the present practice with regard to sacramental wine on

Judaism. I can only repeat the statement that I have made a good deal of times that it is bringing the rabbinate and the Jewish people in general into disrepute and is creating a public scandal. If the bootleggers were lay Jews then your argument would hold good, but since the great quantity of this bootlegging is carried out under the direct authorization of rabbis I feel that it is the duty of a religious organization to protect that holy name. It makes very little difference whether other people are guilty of infractions of the law or not.

I am not concerned about the attitude toward a secular government as you call it. I ought to add, by the way, that insofar as I know there is only one kind of government in this country, but my proposal is that the rabbis themselves should renounce this privilege. Jews from time to time recognize their right and even duty under the compelling influence of their surroundings to alter or modify their own laws. I do not recall any place in the Bible in which monogamy is commanded and as I presume you know monogamy is not absolutely universal among the Jews in the Orient, but in the Western world we have practised it and established definite laws on that subject for a long time. If the Jews deny themselves the pleasure of having two wives, they could also deny themselves the satisfaction of having a glass of wine. . . .

. . . Large sections of the Jewish people have for long periods used for kiddush-habdala and Pesah non-alcoholic wine and I believe that if there were no business interests behind the sacramental wine there would not be so much fuss in the matter. [JTS]

1. Samuel Cohen (1886–1945), Conservative rabbi; executive director of the United Synagogue of America, 1917–44.

TO JUDAH L. MAGNES, NEW YORK CITY

Philadelphia, January 16, 1922

There has been held a meeting of two representatives of each of the three Committees[1] under the chairmanship of Mr. [Harry] Lucas, the secretary of the Joint Distribution Committee. Our own Committee was represented by the Secretary of the Committee, Doctor Krass,[2] and myself. We did not arrive very far. I think that the American Jewish Relief Committee could deal with either one of the other two Committees, but they do not seem able to deal with each other. Rabbi Meir Berlin[3] and Mr. Peter Wiernik[4] have asked me for a separate conference which I have agreed to, with the idea of simply talking things over so that possibly the situation might be clarified. I have had a talk with Mr. Sholem Asch on the subject recently, who wanted to talk it over with me before he went to Europe. In some way, of course, we must have joint action. On the other hand there is much opposition in the Joint Distribution Committee toward any further considerable expenditure of funds in sending representatives abroad. If the three Committees could agree upon one representative for cultural work there would be no difficulty, but the sending of three representatives, I think, would result in much criticism. This is about how the matter stands at the moment. [M]

1. The American Jewish Relief Committee, the Central Committee, the People's Relief Committee, together made up the American Jewish Joint Distribution Committee. See letter to Louis Marshall, December 28, 1917.
2. Nathan Krass (1880–1949), rabbi of the Central Synagogue, New York City, and later of Temple Emanu-El.
3. Meir Berlin (Bar-Ilan) (1880–1949), leader of the Religious Zionist (Mizrachi) movement.
4. Peter (Peretz) Wiernik (1865–1936), Hebrew and Yiddish journalist.

TO FELIX M. WARBURG, NEW YORK CITY

Philadelphia, March 14, 1922

. . . I stayed away from the Zionist movement all these years for two reasons. First, because of its non-religious character and second, because my own visits there and the information that I had about Palestine made me fear that the conditions as described would be the conditions that actually would arise. No small country in the Orient, especially where the race and religious feelings are so strong as they are in Palestine, can absorb any considerable number of newcomers rapidly. I remember very well when I discussed the possibilities with Kamil Pasha, the Grand Vizier in Turkey in 1890,[1] a man who was most sympathetic to the Jewish people, he told me that Palestine could at most assimilate 5000 immigrants per annum.

On the other hand, with the doors shut in so many parts of the world and the conditions as they are in Russia and some other East European countries, any avenues for a settlement even of a few thousand Jews a year ought to be held open. I do not believe that the work in Palestine could ever be satisfactorily done until some organization representing the best minds and abilities of all the Jewish people are put in charge of the work. [W]

1. See letter to Sabato Morais, February 3, 1891.

TO LOUIS MARSHALL, NEW YORK CITY

Philadelphia, March 16, 1922

I have your letter of March 15 and thank you for your kind solicitude about me. I do not think my present difficulty is due to overwork, but is a recurrence of a trouble that I had about four times in the last twenty years. However, I am in entire agreement with you as to the many activities both for myself and for you.

You may remember that when we got back in 1919, I made a distinct proposition to you and Mr. [Felix M.] Warburg with regard to some division of labor all around, suggesting that as we were all devoted to public work, there was no need of our all doing the same work. I proposed then that I should stick to educational work and give up everything else, but you wanted me to stay in the American Jewish Committee and Felix wanted me to stay in the Relief, and those were the two things that take the most time; at least if they do not take up time, they take up anxious thought.

I am very delighted to hear of your splendid result in New York in the Relief Campaign. . . . I think that this campaign pointed the right way for your own very big city. Brooklyn is a town as so is Washington Heights. I am also very gratified at the excellent work that Rabbi Drob[1] did. I have always felt that he was a man of real ability with an indisposition to employ it except under rather considerable pressure.

As for the excellence of the work through the synagogues, that is as it should be. I would much rather the Jews contribute through their synagogue than through the fur trade or even as bankers. The reason that our synagogues have been left so poor is because we have taken so much away from them.

As for the reorganization of the work of the Joint Distribution Committee, I believe that the South and West should have a little more voice in the distribution of the funds which they have helped raise and actually give. We have been working on the theory of representation by political tendency rather than representation on the basis of the donor. I am practically the only person who does not live in New York who has had any real voice in the work of the Committee. I believe that if the meetings of the Executive Committee were not too frequent, and they are usually not above once a month, and if they were on a definite date and not subject to change because of one or another person, so that people in Chicago or Detroit or Washington could make their arrangements, then the out of town men would come to the meetings. After all, the people who raise the money are held to certain responsibilities by their communities for the proper expenditure of that money.

I am inclined to think that there ought to be more of an infusion of business men into the Reconstruction Committee and by business men I mean merchants not bankers. . . . [W]

1. Max Drob (1887–1959), Conservative rabbi; became president of the Rabbinical Assembly, 1925–27.

TO SIMON WOLF, WASHINGTON, D.C.

April 27, 1922

. . . You ask my opinion with regard to a passage by Congress of a resolution endorsing the Balfour Declaration[1] and telling me that you are decidedly opposed "on the grounds of hands off in all European tangles."

With the latter sentiment I do not agree. That may be due to our political differences, but I was decidedly in favor of the League of Nations and think that much of the misery and unrest in the world is caused by our refusal to ratify the Covenant. Instead of creating a more ordered piece of machinery to bring about peace in the world, instead of perpetual war, we have Washington conferences and Genoa conferences and I dare say others, all of these being simply to get America into a concert of nations without forcing us into the League.

But since our Government has thus far declined to enter the League, since we would have nothing to do with Armenia or anyone else, I regard the proposed congressional action as simply a bid for votes. Your high class republican Senators, with Senator [Henry Cabot] Lodge at their head, will pass a resolution that will get the votes of the Jews, votes of the soldiers, votes of anybody that will carry them back into the United States Senate. This is my opinion from the American point of view.

As a Jew, I do not favor the resolution. I did not favor the Balfour Declaration and I did not favor the Zionist platform. I regard the Jews as a religious people and not as a political entity. Had the movement taken the place of a recognition of our sentimental and historical claims to Palestine, even with the view at some future time of the creation of a Jewish commonwealth, I should have favored it, but I am out of tune with the movement engineered to a considerable extent by politicians and non-religious Jews. . . . [W]

1. On May 4, 1922, the United States Senate would pass a resolution in favor of the restoration of Palestine as a National Home for the Jewish people. The House of Representatives would pass a similar resolution.

TO LOUIS MARSHALL, NEW YORK CITY

Philadelphia, June 19, 1922

I am thinking of writing a letter to the *American Hebrew* calling attention to the entire omission or reference of any kind to the [Jewish Theological] Seminary Commencement in their issue of this week, although full information was sent them. This is bad journalism and, aside from that, indicates a new form of militancy against the Seminary by silence.

I noticed in the statement of Mr. Alfred M. Cohen, the President of the Board of Governors of the Hebrew Union College, that they are proposing to establish a College or branch in New York.[1] I do not know how the Seminary is going to fare with three other more or less competing institutions in New York City. Our depleted Faculty is a source of real danger to us in that I fear dissatisfaction on the part of the students if it should be continued and I earnestly hope that by the early autumn, if not sooner, the results of the campaign will be of such a nature as to warrant our making some provision for bible and philosophy this year. After all, students are human. They know Professor [Louis] Ginzberg as a Talmudist and they do not readily take to his biblical teaching and Professor [Alexander] Marx is an historian and bibliographer and reading philosophical texts with him does not meet the subject. I have real hopes that we will be able to do something next year, since the Alumni give me very encouraging reports. I am writing them to let me have the actual results of their work by the first of July, as I do not trust much to the enthusiasm of the Summer.

I am enclosing you a copy of a letter which I have received from Mortimer Schiff. What the reason is for his change of heart, I do not know. I can only assume that he does not desire to have his name connected with the Seminary in any way, however slight, and that all we may expect from him is a moderate annual contribution and an occasional gift to the library. At all events, I have done everything that I could in some way to keep up the attachment of his name to the Seminary and feel that any further efforts in that direction would be fruitless. [AJA]

1. In 1922 Stephen S. Wise founded the Jewish Institute of Religion in New York for the training of rabbis. It would merge with Hebrew Union College in 1950. See letter to Edwin Kaufman, December 31, 1920.

TO LUCIEN WOLF, LONDON

August 22, 1922

. . . It occurred to me that it might be of service to you if I give you a purely personal view of what seems to me to have happened in the American public mind during the last few years on the subject of immigration. I may be wrong in my analysis, of course, but I think you may assume I have watched the situation and am at least in as good a position to reach a conclusion as another.

There has, of course, for a long time, been an uneasiness in certain sections of the country with regard to the large influx of foreign non-English speaking population. In the South this has for many years assumed the complection of a race question; the southern whites have said in effect: "We have a negro problem on our hands and we do not want another problem." In the South there was no Jewish migration to speak of, but the migration that the people there objected to was that of the Italian and Syrian. I state this to indicate that the Jewish question had nothing to do with the strong growth of anti-immigration sentiment in the Southern part of the United States. Nor was it an economic question, because as you know, the South is still very sparsely settled.

Previous immigration restriction movements have, as you know, taken the form of a literacy test, and while these bills were vetoed successively by Presidents [Benjamin] Harrison, [Grover] Cleveland, [William H.] Taft and [Woodrow] Wilson, such a bill was finally passed over President Wilson's head when other bills which he vetoed were likewise being passed over his head.

The War caused the spread of an anti-immigration sentiment to practically every part of the United States. This according to my diagnosis was due to the following causes: During the period that America was not in the War, the Austrian and German ambassadors were organizing their former nationals in the United States just as though they had been on their own territory. The Austrian ambassador did this openly, the German ambassador secretly. As a result, a wave of uneasiness spread throughout the entire native population.

A great many people, however, still cherished the idea of America as an asylum for the persecuted and oppressed and had also conceived the notion that through our public school system, the immigrants, who had reached as much as a million a year or over, were being surely molded into the American body politic. When the draft law was passed and our Army was assembled, this theory, which had been strengthened by Mr. [Israel] Zangwill's phrase of the "melting pot," was rudely overthrown. It was found that we had tens of thousands of citizens who did not know enough English to get the word of command; that even in a state like Massachusetts there were two entire regiments of which this was true. One of [Theodore] Roosevelt's last phrases was that it appeared that we had not developed a nation, but a polyglot boarding house. In other words, America drew back in affright at the great numbers of what it considered undigested human material in its midst, and for good or ill, and I believe without reference whatever to any economic advantages or disadvantages, it has decided that this country is no longer a field for immigration. The present limit of three percent may become two percent or even less. The forces that are operating toward this restriction are too numerous and powerful to be overcome. The American Federation of Labor, in spite of its fine phrases, is one of the most potent of these influences. The old line families of New England and the South are just as determined. Right here in Philadelphia, all of the publications controlled by Mr. [Cyrus H.] Curtis, himself a New England man, are militantly restrictionist. By that, I do not mean solely the *Public Ledger,* which is one of the most read papers in Philadelphia though local in its influence, but the *Saturday Evening Post,* which is said to circulate two million copies and is read in every city, town and village in the United States, has practically as its sole editorial policy the restriction of immigration.

Our scientific men, especially the biologists and the anthropologists, have taken up the subject of the mixed race which they declare is being produced here and have issued all kinds of warnings against it as tending to degeneracy. Professor Henry Fairfield Osborne of Columbia, probably the most distinguished man in the biological sciences in America, is taking this ground and Professor Conklin[1] of Princeton, a very eminent zoologist, is following the same line.

These views, you will see, therefore are being spread not only among the masses through a five-cent paper like the *Saturday Evening Post,* but in college and university circles by leading professors. All of this, whether mistaken or not, is I think honest; that is to say, the people who are promulgating these ideas are sincere in their conviction that the American people, the American spirit, and the English language are seriously threatened. Our statisticians, of course, help this along. A statement was given out only a few days since, indicating that over 960,000 persons in New York City had Yiddish as their mother tongue. The recent anti-Semitic propaganda which was introduced and fostered by Russian émigrés of the Monarchist persuasion, will have little permanent effect, although it may be responsible for the percentage talk at a great university like Harvard, but it has undoubtedly furnished weapons for the anti-immigrationists since it so sedulously depicted the bad characteristics of the Jew. While the Jewish question, therefore, may have had something to do with the further restriction movement through [Henry] Ford's extensive propaganda, I think that it is much broader and more deep seated, and that with such modifications as we may be able to secure from time to time on the theory of allowing families to join their relatives in this country, the United States is forever closed as a field for immigration. Others might dissent from my view, but I believe that you will be well advised if in your further work in behalf of the unfortunate refugees you will accept this analysis as correct. Any attempt to take any step in behalf of these unfortunates being admitted to the United States will have an effect exactly opposite from that desired and might close the door to everybody. At least under the present arrangements[2] I understand 60,000 Jews are coming into the United States each year. [AJC]

1. Edward G. Conklin (1863–1952), professor of zoology at Princeton University.
2. Legislation passed in 1921 limited the annual immigration to the United States from Europe and Asia to 150,000.

TO LOUIS MARSHALL, NEW YORK CITY

Philadelphia, August 25, 1922

I have your letter of August 23. I thought that the word "personal" was sufficient in my letter, but I have adopted your suggestion and have written [Lucien] Wolf a brief note[1] telling him that it would be harmful if my communication or yours should in any way come before the public.

I purposely stated my own view with regard to the future of immigration into this country and could have made it even stronger, had I fully expressed my opinion, which is that nothing but the direst necessity of manpower will ever again open our doors. I do not think it entirely a question of the misleading of public opinion, but rather the militant attitude of the recent immigration and of the social workers who had to do with recent immigration as to the part which the immigrant shall play in America. The early immigration was content and happy to live under the system of law and practice which America had evolved and to merge itself with this even though it formed group organizations. The more recent immigration and its sympathizers have flatly said that they had something of culture and notions of government and life to add to America, thereby modifying and enriching our system. It is this attitude which, in my opinion, has been one of the determining factors in bringing about present day anti-immigration sentiment. [W]

1. See letter to Lucien Wolf, August 22, 1922.

In June 1922 President Abbott Lawrence Lowell (1856–1943) of Harvard University proposed the limitation of Jewish enrollment at that institution, just as other institutions were imposing quotas on Jewish students and faculty. Such an action, reminiscent of the restrictive policies of anti-Semitic European institutions, could not but provoke the outrage of the American Jewish community. The agitation this proposal aroused was laid to rest in April 1923, when the Harvard trustees reaffirmed a policy of "freedom from discrimination on grounds of race or religion." However, they effectively restricted Harvard's Jewish enrollment by seeking more applicants outside the eastern seaboard. Thus Jewish enrollment dropped from 20 percent in 1922 to about 10 percent in the mid- and late twenties and thirties.

TO LOUIS MARSHALL, NEW YORK CITY

Philadelphia, September 22, 1922

. . . I do not think that the Harvard question can be successfully argued from this point of view. If a university is a seat of learning, then it should become, as President Hopkins[1] of Dartmouth said a few days ago, an aristocracy of brains and nothing else should count. If this theory is to be applied only to the post-graduate department and professional schools whilst the colleges are to be held as a sort of country club in which good manners and sports are the tests for entrance, let us know.

My opinion is that if Harvard cannot be convinced that by making discriminations it is doing an illiberal and uncivilized thing, she will not be won over by an enumeration of our eminent people or our sufferings in the past. How much do you think the mind of President Lowell will be affected by having the name of Mr. Justice [Louis D.] Brandeis brought before him? As I recall, Lowell was one of the active opponents of the confirmation of Brandeis and by no means upon a racial or religious basis. . . . [AJA]

1. Ernest Martin Hopkins (1877–1964).

TO DAVID DE SOLA POOL,[1] NEW YORK CITY

November 7, 1922

. . . I have seen Doctor Lewin[2] of Palestine at considerable length. As far as I am able to judge the work he has undertaken from the 32 printed pages which he showed me, it is a work of great importance and he seems capable of doing it, although of course, this is, like nearly all Jewish scholarly and other undertakings, an individual enterprise. I have advised Doctor Lewin that he should formally submit his project to the young institution here known as the Jewish Academy.[3] This contains a small group of the best Jewish scholars in the United States—and secure either their approval or their criticism of his plan. If they approve of the plan, then this approval ought to be stated and signed by them, and upon the basis of such approval, an endeavor should be made to get up a fund for publication. The sum of money that Doctor Lewin mentioned to me—$100,000—I consider quite impossible to secure at the present time for a single literary enterprise. As you know, there are other enterprises emanating from Palestine and elsewhere now in the air—a Concordance to the Mishna, the manuscript of which I understand is completed, a Concordance to the Talmud which is projected, etc.[4]

I understand that the Jewish Academy is going to meet in the course of a couple of weeks. After I hear their views, a plan might be formed by which a reasonable sum can be secured to aid in the publication of this work. After one volume is printed, it could be put upon the market and the proceeds from it used to aid in printing the next volume. Advance subscriptions could probably be secured from libraries.

Doctor Lewin's idea of having the project financed in part or in whole from the cultural funds of the Joint Distribution Committee upon the plea that such funds would give employment to a few people in Palestine seems to me fantastic.

I should be very glad to get any suggestion from you as to any practical method by which Doctor Lewin can be aided. [D]

1. David de Sola Pool (1885–1970), rabbi of Congregation Shearith Israel, New York City, 1907–56.
2. Benjamin Manasseh Lewin (1879–1944), scholar and educator. His magnum opus was the collection of Gaonic literature entitled *Ozar ha-Geonim*, 12 vols. (1928–43).
3. American Academy for Jewish Research.
4. Hayyim J. Kasowski (1873–1960), Jerusalem rabbinical scholar; produced concordances of the Mishna (1917–27), the Tosefta (1933–36), and the Talmud (1954–[incomplete]).

One of the greatest achievements of Adler's term as president of the Jewish Theological Seminary was the acquisition of the collection of Hebrew manuscripts accumulated by Elkan Adler of London. The Adler manuscripts gave the Seminary

Library one of the foremost collections of Hebrew manuscripts in the world. See Adler's letters to Alexander Marx, September 5, 1919, and Louis Marshall, February 1, 1923.

TO MORTIMER L. SCHIFF, NEW YORK CITY

November 8, 1922

Since our conversation, I have given a good deal of thought to the question of the purchase of the Library of Elkan N. Adler.[1] I asked Professor [Alexander] Marx to prepare a memorandum on the Manuscripts, which he has done, and I had a long talk with Doctor A. S. W. Rosenbach on the subject.

As far as I can gather, in addition to the manuscripts which Professor Marx has pretty fully described in the enclosed memorandum, Mr. Adler's collection consists of about 30,000 titles of Hebraica and Judaica. The collection of books printed in Hebrew in his library is superior to any collection now in private possession. It bears favorable comparison with the famous library of David Oppenheimer[2] which had made the Hebrew collection at the Bodleian Library pre-eminent.

Adler has an unusually large number of incunabula and of printed books of the first half of the 15th [*sic*] century many of them unique. The books in his Library are mostly in very good condition and when he secured an incomplete copy he often completed it from another copy.

Of the special departments in which his collection of printed books is rich, I would mention that relating to the Spanish Inquisition and the autos-da-fé. In this branch of Jewish history he made direct collections in Spain and in America and these collections include a great many manuscripts, which not being in the Hebrew language, are not included in the catalogue published last year by the Cambridge Press.[3]

He has everything published in Judeo–Persian and the greatest collection of manuscripts in this department known anywhere. In an article on Jewish-Persian literature written by the late distinguished Professor W. Bacher[4] of Budapest and published in 1905, Bacher refers to Adler's collection as the greatest collection of Jewish-Persian manuscripts in existence. Elkan Adler himself published a little volume in 1905 at the Oxford Press entitled "About Hebrew Manuscripts" based entirely upon manuscripts in his own collection, one of which is a Hebrew bookseller's catalogue of the beginning of the 12th century.

To return to Adler's printed collection, he has everything published so far as known of the Bnai Israel of India, some of which is printed in Marathi, a modern form of ancient Sanscrit.

As for other collections that are likely to come in the market, the only one I know is that of Doctor [Moses] Gaster which may, of course, be sold some day. Doctor Gaster's library is much smaller than Elkan Adler's, though it contains many rare and exquisite books. It does not in any way compare with Adler's Library in size or importance.

Professor Marx is quite sure that if we secure Elkan Adler's collection, the [Jewish Theological] Seminary would have the largest collection in number of Hebrew books and manuscripts in the world and that only the Bodleian might exceed it in the importance of its Hebrew manuscript collection.

To me, at least, a very great interest attaches to Elkan Adler's Library because of the way in which he made his collections. Naturally he bought from booksellers, but his collections are largely Aleppo, Morocco, Algiers, Tripoli, Persia, Constantinople, the Balkans, Sweden, Portugal, South America, the United States, Russia, India and Aden. Some of these places he visited a half dozen times. I have seen him hunting books in Paris, in fact on certain occasions when I was gathering a collection of maps and geographies,[5] we hunted together, and I know that he has a keen sense for important things and a real ability in getting them if he wants them.

I do not want to burden you with documents, but I should like to send you the catalogue of Elkan Adler's Hebrew manuscripts because I think a look at the book itself with facsimiles of pages from some of the more interesting manuscripts, would give you a better impression than any statement of mine.

If you will allow me to do so, I will send the book to you.

When I spoke to Doctor Rosenbach on the subject of Elkan Adler's library, he fully corroborated everything that Professor Marx had said as to its size and importance from his own point of view. He had, however, within the past year gone over the Library three times he tells me, and that it fills seven large rooms in Adler's house.

As for the price of the Library, Doctor Rosenbach said that Elkan Adler had indicated that the price of the Library was 30,000 pounds. Doctor Rosenbach believes that the Library could be secured for $100,000; that an offer of 22,500 pounds would be accepted by Elkan Adler.

As for the method of approach, Doctor Rosenbach is of the opinion that if the Seminary made a direct offer to Elkan Adler, the price might not be so favorable. Doctor Rosenbach tells me that he expects to go to England in the course of a couple of months and that if by that time we were prepared to authorize him to purchase the Library for a sum equivalent to $100,000, he believes he could effect the purchase for us.

If, when you have time to read this rather lengthy statement, you wish to talk it over with me again, I am at your disposal.

P.S. I would like to add that the collection of Anglo-Judaica is very important, especially the section relating to Menasseh ben Israel, and that this would supplement the Israel Solomons Collection which we owe to your kindness. [W]

1. See letter to Alexander Marx, September 5, 1919.
2. David ben Abraham Oppenheim (Oppenheimer) (1664–1736), rabbi and bibliophile. His collection was bought by the Bodleian library in 1829 and forms the core of its collection of Judaica.
3. *Catalogue of Hebrew Manuscripts in the Collection of E. N. Adler* (Cambridge University Press, 1921).
4. Wilhelm Bacher (1850–1913), Hungarian rabbi and scholar. The article referred to is "Zur judisch-persischen Literatur," *JQR* 16 (1904): 525–58.
5. Adler assembled this collection for the Free Library of Philadelphia. *IHCD*, p. 312.

The development of the yishuv *in the 1920's brought about a revival of the movement for establishing a Hebrew University in Jerusalem, in which a prominent place would be given to an Institute of Jewish Studies. Adler, with his experience in administering institutions of higher Jewish learning, became deeply involved in this project as a member of the university's Board of Governors.*

TO JOSEPH H. HERTZ, LONDON

December 13, 1922

I have your letter of November 23 with regard to the proposed faculty of Jewish Studies in the University in Palestine.

Several weeks ago, I received a lengthy project from Mr. ben Yehuda[1] outlining the courses in the proposed Department of Jewish Studies and giving the names of the Committee in charge: President—Achad Ha-am;[2] Vice President—David Yellin;[3] Secretary—Eliezer ben Yehuda; and Messrs. [Menahem] Ussishkin, Klausner,[4] Pick[5] and Doctor Mayer.[6]

I was asked to give any criticism I had to make with regard to the curriculum and also to cooperate in the securing of funds. I presume, of course, you have seen their plan, but if not, I would say to you that it follows pretty much the programme of the Dropsie College adding, however, Egyptian which we do not teach here and also Greek, Latin and modern languages as well as general philosophy, history and comparative law, this going beyond the scope of either a Jewish or even general Semitic Faculty.

Shortly after I received this document, I learned in the course of conversation that Professors [Max L.] Margolis and [Henry] Malter and Professor [Louis] Ginzberg had received invitations to teach in this Faculty for a period of three years, or if they could not do so, then for one year, and the matter was made so urgent that they were asked to cable their reply. Professor Margolis, who was expecting to be in Palestine in the year 1924–1925, after conference with me, accepted, though I believe not by cable. Professor Ginzberg wrote for further information. Whether Professor Malter has answered or not, I do not know. Meanwhile, a cablegram from Jerusalem has been published in the American papers announcing the invitation of these three gentlemen and of several European scholars.

When James de Rothschild[7] was in this country, he asked me whether I would take an interest in the University when it came along, and I told him that I would if the plan was one such as I could support.

I had two lengthy talks with Professor Otto Warburg[8] on the subject when he was in the United States and found, if I am correct in my interpretation, that there was no plan for the University at all, and as far as I could gather from him, he did not expect such an institution to be established inside of twenty years. What he was proposing was the establishment of small research institutes devoted to specific subjects which would ultimately grow into a University. I saw that he, like others who talked about the subject, was vague, and hoping that he might clarify his own thought, I asked him to give the address at the Dropsie College Founder's Day in March, 1922, and devote it to the subject of a University in Palestine, which address might then be printed as something for discussion, but he had to go to the Pacific Coast collecting funds, and so that plan fell through.

More recently, Doctor [Nahum] Slousch came to see me with a view to the formation of a Committee here for furthering excavations in Palestine under Jewish auspices and I agreed to join such a Committee, but not to be its Chairman. I do not know whether he has found a Chairman as yet or not.

Some time before Judge [Julian W.] Mack and his friends agreed to differ with the other gentlemen of the Zionist persuasion, Judge Mack told me that a Committee was being formed to consider the University and asked me if I would join it. I never heard of the Committee again.

One day during the Keren Hayesod drive here last year, a man unknown to me called me on the telephone and asked me if I would take part in the movement of the University. I asked him to send me the plan of the University and received in the mail the statutes of the Keren Hayesod.

Last summer, before he went abroad, Mr. Sol Rosenbloom[9] had a talk with me and told me that he was prepared to devote a considerable sum of money to the Jewish and Semitic Department of a University if assurance could be given that it would be carried on along traditional lines and not fall into the hands of a group of radicals which might well be possible. At that time, I threw out the suggestion to him that the only way to insure a fairly consistent policy for such a Department would be to place it in the hands of a Board of Governors or Directors representing institutions whose policy was reasonably fixed, as far as anything is fixed in this world of ours. I had in mind that the Jews' College in London, the Seminaries in Paris, Berlin, Breslau, Vienna, Budapest and New York, for example, should each nominate one person who would represent them in this council and there might be two or three resident in Palestine. Such a body collected upon the basis of institutions rather than by individual selection could furnish a reasonable guarantee that a conservative policy would be followed. Mr. Rosenbloom, by the way, tells me that the Committee of which ben Yehuda is Secretary approached him and that while he does not make any criticism of their plans, they are not in the direction in which his interest lies and that he is not disposed to have the money which he has pledged used for this purpose.

I have cited all this to you because I think it indicates that considering the seriousness of the matter, it has not yet been taken in hand in any definite way and it may be also that we in America have different views about the organization of an institution of learning than those prevailing in Europe. I discussed this point with Professor Warburg who seemed to think that a group of men might associate themselves together and become a Faculty, as it were, by natural selection and that some unknown persons might provide the funds and look after the details of management. As a matter of fact, the great mediaeval universities of England, France, Italy and Germany did arise in this way by a sort of voluntary association of masters and pupils, but I very much doubt whether this method can be followed with safety at the present time.

Now I want to discuss for a moment the whole question of a Jewish University in Palestine and I wonder whether the people who proclaimed this plan to the world, engaged in the laying of a corner stone and had pictures printed in magazines and newspapers took thought as to the seriousness of the enterprise. In what I am going to say to you, I do not think it necessary for me to assert that I am interested in learning and in science, though in the present intolerance of public opinion among the Jewish people, any difference of opinion is at once set down to some ulterior or unworthy motive.

A University worthy of the name of the Jewish people and situated in Palestine has much greater responsibilities than any other part of the work done in and for Palestine excepting possibly the initial political movements. These I believe were undertaken without the concurrence of the Jewish people as a whole and without serious reference to how it would affect their standing in the rest of the world. People in Great Britain are probably not able to see this so clearly at the present time because it is easy for them to be at once good British subjects and firm adherents to a mandatory of Great Britain—it is all within the Empire—but no amount of saving clauses prevents the growth of the suspicion in other parts of the world that the Jews have a country elsewhere—a homeland as they call it—and the rest of the world probably heartily wishes that now that they have got that homeland they would go to it.

I question whether it was safe for the Jewish people to put itself in a position which would close to it the lands of the diaspora for, in spite of everything we may say against the diaspora, it has saved the Jews and Judaism. Had we not been exiled from the Holy Land, we would not be here to talk about it.

You may think that these statements are wide of the mark, at least at this date, but at all events, they are as germane as some Talmudic discussions. What I have in mind is that having entered upon the whole question of Palestine without real forethought does not involve establishing a University in the same haphazard way with the expectation that we shall muddle through. Sometimes it is possible to bluff in Politics, but you cannot bluff through a University.

A national University worthy of any country, or if it is to be the National University of the Jewish people—worthy of any people must have underlying a well worked out system of secondary and college education. There must be schools, gymnasia or colleges before you can have a university.

The recognized faculties are, of course, the arts and sciences, a post-graduate or research faculty—let us call it the philosophical faculty—and the professional faculties: medicine, law, engineering, etc.

An institution of such a diversified nature, requiring specialists in every direction, must necessarily expect a considerable body of students. It is not unreasonable, if you include the professional schools, to project a university say for 2000 or 3000 students.

Now these students in the national Jewish university will, of course, not be recruited from Palestine alone, but at the present time a very great number of Jewish students would be expected to come from various parts of the world and undoubtedly would come. In countries of large populations with diversified interests—or let me be more specific and say in America—students, as you know, find it possible to support themselves through their college and university periods. I take it that these opportunities are in the main lacking in Palestine and that unless the University should become a rich man's university, so that only students would attend who could be supported by their own families, the cost of the support of the students themselves would form an intolerable burden upon the budget of such an institution. Creating a university for which the Faculty has to be provided and supported, the libraries and laboratories have to be established, the buildings have to be put up and all the students supported, instead of their tuition fees forming a part of the income of the University, would require a sum of money which I do not think any one has reason to expect would be available.

I am inclined to think (knowing that prices in Palestine are at the present time about as high as they are in America) that you would have upon this basis to reckon, say in the postgraduate department alone, that every student will cost $1500 per annum counting his support and the cost of the maintenance of the institution. This figure is low and does not include such faculties as require the upkeep of extensive physical apparatus or an astronomical observatory or a great chemical laboratory or anything of that sort. On my calculation an upkeep of a university with 2000 students would be Three million dollars per annum and this entirely with the capital outlay which would run into many millions.

I put the vulgar money matter first because it is important, though really not the most important. Let us assume that the funds can be provided for the University and that the proper faculties can be secured. It would be, I take it, a necessary part of the policy of the institution that all instruction should be given in the Hebrew language and that the current use of Hebrew should be furthered in every way. I assume further that the students might learn Arabic and English, probably as you and I learned French at College, but that to all intents and purposes Hebrew would be the language which they could best handle. Now what is going to become of the generations of students thus educated in Palestine? Will Palestine be able to absorb them? How many engineers or chemists or physicists or astronomers or even physicians and lawyers can Palestine absorb in any time that we can foresee? Of necessity the students trained in Palestine will have to go to other countries to practice their professions and I am very much afraid that they will have to go to these other countries with all the disadvantage of being foreigners in them. This disadvantage can be overcome, but it is a great handicap. If a Jewish scholar or a scientific man is to live his life in England or in Germany or in Holland or in Austria, he is the better off in the long run for having been brought up in those countries. A year or two of travel or at a foreign university may be useful, but the most serious danger in my opinion would be that of directing the Jewish youth in large numbers to Palestine with the idea that they will then be able to serve the Jews or science at large usefully in Palestine and in all parts of the world. I do not say that this consideration is controlling, but I do not know that anyone has taken it into account. It is very fine to talk about a great Jewish cultural center in Palestine, but we are not like the biologists experimenting on guinea pigs or white mice, but upon human beings whose careers will either have been made or marred. This aspect of the matter is worth thinking about.

I had floating around in my mind for a number of years the idea of establishments in Palestine which might ultimately develop into institutions of such importance that they would become factors in developing a University. You probably know that from the outset I associated myself with the agricultural station at Haifa and that I was a curator of the Technikum. The one I thought would grow into a faculty of agriculture and botanical science which would be of importance to the country and the other of mechanic arts which would also be of great service. My experience with these two institutions and the bitter disappointment which I had almost convinced me that it would be inadvisable for me at any time to have anything to do again with the government of policy of an institution in Palestine. I realized that after all the only purpose of association of an American with them was his supposed usefulness in securing funds and that any attempt to direct or control or even advise about the policy of the institution was either resented or ignored. It is not that I am particularly anxious to have my advice taken, but that when I interest people in a project they hold me responsible for such a project taking a proper direction.

Now you will realize from this very long and rambling statement that I have made to you that I am not old enough yet always to profit by my past experiences and may be willing—though I do not say I am—to make a third mistake with regard to Palestine.

I had read the statement in the *Jewish Chronicle* about your meeting before you sent it to me and assume it to be reasonably accurate although unauthorized. Your sending it to me is a sufficient voucher for its authenticity even if the pages of the *London Jewish Chronicle* are not.

When I read the debate I confess willingly that I found myself a little more in agreement with Doctor [Chaim] Weizmann than I ever expected to be. His dictum that "there is no bridge between Pinsk and Washington" (I do not live in Washington any more, but I used to) may be correct, but still when Pinsk goes to London, it might sometimes get into a western habit of thinking and I believe that Doctor Weizmann has pointed out the difficulty which both you and Doctor Israel Abrahams from your respective points of view are inclined to ignore. The creation of a purely objective, scientific faculty for the subjects which would form a considerable part of the curriculum of this Jewish department is in my opinion impossible. There *is* no such thing as objectivity in science, excepting in the mathematical and physical sciences, and even in these, the personal equation must be taken into account. It is a well known fact that astronomers have been able to correct the observations of each other by making allowances for the personal equation but that is impossible in any department of learning in which opinion plays a part and is entirely impossible in my opinion in Jewish learning at the present time. Some *tendenz* Jewish learning is sure to exhibit and it ought to.

Now if that is agreed to and it is proposed to establish a faculty of Jewish scholars who have a reasonably consistent attitude toward Jewish tradition and a way can be found to do this, I would be glad to help in working out a plan for it. The joke about Doctor [Adolph] Büchler's orthodoxy does not help the case. If, for example, the Biblical Department is to follow the higher Biblical criticism of Germany, England and America, then I for one would think it better if the Faculty were not established. I can see no point in the restoration of anything to Zion which would mean destroying the only foundations on which it is worth while to have Zion stand. I think you know me well enough to believe that I am not one of the fanatics, but upon this point I hold convictions which I assume you share.

I understand the anxiety of Mr. Yellin and the others for the creation of this faculty. They see the Schools of Oriental Research growing up and strengthening themselves. They see the Dominicans, the American, British and other schools, the Arabic University and they feel they must jump in. But are we prepared for the leap? Is the Jerusalem Committee one which has the training and experience to establish an institution of the kind that would do credit to the Jewish people? The names of the Committee, all estimable men, no doubt, in their several fields, do not inspire me with confidence.

Therefore, my dear Doctor Hertz, I am not yet prepared to say any more than that, since you think that for political and geographical reasons London would seem to be the natural clearing house for such a scheme and it is your idea "to create and concentrate the best available expert opinion by means of the circularization of memoranda," this lengthy letter of mine may be regarded as a contribution to be considered by the experts of the clearing house.

But if there is to be such a clearing house and if there is to be a real effort to establish a proper institution, then I think the Committee in Jerusalem should be called off from inviting men to become temporary or permanent professors and requesting them to reply "by cable," and from announcing their names before their acceptances have been received. This seems to me carrying the propaganda and publicity plans just a little too far.

I should be very glad, indeed, if you have the patience to read this long diatribe, to know how some of the views strike you. I put these in the form of a letter because I do not feel that I have got to the point of preparing a formal memorandum, but I nevertheless am quite earnest about the things I say and if I can be shown to be wrong in any of them, I am willing to be shown.

As I owe a response to Mr. ben Yehuda, I am enclosing to you a duplicate of this letter which you may be willing to send to him to facilitate discussion using London as a Center. If you do not care to do this, please let me know. I shall write to him direct. [W]

1. Eliezer ben Yehuda (1858–1922), Hebrew journalist and lexicographer, considered the father of modern Hebrew.
2. Pen name of Asher Ginzberg. See letter to Solomon Schechter, October 25, 1910.
3. David Yellin (1864–1941), scholar, educator, and leader of the Jewish community of Palestine; chairman of the Vaad Leumi (National Council of the Jews of Palestine), 1920–28.
4. Joseph Gedaliah Klausner (1874–1958), professor of modern Hebrew literature and, later, of Second Temple history at the Hebrew University.
5. Hermann Pick (1879–1952), former librarian of the Prussian State Library; representative of Mizrachi on the Zionist Executive.
6. Leo Ari Mayer (1895–1959), orientalist and archaeologist; inspector of the Palestine Government Antiquities Department, 1921–29; professor of eastern art and archaeology at the Hebrew University, 1932–59.
7. James de Rothschild (1878–1957), British politician and philanthropist; active in many Zionist enterprises.
8. Otto Warburg (1859–1938), third president of the World Zionist Organization, 1911–20; became professor of botany at the Hebrew University.
9. Solomon Rosenbloom (1866–1925), banker and philanthropist; endowed the Institute for Jewish Studies at the Hebrew University; treasurer of the Palestine Development Council.

TO LOUIS MARSHALL, NEW YORK CITY

Philadelphia, February 1, 1923

I have your letter of January 31 and from Doctor [A. S. W.] Rosenbach a copy of the cable that he forwarded. After my talk with you and Mr. [Mortimer L.] Schiff on Monday, following Mr. Schiff's advice, I went to see Doctor Rosenbach and he sent a cable offering 20,000 pounds net for the [Elkan] Adler Library. This was declined with the two words "Sorry. Impossible." I tried to see Mr. Schiff all day Tuesday but missed him everywhere. I did see Mr. [Felix M.] Warburg and asked his advice as a business man and he said the matter would never be settled by cable and that we might as well wait until Doctor Rosenbach went over, but I was a little fearful about taking the risk on a fluke and asked Doctor Rosenbach to consult with you and Mr. Schiff. I am glad that your judgments coincided and that the second cable was sent.

Since I spoke to you on Monday, Doctor [Alexander] Marx told me that Mr. Oko,[1] Librarian of the Hebrew Union College, called on him and told him that he was making efforts to get up a collection to secure this Library. Doctor Marx told Mr. Oko that the Seminary was in the field and Mr. Oko said that he had not known this and would not enter into competition.

I should not have been in haste about the matter if it had not been for the presence in New York of Israel Abrahams who of course knows Adler's Library and its merits very well.

Doctor Rosenbach told me that when Adler spoke to him originally, the pound was $4.20 and that he had calculated that for $100,000, the equivalent of 22,500 pounds, the Library might be secured, especially if we would allow Adler to remove from the Library the Shakespeare quartos and his general stock of English literature. Rosenbach, on the other hand, thought we ought to include all the pictures that Adler had. I thought this would make quite a difference to Adler as a good many of them were family portraits and relics, and Adler's nieces, the daughters of the late Doctor Herman Adler, might make a difficulty if he undertook to sell them. I do not think we would care to have them anyway, especially as we have a splendid collection of pictures through the Solomons collection, so I thought if we omitted to mention them it would help in the purchase.

While I know that Doctor [Stephen S.] Wise has been given information about the Library, I do not believe that he need be very seriously considered, although he does have a way of getting funds from time to time. . . .

. . . You will probably have heard before this that our Federation campaign for $1,250,000 has resulted in pledges of $1,414,000. In addition to that, the Gimbel Brothers have given $100,000 in 7% bonds of their Company to the Federation in memory of their brother, Jacob,[2] which insures an income of $7,000 a year from that source. While of course there will be found some duplication, as there always is in such campaigns, I believe that Federation will net at least $1,250,000 on it and help us to carry on our work and make much needed improvements.

It may be of use to note, for future campaigns in New York and elsewhere, that the Chairman of this drive was a man about 34 years of age, born in Warsaw, and I believe that the latter fact had very considerable to do with the success of the campaign, because Mr. Greenfield[3] for the first time really rallied the immigrant Jewish element to the Federation and has not alienated a single member of the older settlement. [W]

1. Adolph S. Oko (1885–1944), librarian of Hebrew Union College; associate and contributing editor of the *Menorah Journal*, 1921–40; became editor of the *Contemporary Jewish Record*, 1943–44.
2. Jacob Gimbel (1851–1922), founder of the Gimbels department store chain.
3. Albert M. Greenfield (1887–1967), Philadelphia banker, philanthropist, and communal leader.

TO ELKAN N. ADLER, LONDON

April 23, 1923

Your letter of March 27 reached me in a time of great sorrow. Mrs. Adler's mother, Mrs. Friedenwald,[1] died on April 13 and just one week later I was called to the death bed of Judge [Mayer] Sulzberger. As you well know, it was from him that the impulse which led to the establishment of a great library here came, and he was its constant and generous friend. Although he had been ailing for some months he was greatly interested in knowing that the plans which he made years ago were being fulfilled through the addition of your splendid collection and those we already possessed.

Now as to the physical facts. With the exception of seven of the cases, the remainder were delivered in our building on April 17. Those seven cases have been retained at the Custom House for closer examination. I fancy that they lit upon the case which contained the copies of the Catalogue of your MSS, and got the impression that we were importing modern books in large numbers for sale. I anticipate no difficulty however—only a little delay. In order to safeguard both you and your interests, I at once effected an additional insurance of £35,000 upon the contents of our building.

So far the six boxes indicated by you containing the most valuable incunabula and MSS have been opened. A great number of the important MSS and some of the incunabula, however, Doctor [Alexander] Marx informs me, must be found in other cases. Doctor Marx is very enthusiastic over the incunabula and some of the MSS he had a chance to examine superficially and he feels sure that as far as printed books go we will be second to no other collection. Owing to our lack of space it will take considerable time before he will be able to give me a full account of the Library. He is very anxious to get your annotated copy of Schwab's *Incunables Orientaux*[2] to guide him in the checking and arrangement of the books.

While a considerable portion of the printed books will no doubt turn out to be duplicates, many of the rarest books will be needed to complete our copies so that the duplicates returned will not always be as complete and good copies as those you sent. Doctor Marx tells me that he already found seventeen new incunabula including some printed on vellum which we have only on paper and that he hopes to find more since, e.g. the *Proverbs* of Lisbon 1492 which are credited to you in the *Jewish Encyclopedia* have not turned up yet. The non-Hebrew incunabula he came across so far are mostly not in our collection.

Of the books you retained we do not possess the *Jewish Chronicles* of 1888–95 and vols. VI and VIII of the *Transactions of the Jewish Historical Society of England*.

I fully understand that it is very hard for you to be suddenly separated from your Library to which you have devoted so much paternal love and care and which you have brought up for more than a third of a century. But you can be sure that your "daughter" will find a proper home. The union with her younger cousin will be very beneficial for both.

I hope the combined libraries will continue to grow and will prove a real boon to the development of Jewish scholarship in this country. I am sure, it is a cause of great satisfaction to you that the great Library you have gathered so successfully will remain in Jewish hands and not share the fate of other Jewish collections. England, after all, is so rich in treasures of Jewish literature that she will not begrudge us our place in the sun and we are happy to have brought together the largest Jewish collection that ever existed to the largest Jewish community that ever dwelt in one city.

I am looking forward to your visit of which you write. [W]

1. Jane Ahlborn Friedenwald (1847–1923).
2. Moise Schwab (1839–1918), orientalist and bibliographer. The work referred to is *Les Incunables Orientaux et les Impressions Orientales au commencement du XVIe Siecle* (Paris, 1883).

TO EDWARD CALISCH,[1] RICHMOND, VIRGINIA

April 24, 1923

I was present at a meeting of the Council of the United Synagogue last night, when your letter suggesting a protest against the Soviet Government's attitude toward all religion was read.

At my suggestion it was decided to ask the advice of the American Jewish Committee, and I earnestly request that you take no action until such advice can be secured.

I am sure you understand that I fully share your indignation and that of others against the systematic attempt that is now being made to strangle religion among 180,000,000 people. It is true that they permit churches and synagogues and mosques to be opened and thus make a parade of their liberality, but it is also a fact that teaching religion to any person under the age of eighteen is a crime.

My reason for suggesting delay, however, is that we are bound to consider how our protest would react upon the Jews in Russia. The Joint Distribution Committee has succeeded in establishing itself there. If any act of ours would cut off the possibilities of relief and reconstruction work just now, it would also be a great disaster. I do not say that it would, but at least that aspect of the subject should be considered. [AJC]

1. Edward Calisch (1865–1946), rabbi and author; president of the Central Conference of American Rabbis, 1921–23.

Article 4 of the Palestine Mandate recognized a "Jewish Agency" as representative of World Jewry in the development of the Jewish National Home. Though at first the Zionist Organization took the role of "Jewish Agency," it was quickly recognized that non-Zionist elements would have to be incorporated into it in order to tap the vast financial resources needed for Palestine's development. Negotiations to expand the Jewish Agency to include non-Zionists began in the early 1920's but were not successfully concluded until 1929.

TO SOLOMON ROSENBLOOM, PITTSBURGH

May 10, 1923

. . . It may interest you to know that on May 9 a gathering of about 30 men took place at Judge [Horace] Stern's home at which Doctor [Chaim] Weizmann was present and since the economic details were less dwelt upon there was more opportunity to consider just those aspects of the importance of the re-construction of Palestine in which you have evinced so much interest.

We especially had more time to discuss the nationalistic aspect and I think that whatever his views may have been in the past, Doctor Weizmann at present has no desire to emphasize this issue at least in America and Western Europe.

I am also convinced that for practical reasons it is necessary that the Jewish Agency should be reconstructed so that it is really representative of the best abilities in Jewry, because the highest kind of administrative talents are required, and these have not existed in the small party group which has heretofore conducted the Palestinian work. Doctor Weizmann said that he would urge this view before the next Zionist Congress. . . . [W]

TO HERMAN BERNSTEIN, NEW YORK CITY

June 25, 1923

You call my attention to the jacket of the book entitled "The Jews of America" by Burton J. Hendrick,[1] the material of which has previously been published in the "World's Work," and you ask me to express my opinion on it. Well, the only opinion that I could express would be based upon the jacket because I have not read the articles and I do not propose to read the book. I am growing weary of the way in which magazines and publishers are commercializing what people call "the Jewish question." The Jews, in my opinion, have over-advertised themselves. They got more publicity about their societies and their affairs and their parades and their movements than they were entitled to in accordance to their numbers or their importance. By this process they have rendered it profitable to write about the Jews and they are so self-conscious that they seem to like to read about themselves, and hence, in a way help to make a market for their own detractors.

The idea that the German and Spanish Jews form one stock and the Polish or Eastern Jews form another stock is fantastic to the highest degree, and this statement alone brands the author of the book as one unfitted to write on the subject. Not having read the articles and not intending to read the book, I am put in the position of the gentleman who received a book to review and placed it upon his desk. When the editor urged him for a review he wrote, "I have looked upon it nine several [sic] days and now I know that it is bad."

My own opinion of the best reply which the Jews could make to Mr. Hendrick, or anybody like him, is to continue to attend to their own affairs, do their proper share of the work of the Jewish community, maintain their traditions, practice their religion, and become as near as possible ideal citizens of the State. Let us put our energy back of these ideals and leave whoever will write about us if he must.

I am surprised that a firm like Doubleday, Page and Company are making themselves the vehicle for this sort of stuff. [AJC]

1. Burton J. Hendrick (1871–1949), American historian; wrote anti-Semitic articles in many leading journals.

TO LOUIS MARSHALL, NEW YORK CITY

Seabright, New Jersey, July 4, 1923

I had a talk with Mortimer Schiff yesterday. He offered to supply the additional funds required to complete the purchase of the Elkan Adler which I think will amount to about $12,000. Louis Bamberger[1] whom I met the other day offered to aid in completing the purchase but I felt that Mr. Schiff should be allowed to have the Mitzvah.

I also discussed with him the question of a [Jewish Theological Seminary] building. Mr. [Felix M.] Warburg seems to have converted Mr. Schiff to the idea of the retention of the present building for a Seminary building but Mr. Schiff believes that we should purchase a building either alongside on 123rd St. or on 124th which should be devoted exclusively to the Library, leaving the present building for teaching and assembly purposes. I told him about Mr. Dix's[2] bequest and my belief that if Mr. Dix lived a number of years the bequest would be converted into a gift for a Dormitory. The upshot of the conversation was that Mr. Schiff requested me to secure prices on the two pieces of property east and west of the Seminary building as well as the piece immediately north of it. This I shall proceed to do through Mr. Samuel A. Herzog.[3] . . . [AJA]

1. Louis Bamberger (1855–1941), businessman and philanthropist; helped endow the Institute for Advanced Study at Princeton University.
2. Henry A. Dix (1850–1933), clothing manufacturer and philanthropist; in 1923 sold his business to his employees and gave large sums to charity.
3. Samuel Adler Herzog (1882–1946), Adler's nephew; real estate developer and lawyer.

TO LOUIS MARSHALL, NEW YORK CITY

Philadelphia, July 24, 1923

I see from the *New York Times* that you are not spending all your vacation at rest; so I am going to trouble you with one thing more. I enclose you a clipping which appeared in the *Philadelphia Ledger* of this date, July 24.[1] I understand that the *Public Ledger's* Foreign Service extends to quite a number of other important papers—the *Brooklyn Eagle*, the *Boston Transcript*, and probably other important papers in various parts of the country.

I have ascertained from the Syndicating Manager of the Ledger Service that this cablegram (which by the way he said he had not seen when I called it to his attention) did not come from a regular staff correspondent of the

Ledger, as they have no staff correspondent at Warsaw, but was probably purchased for them from a local service by their staff correspondent either in Berlin or at some other point on the Continent.

You will see that the idea is to establish a numerus clausus for visas. My own belief is that this does not represent any thought-out policy of the Polish government, which is probably anxious to get rid of Jews, but rather some kind of deal by which the coal mines of Pennsylvania can secure labor, officials in Poland naturally being recompensed for this service, and that this is a flier, to try out American public opinion on the subject.

That there will be local protest of course there can be no doubt. The Syndicating Manager, Mr. J[ohn] E[lfreth] Watkins, told me that he thought it was a rotten article, and advised me to write a personal letter to Mr. C[yrus] H. K. Curtis on the subject, saying that he was sure it would have attention. Before taking this step I should like to have your view of the whole subject and especially of another aspect of dealing with it.

It occurred to me that the Polish government's minister at Washington might have this statement presented to him and be asked whether in fact this represents the policy of the Polish government—whether, in other words, they are treating emigration on an economic basis and actually considering their own citizens as subjects of export and making definite shipments of labor.

The article seems to me to be cynical to the last degree, and I can hardly think that any government would stand for such a statement.

Even if you decide either in favor of or against bringing the matter to the attention of the Polish minister or of dealing with it in some other public way, I still think that I ought to bring it to Mr. Curtis' attention privately, so that his paper would stop publishing material of this sort. [W]

1. The article concerned a plan by authorities in Poland to check the flow of Jewish emigration to the United States by putting a quota on the number of Jews allowed to emigrate, provided, of course, that the Jews in the United States would not raise a protest.

TO MORTIMER L. SCHIFF, NEW YORK CITY

Philadelphia, July 31, 1923

While the last paragraph of Professor [Alexander] Marx's letter has not to do with the question of space for the [Jewish Theological Seminary] Library, I thought I had better send it to you just as it is. I think he is right in saying that it would be helpful to him to see the sketches made by Mr. Arnold Brunner[1] and I have no doubt that Mr. [Felix M.] Warburg will permit him to see these.

As for Doctor Marx's general view with regard to the development of the Library in size, his figures are to me a little startling. I had never contemplated a library of 200,000 volumes, and yet, his vision, which is younger and better informed, may be truer than mine. It is unquestionably a fact that the two departments which he mentions, those of the Bible and Palestine, are capable of great expansion in our Library. Whether we should go into general Semitics is a matter of policy, which the Library Committee ought to consider some day and which even the Directors of the Seminary should finally pass upon. In the Seminary Library so much of general Semitics as will furnish a background for Biblical studies and Jewish history is required. This would mean the general books on Egypt and Assyria, Babylonia, the whole course of the Mohammedan movement, etc. But it is a question in my mind which I have by no means settled as to whether we should contemplate completing these fields by scouring the entire literature, Egyptian, Arabic, Babylonia, etc. One field which will undoubtedly require attention some day is that of philosophical theology and comparative religion, and it may be that Doctor Marx is not far out in his ideal. At all events it is a fine thing to have an ideal.

He evidently wrote his letter with the idea in mind that we should acquire an adjacent building or buildings, maintaining the present Seminary entrance as the main entrance, sealing up the entrance of any newly acquired building and providing for the administration of the Library from the top floor down. I gather your idea to be rather the contrary—that the Library should be a place which could be entered independently of the Seminary building. If this were so the arrangement would have to be reversed: the offices for the administration of the Library, catalogue rooms, reception room, etc., would have to be on the first floor, or certainly some of the offices would, because the entrance would have to be guarded. The bindery I should think would be on the first floor or in the basement, not on the top floor. The Librarian's office, with the bibliographical apparatus, should probably be at the top of the building, where the manuscripts and rare books are kept, and the Assistant Librarian and Secretary, etc., would be near the entrance.

As I keep turning the matter over in my mind several other thoughts occur to me which require consideration. The item of insurance is a rather heavy carrying item at the present time, and aside from that, it is an absolute duty to take every possible safeguard against fire. There is always a greater danger of fire when a building does not stand independently, because the danger comes from within as well as from one's neighbors. The danger from within can at least be reduced by not having fire in the Library building itself. If we should therefore have two structures adjacent, as a matter of economy they ought to be heated from a central heating plant, and that heating plant, I think, had best not be in the building in which the Library is stored. This is perfectly feasible. When the Dropsie College was constructed, we placed the heating plant in a small, separate, outside, underground structure, the entrance to which is separated from the building in which the Library is kept by fire-doors, and as a result we secured the lowest insurance rate ever granted to a building in Philadelphia. In fact we are no longer paying insurance, but receiving premiums. Of recent years my attention has been called several times to the fact that the system of steam heating is slowly injuring our Library. This injury is not so very pronounced among the manuscripts and rare books, because Doctor Marx has been willing to freeze himself, and except on the very coldest days no heat is permitted to go into the manuscript room; but in the rest of the Library our leather bindings are slowly and steadily going to pieces. This is rather a pity in the case of older bindings, and a matter of considerable expense in the replacement of the more recent bindings. . . . [W]

1. Arnold W. Brunner (1857–1925), architect and civic planner; designer of many American synagogues, including Shearith Israel in New York City.

TO ALEXANDER MARX, NEW YORK CITY

New York City, August 24, 1923

With regard to the Judah Halevi volume,[1] my idea was that if we printed both the prose and the metrical version, we should not print the Hebrew twice of course. The volume will not be a very large one, because it will lack the extensive notes that the Gabirol volume[2] has. I would still like to know from you whether in your opinion it is necessary to ask Dr. Brody's[3] permission or that of the Mekize Nirdamim[4] to use his text or whether you have ever personally corresponded with him about it. If you have already written to Brody and he is aware of our views, there is no need for me to write.

With regard to the library building, I have had a further interview with Mr. [Mortimer L.] Schiff and we have agreed to await the return of Mr. [Felix M.] Warburg until some sort of conclusion is reached. Mr. Schiff agrees with you and me that [Arnold W.] Brunner's plan is inadequate and that something more comprehensive ought to be created. There is no thought of separating the library from the Seminary by any physical distance, but I feel that in view of the fact that this is not merely an ordinary working library but a great collection of books and manuscripts, it should be used in such a way that students and scholars who desire to use it for research purposes should be able to do so without encountering the almost necessary distraction that occurs in a building which is used by students, who may sometimes even have the right to shout and sing, and by many people who would not aid in preserving the quiet and calm that are necessary for the library.

I want to say that I do not share your difficulty in regard to the alcove system, even for rare books and manuscripts, just as I have become convinced that the present manuscript room has one error in the plate-glass doors. One has to choose in the case of rare books and manuscripts between dirt and other forms of decay. I believe that all books must breathe and I have therefore come to the conclusion that even for rare books and manuscripts, open cases with a grill to protect them are better than locked cases with glass doors. If you have a grill, you can permit the alcove system, because it is more difficult to steal a book in that way than even through glass doors, which can be broken. The rarest books and manuscripts have to be put in cases under this system. I have always been enamored of the appearance of the old Bodleian Library where, you will remember, the alcove system is employed and in Washington in the Library of Congress and in the Smithsonian, even for manuscripts and other rare things, the alcove system with grills is likewise used. My notion is that if and when we make the change, this change ought to be based upon a very careful study of what is best in all modern libraries and even then we are allowed to have some ideas of our own. [JTS]

1. *Selected Poems of Jehudah Halevi* (Philadelphia, 1924), a volume in the Schiff Library of Jewish Classics. The translator, Nina Salaman (1877–1925), made literal translations of all the poems, and rhymed translations of some.
2. *Selected Religious Poems of Solomon Ibn Gabirol* (Philadelphia, 1923), ed. Israel Davidson and trans. Israel Zangwill. This was the initial volume of the Schiff Library of Jewish Classics.
3. Heinrich Brody (1868–1942), chief rabbi of Prague; editor of the *Diwan* of Jehudah Halevi.
4. Mekize Nirdamim was a society founded in 1862, in Lyck, Poland, for the publication of scholarly editions of medieval Hebrew literature.

Sephardic Jews founded the North American Jewish settlement. Later waves of Jewish immigration, however, had made them a small proportion of American Jewry. Adler, who had a lifelong affinity for Sephardic Judaism, based on his connection with Congregation Mikveh Israel in Philadelphia, supported any effort to better organize Sephardic Jews in America.

TO HENRY PEREIRA MENDES

August 29, 1923

. . . As for the larger question of the union of English-speaking Sephardic congregations,[1] I think well of the idea. But the method of its accomplishment is not so simple. It resolves itself both into the matter of leadership and preparation for the ministry. Whatever one may think of [Moses] Gaster's scholarship, his selection as Haham at London and the virtual destruction for all purposes of training of Montefiore College, Ramsgate,[2] was a great blow to the western Sephardim. I do not see myself how they can readily recover from it, unless some one arises or is selected who will have the confidence of all of the English-speaking Sephardim and who will be vigorous enough and active enough to strengthen such congregations. Alcalay[3] was to my eye a very important and imposing figure, but he is in Serbia. [David de Sola] Pool has broadened out very greatly in the last few years and if he would confine himself to congregational work might prove a man of very considerable importance. But he is not likely to do this, as his interest in large communal problems, especially educational problems, has grown, and, I think, become important in the Jewish community in New York. My feeling is that the English-speaking Sephardic congregations are too few and too weak to initiate any movement of this nature, but that by co-operation with Holland, France, Gibraltar, Morocco and the whole of the vast Sephardic community in North Africa as well as in the Orient they could do something. After all, I presume that Bagdad is fast becoming an English-speaking country, since Mesopotamia is a British mandatory, and indeed Bagdad contains one of the ablest Jewish communities in the East. Even China can be considered. I am not at all sure that some of the Sassoons should not be drawn into such an effort. You see, my dear Doctor Mendes, that I feel that if you are going to initiate a union, it ought to be one that is worth while, and while it presents greater difficulties, it is the plan that ought to be held in view. Naturally it would be helpful if a rapprochement between the English-speaking Sephardic congregations could be effected first.

I confess, however, that there is something larger which would appeal to me more. I mean a movement that would obliterate the differences between

Sephardim and Ashkenazim. We ought to have a book of common prayer. The Ashkenazim have much to learn from the Sephardim in the conduct of the service, and the Sephardim have many beautiful things in their prayer book which the Ashkenazim lack. The Ashkenazim have things in their prayer book and in their service which would be of great advantage for Sephardic congregations. I have always thought, for example, that the use of the first two verses of the Shema at the taking out of the Torah in the Ashkenazic service is immensely more impressive and more important than the Sephardic service at that point. If Palestine is going to help us in a religious way at all, it ought point the way to a union, and one of the first steps toward this would be the adoption of the Sephardic pronunciation. If the Ashkenazim would adopt in their synagogues the Sephardic pronunciation, which they seem entirely willing to adopt in the use of Hebrew as a spoken language, we would take an immense step forward toward union. . . .

. . . Now as to your final suggestion about dying in harness, I would say that so far as I am concerned I have no such feeling at all. But I believe that when people who have worked very hard all their lives get older and are in position to sit down and think, they may be of much more use in the world than if they try to stay in harness. I always admired Judge [Mayer] Sulzberger's renunciation of active life and the very great use he made of the last nine years of his life in his Biblical studies, which were a satisfaction to him and, I think, very useful to Biblical science. Doctor [Solomon] Schechter had in mind retiring within a year or two if the Seminary authorities were able to arrange for it. He wanted to write his book on Jewish Charity. You did not ask me for advice, but since you wrote me this intimate letter, I am going to throw out a counter-suggestion to you. If I were in your place—indeed even if I were in my own place and felt that I were able to do it—I think I should go to live in Newport.[4] There is no city in America about which such fond Jewish memories cluster as Newport. To you it must be especially dear, and if with mild efforts you could keep that old congregation in some kind of proper way and link it with its ancient tradition, you would be doing, I believe, a very great service, and one which would not tax your strength. From there better than from any larger place you might carry on the correspondence which might ultimately bring about a union of the Sephardic congregations and at least follow up the suggestion of some closer union of all congregations. How do you like the picture? . . .

. . . You of course have read of the coming of the Elkan Adler Library to the Seminary, and its reception means further expenditures for us. We must have a new building and further endowments to care for all those things, and we are going to start a campaign in October to raise a million dollars to add to our endowment fund, which I hope we shall be able to do.

I trust that this very long letter will not worry you, and am with kindest regards to yourself and Mrs. Mendes, and best wishes for the New Year, in which my entire family joins. [D]

1. The Union of American Sephardic Congregations was founded in New York City in 1929.
2. Montefiore College, founded in 1869 by Sir Moses Montefiore for the training of Sephardic ministers. It was closed in 1901 and not reestablished until 1952.
3. Isaac Alcalay (1881–1978), chief rabbi of Serbia and later of Yugoslavia. In 1941 he escaped to the United States and became chief rabbi of the Union of American Sephardic Congregations.
4. City in Rhode Island with the oldest surviving synagogue in the United States, the Touro Synagogue of Congregation Yeshuat Yisrael, dedicated in 1763.

When it came time for Adler's daughter, Sarah, to go to college, the Adler family found itself confronted with the unsympathetic attitudes evinced at the time by many institutions of higher learning toward Jewish religious sensibilities.

TO MARION PARK,[1] BRYN MAWR, PENNSYLVANIA

Philadelphia, September 19, 1923

I have received your letter of September 18th and, as you may imagine, I am greatly disappointed. In view of your statement "that the College has always been unwilling to grant similar requests for changes in its examination schedules made by Jewish and Catholic students'"[2] my daughter will be obliged to forgo the advantages of an education at Bryn Mawr.

Might I be permitted to say to you, not as one solely interested in a particular person, but for the common good of our America and indeed of humanity, that the precedent of your College on this point is one which hardly, in the long run, can make for this common good even though it renders the administration of the College easier.

Bryn Mawr College, I understand, is non-sectarian, but I take it from your letter that this does not mean that it is no doubt non-religious or anti-religious. Its schedules allow for the religious observance of students of the Protestant faiths. The only result it could have upon students of the Catholic or Jewish faith would be to break down their religious morale at a time when religious conviction is so greatly needed in the world.

Bryn Mawr College, I believe, was founded by a distinguished member of the Society of Friends and its Trustees belong to that Society. I remember being present either at the opening of Bryn Mawr or at the dedication of one of its most important halls and James Russell Lowell[3] delivered the dedicatory address. I thought–at the time maybe a young hopeful man–that here would be an institution founded by a man belonging to a sect which had itself been bitterly persecuted, which would always recognize and accord the student religious tolerance. I have myself passed through the University of Pennsylvania, through Johns Hopkins University, where I was also a teacher, and spent sixteen years on the staff of the Smithsonian Institution, and was never required or even expected to disregard any of my religious observances.

The Dropsie College, founded by a Jew, whose Governors are all of the Jewish faith, but which is open without regard to creed, color, sex or nationality, has from the day of its opening arranged its calendar so that the Christian and Jewish Holidays may be observed by every student.

I am writing not in anger, but in sorrow, and would not ask any more for my own daughter than I would ask for any student who desires to observe her religion. [W]

1. Marion Edward Park (1875–1960), president of Bryn Mawr College, 1922–42.
2. In this particular instance, the entrance examination was scheduled for a Saturday.
3. James Russell Lowell (1819–91), American poet and diplomat.

Kaplan and his vision of Judaism continued to trouble Adler.

TO MORDECAI M. KAPLAN, NEW YORK CITY

September 21, 1923

I am in receipt of your letter of September 16th.

The correspondence published in "The Light of Israel" for July 27th was printed without my knowledge and consent and its publication was a breach of faith.[1] I greatly regret that I entered into correspondence with Mr. Israel with whom I had no acquaintance and that correspondence of this nature was forced upon me. While this may not be pertinent to your objection to the part of the correspondence which you quote, I think you will see that my object was to prevent published attacks upon the [Jewish Theological] Seminary. In this attempt I failed in the particular instance before us owing to the fact my confidence was not observed. For the statements of the Editor, I am, naturally, not responsible.

Shortly after the publication of the articles by you in the *Menorah Magazine* about three years ago, we had a talk and I told you that the articles were giving me a great deal of trouble both because of interviews which people sought with me about them as well as correspondence from various parts of the country.[2] The view that I took was that the opinions you expressed were individual, that the Seminary as a whole did not share them and was not responsible for them, but that Judaism judged men not by their opinions but by their deeds and that I had full confidence that your life was in accord with the Jewish tradition.

I also did say, and I understand it to be the fact, that the body of Jewish knowledge which is imparted by the Faculty of the Seminary to the students—I mean Bible, Talmud, Codes, History, Literature—is taught by other masters and that your special function in the Seminary Faculty is to instruct the students how to apply this knowledge to the preparation of sermons. This latter is certainly a most important part of the work of the Seminary which you have done very well and I had no intention at all of belittling it, but in defending the Seminary against possible attacks that it was dominated by your views, I think that my statement was justifiable. I overlooked the course in Midrash because I considered it a minor part of your work and possibly, even if incorrectly, do not give it that prominence in Jewish theology which you ascribe to it. As all the people who approached me were discussing the Seminary proper, I did not include the Teachers' Institute, where, of course, the range of your authority both as Principal and Teacher is much wider.

Naturally, you realize, as I do, that a discussion of the particular point you raise only touches the surface of the subject. I daresay we both realize the facts. We differ in our views upon aspects of Judaism as I believe you differ from most of your colleagues in the Seminary Faculty. You have shown great ability as a teacher and organizer and have made great personal sacrifices for the Seminary. We are all modern men, we do not engage in inquisitions or excommunications or heresy hunting and we are brought up in the general doctrine of academic freedom. How far this applies in a theological seminary which teaches subjects that are bound to be treated subjectively, in which faith, tradition, even inherited prejudice if you please, must have a part is a subject we have never discussed but which probably ought be discussed either between us or with the entire Faculty. We have all been personal friends and we must continue to be, but I think we are civilized enough to recognize and even to discuss our differences without destroying our friendships. This is more important for us to reconcile than a chance remark of mine in a letter.

I shall be glad as soon as the holydays are over to have a full talk with you on the subject. [AJA]

1. In July 1923, the editor of *Idishe Likht,* S. A. Israel, published his correspondence with Adler regarding Kaplan's position at the Seminary. Israel desired to have Kaplan removed from the Seminary as a source of "poisonous doctrines" while Adler temporized that Kaplan taught homiletics and not theology.

2. See letter to Edwin Kaufman, December 31, 1920.

TO MARION PARK, BRYN MAWR, PENNSYLVANIA

Philadelphia, September 24, 1923

I wish to acknowledge your kind letter of September 21st, which reached me on Saturday, September 22nd, and to thank you and Doctor Jones for your offer to propose to the Entrance Examination Committee, which meets on September 29th, that an exception be made in the case of my daughter and that she be granted a special examination later in the term. I also note your statement that College examinations at the end of each semester do occur on Saturday.

While I recognize the generous spirit in which the offer to refer the matter to the Entrance Examination Committee is made, I cannot avail myself of it.

Your letter of September 18th, received on the 19th, in which you stated that Bryn Mawr College had always been unwilling to grant similar requests and that it did not seem wise to break the precedent, I considered final. On the same day, September 19th, I telephoned to the Registrar of Barnard College asking for the Register. In it occurs the following statement:

> Candidates who find that examinations are fixed for days set apart for religious purposes by the church to which they belong, and who are prevented by conscientious scruples from attending such examinations, are requested to make application to the Committee on Admissions through the Registrar of Barnard College for equitable relief.

In view of this statement, I at once proceeded to Barnard College on September 21st. My daughter applied for admission on the basis of her College Board Examination credits and was permitted to take a re-examination in Geometry which was in progress that afternoon. I have been notified that she has passed the examination and that she has been admitted as a student at Barnard College. While for many reasons I would have preferred her attending Bryn Mawr, I could not wait any longer and possibly cause her to lose an entire year. I realized the difficulty on August 29th and addressed you a letter on that day and it was not until September 19th that your letter of the previous day reached me. Its wording was so definitive that I felt obliged to make other arrangements at once. [W]

Magnes had moved from New York to Jerusalem, where he was to take charge of the fledgling Hebrew University with which Adler and American Jewish scholarship were vitally interested. Over the years, Adler was to maintain a steady correspondence with Magnes on university and Palestine affairs.

TO JUDAH L. MAGNES, JERUSALEM

October 22, 1923

I was very glad to receive your letter of September 24 if only to hear from you. Mr. [Louis] Marshall had told me that you had been ill and I am glad that you are back at the old stand. I learned from the Jewish papers that you had taken part in the services on Yom Kippur.

With regard to the Department of Hebrew Studies in the Jewish University, I would say that I had already heard a somewhat similar statement from two sources. When Doctor Zeitlin[1] returned from Europe he told me that he had had a long talk with Israel Levi[2] and that Levi did not assent to the faculty chosen by Doctor [Joseph H.] Hertz and his friends. Israel Levi has another suggestion with regard to the general oversight which European and American scholars would give to the proposed Department. He urges that the small Jewish Academy which we have started here[3] should be paralleled in various European countries by similar academies, and that out of these we should make a sort of council of academies, which would represent the Jewish scholars of the world, and that this council should be responsible for the drafting of the plan for the Department of Hebrew Studies, and I presume also for the nomination of professors. Professor [Henry] Malter, who met Doctor Chajes[4] and others in Carlsbad, also told me that they too had the idea of a sort of international Jewish academy, which would make itself responsible for the scholastic direction of the Department of Hebrew Studies. At this same conference, however, a serious discussion took place, which was not settled, concerning the headquarters of this academy. Some favored Jerusalem, some favored more or less central points in Europe. It was the general agreement, I believe, that for practical purposes London would be the best place, as being more central for American scholars, but that there was nobody in London who would be acceptable as a sort of head for the academy.

I am of course not in position to express the views of the men here without consultation with them, and I am not sure whether you would want me to communicate your letter to them or not. I advised Doctor Zeitlin, however, to take the matter up directly with Professor [Louis] Ginzberg, who is president of the Academy here, and if the Academy itself wishes to take the matter up directly or desires me to act as intermediary, I am satisfied with either course. Here the opinion does not tally with what you express concerning the men heretofore chosen. Doctor Tchernowitz[5] is not considered by some of our men a very eminent scholar. [Samuel] Krauss in some ways has a much wider reputation, but I was told that Krauss speaks no Hebrew. It is not impossible that it may be necessary from time to time that we waive the Hebrew requirement, as a good many scholars, at least of middle age, who know Hebrew very well, are not accustomed to speak it. [Lajos] Blau is in my opinion an eminent man. However, from the very beginning it looked to me as though the choice rather fell upon men who needed positions because of European conditions than upon men of the greatest eminence who would be selected for the purpose.

Personally I am in complete agreement with the idea that the Dean need not be a biblical specialist. He might be a rabbinical specialist or a philosophical specialist if you choose.

I do not think that there is any desire on the part of anybody in America to parallel the school at Beirut, and if there are men of sufficient ability in Palestine to manage both the financial and the academic aspects, all the better, but I am not at all sure that this is the case as yet. With regard to the financial management, my difficulty is that one does not know where certain designated funds go. For example, you speak of £3000 voted by the Zionist Executive in London. I have been told that Baron Edmund de Rothschild[6] had set aside £3000. Are these the same £3000 or are there £6000? I understand from Mr. [Felix M.] Warburg after a talk I had with him that he gave Doctor [Chaim] Weizmann $10,000 for the University. Is this in any general fund or is it assigned to this particular school of which we are speaking? Mr. Albert Greenfield of Philadelphia in the same way gave $5000, which he designated for the University. There probably have been other designations for the University. Do these go to the Zionist Executive in London and do they designate funds as they see fit to different departments of the University? There is still an offer pending, I believe, from Mr. [Solomon] Rosenbloom, for the endowment of a chair. What responsible persons are there by way of trustees who will hold the fund for the endowment? Mr. Rosenbloom when he last spoke to me was insistent that he would not turn his funds over to the Zionist Executive. All this points, it seems to me, to a certain more definite organization than has yet been effected. There still seems to me to be a need of trustees to hold trust funds which may be given them safely, to invest them, and to pay over the income to some authorised person or persons. Such funds ought not to be lodged in Palestine, because the opportunities for safe investment are, I presume, not so great in Palestine as they are in America or England. The likelihood that any funds turned over to the Zionist Organization even by way of capital will be commingled with other funds is so strong that I doubt whether any serious amounts will be entrusted to them. Now these are all difficulties that cannot be readily blinked. I have so many things on my hands and am so far away both from conditions in Palestine and from actual contact with people in Europe that I am not the person to solve them, but at least I see the difficulties, and may be you, with your considerable experience in Palestine and your knowledge of conditions in America and the world over, can yourself evolve a plan. Please remember that when I say trustees I mean trustees of funds, not necessarily directors of the institution.

A very important defect in the whole matter is indicated by your own statement concerning the report that it was Doctor [Chaim] Weizmann's intention to have Doctor Chajes appointed Dean or Head of this Department of the University. Such an act would indicate a form of autocratic authority which is now exercised nowhere else in the world. I question whether any of the recently set up autocrats of Europe would go so far as to name the heads of universities or deans of departments. And all this from a democratic man! One might be led to suspect that there is something other than purely scholastic in the selection of Doctor Chajes, whose activities in recent years have not been confined to scholarly pursuits. I would not complain of this in the headship of the University, say the post of chancellor or president, or something like it, but the dean of a particular school in a University can only remain the dean, I believe, so long as his attainments are at least equal to those of the other members of the Faculty.

Upon second thought I see no reason for not communicating the contents of your letter to some of my colleagues, and I shall do so, with the understanding that I shall communicate their opinions to you after I get them. I assume that you have been made acquainted with all my correspondence with Doctor Hertz, because I know that Professor Otto Warburg and others saw it quite a good many months ago.

With regard to any real or continued help from America, I would say this: at the present time we are all very much encouraged with the campaign for a million dollars that we have undertaken for the Seminary. The interest shown in the initial conferences is far beyond our expectation, and in fact the conference held in New York on October 7 exceeded both in numbers and enthusiasm and in its representative character from various parts of the country any of the conferences I have ever seen, not even excepting our best relief conferences. Both Mr. [Louis] Marshall and I are now of the opinion that if this campaign succeeds we will be prepared immediately upon its heels to inaugurate a campaign for the great educational fund, and it has been our thought from the beginning that a percentage of the funds thus derived shall be set apart for the support of education in Palestine and also for help here and there for such institutions in Europe as may still require it. I do not believe that it would be safe to set up an institution in Palestine upon the chance of sums collected here and there by small communities. You cannot compare the Department of Jewish Studies in this respect with, say, a medical department, where there is a very large number of men who are making reasonably good incomes. The Jewish scholars are few in number, and have no incomes at all to speak of. [W]

1. Solomon Zeitlin (1892–1976), professor of rabbinic literature at Dropsie College; succeeded Adler as editor of the *Jewish Quarterly Review*.
2. Israel Levi (1856–1934), chief rabbi of France, 1919–32; editor of *Revue des Etudes Juives*.
3. See letter to David de Sola Pool, November 7, 1922.
4. Hirsch Peretz Chajes (1876–1927), Viennese rabbi, scholar, and Zionist leader.
5. Chaim Tchernowitz (1871–1949), talmudic scholar and author; editor of the Hebrew monthly *Bitzaron*.
6. Edmund de Rothschild (1845–1934), philanthropist and, especially, patron of the Jewish settlement in Palestine.

Adler remained firm in his stand against diaspora Jewish nationalism, which characterized the American Jewish Congress. The Congress, which had reestablished itself immediately after its planned demise following the First World War, conflicted with everything for which Adler stood.

TO ISRAEL ZANGWILL, NEW YORK CITY

October 25, 1923

. . . I am sure that no one would disagree with you as to the right of Judaism as a religion to organize itself nationally or even internationally. Your statement that the case for political nationalism in the diaspora is far more dubious is the one that I want to write about, because I think that you may yourself not to be completely aware of the important part which the claim of political nationalism in the diaspora has played in preventing a union of Israel.

During the four or five anxious months in Paris in 1919, when one might have supposed that a united front could and should be presented for the purpose of obtaining some measure of security and justice for the great Jewish population of Eastern Europe, it was this theory of political national-ism—and this only—which stood in the way.

From March 30 to April 6, 1919, a series of conferences and meetings of representatives of Jewish organizations, then in Paris, was held at the call of the Chief Rabbi of France, Israel Levi and after organization Mr. [Louis] Marshall was called to preside over these conferences. The entire effort was to secure a formula for the protection of minorities—all minorities—which might be presented by a united delegation to the Peace Conference. That minorities should have equal rights with the majority in the matter of the practice of their religion was of course agreed by all. With very little dissent a like agreement was reached with regard to the maintenance of linguistic rights. The only subject of dispute was with regard to the claim of "national rights." At one period of the discussion Mr. [Nahum] Sokolow asserted, speaking particularly for the Jews of Poland, that they desired what might be called "ethnic" rights, and that the word "national" was not essential so long as the thing were secured. Others like Doctor Thon[1] and Mr. [Menahem] Ussishkin declined to follow Mr. Sokolow, and insisted on "national" rights. Doctor Thon, for example, baldly stated that "the Jews are a nation, not a religious sect; and we wish the world to know it." Mr. Ussishkin voiced the demand that the Jews as a people of fifteen millions should, as such, be admitted to the League of Nations. At one period of the discussion it almost seemed that Mr. Sokolow and Mr. [Claude G.] Montefiore found themselves in agreement, but Mr. Bentwich[2] turned out to be an uncom-promising nationalist, and almost the last word in the conferences was spoken by Mr. Sokolow in reversal of an earlier statement. As to the sugges-tion to leave out the word "national," his answer was: "No."

Even this, however, was not accepted as a final defeat for an attempt at union, and a committee of seven was appointed to endeavor to present a uniform formula, but "national" rights were the stumbling-block. In spite of the fact that Mr. [Herbert] Hoover told me as early as April 19 that the term "national" minorities could not secure the assent of any delegation, and that President [Woodrow] Wilson made a similar statement to Mr. Marshall and myself later, the astute Jewish statesmen of Eastern Europe, supported by one or two from Western Europe, continued their demand (that was always the favorite word) for "national rights" which meant, of course, national rights in the diaspora.

As you know, the word "national" was never inserted in the treaty, the formula reading "racial, linguistic, and religious minorities." While I do not believe that more could have been secured—and in form at least it was ample—I firmly believe that the insistence upon this phrase, which of course meant the thing, prevented a union upon Palestine and many other matters that would have worked greatly to the advantage of the Jewish people.

And since I have said so much to you, and I know you are willing to accept criticism as well as to offer it, may I not point out that you yourself, while recognizing the danger, unwisdom, and even the unhistorical character of the claim for diaspora nationalism, are yet doing your share toward promoting it? You gave, by your presence, support to the idea of a Jewish Congress in America which is ultimately based upon the theory of diaspora nationalism. Aside from the fact that the Jews of America are in an overwhelming majority unwilling so to organize themselves, even if they would be willing, they would be acting against the very theory that you propound, because this organization is solely upon a political basis. I think you must recognize, if you will consider it carefully, that a plebiscite of all the males and females above the age of eighteen of one section of a great population, demanding no other criterion than the payment of a poll tax of ten cents, is so absolutely akin to the general political elections of this country or indeed of any other country that it would require a very high-powered microscope to discover the difference between it and a regular political election. And if you add to this the utter impossibility of creating any piece of machinery whereby the honesty of such an election could be assured, I think the matter is reduced to an absurdity.

If you do not believe in diaspora nationalism or, since I am concerned for the moment with the United States, if you are not prepared to take the responsibility of advising the Jews of the United States that they should politically organize, then I think the culmination of your sacrifice of time and really distinguished effort would be further to advise the Congress to disband.

How you can reconcile your own views with the advice that there should be a Jewish vote, I confess I do not understand and I hope I may be permitted to remind you in this connection of a remark that you once made to a gentleman who persisted in biting off the conversation and who expressed rather confused philosophical views: "Sir, you misunderstand yourself." I was not present, and if the story is not true, you were nevertheless worthy of it.

Some twenty years ago or more, I think, when we differed about something or other, you told me that I was not of the world and had retired to my academic seclusion.[3] I wish I might have. But the events of at least the last ten years and more dragged me forth from this sheltered position, and in the course of that time, I have mingled a great deal with my fellow-Jews, somewhat in other parts of the world and certainly in America. Though I have never travelled in an aeroplane, I have met them upon the earth, face to face, and even heart to heart, and I am convinced that the Jews of America as a whole have no intention of taking your advice, really to organize themselves into a congress upon the basis of a plebiscite depending upon manhood and womanhood suffrage. The Jews of America may be an untutored lot, and still somewhat in the pioneering stage, but they have old roots in this country, and it does not take long to strike roots in America. They have learned to organize themselves, locally and nationally, for religious, educational, scientific, and philanthropic purposes. They have shown upon occasion that they are willing to meet together, through delegates of these organizations in conference, when important matters affecting them all require any action. They would have done this, in my opinion, upon a much larger scale, had not the Zionist Organization of America in 1916 refused to enter such a conference and supported the congress idea as a substitute. The congress idea in America has never been anything but a tail to the Zionist kite, and up to this time at least no cause has been injured by this mistaken policy more than the cause of Palestine.

Just at the present time, I believe, the setting of Jewish opinion and of world opinion aright upon this question of Jewish nationalism is the most important service that any Jew could render to his people. Please think over both my agreement with this part of your address and my criticism of it, and see whether I am not right in the assertion that a man who disapproves of diaspora nationalism must also disapprove of political Jewish congresses and a Jewish vote. [AJC]

1. Osias Thon (1870–1938), Polish rabbi, Zionist, and communal leader. He was a representative in the Polish Sejm (Parliament), 1919–31.
2. Norman Bentwich (1883–1971), English Zionist leader and author; attorney general of Palestine, 1920–31; subsequently professor of international relations at the Hebrew University, 1932–51.
3. See letters to Israel Zangwill, November 1, 1905, and December 31, 1905.

TO HARRY SCHNEIDERMAN, NEW YORK CITY

October 29, 1923

I am sending you herewith specimens of anti-Jewish literature now appearing in Germany, which I would like to have laid before the Executive Committee [of the American Jewish Committee] at its next meeting. These were brought to my attention by Doctor Jacob Goldstein of Darmstadt, who is now in this country. He has discussed this subject briefly with Mr. [Felix M.] Warburg, and I had a talk with him about it too. He intends to see Mr. [Louis] Marshall, if he can, before the meeting, but in any event the present form of anti-Semitism in Germany is the attempt to win the working classes over to it by cartoons, literature, etc. indicating to the workingman that it is the Jewish capitalist who is at the bottom of his ruin. In the past anti-Semitism in Germany was confined to the court and reactionary classes and university people, whereas the workingmen, at least those who belonged to the Socialist Party, had always refused to have anything to do with it. This is a matter of importance, and ought to be given an early place on the agenda. [AJC]

TO SHAIA D. TULIN,[1] HARTFORD, CONNECTICUT

October 31, 1923

. . . You ask whether the [Jewish Theological] Seminary favors the playing of the organ in a Jewish synagogue on Friday night.

The Seminary is a teaching institution, and does not undertake to pass upon the conduct of congregations. Its sister body, the United Synagogue of America, has a Committee on the Interpretation of Jewish law, of which members of our faculty and some of our graduates are members. This committee makes formal reply to inquiries submitted to us by congregations. I do not know whether the question you raise has ever been formally submitted to it.

I realize, of course, that this is not a specific answer to your question. The Seminary conducts a small synagogue of its own. In this synagogue there is no instrumental music. It is the hope and desire of the Faculty of the Seminary that as our graduates go out they will establish services of the same general character as those they see in the Seminary synagogue. Nevertheless, it is fair to say that the Seminary does not prohibit its graduates from going to synagogues in which the organ is used, if these men themselves have no objection to it. When the Seminary was founded, the founders were men like Drs. [Sabato] Morais, [H. Pereira] Mendes and [Bernard] Drachman, who rigidly adhered to the ancient tradition, and men like Dr. [Alexander] Kohut, [Marcus] Jastrow, and [Benjamin] Szold, who had permitted the organ and other changes in the ritual. The life of historical Judaism seemed to be at stake, and these divergences were not deemed sufficient to prevent unity and cooperation. This view the Seminary still maintains. We have made absolutely no changes in the old traditional practices ourselves. We prefer greatly that congregations should follow our example and not make changes. If a congregation, otherwise conservative, has made a change such as the admission of an organ, we do not object to a Seminary graduate entering the service of such a congregation if he has no scruples on the subject. If he has, we always endeavor to place them in a congregation where no innovations have been made.

I trust that you will understand the policy which I outline in this informal way and without consultation with any of my colleagues. We face the condition in the American synagogue and are doing whatever lies in our power to preserve as much of the tradition as we can. We prefer the traditional synagogue without change in method of worship or liturgy—orderly and decorous—with an English sermon and a good school. Where a congregation has departed from this but is yet minded to be conservative, we do not withdraw our aid from them, but prefer to give them our help, support, and fellowship, so that at least as much of the traditional service shall be maintained by them as possible. Were we to refuse this, we should simply drive them into the reform or radical wing, where they themselves do not wish to go. [JTS]

1. Shaia D. Tulin (1848–1936), Hartford merchant, communal leader, and philanthropist.

TO JUDAH L. MAGNES, JERUSALEM

November 9, 1923

Sometime since I wrote you with reference to the Palestine University, that I would confer with some of my colleagues here, and especially with Professor [Louis] Ginzberg, who is President of the American Academy for Jewish Research.[1] Professor Ginzberg, unfortunately, was not well for a time, and it is only within a few days that I could have a talk with him and get the joint opinion of himself and the others.

I have, I think, told you before that the men in this country were not at all impressed with the plan of the London Committee, and this did not at all refer to the financial end. It is the view of the men here that if there is to be a department of Jewish studies in the proposed University, its general plan should be carefully made up by the best Jewish Scholarship available, and not by Committee "A" or Committee "B" because they happen to be located at a given place. Thus, if the Committee in Jerusalem is going to take the initiative in securing cooperation, I think it would be advisable that it should put itself into direct communication with Professor Ginzberg as President of the Academy here. It is the view of my Colleagues, too, that the Committee in Jerusalem should enter into communication with the Jewish Academy in Berlin.[2] The fact that Germany is not in a position to give material aid at the present time should not exclude Jewish scholars in Germany from giving advice in a matter which affects Jewish Scholarship everywhere.

Quite without reference to the University in Palestine, but yet as affecting the whole question, I would say to you that I have had conferences with Professor [Henry] Malter and Doctor [Solomon] Zeitlin, both of whom were in Europe this year, and the latter had an extended conversation with Israel Levi in Paris. More recently Professor [Richard] Gottheil has been writing actively on the subject. They are all groping after some organization of Jewish Scholarship which would strengthen the hands of the Jewish scholars and render possible even the undertaking of some of the greater tasks on a cooperative plan. The difficult question is, where the seat of such a movement should be. I think that for sentimental reasons everyone would prefer Jerusalem as the center. But the feeling also is general, that with all due respect to the fine set of men in Jerusalem, who have formed a Committee, and who undoubtedly represent all Jewish intellectual life in Palestine, they cannot be said to represent the Jewish Scholarship of the world. Everyone hopes that the time will come when Palestine can take over this work, but I have not found anyone who believes that the men are strong enough to do it yet.

Professor Ginzberg, while agreeing with you that the work should be started as soon as possible, is not at all convinced that the way to start is to definitely appoint a Faculty. But that it would be far more advisable to plan the Jewish Department for three years by extending an invitation for this period to the most prominent Jewish scholars all over the world for a year at a time. In this way the Institution might attract to itself the most prominent Jewish scholarship in the world. Its prestige would at once be established, and the combined experiences of these men, together with their becoming familiar with conditions in Palestine, would undoubtedly, aid the development of a permanent policy much sounder than can be secured by consulting scattered committees through correspondence. [W]

1. See letter to Judah L. Magnes, October 22, 1923.
2. Akademie fuer die Wissenschaft des Judentums, founded in 1919.

In 1924, after nine years as acting president, Adler was appointed president of the Jewish Theological Seminary.

TO LOUIS GINZBERG, ALEXANDER MARX, AND ISRAEL DAVIDSON, NEW YORK CITY

Philadelphia, February 1, 1924

I am in receipt of your letter of January 30, which I shall lay before the Board of Directors at their next meeting. The subject of the salaries of the members of the Faculty would undoubtedly have engaged the attention of the Directors when the budget for the next academic year was taken up, but I am sure that your own forceful presentation of the situation will receive the most careful and sympathetic consideration from the members of the Board.

It is needless for me to tell you that I have been painfully aware of the difficulties under which you have so faithfully labored for the Seminary. The greater part of the Seminary's income—indeed more than its income—has gone into salaries, and only enough has been used for physical purposes to prevent the building and its appliances from falling into decay. I think you are all aware of the fact that even with the present insufficient salaries our outgo has been considerably larger than our income. With the hope for success of the present effort to improve the financial condition of the Seminary I shall make every endeavor to meet your wishes, and I am sure that my colleagues on the Board will be only too happy if the Seminary is in position to grant your request. [W]

TO AARON FINGER,[1] WILMINGTON, DELAWARE

Philadelphia, March 24, 1924

It was our belief when we first called upon the Jews of America, last October, to contribute the sum of $1,000,000 as an endowment fund for the Jewish Theological Seminary—that the campaign would be over by December 1st.

But we have been disappointed. Instead of being able to close the campaign by the middle of December, at least, the total that has been raised up to date is $900,000.

I have been told that against a quota of $5000, Wilmington has raised $800, part of which goes to another organization. Surely, you cannot allow this condition to continue. The success of the campaign depends upon each city doing its part and filling its quota. You and Rabbi Abeles,[2] with the help of some of the community ought to be able to finish out this work in short order.

We felt sure that the Jews of America would realize the urgency of supporting this institution which is training Rabbis and teachers for the Jewish communities of America, men who are perpetuating our faith in the hearts and minds of our people and winning respect for Israel among our neighbors. We felt sure of an immediate and generous response to the eloquent plea of Louis Marshall "to keep alive on the altars of Israel, the holy fires of our faith."

Every Jew who has any Jewish self-respect must realize the pity and the shame of this situation. Every Jew must realize that unless this campaign succeeds—that unless the entire million is actually raised—we will have deserved the criticisms made against us as a materialistic people, having no regard for the finer things of life. If this campaign fails, it will be a disaster for the Jews of America.

This must not be permitted to happen, and I am sure that the Jews of your community are unwilling that it should happen. Call a meeting of the leading Jewish citizens of your town, place this matter before them, tell them the truth as I am telling it to you. If they have already contributed they will be very glad, I am sure, to give a little more, and to get others to give. And if the facts are placed before them at a meeting they would be glad to do it. In any case act promptly because the honor and the future of American Jewry are at stake. [D]

1. Judge in Wilmington, Delaware.
2. Moses J. S. Abels.

TO LOUIS MARSHALL, NEW YORK CITY

Philadelphia, April 30, 1924

I am in receipt of your letter of April 29, enclosing the letter of the Macmillan Company of April 18 concerning the publication in English of Doctor Joseph Klausner's book which they entitle "Jesus, the Hebrew Moralist," and which in Hebrew is "Jesus the Nazarene, his Time, his Life, and his Teachings."[1] The book appeared in Hebrew in 1922, in Jerusalem, and is one of the first unfortunate products of that scientific and cultural revival about which we have talked. Klausner, who published a book some twenty years ago on the messianic hopes of the Jewish people at the time of the Tannaim,[2] later went to Palestine, became the editor of *Hashiloah,* and has been a profuse writer in Hebrew periodicals. I am rather surprised at the statement of Macmillan's that Professor George Foote Moore is keen to have an adequate translation into English, because in a review of the book which Moore published in the *Harvard Theological Review* for January, 1923, he writes: "The chapters on the teaching of Jesus (pp. 395–448) are the part of the work in which Christian scholars would find the greatest intrinsic interest"; and later he adds: "A translation of this part of the volume at least would be well worth while." Moore himself does not speak with entire favor of the book by any means, and in order to show the Jewish critical attitude he summarises an article in *Hatoren* for August, 1922 by Armand Kaminka,[3] and says that Kaminka's main attack upon Klausner is that he sees in it "an unbecoming disposition to truckle to Christianity." The whole article of Moore is well worth reading. It covers 8 or 10 pages, and if you have time to read it, I shall be very glad to send you the volume. A similar unfavorable review of the book was published in the *Jewish Quarterly Review* for July, 1923, written by Doctor [Solomon] Zeitlin, pp. 132 to the end of the article, in which Zeitlin beside criticising him in a great deal of detail combats his view that "Jesus, for the Jewish nation, is the ethical man par excellence." Zeitlin's review is extremely severe, but not so severe as he wrote it, because I toned it down somewhat. Aside from the view that Kaminka expresses, that Klausner, probably for political reasons, truckled to Christianity, the book itself is highly unscientific. I have discussed it with quite a number of men, and they all seem to think that it is a very unfortunate product of Jewish learning. Klausner has made a very big book on what is apparently a journalistic plan. He has read all the books he could about Jesus and made extracts from them and arranged them. Not infrequently he makes statements on opposite pages which are totally divergent, showing that not only is he not a very good author, but he is not even a good editor. I think you will gather from this my opinion, that insofar as we are concerned the less circulation the book has the better.

If you should not happen to have your *Jewish Quarterly Review* handy and want an extra copy I shall of course be glad to send you one.

I do not suppose that you want to object to Macmillan's publishing the translation, since that is well within their right, but certainly I see no reason why Jews should support it. [AJA]

1. The book, entitled *Jesus of Nazareth: His Life, Times, and Teaching,* translated by Herbert Danby, was to be published by Macmillan in September 1925.
2. Klausner's book, *Ha-ra'ayon ha-meshihi be-Yisrael* (The Messianic Idea in Israel) was first

published in three volumes in Cracow, 1908–22. An English translation was published in New York, 1955.

3. Armand Kaminka (1866–1950), Jewish scholar; lecturer at the Vienna Rabbinical Seminary; secretary of the Vienna Israelitisches Allianz.

TO FELIX M. WARBURG

May 19, 1924

I am writing you the enclosed letter simply commenting upon your report, although as I indicated to you yesterday I did not see that the Joint Distribution Committee is going to deal with this subject. What you told me about the postponement of the Russian question until Doctor Rosen[1] could come over here makes me think that there is no use in commenting upon that subject. Since I saw you I have had a talk with Doctor Bramson of the Ort,[2] who seems to me a rather capable man. The Ort wants to make a campaign in this country for $750,000—yet another campaign. I still have a feeling that our best use of any funds that we have available for Russia will be in the direction of agricultural and technical training, and if you think agriculture should be more encouraged than handicraft, which possibly is quite advisable for so predominantly an agricultural country as Russia, that condition might be made with the Ort if we should hand over funds to them.

With regard to the [Hebrew] University, I believe that the first step is the selection of trustees who could receive and handle funds. Mr. [Solomon] Rosenbloom, as I think I told you, is proposing an endowment fund, that is, the endowment of a chair or may be two chairs, and he was at least not prepared to give up the expendable fund. I think if that skeleton part of the organization could be brought down to earth first it would be very important.

With regard to the question of the teaching staff or the curriculum, I do not believe that I would be valuable in the matter, or at least that my views would be accepted as representative of any particular group. I would very strongly urge even at the initial stage that Professor Louis Ginzberg, as President of the American Academy of Jewish Research, who as I told you over the phone is now president of an organization which includes scholars from the Seminary, the Yeshiva in New York, the Hebrew Union College, the Dropsie College, and even men like Professor [David S.] Blondheim of Johns Hopkins University and Professor [Isaac] Husik of the University of Pennsylvania, is the man who ought to be named distinctly as the American representative to discuss these matters, and it would be worth while even to ask him to go to Europe for the purpose. I do not often make statements so definitely as this, but I am sure that what I am suggesting to you is very

important. I think that Jewish scholars are getting a little tired of my ubiqui-
tous presidency, chairmanship, etc., and I think rightly so.

There is, however, another and larger aspect of the matter which I would
like you to consider, which has come into my mind since our talk. This effort
in Palestine is one that ought reasonably to represent as much of Jewish
scholarship as is attainable. Now it happens that Doctor [Judah L.] Magnes is
in Palestine; Doctor [Joseph H.] Hertz by reason of his position in England,
has to be considered; and you and Baron Edmund de Rothschild as donors of
considerable funds are willing to have your views expressed on scholastic
points by Israel Levi and myself, or as I would prefer, Professor Ginzberg. It
seems to me, however, that the mere fact that certain countries are today
financially down and out should not preclude their participation in these very
important initial stages. I need not tell you that at least for seventy-five years
Germany was the home of Jewish science. Italy, in spite of her comparatively
small Jewish community, has had very distinguished scholars in the past
hundred years, and still has some, the dean of them at the present time being a
man like Professor Umberto Cassuto.[3] Then too Prague and Warsaw, Vienna
and Budapest are great centers, or at least have been great centers, of Jewish
learning. It would seem to me to be rather a pity that the program for the
Jewish department of the University of the Jews should be cut and dried by
two, three or four men. Such an arrangement would leave, I fear, a certain
amount of resentment, and may also deprive us of a good deal of useful advice
for the present and help for the future. Maybe after you have seen Mr.
Rosenbloom you will let me hear from you again on this subject. [W]

1. Joseph A. Rosen (1877–1949), agronomist; head of the Joint Distribution Committee's
programs in the Soviet Union (Agro-Joint).
2. Leon Bramson (1869–1941), communal worker and writer; an official of ORT (Obsh-
chestvo Rasprostaneniya Truda sredi Yevreyev)—Society for Manual Work among the Jews,
founded in Russia in 1880.
3. Umberto Cassuto (1883–1951), Italian Jewish historian and biblical scholar; at the time
director of the rabbinical seminary in Florence; subsequently became professor of Hebrew
language and literature at the universities of Florence and Rome, and professor of Bible studies at
the Hebrew University.

Memorandum regarding the University of Jerusalem

June 1, 1924

It is proposed that the American donors of Funds for the School of
Jewish Studies in the University of Jerusalem shall select Trustees who will
invest Endowment Funds and hold expendable Funds to be paid over from

time to time upon proper vouchers. These Trustees should include the Donors and three other persons whom they should select. It is suggested however that these Trustees should be known to have a sympathy with the purposes of the Trust. The trustees should operate under a Trust agreement without the necessity for incorporation at the present time.

They should request that all funds for this Department which may have been appropriated by the Zionist Organization or contributed through the Keren Hayesod or donated by any individual should likewise be placed in the hands of Trustees and be subject to draft upon the presentation of proper vouchers. With regard to the Board to direct the Educational policy it is proposed that so far as America is concerned this shall be done through a special Committee of the American Academy of Jewish Research which at present consists of Professors Louis Ginzberg, Alexander Marx and Israel Davidson of New York, Cyrus Adler and Henry Malter of Philadelphia and David Blondheim of Baltimore. This Committee has held a lengthy meeting (all present except Professor Malter), and after considering all previous plans proposed makes the following suggestions:

That the subjects to be provided for in this department shall be the following:

Hebrew Philology	Jewish Literature
Philosophy of Judaism	Jewish History
Jewish Law	Palestinian Geography, Archaeology and Epigraphy

That in order to render this Department of the University comprehensive the Cognate subjects should be included under the following headings:

Arabic Language, Literature, Judeo-Arabic	Egyptology
	Ethiopic
Aramaic, Syriac, Samaritan	Pheonician
Assyriology	

It is the view of the American Committee that no Chair should be filled for a period of three years and for that length of time the work should be conducted upon the following basis: Various Jewish institutions of learning throughout the world should be requested to permit one or another of their Professors to reside in Palestine for a period of one year and lecture upon their specialty from among one or another of the general subjects outlined above. It is the view of our Committee that if this plan were followed after a period of three years a considerable number of the Jewish scholars of the world will have been in Palestine, become acquainted with its conditions and the needs of students there and a definite plan could be arrived at as the result of experience instead of one being created ad hoc.

If it appears necessary to inaugurate this Department in October 1924 the contribution offered for America would be Professor Max L. Margolis as Professor of Hebrew Philology and Professor Louis Ginzberg as Professor of Jewish Law. Professor Margolis has already gone to Palestine and provision can be made for his lectureship by a Philadelphia Committee. I am prepared to recommend a leave of absence for Professor Ginzberg as an earnest of the interest of the Seminary in this plan. As for European scholars who might be invited for one year or another we suggest the following:

Doctor Immanuel Löw[1]—Archaeology
Doctor S. Dubnow[2]—History
Chief Rabbi Israel Levi—
Doctor Ludwig Blau—Archaeology
Doctor Michael Guttman[3]—Jewish Law
Doctor A. Buchler—Jewish History
Doctor Joseph Horovitz[4]—Arabic
Prof. Eugene Mittwoch[5]—Arabic
Chief Rabbi Joseph Hertz—Philosophy of Judaism

These names are merely suggested from among a number to indicate the type of men. Doubtless the European scholars can suggest many others.

We feel moreover that Jewish scholars in Europe should be requested to organize themselves into an Academy or Academies through an organization Committee which would operate in association with our own body in America. We feel that if a Committee for the organization of such an Academy were created in Europe that it might also function as the Organization Committee in Europe for the Jewish Department of the University of Jerusalem. Doctor Hertz and Doctor Israel Levi and Doctor Simonsen[6] of Copenhagen would be the gentlemen to call such a body together, and although his specialty lies in another direction we think that Doctor Haffkein [sic][7] of Paris should be co-opted on this initial Committee both because of his experience and his deep interest in Jewish learning. The Palestinian

Committee should appoint an administrative official who is prepared to act on the spot as the administrator of the Department and co-ordinate the work of the visiting Professors.

It is believed that if this scheme is followed Jewish learning will be represented in a distinguished manner in Jerusalem during the next three years and that as a result a definite plan will be organically evolved.

Professor [David S.] Blondheim will be in France this summer and Professor Marx in Germany. They will undertake to place this subject before scholars in those countries. Meanwhile if approved this plan will be communicated to Doctor Hertz in England. In view of the fact that the subject which Mr. [Solomon] Rosenbloom especially desires to foster would come under the general heading of the Philosophy of Judaism, we suggest that in order that his views be carried out he stipulate in his foundation that the occupant of the Chair which he founds shall be known to the Board of Governors to hold the traditional point of view. This Board of Governors shall ultimately become responsible for the educational policy of the Department and for the selection of the Faculty. The Palestinian Committee should select two representatives on this Board. The American representatives should be the special Committee of the Academy. The European scholars should be appointed either upon the basis of an Academy which they may form or upon that of their local institutions of Jewish learning. It is the hope of our Committee that out of this plan there might develop a general Jewish Academy greatly to the advantage of Jewish learning and that if men of the positions of the Chief Rabbis of England and France would actually join in this plan it might further result that a Center of authority for Judaism would be established.

These latter ideas are not essential to the plan but indicate our belief of the great advantage to Judaism and to Jewish learning which might result from it both in Palestine and throughout the world. [W]

---

1. Immanuel Löw (1854–1944), Hungarian rabbi and talmudic scholar.
2. Simon Dubnow (1860–1941), noted Russian Jewish historian.
3. Michael Guttman (1872–1942), talmudic scholar, professor at the rabbinical seminaries of Breslau and Budapest.
4. Joseph Horovitz (1874–1931), Arabist; professor of Semitic philology at the University of Frankfurt am Main.
5. Eugen Mittwoch (1876–1942), German Jewish orientalist; professor at the University of Berlin; subsequently director of the Berlin office of the Joint Distribution Committee.
6. David Jacob Simonsen (1853–1932), Danish rabbi and scholar; former chief rabbi of Denmark, 1891–1902.
7. Waldemar Mordecai Haffkine (1860–1930), Russian Jewish bacteriologist; developer of the first successful vaccine against cholera.

As a scholar who had taken an important role in devising a system of international scientific exchange, Adler decried the postwar trend of publishing scholarly research in minor languages—such as Modern Hebrew—which could not be read by the majority of the world's scholars.

TO JUDAH L. MAGNES, JERUSALEM

June 6, 1924

I have delayed replying to your letter of April 16, because there were a number of people I wanted to see before I took the matter up with you. Mr. [Felix M.] Warburg now tells me that he has already sent you a copy of the memorandum which I handed to him and to Mr. [Solomon] Rosenbloom on the first of June. As that was very hastily written and contained a number of errors I am sending you a corrected copy herewith.

As for the letter of Doctor [Leo Ari] Mayer, I would say this. His work, if it is thoroughly done, is of course most valuable. I am not at all certain, however, that the idea of having the entire work printed in Hebrew is good, even if it were not a question of securing a publisher. You yourself know that Palestine's inscriptions in Hebrew, Greek, etc. would be of great interest to a large body of non-Jewish scholars. The non-Jewish scholars are, I believe, not going to learn current Hebrew, and if a scientific work of this kind is for theoretical reasons printed exclusively in Hebrew its influence and usefulness will, I believe, be greatly limited. I would suggest as a policy with regard to this particular book that the introduction and notes be given in Hebrew and English. I have before me at the present moment the two volumes of the *Scripta Universitatis et Bibliothecae Hierosolomytanarum,* and I notice that some modern languages, German, English, have been admitted along with the Hebrew, even in the volume devoted to Orientalia and Judaica, and that Nijhoff[1] is apparently the publisher. Why would he not take up such a volume as Mayer's, which would have a much greater appeal than a volume of miscellaneous articles.

I believe that this publication would be very properly a publication of the Jewish department of the University, and I think it not impossible that in view of the fluid condition of Mr. Warburg's fund that could be drawn upon for the purpose if it would be found necessary. Naturally there will be sale for such a book, but there would be much greater sale if the introduction and notes were rendered in some language beside Hebrew.

I have recently been talking with a number of scholars in this country, none of whom were Jews, who were seriously considering the very great difficulties which scholars now had to face in view of the nationalistic revivals, large and small. Up to a comparatively recent time, a scholar who knew Latin, English, French and German could reasonably keep abreast of the scientific world. At present the Russians write in Russian; the Latvians in Lettish; the Czechs in Czechish; the Poles in Polish; and of course the Rumanians in Rumanian; the Irish in Gaelic; and now the Jews in Hebrew and the Japanese in Japanese. For a considerable period, as you know, the Russians published their scientific works either in French or German; the Japanese were using English, etc. Now the thing that really will happen is that a large body of the scientific discovery made in the smaller countries will be ignored or lost even to the general scientific current. The international languages apparently have failed. There is a serious proposition being made for the revival of Latin as an international language of science, or at least for the printing in Latin of a summary of the important results of all scientific papers. Now that you are giving your attention to an institution of higher learning, you ought to think about these things. It seems to me that there is but slight satisfaction in a man's doing a piece of scientific work and having it published with the knowledge that it must be inaccessible to a very large proportion of scholars.

I am going to Europe very shortly and I am expecting to take the first vacation in my life, have no conferences, and engage in no work of any kind. I am sure you will not begrudge me this. . . . [W]

1. The publishing firm of Martinus Nijhoff, The Hague. The two volumes were *Mathematica et Physica* and *Orientalia et Judaica* (Jerusalem, 1923).

TO FELIX M. WARBURG, NEW YORK CITY

October 17, 1924

When I last saw you, you handed me, among other things, Doctor [Judah L.] Magnes's statement concerning the meeting on the Palestine University and his letter to you, which I promised to consider and discuss. Maybe I can best discuss it in writing and then if there are any points in which you do not agree we can talk about them later.

I had the impression that what we had been discussing in recent months was not the policy of the whole University but only of the Department or Institute of Jewish Studies. Doctor Magnes has either mingled these two or prefers to take up the subject of the University as a whole. Of course, the subject of the University as a whole was not the one which the London Conference was called to consider nor were the men particularly qualified to consider it. If it is feasible to establish the University in Palestine, comparable in importance and dignity if not in size to the great universities in Europe and in America, it is naturally the experience of these universities which should be taken into account. There would be a philosophical faculty, professional schools, and the only one that would differ very strongly, except as local conditions require, from the great universities is the Institute of Jewish Studies, which ought to be much more important than their Semitic Departments. I take it for granted that the Founders of the University have in mind at present one after the European model rather than the American model, which means that they are mainly considering post-graduate studies and not what we call the college.

To return to Doctor Magnes's memorandum and to take particularly his example with regard to the method of approach, I cannot but feel that his view, if it represents that of his colleagues in Palestine, is incorrect. If Greek and the history of Greek civilization are to be studied and are to be considered from the point of view of the Jewish contact with Greek civilization, a totally incorrect perspective would be obtained. One cannot acquire the genius of a language or literature from translations. The Greek translations of the Bible, the Septuagint, Aquila, etc., can no more form a starting point for the study of Greek language and literature than would a German translation of Shakespeare for German literature. Philo,[1] while he has his importance of course, is not fundamentally important, either from the point of Greek literature or of Jewish literature. If anything, the philosophy of Philo furnished the real philosophical basis for Christianity and I am not at all certain that the Jewish consciousness was wrong in ignoring him for so many centuries. But even if my two estimates of these works cited by Doctor Magnes are wrong, I still think that he is wrong both from the linguistic and literary point of view. I naturally agree that the professors ought to and must know about the Jewish contact of these various subjects and the specific Jewish interest, but should these contacts be made the starting point, the men trained there will be so narrow and one-sided that they can never attain to a place in the scholarly world, and while Doctor Magnes in his statement guards against this, the method will not guard against it.

A university press is of course an important adjunct of every institution, but a very expensive affair, and it is a question whether it is essential at the very beginning, and it is also a question, in my mind, whether it is essential that each professor that comes to the University should be required to take up a piece of research and finish it within the time that he is in Palestine and deposit it for publication. After all, the universities are initially carried on for students, but sometimes people seem to think that they are carried on for the professors. I believe that in the initial years the professor ought, beside giving his lectures, spend a great deal of time with the students themselves and if he succeeds in training them to a method of research he will do better than actually adding one to his own list of papers. Doctor Magnes makes rather a point of defending [Joseph G.] Klausner and charging that he has had contempt and contumely heaped upon his head. Now I think that he is a little unfair in asserting that this is because Klausner is a Palestinian. Whatever may have been said about him in the past, his work on Jesus has been viewed by nearly all of my associates both in Philadelphia and New York as a distinct betrayal of Judaism and this aside from what they consider his improper method from the historical point of view. . . .[2]

. . . Now with regard to Doctor Magnes' suggestions concerning the American Committee, I also doubt whether they are good or at least if they do not show some confusion. Judge [Julian W.] Mack as an advisor for the general University policy and as an advisor for the Department of Jewish Studies is quite another matter. The selection of Professors [Israel] Davidson and Mann,[3] of New York and Cincinnati respectively, would I think arouse resentment and I believe that a much safer way would be to let the Jewish scholars in America, through the Academy, select their own representatives. I have the highest regard for both Davidson and Mann, but if these two Faculties are to be represented, [Louis] Ginzberg is the senior of Davidson, and [Jacob Z.] Lauterbach is the senior of Mann, and these human considerations have to be borne in mind. I doubt whether either of these two men would accept, although of this I am not sure. Well, I think I have written enough to-day, but there is only one point I wish to add: Mr. [Solomon] Rosenbloom appears to be unreconciled. I am enclosing you a copy of his letter to me and a copy of my letter to him. . . . [W]

1. Philo Judaeus (c. 20 B.C.E.–50 C.E.), Jewish philosopher of Alexandria.
2. See letter to Louis Marshall, April 30, 1924.
3. Jacob Mann (1880–1940), professor of Jewish history at Hebrew Union College.

The organization and rationalization of Jewish charitable fundraising was one of the great tasks facing the American Jewish leadership of the 1920s.

TO LOUIS MARSHALL, NEW YORK CITY

November 18, 1924

I have been wanting to write to you for some time in response to various letters which have come to me from the Emergency Committee on Jewish Refugees about the campaign in Philadelphia. The assumption seems to be throughout these letters that I was to take the initiative in Philadelphia. It further appears that no national conferences or public meetings are being scheduled for this appeal and I also learn, through having been present at the meeting of the United Synagogue, that that Institution and I presume other national institutions were asked to make an appeal through their constituents and a quota (it seems to me a very small quota) was set for the United Synagogue. As there are about ten congregations in Philadelphia which are members of the United Synagogue, they would have their requests for assistance made through the national office of that Institution. I imagine that the Union of American Hebrew Congregations and the fraternal orders are also being appealed to in the same way.

I am sure that it is not necessary for me to tell you that campaigns for funds cannot be managed on this double plan. If Philadelphia or any other city is asked to contribute a definite sum of money and a local committee takes the matter up, then the territory cannot be canvassed in any other way. I can very well imagine that under the present plan if a synagogue had been approached as a body, its membership could not be approached again.

Our situation here in Philadelphia is at present as follows:

Last spring, at the request of Mr. Leon J. Obermayer[1] and Mr. Morris Wolf[2] of the Young Men's Hebrew Association, a meeting was called by Mr. Jules Mastbaum[3] of some twenty-five men to consider the question of the regulation of drives and campaigns in Philadelphia, whether for local or national or international purposes. An agreement was reached there that this Committee should be called together whenever such requests came, in order that these campaigns might be arranged in such a way as not to interfere with local campaigns and not to unduly tax the time of the public. We have at the present time, as you know, a necessity for a small campaign for the Jewish Welfare Board. I received a letter to-day from Mr. Moskowitz[4] telling me that some of the "leading Jews of Philadelphia" at Mr. Lewisohn's[5] meeting pledged Philadelphia to $150,000 and asking me to call a preliminary meeting on November 20th. I am going to explain that I am going to do no such thing and am asking for the names of the persons who made this pledge. I think you can see yourself the usefulness of the plan which we have outlined for ourselves in Philadelphia and that if it is not carried through all of everybody's time will be taken up with these campaigns. If you are in agreement with this plan, I am willing to lay the matter before the Committee on the Co-ordination of Campaigns and be guided by their judgment. Just for your own information and since I know that you cannot possibly control all the things that are done in your name, I want to say that this idea of asking one man in a letter to say on a return postal card what his community will do may be suitable for small towns, but certainly not for large cities. Pledges or promises of this kind made by an individual are worthless, unless the individual is able to make up the deficit out of his pocket and you know how rare one like that is.

I am not at all convinced that I am the best man to manage this campaign and it may be that the people here may feel a necessity to combine the Jewish Refugees Fund, the Ort Fund, and even the Jewish Welfare Board in one campaign permitting designations. However, I am not pre-judging that. . . . [W]

1. Leon Jacob Obermayer (b. 1886), Philadelphia lawyer and communal worker; president of the Philadelphia YMHA and YWHA, 1915–26.
2. Morris Wolf (1883–1978), Philadelphia lawyer and communal worker.
3. Jules E. Mastbaum (1875–1929), Philadelphia philanthropist and communal leader.
4. Henry Moskowitz (1879–1936), social worker and Jewish communal leader; an executive of the Joint Distribution Committee and ORT.
5. Adolph Lewisohn (1849–1938), philanthropist.

TO FELIX M. WARBURG, NEW YORK CITY

December 1, 1924

I have a letter of your Secretary of November 25th with regard to the visit of Doctor Illoway[1] concerning the work of Professor Henry Malter. The facts are as follows: Professor Malter was invited by the Classics Committee [of the Jewish Publication Society] to prepare a critical text of one of the tractates of the Talmud—Taanit—for the [Schiff] Classics Series, together with a translation, introduction, etc. This has been done and the volume is now in type.[2] In the course of his studies, Professor Malter found that the text of the Talmud had grown very corrupt and moreover that they all followed one edition which had been based on one manuscript. For the purpose of his own critical text, he has examined about thirteen manuscripts and has established, as a result of some seven years' work, what he considers a correct text.

It has been long the hope of Jewish scholars to secure an accurate text of the Talmud, and Professor Malter and many of his colleagues believe that he has arrived at a method which if followed in the case of other tractates would finally result in the best text. This entire work can only be done by numbers of scholars working in various parts of the world and Professor Malter believes that the publication, as it were, of his laboratory method would indicate how he arrived at his result.

The Classics Committee very carefully considered the question of the publication of this by-product of Professor Malter's work and they all came to the conclusion that it could not properly be published in the Classics Series. For one thing, the form alone forbade it, because this present work of Professor Malter would have to be prepared on a large page, at least a good size quarto, in order to illustrate his method. The American Academy for Jewish Research has unanimously agreed that this work of Professor Malter should be published but they are at present without funds. I think that if you are disposed to help, and I believe that this would be a real contribution to scholarship, the best method would be not to give this help to Professor Malter as an individual but to the Academy, in order that they might publish this work and thus launch a series of publications.[3] [D]

1. Henry Illoway (1848–1932), New York pediatrician and Jewish scholar.
2. It was published in 1928 as *The Treatise Ta'anit of the Babylonian Talmud*, the fourth volume in the Schiff Library of Jewish Classics, issued by the Jewish Publication Society.
3. Malter's work was published by the Academy as *Treatise Ta'anit of the Babylonian Talmud* (New York, 1930).

The Hebrew University, begun as a graduate and research institution, did not develop an undergraduate program until 1949. This left a gap in the Palestinian educational system, which concerned Adler.

TO FELIX M. WARBURG, NEW YORK CITY

December 12, 1924

. . . I do not like to set up my judgment against that of people who are on the ground but I have very great hesitation in thinking that the policy of not admitting students of regular University grade is a wise one or even a fair one to students in Palestine. There are three, in fact, I believe four Palestinians at the Dropsie College now who came here because they could not continue their studies any further in Palestine. That, of course, is understandable but what of the future? I just got in the mail an application from a student who has done everything he could in Palestine and who wants to come here. Why should such men be put to the expense and dislocation of coming to America, especially when I think it was generally understood, and students had a right to so understand it, that the University in Palestine would be for them and not merely for a select few of the very highest grade. It seems to me that after all the talk about University the effort is now being made to establish research Institutions more of the grade of the European Academies or the English

Royal Society than of the grade of the University teaching and that if this policy is followed out there will be a hiatus between the Teachers Seminary and the Gymnasium on the one hand and the Research Institute on the other and that native born Palestinians will be forced to visit Europe or America for what we understand to be their University Studies. . . . [W]

TO LOUIS MARSHALL, NEW YORK CITY

January 2, 1925

I had your letter of December 27 enclosing the correspondence which passed between Mr. Simon Miller and Mr. Nathan J. Miller[1] concerning the distribution of Professor [Israel] Davidson's *Thesaurus of Jewish Poetry*.[2] As you may imagine, this has been a subject of a good deal of discussion between Professor Davidson and myself during the past few months. Professor Davidson has been engaged on this work for a quarter of a century. The present volume is the first of four volumes. The publication of the first volume has been made possible through the goodness of Mr. Nathan J. Miller but neither Professor Davidson nor the Seminary has any fund in sight for the publication of the succeeding volumes.

It has seemed to us, therefore, quite worth-while to endeavor to sell the first volume at a price which would yield a fund to print the second volume and thus to go on with the succeeding volumes. I have conferred with Doctor A. S. W. Rosenbach on this subject and he believes that a reference work like this could be sold. At all events, it is worth trying. Certainly I think Mr. Simon Miller's suggestion for free distribution to seminaries and Jewish seats of learning should not be adopted. All such institutions buy books and there is no reason why they should not buy this one.

It is always possible to give books away, but I should like to see the experiment tried first of placing this book on the market and, by circularization of the great public libraries, the universities and seminaries here and abroad, see if it is not possible to sell a reasonable part of the edition. If we fail, we can always make presents.

There must always be a number of review copies and Professor Davidson thinks that a better result will be reached if these are sent to individual scholars who will agree to write reviews for particular periodicals instead of sending them direct to the publisher on the off chance that he may or may not assign them to the proper person. In this way, a number of individual scholars will receive free copies.

I do not like to oppose my judgment to that of men like Mr. Simon Miller and Mr. Nathan J. Miller, both of whom have shown such a deep interest in the promotion of Jewish literature, but it seems to me that Professor Davidson's *Thesaurus* presents a rather unusual case. It is a work of reference and has not and is not likely to have any competitor for several generations. The edition is limited to five hundred copies. It is written entirely in Hebrew and hence is available to scholars all over the world. Granted the initial capital was supplied through the generosity of Mr. Nathan J. Miller, I feel that the experiment should be made to determine whether it cannot be continued on a business basis. [W]

1. Nathan J. Miller (1873–1927), banker and philanthropist; with his wife, Linda (1877–1936), subsidized the publication of Davidson's work.
2. *Thesaurus of Medieval Hebrew Poetry*, 4 vols. (New York, Jewish Theological Seminary, 1924–33).

The new American immigration law, which had just come into force, imposed an even more stringent quota on the number of immigrants allowed into the United States. This meant that a number of people with passports and visas for the United States were being denied entry. The American Jewish Committee, still fighting to keep the doors of the United States as open as possible to immigration, attempted to lobby Congress on this issue.

TO LOUIS MARSHALL, NEW YORK CITY

February 24, 1925

On Sunday, February 22, Judge [Horace] Stern and I had an hour's interview with Senator Pepper[1] with regard to the joint resolution concerning the refugees. Senator Pepper seemed to be quite familiar with the subject and showed to us the Congressional record of February 17 containing the debate started by Senator Willis[2] and indulged in between Senator Reed[3] and Senator Copeland[4] concerning the Copeland resolution. He seems to be very much impressed by a statement made by Senator Reed concerning the strike of the transmigrants in Cherbourg. We told him that if that was intended as an intimation that most of these immigrants were communists it was beside the mark as none of these people held a visa from a consul in Soviet Russia because we had no consuls there. Senator Pepper said that he was impressed by the justice of our position and that he would personally undertake to see Senator Reed and the Committee and urge the passage of the resolution and that he would let us know the result of his efforts. He further said (as he put it, in order to be frank) that for the sake of party discipline and regularity he wished us to understand that if the Committee did not report the resolution favorably he would not bring the matter up on the floor or support it against the Committee. We told him that we would be satisfied if he would confine his effort in getting it through the Committee because if he could not we did not suppose it would come up before the Senate this session anyhow.

Senator Pepper also asked us whether we would hold ourselves in readiness in case he desired us to appear before the Committee and we told him we would. Thinking there might be some point in the discussion which we had overlooked I telephoned Mr. [Harry] Schneiderman Sunday night and asked him to look up the Congressional record of February 17 and furnish Judge Stern and myself with a memorandum concerning the points raised. He prepared such a memorandum which is very clear and detailed and sent it to Judge Stern and myself. The Judge is of the opinion that until we hear from Senator Pepper further we should hold this memorandum. . . . [W]

1. George Wharton Pepper (1867–1961), U.S. senator from Pennsylvania, 1922–27.
2. Frank Bartlette Willis (1871–1928), U.S. senator from Ohio, 1921–27.
3. James A. Reed (1861–1944), U.S. senator from Missouri, 1911–29.
4. Royal Samuel Copeland (1868–1938), U.S. senator from New York, 1923–38.

TO JUDAH L. MAGNES, JERUSALEM

March 2, 1925

I received your letter of January 13th with its enclosures concerning the regulations for the Institute of Jewish Studies of the Hebrew University.

I do not know that Mr. [Felix M.] Warburg has constituted a Committee, but he, Judge [Julian W.] Mack, Mr. [Louis] Marshall and I have met once or twice to talk things over. I have said to them definitely that unless the Jewish Academy here is constituted the consulting body in scholastic matters, I cannot go along with them as any other course would result in a breach between the Jewish scholars here and myself and this I am unwilling to contemplate. With Mr. Warburg's assent, I laid all your proposals before the Academy a few days since and was present at their meeting. You will receive their advice direct from Professor [Louis] Ginzberg and I think their conclusions are sound. Upon the whole, I believe you are working toward a definite basis.

A very important matter for the University to determine as a whole is whether it intends to grant degrees. If so, it must adopt standards of admission and residence which will make its degree recognized by European and American universities.

I am trying to interest people in the University and did secure a subscription for five thousand dollars ($5000) the other day from Jules E. Mastbaum of Philadelphia. On February 26th, Mr. Warburg gave a dinner at his house at my suggestion just to discuss the University. Julius Rosenwald, Louis Marshall, Herbert Lehman,[1] Paul Baerwald[2] and others of our friends were there. Doctor [Chaim] Weizmann and Colonel Kisch,[3] however, talked about the whole Palestine problem and Jewish question and while I tried to hold the company to the University, I am not sure that I succeeded. Of course, there was no idea of asking for funds but only to favorably dispose the minds of those present to the University.

To me it seems a very hazardous thing to open a University on a shoe-string and I shall do what I can to make the shoe-string a little stronger, but naturally I have my own institutions here to look after and that is aplenty. [W]

1. Herbert H. Lehman (1878–1963), banker and politician; lieutenant governor of New York, 1928–32; governor, 1932–42; U.S. senator, 1949–56.
2. Paul Baerwald (1871–1961), banker and philanthropist; treasurer and subsequently chairman of the Joint Distribution Committee.
3. Frederick Hermann Kisch (1888–1943), British officer and Zionist leader; a member of the Zionist Executive in Jerusalem; director of the political department, 1922–31; killed in action in North Africa during the Second World War.

TO SOLOMON ROSENBLOOM, PITTSBURGH

March 20, 1925

I have been very much interested in the correspondence between yourself and Doctor [Judah L.] Magnes, and in accordance with your request am expressing my opinion on his two recent letters. It is necessary to differentiate between the general departments of the University of Jerusalem and the Department of Jewish Studies. The latter is the Department in which you are especially interested and in which apparently the discussion revolved around the use of the phrase "academic freedom." This is a very difficult subject and one over which a great deal of ink has been spilled, but I think after all a reasonable consensus of opinion has been reached about it. Academic freedom does not refer to the selection of professors. No person has an inherent right to be a professor in a particular institution and the governing body, whatever it may be, whether Trustees or Faculty, indicates their trend of opinion by the selection of professors. Academic freedom means that once a professor is in a given institution he may teach the subject for which he is selected according to his lights—in other words, according to what he believes to be the truth. It further means that a professor is free to express his opinions on any subject just as any other man is, but when he expresses his opinions outside of the field for which he is elected, it is his duty to make it clear that he is speaking in his own name and not in behalf of his institution. Even within this limit there is a courtesy among university professors that they shall not attack the conduct of departments within their own university. For example: it would be outside of courtesy and the proper policy if the professor, let us say, in the Department of Jewish Studies should attack a professor in the Medical Department for permitting dissection. And on the other hand, it would be against the courtesy and proper policy if the professor in the Medical Department should attack the Professor of Talmud for any instruction that he was giving. Experience has dictated this necessary to the harmonious conduct of a university.

In sectarian or particularist universities, there is a further limitation. If the institution starts out with a certain definite point of view and the professor understands this when he enters, there is an implied contract that if he should renounce those views, it would be his duty to resign from the university.

The question as to how far these general propositions apply to the new Hebrew University depends upon what the founders themselves have in mind. If, for example, they mean to establish a Hebrew University which shall differ from other universities only in the fact that the language of instruction is Hebrew, there is no point in any further discussion. In the Department of Jewish Studies, all that this would mean would be that the instruction should be given in the Hebrew language; that the Professor of Bible might be from the neighboring Dominican School. I assume that this is not the point of view and that so far as the Department of Jewish Studies is concerned, it is not going to be merely Hebrew but also Jewish.

Once this is granted, the question does arise—what sort of Jewish? Surely it must be recognized that there are differing points of view. There is a main stream of Judaism which we may call rabbinic or traditional. This represents the orderly development of Judaism from within through its written and oral law, modified no doubt by time and environment, but always basing itself upon its own constitution. All other forms of Judaism in the past or present were particularist or sectarian.

Doctor Magnes lays great stress on the truth no matter where it leads. So do we all. But absolute truth is difficult to attain and this more especially in departments of knowledge where opinion—not to say prejudices or predi-lection—plays a part. Prejudices play a part even in opinions about matters in the realm of the physical sciences. Let me give you a very extreme instance: The very distinguished Professor [Albert] Einstein has announced, over a period of ten years or more, some extremely important discoveries and theories affecting the conceptions of the world and the universe.

Quite naturally enough matters of this importance aroused discussion in the non-scientific world. Anti-Semites denounced Einstein as entirely wrong or a plagarist and Jewish journalists the world over proclaimed him as absolutely right. Probably neither group had the slightest idea of what Professor Einstein was talking about.

How could it be supposed in the light of discussion like this that any subject connected with Jewish learning can be studied from a purely objective point of view. Things that affect the lives or have affected the lives of millions of people over the course of many centuries, whether it be the Bible or the Talmud or the Jewish Law, can be approached from two definite points of view. The one is the acceptance of the ancient document until it is proved to be wrong. This in effect is the traditional view. The other point of view is the sceptical which doubts the ancient document and more particularly in this instance the Bible, unless there are other ancient documents to corroborate it. And this latter is definitely not the Jewish point of view. The moment that the latter attitude is assumed, Jewish learning becomes the object of analysis and not the subject of study.

And then too, these subjects which we are discussing ought to be approached with a certain sympathy. The person who believes that the Bible is largely made up of fictitious documents or the Talmud is a collection of rubbish might be able to read and explain and discuss every point in both of these great collections of literature perfectly and yet would never advance the knowledge of either.

I confess that I am in agreement with Doctor Magnes as to the impossi-bility of the Department of Jewish Studies ultimately developing into a Sanhedrin. If there is to be a re-establishment of some authoritative Jewish legislative body that must come from the people themselves and not from any academic authority. If, for example, the Chief Rabbis in countries where such functionaries exist represent their people, and could from time to time assemble in Jerusalem in order to bring about a greater uniformity in practice on the part of the Jews the world over and also settle in a legal way matters of vital importance which no one Rabbi feels the right to settle for himself, that would be a great blessing and it would certainly be helpful if there were one or two men in Palestine of sufficient position to take their part in such a counsel, but as I have said above for such a restoration the people must be behind the move.

My own suggestion to you is that you place the funds you are willing to devote to the University into a trust with power to nominate the incumbents of the chair or chairs you intend to found, the Trustees to be representatives of certain institutions whose point of view conforms with your own. There would be, of course, within the governing body of the University the right to reject the nominations of these Trustees but they could not initiate one. This I think would safeguard your point as far as it is humanly possible to do so, and it would for an indefinite time secure in this Department of Jewish Studies of the Hebrew University teaching which would tend toward the maintenance of Rabbinic Judaism which I think has a right to make all efforts to perpetuate itself.

I am inclined to think that in fact Doctor Magnes does agree with you on this point, but there is a certain exhilaration in the atmosphere surrounding the establishment of the new University which makes the people there believe that the absolute ideal can be attained, at least on paper.

If there is any point which I have left untouched and upon which you desire my opinion, it is quite at your service and I have no objection, of course, if you care to send a copy of this letter to Doctor Magnes. [W]

TO SOLOMON GOLDMAN,[1] CLEVELAND

March 27, 1925

To-day Mr. Katz of Cleveland visited me and talked over with me the conditions in your Congregation. He also brought a letter from the Union of Orthodox Rabbis suggesting that the difference between a section of the Congregation and yourself concerning the seating of men and women to-gether should be brought to my attention.

I am aware of the fact that there are always two sides to every question and am not presuming to give an ex parte opinion. It seems to me that the question—if there was a difference—should have been submitted to the Committee on the Interpretation of Jewish Law of the United Synagogue.

My object in writing to you now is to urge you not to put this proposed change into effect at the approaching Passover, as it is likely to create a disturbance and a Hillul ha-Shem,[2] of which the Center has already had enough.

If the attitude of the Seminary means anything to you, it would be not at any time to force or even encourage changes in the ritual or the practice of a

Congregation. We have not refused the fellowship of the Conservative Congregation, but it has not been our purpose to depart from the main stream of Rabbinic Judaism.

I recognize that we cannot control either the Rabbis or the Congregation, but I have always hoped that the result of the Seminary's teaching would be the maintenance of the traditional worship.

For men brought up in traditional Judaism, the proposed change is a matter of conscience not to be settled by a majority vote.

I earnestly hope that you will persuade your people to delay action in this entire matter until it can be sanely considered and wisely and properly settled. [W]

1. Solomon Goldman (1893–1953), Conservative rabbi in Cleveland, 1919–29, and in Chicago, 1929–53; president of the Zionist Organization of America, 1938–40.
2. Desecration of God's name.

TO EPHRAIM LEDERER, PHILADELPHIA

April 22, 1925

The bearer of this letter is Doctor Nathaniel Reich,[1] whom I believe you know and who is a member of the Faculty of the College. He is desirous of going to Austria this summer to see his family and then to England to engage in some research work. He has just taken out his first papers. His idea is to go abroad on his Austrian passport. In view of all the new laws and regulations, I am wondering whether he can do this and be certain to come back with safety. When Doctor Reich came to this country in January 1922, he came as a non-quota immigrant for the purpose of engaging in research work in this country and stated that he did not intend to settle in America. Since then, as you know, all sorts of new laws have been passed, among them the law about which I spoke the other day: that persons who come as students or for research work are regarded as temporary residents and no person can come over to engage in teaching work unless he had been two years previously engaged in the same kind of work in the country of his origin.

Doctor Reich anticipates no difficulty and of course I do not want to throw any difficulties in his way, but it seems to me that his course of action in going over on an Austrian passport may not make it possible for him to return as a non-quota immigrant.

I know that you will advise him wisely both in his own interest as well as in the interest of the College. We have a very small Faculty and cannot afford to be without a professor next year. [D]

1. Nathaniel Julius Reich (1882–1943), professor of Egyptology at Dropsie College, 1925–43.

TO FELIX M. WARBURG, NEW YORK CITY

May 28, 1925

. . . I have not seen Doctor [Judah L.] Magnes yet and do not know what, if any, has been the practical result of his visit here so far as the benefit of the [Hebrew] University is concerned. I am wondering what your own plans are at this dinner and would be glad if you would drop me a line. As for the dinner in Philadelphia I am not particularly disposed to make it a money gathering dinner unless there seems to be a voluntary impulse in that direction, though quite a number of the men who could not attend have written to me offering their financial and moral support to the University. Since the likelihood is that no adequate endowment can be secured for the University in its present state I think that the most that could be hoped for is a sustaining fund for a period of two or three years and if it falls in with your plans I was thinking, unless the people come forward and offer, to propose at the outcome of the dinner and under the inspiration of the presence of Doctor Magnes the appointment of a Philadelphia Committee to join any Committee that you might form. You will recall my offer to you to act as your assistant in anything that you will undertake for the University, and that offer still holds good.

That does not mean that I am convinced of the correctness of all the details of the plan and I hope when I see Doctor Magnes to have a very amicable difference of opinion with him, indeed to convert him or be converted by him. After giving the matter a good deal of thought I am still of the opinion that the University ought really open with a reception of students who are of the University grade and not limit itself to research Institutes. On the other hand it will not at all be necessary for the University to open all of its departments at once. The Institution of Jewish Studies is open and if, say, medicine and one other subject were added and a start made with three faculties or even two faculties, this would be better than trying to start all subjects at once on the research scale. . . .

I can hardly think that it is the path of wisdom to totally disregard the experience of eight centuries of higher learning and make this new experiment. I am writing this to you both for your own consideration and in case you happen to see Doctor Magnes and care to show it to him he will know the lines upon which my mind is moving. [W]

TO LOUIS MARSHALL, NEW YORK CITY

October 8, 1925

Mr. [Harry] Schneiderman has handed me in confidence your correspondence concerning the Haym Salomon Memorial.[1] I have myself taken no interest in the creation of the Memorial because such things as a rule do not interest me. I do not think, however, that it has been the opinion of sober historians that there was anything mythical about the Salomon story. Professor Herbert B. Adams of Johns Hopkins University found what was probably the beginning of the story among the papers of Jared Sparks[2] and he took the responsibility of publishing them in the second volume of the publications of the American Jewish Historical Society.[3] There were notes to this paper by Professor [Jacob H.] Hollander and can be found in this second volume on pages 5 to 19. In volume three Professor Hollander gave some more references but I am not going to load you up with them.[4]

The article on Salomon in the *Jewish Encyclopedia* was written by Doctor [Herbert] Friedenwald, after very careful investigation as I happen to remember, including the study of the manuscript diary of Robert Morris.[5] It has always seemed to me that Salomon's services were just as much to the French and Spanish as to America. I have no doubt but that he rendered great service as a broker during the latter part of the Revolutionary War. Robert Morris himself indicates this. What I always thought unjust was that he should be claimed as the financier of the Revolution. In other words, it seems to me that our friends who want the Memorial have over-estimated Haym Salomon and your Art Commissioner of New York has under-estimated him. Herbert B. Adams would certainly not have lent his name to the first serious publication on the subject if he had not been convinced of its authenticity. I am by way of having forgotten a good deal about what I knew on the subject many years ago but I am also convinced of the fact that in the days when money was extremely scarce and very important Haym Salomon rendered notable service to the struggling republic. It seems to me that in such a matter probably the methodical thing to do would be to ask the American Jewish Historical Society to furnish, through Doctor [A. S. W.]

Rosenbach, as complete a statement as it can about Haym Salomon, an exhibition of the documents, and if Doctor Rosenbach is willing, to express a sober opinion on whether the merits of Salomon are such as to justify a popular movement for a Memorial. What do you think of this plan? I am sending a copy of this to Mr. [Harry] Schneiderman. . . . [W]

1. Haym Salomon (1740–85), American Jewish merchant and Revolutionary War patriot. The Federation of Polish Jews initiated plans for a monument to Salomon in New York that did not come to fruition.
2. Jared Sparks (1789–1866), American historian, best known for his edition of *The Writings of George Washington*.
3. "A Sketch of Haym Salomon from an unpublished MS in the Papers of Jared Sparks," *PAJHS* 2 (1894): 5–19.
4. "Some Further References Relation to Haym Salomon," *PAJHS* 3 (1895): 7–12.
5. For these excerpts, see Morris U. Schappes, "Excerpts from Robert Morris' 'Diaries in the Office of Finance, 1781–1784,' Referring to Haym Salomon and Other Jews," *AJHSQ* 67 (1977): 9–49, 140–61.

In September 1925, an agreement was reached in Philadelphia between the Zionists and the Joint Distribution Committee regarding a combined fundraising campaign with a national goal of $15,000,000 to be used for relief activities in Eastern Europe and Jewish agrarian settlement in Russia as well as for the building of the Jewish National Home in Palestine. At the convention of the American Jewish Congress that October, Stephen S. Wise charged that the JDC had broken its word and that, in circular letters sent out to organize the campaign, only the JDC projects were mentioned while those of the Zionists were ignored. Despite attempts at mediation by Louis Marshall, the Zionists broke away from the United Jewish Campaign and set up the United Palestine Appeal.

TO LOUIS MARSHALL, NEW YORK CITY

Philadelphia, October 28, 1925

. . . Between Cincinnati and the Congress in Philadelphia I have heard a great deal of talk about the Joint Distribution Campaign and the "peace of Philadelphia." I think that unless something is done we are in for a greater rift than we have had for a long time and while it may be a mere pretext, and possibly is, the whole issue is being made on David Brown's[1] letters. I have suggested something in the report of our Committee which may help the situation although of course I do not think we shall have any peace as long as Mr. [Stephen S.] Wise is in the field. It seems to me that he is now aiming at the leadership of the World Zionist movement, and from incautious remarks of various Zionists I am of the opinion that he can form a party behind him in America for this purpose. The European diplomats, however, will probably beat him out in the long run. [W]

1. David Brown (1875–1958), business executive; executive vice-president of the JDC; chairman of the United Jewish Campaign. He was a firm opponent of the idea of a Jewish state.

Preparing the biography of Jacob Schiff was a delicate task for Adler at times.

TO WILLIAM H. TAFT, WASHINGTON, D.C.

Philadelphia, December 2, 1925

. . . With regard to your inquiry as to whether I intend to use your letters, may I temporize? At present I am engaged in bringing together materials for the book. How much use I shall make of letters depends upon the volume secured. As the book is to be a Biography of Mr. [Jacob H.] Schiff most of the letters printed will be his own and I shall use the full replies to them only in very rare cases. The replies will in the main be useful to me to "paraphrase," as the Diplomats say, in order to make the narrative continuous.

Your letter to Mr. Bannard[1] I shall not use as it was obviously personal and I think that Presidents and even ex-Presidents are entitled to their privacy.

You may trust me to avoid any indiscretion and if I find it necessary to the narrative to present your own point of view I shall do so with entire fairness. [LC]

1. Otto T. Bannard (1854–1929), lawyer and banker.

PART SIX
1926-1932

The years 1926–1932 saw Adler ever more involved in Palestine, through the Hebrew University, and, especially after 1929, through his membership in the enlarged Jewish Agency. Other major challenges which presented themselves included the world economic crisis, beginning in 1929, and the shadow of Nazism which hung over Germany.

TO ISRAEL EFROS,[1] BALTIMORE

January 14, 1926

I have been thinking for some time about the letter of Doctor [William] Rosenau which I return herewith. It seemed to me that it was rather a difficult position that you placed me in by simply sending me this letter without a word of explanation from you and then expect an opinion which might be used in a public way and therefore commit me on matters in which principles of importance are involved. While I am not particularly inviting a personal conference, such conference has frequently been sought on matters of much less moment. As it stands, I have not a single word as to the point of view of your College and must rely exclusively on the statement of Doctor Rosenau.

It appears from this correspondence that the Baltimore Hebrew College had on previous occasions approached the Reform Rabbis for support. Since the Baltimore Hebrew College made this approach, they no doubt expected and were prepared to make certain concessions if an agreement could be reached, but I have no hint as to what these were.

It appears further from Doctor Rosenau's letter that an agreement was reached on a curriculum and that if certain conditions are met the Reform Rabbis will give up their plan of starting a distinct training class for teachers of their own congregations and pledge their support to the Baltimore Hebrew College.

Now as to the conditions: 1) I suppose you have no objections to sending a copy of the curriculum to each of the Rabbis for study and modification but the question then would be whether you or your Faculty or the Board of

Trustees would accept all of the modifications made by each of the Reform Rabbis. I do not see how such a matter can be settled on paper. It ought to be the result of a round table conference and not of an ultimatum. 2) Persons who have completed the course fitting them to teach in one-day-a-week religious schools shall be graduated and certified as such. I consider this a perfectly proper condition and ought to be agreed to. 3) Means that the Reform Rabbis shall determine instructors to be employed in the training of specific teachers referred to. While it is true they are calling it an Advisory Committee I suppose the advice would have to be accepted as final. This brings me to raise the question as to what the plan really is.

If it proposes that the Baltimore Hebrew College shall have two separate departments in one of which the education shall be carried on strictly in conformity with Reform practices and principles and observances and that there should be another department in which the traditional view should prevail, while this is possible, I think you would be creating a difficult and wasteful situation. There seems to be a theory involved here that only Reform congregations have one-day-a-week religious schools and on the other hand that teachers in such schools require an entirely different education than teachers in other schools. Let me be specific. Do they mean that their teachers shall not be taught any Hebrew or if they are taught Hebrew that they must be taught Hebrew by a person of their own choosing or a Reform Rabbi? Of course, there would be no objection to a Reform Rabbi being on the teaching staff if he were teaching the subject for which he was qualified. I think, for example, that Doctor Rosenau, though a Reform Rabbi, could very fairly lecture on the history of Jewish ceremonies and it would be proper that he should indicate that there is a difference in the observances between the traditional and reform Jews. I can imagine pedagogical method to be taught even by non-Jews, although I do not suppose you are driven to such a testimonium paupertatis.

Strange as it may seem, Number five, which looks like a slight matter, presents a real difficulty to me because it is so obvious, and if I were you I should not agree to do it. If the covering of the head is left optional, it will be a notification to all of the young people that there is no matter of principle involved here and I think that your present students would lose a good deal by such a policy, for if you have taught them that it is a matter of respect to cover their heads when they read the Bible, you will find it difficult to maintain that attitude if either the instructor or the other students do not observe it. I was present at the dedication of Doctor [Louis] Finkelstein's Synagogue in the Bronx recently and the Pastor of a neighboring Baptist Church not only found no difficulty in covering his head but even did it without being requested to do so and seemed to consider it quite natural. Cannot our Reform brethren adopt the same frame of mind? Surely their Jewish consciousness has not so completely changed that they regard it as *disrespect* to be covered in the presence of the Torah. [D]

1. Israel Efros (b. 1891), rabbi, poet, and Jewish scholar; founded the Baltimore Hebrew College in 1919; held university posts in the United States and Israel, including the presidency of Tel Aviv University.

During the mid-1920s there was a move to amalgamate the Jewish Theological Seminary and the Isaac Elchanan Theological Seminary in New York into one institution. It was felt by many, Adler included, that the religious philosophies of the two schools could be harmonized and that the American Jewish community could better support one traditional rabbinical seminary. The attempt was a failure and was abandoned in 1927.

Memorandum

February 22, 1926

Rabbi B[ernard] L. Levinthal called on me today and we spent several hours in discussing the affairs of the [Isaac Elchanan] Yeshibah and the Seminary.

His general statement was that at the present time the Seminary was much better equipped than the Yeshibah but that for the future of the Yeshibah he had great hopes. He felt that the question to be discussed was not so much a merger but a co-ordination and that in any event the question was not one of organization but of idea. (I may say that throughout the discussion he at no time raised the question of greater or less orthodoxy.)

His idea of the Yeshibah is distinctly not that of a Theological Institution. To him it is indifferent whether the student who resides at the Yeshibah becomes a lawyer, or a physician, a banker or a merchant. The main idea is that he shall become imbued with a knowledge of Torah always with the hope that he will thus become a center for its observance and propaganda. He says that since Revel[1] has been President, the Yeshibah has become more of a Theological Seminary than heretofore but his main thought is that there shall always be an Institution for the study of the Torah for its own sake and without reference to a future profession. If Rabbis or scholars eventuate, that is part of the work.

They also have a High School for secular and religious purposes and a Teachers Institute—all told about 500 students. Their annual budget is $175,000.

In criticism of the Seminary, Rabbi Levinthal advanced the following points:

By insisting upon a college education, we curtailed the amount of time which could be devoted to Jewish studies. His impression was that a High School education sufficed. He also expressed the opinion that we devoted proportionately too little time to Bible and Talmud and far too much to what he considered non-essential—History, Poetry, etc. I found that his information was based upon a vague notion of our curriculum which I gave him for study. He also asked for the full course for the Hattarat Horaah [rabbinical license] which I promised to send him. He said that after studying these he would ask for another interview. He seems to have faith in the general Jewish College about which Revel has been talking. He would welcome a Cantors' Seminary which he deems important and also the idea of having in the general scheme the School for Jewish Social Work and Y Secretaries.

I got the general idea that he was favorably inclined if some measure of autonomy were granted to the units within the larger organization. He also raised the question as to what would become of their teaching staff which he says contains very good men. I told him that if there were an enlarged institution I would strongly favor the introduction of the tutorial system.

With regard to his general ideas of the need of an institution for Jewish learning which is not Rabbinical, I think he is right. The increasing number of students at the Dropsie College shows this. Quite without reference to this question of merger, the subject is gradually forcing itself upon the Seminary. We have at the present time about twelve students who I think will never make preachers. Some of them may become scholars, yet if they persist in endeavoring to be active Rabbis occupying pulpits, they will in the future become a liability to the Seminary. I am expecting to discuss the question at the next meeting of the Faculty. [AJA]

1. Bernard Revel (1885–1940), educator and scholar, leader of modern Orthodoxy; in 1915 reorganized the Isaac Elchanan Theological Seminary, opening it to laymen and teachers as well as rabbinical students; in 1916 founded Talmudical Academy, the first combined academic high school-yeshiva in the United States; in 1928 founded Yeshiva College as an extension of the Rabbi Isaac Elchanan Seminary and served as its first president.

TO ISRAEL DAVIDSON, JERUSALEM

Philadelphia, March 16, 1926
. . . I am not at all surprised at what you tell me about the European libraries. One can only work in Continental libraries, at least, if one has plenty of time and however at fault we may be in America, our library

administrators do much more for students than Europe does. I am happy to know that you have had such a pleasant and comfortable trip thus far and assume that you have enjoyed good health. Both at the Dropsie College and the Seminary, all of our staff have remained reasonably well and this in spite of the fact that they are surrounded by influenza, a good deal of it quite serious.

At a meeting of the Board of Directors held yesterday, the resolution of the faculty to give an honorary degree to Bialik[1] was approved and I have now sent a formal letter to the distinguished poet asking him whether he will accept. I must say that his visit to this country is being used purely for propaganda purposes and that he and some of his fellow Palestinians are quite hostile to the work we have undertaken on behalf of the Jews of Russia, Poland and Eastern Europe. It is curious how residence in Palestine seems to glorify a man's spirit and make his heart shrink. There seems to be a sort of callousness growing up about the great mass of Jews in Eastern Europe. Apparently the theory is that unless they can go to Palestine, they might as well die anyhow, however this is quite an improper letter for me to be writing to you when it will reach you during the holiday.

I know that you, yourself, so far from being hard-hearted, are very soft-hearted and with your rachmonus [quality of mercy] removed from the faculty, there is a tendency to be much more severe in the matter of admissions to the Seminary, whereas it is not impossible that an exit may have been facilitated which you would have prevented. [W]

1. Hayyim Nahman Bialik (1873–1934), Hebrew poet and Zionist activist.

TO JACOB KLATZKIN,[1] NEW YORK CITY

March 26, 1926

I think you can judge from your presence the other night at the meeting of the Jewish Publication Society that the Society has troubles of its own and certainly could not embark upon any new enterprise. It seems to me, therefore, that so far as the people you have been to see are concerned, I may express it as a general sentiment that your visit is ill-timed and unless you yourselves happen to know of some person who is particularly interested in this subject, there is little likelihood of engaging the interest of most of the men who are usually sympathetic to Jewish literary and scientific projects.

I am not at all pre-judging the question as to whether the time is ripe for another *Encyclopedia*. This is something which the Academy could deliberate upon and express an opinion, at least so far as American scholarship is concerned. There are many great projects which Jewish scholars ought to undertake. There is a real need of a new edition of the Masoretic Bible, which we would be glad to undertake in this country if we had the means. There is need for a critical text of the Talmud. There is need for a Concordance to the Talmud. Hundreds and hundreds of valuable Hebrew manuscripts lie unpublished in our libraries. I cannot, therefore, with great fervor encourage a project which seems to me not to be properly timed. I believe that if the sum of money which you gentlemen think will be required, and I think you have underestimated it, could be put at the service of Jewish scholarship to do more what I would call spade work within a period of maybe ten years, then I think by the co-operation of all countries and all institutions a great encyclopedia could be produced.

Since I have seen you both, I have been giving a good deal of thought to the subject and the above represents my reasoned opinion. However, as I said before, the best way to get the consensus of opinion of Jewish scholars in this country would be to arrange for a meeting through Professor [Louis] Ginzberg with the Jewish Academy if you think this would be useful and desirable.

I admire your energy very much and also your courage in undertaking such a project in these difficult times, but I myself have in the course of my life been obliged to give up and defer many important projects upon which my heart was set and always found other work to do.

So far as my opinion goes, the American public should not be asked at the present time to support this project. If the Committees in Europe think that in view of all the circumstances and existing conditions there the *Encyclopedia* is an object for which important sacrifices must be made, they are naturally entitled to their own judgment. [W]

1. Jacob Klatzkin (1882–1948), journalist and scholar; an editor of the German *Encyclopedia Judaica* of which ten volumes (Aachen to Lyra) were published in the years 1928–34. He came to the United States to seek support for the project.

TO JUDAH L. MAGNES, JERUSALEM

April 7, 1926

. . . You say that you do not read American papers, but that a sort of paralysis seems to have fallen upon us. It may be fortunate for your peace of mind that you do not read our papers—but the condition is confusion rather than paralysis. Before I got back to America last autumn, a great row had been started at the Philadelphia Conference for the JDC by the Zionist representatives. Apparently, the row was composed, but it flared up all over the country. In December a new row was started over a popularization by Stephen Wise in a sermon of Klausner's book and while after a month's agitation this too was apparently settled, its aftermath is with us and will continue for many a day. The most violent period of polemics which you can remember in America was but an April shower compared with this storm. It has separated people, split communities and apparently for the time being rendered the reconstituted Jewish Agency impossible.[1]

I know there is a disposition to hold Mr. [Louis] Marshall responsible for not re-convening the non-Partisan Conference, but I am satisfied that an overwhelming majority of those who attended the previous conferences would not have responded under present conditions. I am not telling you this to pain you, but think you ought to know the situation.

If you have any plans for a meeting at which you want me present, will you not let me know at the earliest possible moment? I am going to England and Germany for some work which will necessitate my making definite appointments in advance and so must arrange my calendar well before I cross. . . . [W]

1. See letter to Louis Marshall, October 28, 1925.

TO FELIX M. WARBURG, NEW YORK CITY

May 26, 1926

As I do not know how much of the discussion which took place at the meeting yesterday in regard to the draft of the constitution for the Hebrew University will be recorded, I want briefly to state some of my criticisms to the plan now presented, and to bring forward one new point which I did not touch upon at all.

Under the general objects of the University, I take exception to item "3" which reads:

3. To act as the central academy of Jewish studies and as an academy of the Hebrew language.

The University cannot at the same time be the Academy. Membership in the University would be limited to the faculties. So far as the Institute of

Jewish Studies is concerned, it is fantastic to suppose that for any time that anybody can foresee in the near future the faculty of the Institute would in any way include all those persons who ought to be members of the central academy of Jewish Studies. If the members of the faculty of the Institute wish to take the initiative in creating an academy in Jerusalem which later on, if it were strong enough, would grow to be the central academy, that is another matter, but anything like bombast should be avoided in a solemn document of this kind.

Under the heading V1a#A. "Composition of the Board of Governors," there is a use of the words "Jewish scholarship" which I think is not intended. It is plain that all science and learning are intended, whereas "Jewish scholarship" has a very distinct meaning. I presume the intention is "scholars who are Jews." I also do not think that in such a document a phrase like "important individual donors" should be used. There ought to be every reason to hope that there will be a great many individual donors and to decide who is important and who is not will be an unpleasant task. The purpose can be carried out without placing this in the constitution.

Under "B. Functions of the Board of Governors" a clause like "4. To meet once a year" is out of place. That is not or at least should not be a function.

Under "C," with regard to the presidential board, I think that the board must be three so as to prevent a deadlock.

That the chairman and deans should be elected annually from among the faculties seems to me highly inadvisable, especially in a new institution. You have no permanence of policy at the beginning and there will be no responsible officers to look to.

The one matter that I did not mention yesterday which I consider of great importance is the creation of two faculties—a faculty of science and a faculty of humanities. This is a division on the basis of an academy rather than of a University. It is obvious that every department will eventually have its own faculty. If there is a medical school or engineering there is no reason why they should be lumped together. The two would have very little to do with each other and there is no reason why the professors in one should pass upon the policies of the other. What I am particularly concerned about is the so-called faculty of humanities, because in the long run I think that this will submerge the Institute of Jewish Studies. I think there is a technical error in stating that the faculties shall grant diplomas and degrees. They make the recommendations. This granting of diplomas and degrees is the act of the University, under its seal.

I am sending this to you really as a memorandum, in addition to the discussion we had at the meeting. [W]

TO ABRAHAM FLEXNER,[1] NEW YORK CITY

June 4, 1926

I am wondering whether you could give me any advice on the following subject. It is a matter of public knowledge that Mr. John D. Rockefeller had sufficient interest in Egyptology and in Egypt to offer a great sum of money to further that science for a museum and for research work and for various reasons this fell through. There is very great need for a fund for Oriental archaeology, philology and research in general. These fields have been reasonably starved as you probably know. Egypt, naturally, has been in the limelight and will continue to be because of the beauty of the objects found there, but there are hundreds of sites in Mesopotamia which would probably yield much greater scientific results. There are innumerable sites in Palestine, Syria and Asia Minor which require excavation.

In addition to field work, we also require the training of scholars because, after all, there is little point in getting material out of the ground with nobody to study it. At the moment, I can call to mind not more than four Egyptologists in America. The tragic death of Professor Ember,[2] of Johns Hopkins University, the other day, removed the fifth. There is great need for the encouragement of the training of such men in America and also there is great need for a publication fund. In other words, what the Near Eastern science needs is an encouragement like that given to medical science or to the natural and physical sciences and so far it has never had this or anything like it.

At the moment, I am taking the matter from the point of view of two American schools now established in the East. I mean the American Schools of Oriental Research at Jerusalem and Bagdad. The one in Jerusalem has been in existence for over twenty years. Its running expenses are provided for by some forty or fifty American colleges and universities. It has a proper building, which was given to it by the late Reverend Doctor Nies[3] and he also left a fund for the running expenses of the School at Bagdad amounting to about $200,000.00. But these present incomes are simply incomes to keep house, as it were; there is no fund for excavations and no fund for publication. I cannot imagine any way in which the study of these countries around the Mediterranean, especially those which illustrate the Bible and all the things that have flown therefrom, could be stimulated than by such a foundation. . . . [D]

---

1. Abraham Flexner (1866–1959), scholar and educator, noted for his survey of American medical schools; the first head of the Institute for Advanced Study at Princeton University.
2. Aaron Ember (1878–1926), professor of Egyptology at Johns Hopkins University. He perished in a fire.
3. James B. Nies (1856–1922), clergyman and orientalist.

TO JUDAH L. MAGNES, LONDON

Berlin, July 21, 1926

I have received in London your cable of July 19th, in which you tell me about Mr. [Felix M.] Warburg's proposition of thirty-one (31) members of the Board [of Governors of the Hebrew University]—eight (8) Zionists, seven (7) non-Zionists, four (4) European, four (4) American scholars, four (4) European, four (4) American patrons, and ask my opinion if I dissent.

I assume that this refers to Mr. Warburg's letter to Dr. [Chaim] Weizmann of June 23rd, in which Mr. Warburg says that he is sending a copy to you, to myself and others. At all events, I do not wish to be quoted in any personal way on this matter.

I find that after I had left America, a meeting of the American Committee was held on June 15th and at that meeting, certain action was taken which seems to have produced the various misunderstandings about dates of meetings in London, Paris, etc.

When I was in London, I spoke to the Secretary of the University Committee, Mr. Leo Kohn,[1] and gave him my views, not on any individual governors, but on the whole scheme of governors as laid out in the draft for a constitution. In order that you may have the opportunity to consider this, I am enclosing you a copy. From this you will see that my personal opinion is that people ought to be elected governors not because they are Zionists or non-Zionists or scholars or donors or anything else, except that they are the kind of people whose experience and temperament would make them useful in the general administrative body of a university.

While in London, I had an hour's talk with Dr. Weizmann but he was principally concerned about the [Jewish] Agency. I also had a talk with Mr. Norman Bentwich, but at that time he had no information as to the dates at which the meetings were to be held.

Commenting upon Mr. Warburg's letter, I would say that it would seem to me inadvisable to say in the constitution that the Board of Governors shall consist of thirty-one members. If thirty-one has to be the maximum number, then the phrase should be to "consist of not more than thirty-one members," so that the entire Board need not be filled at once.

As to the division in these classes, I have expressed my opinion in the enclosed memorandum, but I assume that Mr. Warburg and the gentlemen in New York have made these proposals with a view to meeting what they suppose might be the requirements of the Actions Comité, and I certainly do not want to put any spoke in the wheel. In the opinion of Mr. Warburg and the others in Europe, the paramount issue is to have such action taken by the

Actions Comité as will result in making the University an autonomous institution which can then govern itself irrespective of any political consid- erations, and with this thought I am in the heartiest concurrence.

I do not like in a letter to discuss individual names but I think it is rather funny, just to speak of myself, that I should be down as an American non-Zionist, and let us say, Mr. L. C. Lewinstein, whom I do not happen to know, should be down as an American scholar.

The insistence of yourself and others of the presence of Dr. Stephen S. Wise on this Board is not likely to make for my continued cooperation, at least, if I have to sit in the room with that gentleman very often.

Dr. Harry Friedenwald, who is undoubtedly greatly interested in the University, is notoriously neglectful of all of his duties outside of his medical, professional work in Baltimore. I know two educational boards of which he is a member, not a meeting of which he has attended in ten years and I do not recall that he even deigns to send an excuse for non-attendance.

These are some remarks in passing about the American selection. I have never been able to understand how a gentleman like Mond,[2] who is almost notoriously in the Church, can be regarded in any way as a representative of any Jewish interest, but apparently Zionism makes strange bedfellows.

Don't think I am in a bad temper. As a matter of fact, I am quite amiable. I am afraid that I have been too amiable in my language to many people in the past and they don't seem to get a proper understanding of one's intention without a little harsh language. A very wise man once said to me that the only people who got anything they wanted were those who make themselves excessively disagreeable about it. . . . [W]

1. Leo Kohn (1894–1961), Zionist diplomat.
2. Alfred Moritz Mond, Lord Melchett (1868–1930), English industrialist and statesman. A firm supporter of the Zionist cause, he became joint-chairman of the Jewish Agency.

TO FELIX M. WARBURG, NEW YORK CITY

Paris, August 12, 1926

When I was in Hamburg your brother Max said that in the present condition of the world to be a Jew and a German and a banker was a hard combination, and indeed I never wanted to be a banker as you know, but now I have changed my mind. For three solid days—and nights up to midnight— the Curatorium of the Institute of Jewish Studies of the Hebrew University of Jerusalem has been meeting and now I am prepared to change places with you. I should like to be in position to give the money to the University and let you attend the meetings. [Judah L.] Magnes has become a miracle of patience. I am really glad that I was not at the London meeting because I feel sure that had I "assisted" there I should never have come to the Paris meeting and probably I could do more service in the latter.

There were 18 people present including Mrs. Rosenbloom[1] who "represented Judge [Julian W.] Mack." None of the Germans came although Professor Freimann[2] of Frankfurt told me he would. It was not on account of the valuation because you can save money now by leaving Germany and coming to France.

To come back to the meeting. You know I am a seasoned "joiner" and have probably attended more meetings in my life than anybody except yourself; but in all this long life of mine I have never witnessed such a combination of intellectual arrogance, vanity, and verbosity. The greater part of the first two days was spent on the report of the last year and the re-election of the staff or the discussion of why someone else was not elected. The minor matters of administration were badly done. The annual report was sent from Jerusalem eight weeks ago but no copies were made and German was the only language known to all present. Magnes had to translate into that language from Hebrew. The report and its discussion occupied from 10:30 A.M. to 5 P.M. of the first day, and then throughout the whole meeting the Curators acted as though they were the Faculty and not the Board of Governors.

Other documents to be discussed were not in as good shape as the report. There were never sufficient copies; they did not correspond. Matters that had been withdrawn by the Faculty in Jerusalem were not crossed off and hence were discussed at great length in spite of Magnes' statement that they had been withdrawn. These are minor difficulties in administration which can and should be corrected but in the main they depend on the dual government with its two sects in London and Jerusalem. London is determined to keep Jerusalem in a subordinate place and Jerusalem is determined to get London out of the way. You notice I do not mention [Joseph H.] Hertz and Magnes because I think the real difficulty far transcends a personal matter. Hertz according to his light means to be fair—he at least is a fair chairman to the extent that he allows a wide latitude in discussion though a little over-prone to express his own views in advance, but he has an exalted sense of his position as the Chief Rabbi of the Jewish Community of the greatest Empire on Earth and his arch-episcopal grandeur is a little hard to bear. Three Chief Rabbis are a good many to have in one Board. Of the three, Israel Levi is the best and while his nerves are jumpy—all France is that way just now. He retains much sweetness with his dignity. But every subject which came on the carpet in the table he discussed. In fact discussion was the order of the day. The simplest routine statement which was put forth in any report on proposal was discussed. The question was never asked—is there any objection to this but always this way—we must discuss it. The treatment of the budget would have moved you to laughter or to tears as the case may be. Every item was subjected to a scientific discussion.

You will assume from all this that I was of no use at all and maybe you are right. In the innocence of my heart I did try the first day to damn up this Niagara of words but saw it was no use and hence fell back on the plan to allow the combatants to exhaust themselves and then write out a resolution which brought some questions to a head.

Now for a few details. Quite a number of the discussions were more or less personal, the gentlemen seeming to feel that Magnes was doing too much on his own and hence must be brought to book. Dr. [Adolph] Buchler of London was the arch-Inquisitor and I cannot help but feel that there is a sort of malice in that gentleman's character which makes him very hard to deal with. Most of the personal attacks came from his quarter and Magnes, while as I said at the beginning has become an angel of patience, is not entirely a lamb. Dr. [Hirsch P.] Chajes too is a wily sort of person who would be entirely willing to go to Jerusalem as a Professor provided he could be the head—he knows himself and knows that he could not subject himself to anybody else. This characterization is not a work of the imagination as the gentleman was frank enough to make the statement at a full session. Daiches[3] of London is reasonably bad tempered and reasonably satisfied with himself, and [Hayyim N.] Bialik's trip to America made him much more of an orator than a poet has a right to be. The only new man I fell in love with was Rabbi Senator Rubinstein[4] of Wilna, a man of excellent knowledge and modest manner. You know about his work for the J.D.C. in bygone days. Dr. [Hermann] Pick of Jerusalem is a rather good chap and a man of knowledge but also possessed of a dreadful facility of words—logorrhea Judge [Mayer] Sulzberger used to call it.

The Institution however is going along and a few forward steps were taken. History and Philosophy are still unprovided for and something was done toward Bible teaching—also there will be lectures in Hebrew poetry and in sociology; a limitation was put upon publications not entirely unreasonable though difficult under the circumstances, and two main subjects of discussion—the character of the Institute (research or teaching or both) and the actual seal of administration were postponed for another year.

The Council decided that publications must go to a Committee for approval—this Magnes opposed at length though I think he was wrong in principle. I know that the Smithsonian, Johns Hopkins and the American Philosophical Society require such submission and in the case of the Smithsonian for all major contributions two of three referers must come from outside. The real difficulty is that now every paper will have to be sent from Jerusalem to London. Magnes too, I think, overburdened himself with details—at least he does things which the Registrar or Secretary should do—he has not yet acquired that highest skill of administration, never to do anything that he can get someone else to do. I know you think I have the same fault but at least I can recognize it in another.

I cannot get away from the difficulty in London versus Jerusalem. London writes letters—even involving money—and does not as much as send copies to Jerusalem. Important reports—the one on the teaching of the Bible for example—was prepared in London (no copies made) and Magnes heard it read for the first time in Paris.

Jerusalem on the other hand is a little over sensitive about its position as being the heart of the Jewish world and the importance of its science just because it is developed on the sacred soil (I am not ascribing this to Magnes personally but I read in between the lines of the propositions he brings from the teaching Council of the Institute).

To sum up I consider the present method of instituting the governing council both in its size and personnel one which should be greatly modified. It is too large and it is not composed of the most useful kind of people. It would ultimately drive anyone who is at the head mad. The Institute must in my opinion develop more and more in the interest of the Land and its people. It will be many years before Philosophy or History or even Talmud can be as well studied there as in New York or Berlin but it should throw its strength into archaeology and geography and the study of the climate[,] zoology, botany, etc. as contributory to an understanding of the Bible. It must be satisfied with young men who have their futures before them and not be striving to secure a great name for every chair.

Well I am getting tired of writing and you, I am sure, of reading. As for the University itself I have no real news. The Actions-Committee met in second session and so far I have not seen what happened. I learn that the Constitution of the University virtually as you sent it over has been provisionally adopted for one year. The property has not been turned over. I doubt whether it ever will be. The land of the University belongs to the national fund which does not alienate its property—it might lease this land to the University for ninety-nine years or for nine hundred and ninety-nine years. The Zionist organization has property rights in a building and so has the American

Physicians Committee. There is an under-current that so long as you yourself have executed a special trust and the Rosenbloom money is in a special trust you have pointed the way to the maintenance of these special rights of the National Fund and the Zionist organization. None of these latter statements by the way were made at our meeting. They were retailed to me privately from London.

In spite of anything I have written the work is a good one and must go on. If one only understands that neither Rome nor a University is built in a day—if false expectation had not been aroused by a quasi political propaganda then the growth of a few years would be considered marvelous. The trouble is that the growth does not correspond to the super heated imagination which has been fed by the hot air furnace of the Zionist propaganda.

This is a terribly poor and probably unwise letter. Many things I know should never be written. I believe it was our German friends who invented the phrase gedruckt als handschrift (or should it be manuskrit). Well let this letter be "written as conversation."

Give my love to your wife. My wife authorizes me to send hers to you. I hope to see you soon after we get home. [AJA]

1. Celia Neumark Rosenbloom (1888–1947), wife of Solomon Rosenbloom; member of the board of the American Friends of the Hebrew University; donated funds for the building of the Institute for Jewish Studies at the University in memory of her husband.
2. Aron Freimann (1871–1948), historian and bibliographer; librarian of the Jewish department of the Municipal Library of Frankfurt am Main, 1897–1933.
3. Samuel Daiches (1878–1949), lecturer in Bible and Talmud at Jews College, London.
4. Isaac Rubinstein (1880–1945), rabbi, leader of Mizrachi and of Polish Jewry; from 1922 to 1939 a member of the Polish senate, where he vigorously defended Jewish rights.

TO ELISHA M. FRIEDMAN,[1] NEW YORK CITY

Philadelphia, November 12, 1926

Pardon my delay in replying to your very interesting letter of October 28, concerning the biography of Mr. Jacob H. Schiff.

I would certainly be very much obliged to you if you would let me have your memoranda of the conferences about the formulation of the Balfour Declaration, at least so far as Mr. Schiff was concerned.

Mr. Frederick Strauss[2] has sent copies of his correspondence with Mr. Schiff, regarding the railroad situation after the War, and also some brief personal reminiscenses. He seems to have furnished everything that he could, and I do not think that it will help me to write to him again.

As for your general theory about the writing of biography, and particularly of Mr. Schiff's biography, I would say to you that the plan which you have in mind is a rather larger one than I at present anticipate. Indeed, if the material turns out so as to render it practicable, I am rather inclined to make the biography chiefly out of Mr. Schiff's own letters. I think that in the long run the best contribution that one can make to history through biography is to let the person whose biography is being written tell his own story—in other words, to make the work as nearly autobiographical as possible. In fact I think a book based upon letters is in a way more of an autobiography than a conscious autobiography, because the moment people become conscious of themselves, they philosophize about themselves, and create an image which is somewhat different from the original; whereas by making a biography out of letters, one gets the man as his mind and his heart worked, without reference to the public—in other words, a really intimate view—and in this way, I think, one gets a really intimate view of his times as well as of himself.

However, I am not at all determined yet as to the form of the biography, and I shall certainly bear your kind suggestions in mind. [W]

1. Elisha M. Friedman (1889–1951), economist, statistician, and author; active supporter of the Hebrew University.
2. Frederick Strauss (1865–1937), partner in the banking firm of Seligman and Co.

TO OSMOND D'AVIGDOR GOLDSMID,[1] LONDON

Philadelphia, December 31, 1926

I received your letter of November 30 and wish to inform you as follows.

At a meeting of the Executive Committee of the American Jewish Committee held at the end of October, the subject of the religious position in Russia referred to in your letter of July 19 was brought up for discussion. Doctor Bernard Kahn[2] and Dr. Joseph Rosen were present at the meeting. The matter was fully considered and a general conclusion was reached that more harm than good could be done by the sending of a Commission to Russia. This conclusion, which I believe coincides with your own, was strengthened in me by a conversation that I had with the Grand Rabbin Israel Levi in Paris and by reports brought me by Professor [Solomon] Zeitlin and others who were in Russia last summer.

At the conversation I had with Israel Levi, at which Dr. [Joseph H.] Hertz was present, it was agreed that I should request a representative of the

Joint Distribution Committee whom we then had in Europe not to go to Russia solely on the ground that he was a Rabbi and it seemed possibly harmful to send a Rabbi into Russia even as a relief agent. I accordingly telegraphed him to Antwerp, where he then was, not to go to Russia and he did not.

At this Conference, the Grand Rabbin stated that Doctor Waldemar Haffkine was then in Russia. Haffkine is, as you know, not only an eminent physician and biologist but also an orthodox Jew who would have the confidence of the Rabbis there and Doctor Levi promised me to send Haffkine's report to us to enable us to have his information before forming a judgment.

Meanwhile, I may say to you of my own knowledge that we are fully convinced that the Russian Rabbis do not wish any intervention of this sort; that the government is more and more overlooking the existence of Jewish religious teaching which is carried on in an extra-legal fashion and that we have placed Seventy-five thousand dollars at the disposal of a Committee (it could not be sent direct to Russia) to aid in the work of Jewish education there. We are quite certain that it will reach the proper source and will do much more good than would a demonstration.

We are all convinced that this demonstration would result in a tightening of the laws and destroy a fabric which the Russian Jews have been painfully building up these last few years.

After getting your letter I called on Mr. [Louis] Marshall and reminded him of it. He had thought possibly that Haffkine's report would come in and that we might check it up against our other information. As you know there have recently been some Rabbinical resolutions on the subject adopted at Amsterdam which Mr. Marshall is also considering. He told me that he hoped within a week or ten days to be able to send you a reply. Meanwhile, this personal letter does, I feel sure, represent our opinion. . . . [YIVO-M]

1. Sir Osmond d'Avigdor Goldsmid (1877–1940), president of the Anglo-Jewish Association, 1921–26; subsequently president of the Anglo-Jewish Board of Deputies.
2. Bernard Kahn (1876–1955), European director of the Joint Distribution Committee.

TO SOL BLOOM,[1] WASHINGTON, D.C.

January 3, 1927

I have your letter of December 22 with the enclosures concerning your resolution about Mr. [Henry] Ford and the Federal Reserve Bank.[2] I can understand your indignation and the motives that prompted you to introduce your resolutions, but since you ask me to write you my personal opinion, I shall do so:

In the first place, with all due respect to Mr. Nathan Straus, I think his challenge to Mr. Ford was unwise. The Ford agitation had died down, the sale of Mr. Ford's car was on the decline and he was commencing gradually to lose out as he deserved to. Mr. Nathan Straus gave Mr. Ford the opportunity for an enormous amount of free advertisement and you, I am afraid, have increased this advertisement.

If the Congress of the United States is going to make an investigation whenever a fool or a knave, and I am inclined to think that Ford is a combination of both, makes a charge against any part of the government activity, it would certainly keep itself occupied. Every now and then somebody gets out a statement that Congress is under the domination of Wall Street, but you do not bother about it. There are papers in the South, even Democratic ones, that intimate that the Governor of New York is the hireling of a foreign power. Nobody investigates it.

I do not think the American people consider Ford a national figure at all. From the time of his famous trial[3] and his famous peace ship,[4] most people consider him a fool. That a fool should make money is nothing new. Lots of them do it. I know he has done mischief, but in a democracy and with the right of free speech and the free press this sort of thing is inevitable.

Ford has had one of the cleverest kinds of advertising propaganda, much of which is to make fun of himself. The Ford joke against the Ford car I always believed was manufactured inside of the Ford organization. It may even suit the Ford organization to picture him as the defender of the downtrodden Gentile against the rapacious Jew.

So my dear Mr. Bloom, now that your first indignation has worn off, I think it would be wisest to let this matter drop. I want to say that I have not discussed your letter with anybody and would not have discussed this subject with you had you not asked me for my opinion. [W]

1. Sol Bloom (1870–1949), member of the U.S. House of Representatives from New York, 1923–49; chairman of the House Foreign Affairs Committee.
2. On December 14, 1926, Bloom introduced a resolution in the House providing for a select committee to inquire into charges made by Henry Ford concerning the operation of the government and the Federal Reserve System. It never left committee.
3. A suit for libel brought against Ford by Aaron Sapiro. On June 30, 1927, Ford would present to Louis Marshall an apology to the Jewish people and a retraction of his accusations against them.
4. See letter to Louis Marshall, May 11, 1915.

Mordecai Kaplan's criticism of traditional Judaism, no less strident than his critique of Reform, increasingly alienated him from his colleagues at the Jewish Theological Seminary, and pressures were brought to bear on Adler from Orthodox supporters of the Seminary for his removal. In 1927 Kaplan was offered a position on the faculty of the Jewish Institute of Religion by Stephen Wise. Although he seriously considered this offer, he was persuaded to remain at the Seminary.

TO RACIE ADLER, PHILADELPHIA

February 23, 1927

I saw Mr. [Louis] Marshall before our meeting last night and we agreed that all things considered it would be best to give [Mordecai M.] Kaplan his chance to explain, so our meeting was pleasant enough and largely devoted to the possible situation of the Brush dormitory.[1] There is still a strong hankering after a part or the whole of the vacant lot across the street on 123rd St.

After the meeting, [Max] Drob & Jacob Kohn came over here with me and gave me a full account of their conferences—both said that Kaplan backs down but Drob added that he had less respect for him than before.

Today all or nearly all of the Professors came to see me individually and this afternoon Kaplan. I won't go into the details but for the time being the reaction is won. It seems he got the idea that I intended to dismiss him (or so he says) and hence took this step. This may be true because there is a terrible bit of gossip among Rabbis and Professors and students and possibly also among their wives. I think he was very glad to get out of an awkward situation. I did not tackle the students but thought I would leave that for next week. [W]

1. Louis Brush (1849–1925), lawyer and philanthropist; had left a large sum to the Jewish Theological Seminary for the construction of a dormitory that is named after him.

TO SAMUEL SCHULMAN, NEW YORK CITY

February 25, 1927

. . . I have been approached about the [Simon] Dubnow proposition from half a dozen points of view. Last Summer when I was in Berlin a publisher, whose name I cannot recall, came to see me and told me that he wants to seek my advice about an English translation of Dubnow's history.[1] I told him that I thought it would be extremely difficult to float a ten-volume history of the Jews in America just now, the man haughtily replied to me that he was not bothered about the financial aspects of the matter, but that he wanted advice on the literary side. He said that the translation had been made in Berlin by a person who knew both German and English very well scientifically, but did not possess a style. And he wanted someone who would read the English of his translator. As I did not want the proposition on our hands in America, I suggested to him a young Dr. Cecil Roth[2] of London, who knows Jewish history and has a good style. Cecil Roth is a graduate of Oxford, though not connected with it, but that is what all the patter about Oxford scholars amounts to.

Now as to Dubnow himself. One thing he was at home in, of course, was the history of the Jews in Russia and Poland, which, as you know, the [Jewish] Publication Society secured with great trouble during the War and published in English.[3] The work itself was translated and greatly improved by the late Professor Israel Friedlaender. In that particular section of Jewish history in which he was no doubt mostly at home, he did not in my opinion, show the greatest merit as an historian, but rather as the chronicler of misfortunes and pogroms. While it was immensely useful as a piece of history writing, it did not leave a profound impression on me, and I do not think on any student of history. His earlier conception of the national point of view in Jewish history, as you know, has also been translated and published in English.[4] Then his three-volume history of the Jews was translated and published in English by a private firm in 1925.[5] It seemed to me, therefore, that the English-speaking world had Dubnow's views sufficiently presented to them.

As for Dubnow's further abilities to do a constructive and unifying piece of work beyond that of [Heinrich] Graetz, he does not possess them. He can cast no light on the sources of the Hellenistic period, nor the Arabic period. As for the utility of such a work, it is proposed to issue it in 1,000 copies, which, of course, means only for libraries and a few special persons, and it seemed to me that the layman is not going to read a ten-volume history and the scholar can read it in German, so that I do not see why the Jewish world should get excited to raise funds to enable the MacMillans to put through a money making plan which, if it has any effect at all, will give an undue prominence to Dubnow's conception of all Jewish history, stamp it as the authoritative ten-volume work for a generation or two, and prevent any other real enterprise. Of course everybody would like to do Dubnow a good turn, but I very much doubt, knowing as I do German publishers and American publishers, whether Dubnow would get much out of it. I have written to MacMillan unfavorably with regard to the project. Mortimer

Schiff and Louis Marshall both approached me on the subject, they having been approached on the project, and I told both of them that if they had $30,000 to give away for a Jewish literary enterprise, I know where the money would do more good. [JTS]

1. *Weltgeschichte des judischen Volkes,* 10 vols. (Berlin, 1925–27); published in English as *History of the Jews,* 5 vols. (South Brunswick, N.J., 1967–73).
2. Cecil Roth (1899–1970), English Jewish historian.
3. *History of the Jews in Russia and Poland,* 3 vols. (Philadelphia, 1916–20).
4. *Jewish History; an essay in the philosophy of history* (Philadelphia, 1903).
5. *An Outline of Jewish History* (New York, 1925).

TO LOUIS GINZBERG, NEW YORK CITY

March 23, 1927

I am writing this letter to you personally and not officially, but if you wish to take it officially as President of the [American] Academy [for Jewish Research] pray do so.

For several years Professor [Solomon] Zeitlin has been at work on a book, not a large book, which he has named "Jesus of Nazareth—the Evidence for his Historicity Critically Examined." The book is an extremely interesting one. Some of the material is in criticism of previous writers, a great deal of it original, bringing forward new facts and new opinions. Of the importance of the subject there can be no doubt and just because of this importance I have discussed it a number of times very earnestly with Professor Zeitlin because I felt that anything that was written on this subject, even though the author had no intention of having it become a matter of general controversy, might become the basis of such a controversy and therefore required great caution. I know that Professor Zeitlin has spoken to you about some of the details of this subject from time to time, as he has spoken to other of his friends and colleagues, but he tells me that I am the only one to whom he has shown the complete manuscript.

It has occurred to me that in a subject of such importance an author ought to have the benefit of the best critical opinion he can get before the book is published rather than after it is published and that moreover we had in the Academy an instrument whereby any member might get the advantage of the criticism of his colleagues—in other words, the main points of such a study, by which I mean both the conclusions and the arguments, should be presented as a paper with ample opportunity for discussion before it is thrown out to the world. I wonder how you feel about such a proposition—whether you do consider it a function of the Academy to afford such opportunity for the kind of discussion of which I speak.

To indicate to you how open-minded Professor Zeitlin is on the subject, he has said to me that if I thought the publication of the book unwise he would abandon the matter altogether. I am not willing individually to take such a responsibility because I am not willing to have scientific works suppressed under fear or because I am unconvinced; nor do I say that Professor Zeitlin would agree to withdraw the book even if all the members of the Academy would advise him to do so, because I think he has very strong convictions about it. On the other hand, if the members of the Academy could prove to Professor Zeitlin that he is wrong, he naturally does not wish to publish a book which contains a thesis that cannot be maintained.

I presume too, although this is not the immediate subject for discussion, that if any number of responsible people could demonstrate to Professor Zeitlin that the publication of a book on this subject would be against Jewish public policy, if I may use such a term, in other words if it might be calculated to bring about a great controversy that would seriously injure the Jews, he would also not wish to publish it. Not that he thinks it would, because in this book he neither attacks nor defends the person of Jesus but discusses as dispassionately as he can the question whether any of the documents that are claimed as evidence for his historicity are in effect such documents. Professor Zeitlin is so anxious to get whatever valid criticism of his book that can be secured that if you saw no objection he would be quite willing that the Academy should invite to such a sitting some non-Jewish scholars whose opinion and criticisms might also be valuable.[1] [D]

1. Some time, however, elapsed before a book by Zeitlin on that subject was forthcoming. In 1941–42 he published a long article in *JQR* entitled "The Crucifixion of Jesus Re-Examined," which was later expanded into book form under the title, *Who Crucified Jesus?* (New York, 1947).

TO HIRSCH PERETZ CHAJES, VIENNA

May 25, 1927

I had your letter of March 28th about the Falasha work and about Doctor Jacques Faitlovitch,[1] and since the latter's arrival in this country, I have seen him several times. I, too, have been greatly interested in the Falasha work and have secured for it a very considerable part of the funds received from this country.

That there has been a slackening of interest in this country is undeniable. For over two years, we have had no information of any kind. When funds are supplied, those who supply them expect to hear what is being done. It is not a question of gratitude or thanks, but simply the desire to be assured that some useful work is going forward.

To me, it appears also that the troubles had in the matter of the school building could have been avoided with tact and better management. I believe that a new effort will be made to secure funds in this country, but at the present, I cannot say with what success.

My own opinion as to Doctor Faitlovitch is that it would be best if he could find employment in the Oriental Institute in Jerusalem. As a student of the Ethiopic dialects, they cannot find his superior. Moreover, it would be in accord with his plan of educating teachers for the Falashas in Palestine, which would seem to me much more rational than scattering them all over the world to bring back to Abyssinia the indigestion of many cultures. We do not want to make cosmopolitans of the Falashas, but rather simply to give these folk the opportunity once again to know Judaism in their own environment. [W]

1. See letter to J. Walter Freiberg, February 5, 1912.

Throughout the 1920s and 30s in Europe, attempts were made to ban the ritual slaughter (shehita) of animals, ostensibly on humanitarian grounds. In 1926 campaigns of this sort were being undertaken in various German states and in Hungary as well as in Norway. Shehita was to be forbidden in Norway by law on January 1, 1930.

TO HELMER HALVORSEN BRYN,[1] WASHINGTON, D.C.

May 27, 1927

I venture to bring to your attention the following subject, feeling persuaded that you will recognize the significance of the representations that I take the liberty of making to you:

This Committee has been informed from a reliable source that a bill has been introduced into the Norwegian parliament, intended to prohibit the slaughtering of animals after the method prescribed by the Jewish law, and that in connection with the arguments advanced in favor of the passage of this bill, the statement has been made that only old-fashioned oriental Jews deem this law sacred.

May I venture to say that the observance of this law as a religious practice has been followed by a great proportion of all Jews for over twenty centuries; that it is not a matter of mere form, but is based upon the biblical principle which forbids the eating of blood, and that therefore meat may not be eaten from which the blood is not thoroughly drained. In order to bring about this result, minute regulations have been prescribed with regard to the method of slaughtering. The person who performs this act is required to possess expert knowledge and to be able to determine whether the animal was in a state of health to render its flesh wholesome for consumption. While it is undoubtedly true that some Jews have departed from this law, I venture to say that it is still observed by the overwhelming majority of Jewish people in America and all over the continent of Europe, so that the statement that the practice is confined to old-fashioned oriental Jews is not justified. If such legislation were passed, it would prevent Jews in Norway who adhere to this religious doctrine from eating meat altogether under pain of violating their conscientious beliefs.

I feel sure too that it would make a painful impression upon the Jewish people throughout the world, and particularly in America, and would bring about a belief on their part, which would undoubtedly find public expression that the government of Norway is placing obstacles in the way of conscientious Jews observing the time-honored practices of their religion.

I assume that the passage of this law is being favored by persons who are advocating it from the point of view of the prevention of cruelty to animals. This aspect of the subject has been frequently brought up and has been given careful consideration.

Some years ago a similar question was discussed at the annual convention of the American Humane Association, held at St. Paul, Minnesota, and at the time the Reverend Dr. Moses Hyamson,[2] Professor of Codes at the Jewish Theological Seminary of America, in New York, was invited to give an exposition of the subject. As a result of his explanation the American Humane Association pronounced itself in favor of the method. I enclose you a copy of the paper which he read on that occasion.[3] If you will be good enough to read page 63, you will observe that when this matter was up before some of the greatest physiologists in the world, all were asked to express their opinion as to the humanity of the method of slaughtering, and among those who had expressed their opinion in its favor were the late Lord Lister,[4] Sir Michael Foster,[5] successor of Huxley[6] at Cambridge, Professor Virchow,[7] and other eminent physiologists. I venture, therefore, on behalf of this Committee, and the many organizations which it represents, to invoke the aid of your excellency in conveying to your government the representations herein made, and to assure you that hundreds of thousands of people in America who entertain the highest respect and admiration for the government and people of Norway, would be deeply pained if such a law went into effect.

I fully recognize that it might be said at first blush that this is an internal matter, with which people outside of Norway had no right to concern themselves, but I am sure that upon reflection your excellency will see that if a government like Norway adopts such a law it would give aid and comfort to less liberal governments on the continent of Europe to initiate similar measures and other measures which anti-Semites have from time to time advocated so that the subject is one of general concern. [AJC]

1. Helmer Halvorsen Bryn (1865–1933), Norwegian minister to the U.S., 1910–33.
2. Moses Hyamson (1863–1949), professor of Codes at the Jewish Theological Seminary.
3. *The Jewish Method of Slaughtering Animals from the Point of View of Humanity* (1923).
4. Joseph, Lord Lister (1827–1912), founder of antiseptic surgery.
5. Sir Michael Foster (1836–1907), professor of physiology at Cambridge University.
6. Thomas Henry Huxley (1825–95), English biologist.
7. Hans Virchow (1852–1940), German physiologist.

TO JACOB LANDAU,[1] NEW YORK CITY

July 19, 1927

I have your letter of July 15th. I do remember that you came to me very shortly after you arrived in this country. At the time, I think our discussion was entirely about the Jewish Telegraphic Agency, but I had for a long time thought of something like a Jewish Associated Press. As a matter of fact, Joseph Jacobs and I discussed it many years ago. There was at that time only one English Jewish paper that received any telegraphic news at all and that was the *Jewish Chronicle* of London. All the rest of the papers were made up by the use of the paste pot.

I thought then, and think now, that you had a good project. I think you have a good project in the [*Jewish Daily*] *Bulletin* too. I have at all times suggested the placing of both of these projects on a business footing and in spite of your repeated applications to the American Jewish Committee have warned you against tying up with any communal agency. This I still do.

I would also continuously advise you to pay more attention to news in America. A certain proportion has to be maintained among the Jewries of the world and while the Agency, of course, can best bring foreign news to the American press, the *Bulletin* circulated in America must reach the home interests of its subscribers, as well as their interest abroad. With the stoppage of immigration, the Yiddish press will inevitably decline and an English Jewish daily will have an ever increasing field.

Pardon the sermon. [W]

1. Jacob Landau (1892–1952), founder and director of the Jewish Telegraphic Agency.

TO CHARLES DUSCHINSKY,[1] LONDON

November 3, 1927

I have your letter of October 23. I did not know that Doctor [Adolph] Büchler celebrated his sixtieth birthday and am glad to hear that he is so young. I had no idea that I was his senior by some four years.

I am afraid you will think me very unsympathetic with regard to the suggestions that you make, but I confess that I do not see how it would be any particular credit to dedicate a number of the *[Jewish] Quarterly [Review]* for Doctor Büchler's birthday. The next number, which is reasonably made up, will of necessity look pretty much like the other numbers. Moreover, once this policy started I should be faced with similar suggestions, or it might even be my duty to be on the alert to see that Jewish scholars are so remembered from time to time and the friends of each one would no doubt consider him worthy, so that with the highest respect and admiration for Doctor Büchler I cannot very well fall in with your idea. I hope that you will not consider this ungracious.

With regard to the other proposition that you had in mind about a Jubilee Volume, I want to say that while I have been once or twice in the past years weak enough to fall in with the plan of a Jubilee Volume, I think that it is a very bad custom. Authors are importuned to write articles ad hoc. The classification of such books is the despair of librarians, and unless the articles are published in separates, they are difficult to find. I very well remember that about six months before Doctor [Solomon] Schechter's sixtieth birthday he adjured me most solemnly that if I heard of any plan to publish a Jubilee Volume I should do my best to prevent it, and I did. [D]

1. Charles Duschinsky (1878–1944), English rabbi and historian of English Jewry.

TO LOUIS MARSHALL, NEW YORK CITY

November 16, 1927

. . . I was in New York yesterday and late in the evening my nephew [Samuel A. Herzog] called me up and told me that the contract for the Seminary lot had been signed late yesterday afternoon. There is to be no publicity on either side and of course the deeds have not yet been delivered. That may take a little time.

I spent several hours yesterday with Felix Warburg and Mortimer Schiff, much of the time being taken up in discussing the Schiff Biography. But later, Mortimer, of his own accord, brought up the question of the Seminary Library. I do not recall whether I told you that during the middle of October when the Felix Warburgs were down at Seabright he and I had a little serious talk with his wife and Mrs. Schiff on the subject. It seems that they have discussed it with Mortimer and he has now asked me to furnish him with as nearly an exact statement as possible of 1) the cost of the Library building—that is to say, what amount would be required in addition to the amount we now have on hand. Mr. Warburg roughly calculated this would be $300,000; 2) an estimate of the endowment fund for the physical upkeep of the building, including a sum for necessary repairs from time to time; 3) the amount of endowment required to provide a staff for the Library on the scale that will be required in the new Library building. In other words, it is his thought that if the family should go into the Library as a Memorial, it would be insufficient to provide the funds for the building, but that the endowment for its upkeep should also be provided.

As for the endowment for the purchase of books, manuscripts, binding, etc. he said that was a sum that nobody could provide for an active librarian. I shall try to furnish these figures as soon as I can.

As soon as the land proposition is absolutely settled we ought to take further steps, first to dispose of the apartment houses next door to us, because we will need further cash for settlement; second, as soon as the plans are made to deed over to the Library Corporation the piece of land on which the Library stands. I think that if we follow this plan there is a reasonable hope (I do not want to be too sanguine at the moment) that the Library may be provided for and thus this item taken off the Seminary budget.

I hope you will consider this much at least to have been a good day's work. [W]

TO MORTIMER L. SCHIFF, NEW YORK CITY

January 4, 1928

Monday evening I wrote to your Mother and told her that I had, so far as I could, completed the first draft of the [Jacob H. Schiff] Biography. It will probably take a week before everything that I dictated is written up as I kept my people busy with dictation and they have not had chance to write them up. These sections will come to you shortly. After I have received your comments upon these sections I will then proceed to the following steps: Arrange the book in the order which would seem best; reduce its size, both by elimination of material and by elimination of duplication, of which I know there is some. I would then like to put a second copy into your hands when the book is in that shape, and also maybe seek a little outside criticism. I think too, since the material is all together, that it might be advisable that we earnestly consider the question of illustrations and maybe even get down to that of the publisher.

I want to repeat to you what I said to your Mother—that it has been really a very great satisfaction to me to have spent, as it were, these two years with your Father's life, and I have the feeling at the end that he was a much bigger and more powerful man than I had any idea of. My only fear now is that I have not worthily represented him, but I hope and feel sure that I shall be able to greatly improve the manuscript before it is finally submitted, nor do I think that this process will take very long. [W]

TO MENAHEM RIBALOW,[1] NEW YORK CITY

January 17, 1928

In view of the fact that I am a member of the Committee on the Institute of Jewish Studies at the [Hebrew] University, I do not know whether I should express a public opinion concerning the subject considered at a meeting at which I could not be present. However, since as you say the matter is one of active discussion and great concern, I would say that it is my personal opinion that the offer to establish a chair for the Yiddish language and literature should be accepted by the Hebrew University.[2] The history and development of the Yiddish language is worthy of study and investigation, both as a philological phenomenon and because it was used by a large section of the Jewish people for hundreds of years and produced a literature which, in some departments, has earned the respect of the world. It should be clearly understood that no attempts will be made to alter the language of instruction in the University, or that such a chair would be used for the purposes of propaganda and thus intensify a struggle which is senseless. From a scientific point of view, I think it is incontrovertible that all phenomena which attended the life of the Jews in the Diaspora are worthy of study and research. The Greek of the Bible versions, the Judeo-Latins, if Doctor [David S.] Blondheim's thesis is correct as I believe it is, Ladino, which has been used by the exiles from Spain for 400 years, Judeo-Arabic, which is a dialect of classical Arabic, the dialects employed by the Falashas in Abyssinia, all these in my mind, would have a place in the Institute of Jewish Studies provided endowments were found for them.

If this discussion should result in partisan agitation, it would indicate that the Jewish people are not sufficiently scientific minded to be ready for a University, and this, I trust, is not the case. [JTS]

1. Menahem Ribalow (1895–1953), editor of the New York Hebrew weekly *Ha-Doar*.
2. A chair in Yiddish literature at the Hebrew University was not endowed until 1947.

Decades after his association with Samuel P. Langley, Adler retained his interest in aeronautics.

TO ALBERT P. BRUBAKER,[1] PHILADELPHIA

February 3, 1928

I had an interesting interview with Mr. Harry F. Guggenheim,[2] President of the Daniel Guggenheim Fund for the Promotion of Aeronautics, Inc., 598 Madison Avenue, New York; telephone number, Plaza 8269. He was very sympathetic with the idea of aiding us in arranging for a symposium on the subject of Aeronautics. He said that the question of persons would depend upon the topics chosen. The topics that we discussed were the following:

1. The Science of Aero-dynamics. Its origin and development.
2. The Movement for Aeronautical Engineering Education.
3. The Development of the Airplane Motor.
4. The Airplane Industry.
5. Air Transportation and Operating Companies.
6. Meteorology for Aviation.

7. The Development of Air Navigation Instruments.

8. Aviation and the National Defense.

9. Lighter than Air and Heavier than Air Machines

. . . I should be very glad to discuss with you, if you wish it, in detail some of these subjects. After the Committee is agreed upon the subjects and how many they want, Mr. Guggenheim would then try to get us suitable people for the discussion.

I may say that in the course of my talk with Mr. Guggenheim, I was very much impressed with the uses to which aviation is already being put in America and I think that a presentation of the subject would be very valuable; also the subject Meteorology for Aviation is apparently of the highest importance. The most debatable subject and one therefore which might arouse greater interest is number 9; Lighter than Air and Heavier than Air Machines.

I do not know what plans you made for the next meeting of the Committee, but if you will let me know when you will call another meeting of the Committee or a conference about this matter, I should be very glad to try to meet you and the other gentlemen. [W]

1. Albert P. Brubaker (1854–1943), professor of physiology at Jefferson Medical College, Philadelphia, 1909–27.
2. Harry F. Guggenheim (1890–1971), businessman and philanthropist.

TO FELIX M. WARBURG, NEW YORK CITY

February 6, 1928

Miss Emanuel[1] sent me the enclosed letter from Doctor [Chaim] Weizmann and says that you will let me have the enclosures later. It is very difficult for me to express an opinion about the letter without the enclosures. However, I will try to think without them and see what the salient points are according to Doctor Weizmann's statements. He says that Professor [Albert] Einstein does not "wish to be further associated in any way with a [Hebrew] University in the administration of which he had no confidence." I judge from Doctor Weizmann's letter that he wants the "appointment of an academic head," which means some person other than [Judah L.] Magnes, whom he is not prepared to recognize as such academic head. This, you will remember, was the proposal put forward by Brodetsky,[2] no doubt as an echo of this, and at the time at least definitely resisted by Magnes. He also wants "a permanent executive of the Academic Council," which I should think would mean that if he is to remain President of the Academic Council he should have a constant secretary at his hand to conduct correspondence, consider reports, and do the other things which an active investigator like himself cannot do. So long as the Academic Council is in existence and he is its head, this would seem to me to be reasonable.

In my various talks with Doctor Magnes while he was here I recognized, as did he, the terribly complicated situation even at the present time. I too recognize the strength of Einstein's name. He is considered in many quarters—and rightly so—as one of the foremost intellects of the world. If his proposals are realizable and at all within reason I have no doubt that it would be in the interest of the University to accept them. If, however, they are of such a nature as to be palpably absurd or impossible, from an administrative point of view, then between the University and the man, I would prefer saving the University. This is so far as I can go in my analysis of his letter, until I see the enclosures.

I am coming to New York tomorrow, Tuesday, with a lengthy meeting of the [Jewish Theological Seminary] Faculty in the afternoon and an evening meeting at Mr. [Louis] Marshall's house of the joint Committee to consider the finances of the Seminary, the Rabbinical Assembly and the United Synagogue. I am afraid it is going to be a long and difficult meeting. The representatives of the two other groups will strongly urge, as you know, a joint campaign; probably even one of the Seminary representatives—Doctor Jacob Kahn—will do the same, Mr. Marshall, representing our opinion, will oppose it, and in accordance with our agreement I shall stand with him. I hope all of this will be done in good temper, but I must say that I foresee great difficulties because while the Seminary makes the appeal to the people, the Seminary lacks the machinery to create a campaign, whereas the United Synagogue and the Rabbinical Assembly, which make no popular appeal, possess the machinery ready made which can easily be mobilized.

I assume, from what you said to me the other day, that you will not be present at the meeting and of course I would not urge you to be, but I wish you would think this over and if you have any other view than the one you expressed at the charming little conference at your house, that you would be good enough to say so to Mr. Marshall. We too have complications.

I was wondering whether you could arrange to give me a little time on Wednesday, February 8. I want to try to see Gehron[3] again and then sit down with you and examine the plans a little more closely than we could the other night. At the meeting of the Board of Directors of the Seminary a situation something like this developed with regard to the Building program:

Both Mr. Unterberg[4] and Mr. [Henry A.] Dix, and possibly others, strongly urged the appointment of a Building Committee which, while accepting the Library Building as located, should provide for the further development of the laying out of the plot not only including the sites for the Dormitory and the Teachers Institute, but also some consideration of spaces for future buildings. They did not seem willing to take it for granted that the Arnold W. Brunner Associates should, without question, be accepted as the architects for the entire development. When I pointed out that all this might create considerable delay and that at least preliminary studies would be necessary, it was suggested that I endeavor to make an arrangement with the Arnold W. Brunner Associates for outline sketches for the remainder of the plot upon some definite compensation, with the understanding that that would be their entire compensation and that if they were finally made the architects for all the buildings that this compensation was to be subtracted from their ultimate fee. I have not yet taken this up with them because I wished to tell you about it and also wanted to consult with Mr. Marshall as to the exact wording of a communication to them.

All these gentlemen, as you know, have favorite architects and we have all received dozens of requests for men to be considered. I find these men very workable with and believe, possibly in order to satisfy the sentiment which Mr. Unterberg and others seem to have, that at least for the remainder of the buildings, outside of the Library, the association of a Jew, who is also a good architect, with the Arnold W. Brunner Associates, would be a plan that might satisfy everybody.

I wandered off from the beginning of my request, which was that if you could find a little time for me on Wednesday I would like very much to go over these plans with you. A telephone message to the Seminary any time after 1 o'clock tomorrow, Tuesday, would reach me, or, if I do not hear from you I will call up Miss Emanuel to find out whether you have any time. [W]

1. Felix Warburg's secretary.
2. Selig Brodetsky (1884–1954), English mathematician and Zionist leader; succeeded Judah Magnes as president of the Hebrew University, 1949–51.
3. William Gehron (1887–1958), architect, formerly associated with Arnold W. Brunner. His firm was to design the new Seminary complex.
4. Israel Unterberg (1863–1934), philanthropist; member of the Seminary Board of Directors, 1927–34.

The Committee was concerned with the fate of a number of Jewish refugees in Turkey who were temporarily stranded with no country willing to take them in. At this point the Jewish refugee problem was serious, yet still small. The rise of Hitler would expand it to catastrophic proportions.

TO LUCIEN WOLF, LONDON

New York, February 13, 1928

While, no doubt, what I am going to tell you has reached you from other sources, as a result of the efforts made by various members of our Committee the following is a summary of what was reported at a meeting of the Executive Committee on February 12:

Doctor Bernard Kahn, representative of the Joint Distribution Committee in Berlin, cabled us on January 31: "ACCORDING LAST CONFIDENTIAL REPORT TIME EXPULSION REFUGEES CONSTANTINOPLE EXTENDED FOR ONE YEAR." Doctor Anson Phelps Stokes,[1] who took charge of the Refugees Emergency Fund at Constantinople, reported to us under date of February 8 that "as a result of the efforts of the American Ambassador and of the League of Nations representative at Constantinople, we know from cables received that substantial modifications in this order have now been obtained, which will give the High Commission on Refugees a full year to effect the evacuation."

It seems that considerable subscriptions to aid the refugees was accepted as assurance by the Turkish Government that they would ultimately leave the country and that this is one of the elements in the extending of time. We have received the assurance that the fund collected at the last writing, totalling over $105,000, would apply equally for the benefit of all refugees and it was further agreed that Doctor Bernard Kahn, representing the Joint Distribution Committee, one of the subscribers to the fund, would be added to the Committee in charge of the evacuation work as a representative of the Jewish interest. [W]

1. Anson Phelps Stokes (1874–1958), Episcopal clergyman and communal worker.

TO JAMES MARSHALL,[1] NEW YORK CITY

May 7, 1928

It was very kind of you to send me a separate copy of your interesting article "The Workshop of Israel" which I had already read in the *Menorah Journal*.[2] I am glad to see your optimism about Palestine. I am wondering whether you are not unduly pessimistic about the Diaspora. I think I might show you centers in America, in England, in Germany and no doubt in other countries with which I am less familiar where Judaism has not disappeared entirely even among the youth. But if you are right, to what does your conclusion point? The extinction of all Jews outside of Palestine? Because if this is inevitable then who will feed the beautiful settlement in the Holy Land? It is obviously not strong enough to depend upon itself. Why will you not be one of those to stem the loss of the Diaspora instead of bewailing it. It is still possible to observe the Sabbath in America and to let the Sabbath candles shine through the windows. Yes, even Hannukkah lights. I think the whole matter depends upon where one places the center of gravity of one's life. The Jewish Golden Age in Spain was not maintained by ghetto walls and certainly the environment was none too sympathetic. The hope for Palestine it seems to me does not involve despair in America. Think it over. Maybe you can help along with revival in America too. [JTS]

1. James Marshall (b. 1896), lawyer; son of Louis Marshall.
2. The article appeared in the *Menorah Journal* 14 (1928):361–68.

TO FELIX M. WARBURG, NEW YORK CITY

May 22, 1928

As I have told you, and Doctor [Chaim] Weizmann personally, I very much regret that it is not possible for me to attend the meetings of the Board of Governors and of the Academic Council of the [Hebrew] University. I have, however, carefully considered the agenda both for the Council and for the Governors, and they are almost identical. I am writing you my views on a few of the subjects to be considered, although of course I realize that no one who has not heard the debate on a subject has a right to express a controlling opinion in advance.

With regard to item 3, Disciplinary Measures Affecting the Staff, I would recommend great caution in laying down any hard and fast rules at the present time. It will not be easy to bring men of distinction to the University. If they are met in advance by a series of regulations, which would seem to place them at the mercy of Boards and Committees, they are even less likely than now to give up well settled places and go to Jerusalem. The best way for the University to hold this matter in its hands is to elect instructors, lecturers, and associates for short terms. If they prove non-cooperative or inefficient, their appointments can be allowed to lapse without disturbance. Professors should be elected for life, under good behavior. It is more than likely that no cause for discipline among this group will ever occur and if it does, it is not necessary to establish rules in advance.

With regard to the plan of establishing a School of Agriculture, it seems to me that this would be desirable as soon as it can be effected and I think it should be upon the basis of the consolidation of the existing Institutes in Palestine at the present time.

I favor the affiliation of the Haifa Technicum to the University as soon as its course of studies can be so arranged that it can be usefully affiliated, but it seems to me that it ought to be affiliated as an under-graduate College of Science. In general, what the University needs is a group of supporting colleges or gymnasia, so that it will not be necessary for all young Palestinians who have ambitions for study, and scholarship, to leave Palestine and come to Europe or to the United States. This seems to me to constitute a very considerable danger to the future growth of normal intellectual life in Palestine.

I would favor in the same way an Under-Graduate Faculty of Humanities, but I do not favor any of these things at the risk of diverting funds from the work already in existence. It would seem to me that the best plan for the University would be to develop into proper faculties those Institutes which it has already begun; to consolidate and strengthen them and not to undertake new ventures, unless special and sufficient endowments are offered for them.

Will you kindly present my excuses to the President and members of the Board? [W]

TO LOUIS GINZBERG, NEW YORK CITY

Philadelphia, July 17, 1928

Within the past few weeks it has been brought to my attention that the year 1935 would be the eight hundredth anniversary of the birth of Maimonides. I was reminded of the date by a letter which was forwarded to me from a physician in Cairo who is also an Arabist, and who is looking forward to publishing certain unpublished medical texts of Maimonides and said that he would like to have them ready for that year.[1] The thought occurred to me that we ought to signalize the eight hundredth anniversary of the birth of one of the greatest figures in the middle ages—the greatest intellectual figure produced by the Jews. But the publication of a few of his medical manuscripts would seem to me quite insufficient. I have talked with

Professor [Alexander] Marx and Doctor [Abraham A.] Neumann and Skoss,[2] just as I happened to meet them, as to whether some real notice should not be taken of this event. I have also had some correspondence with Professor Sarton[3] of Harvard on the subject.

It seems to me that an ideal thing to do would be to publish a definite text of the works of Maimonides. Whether such a thing is feasible within a period of seven years I do not know. At least a plan can be made and a company of scholars started on the work. As you know even the well known texts of Maimonides are no longer available to students. Certainly to my knowledge there are no texts of the Guide in Arabic which can be purchased, and many of the texts require critical editing.

My object in writing to you is this: First, I would like to know what you think of the idea yourself. Second, if you think that something ought to be done, and something important, I am wondering whether in your wanderings you would confer with scholars in Europe and find out whether they have set any plan on foot, or if not whether they would be likely to fall in with a plan such as the one I have outlined.

I want to say myself that I would be very little interested in any plan to get up a volume of miscellaneous papers about Maimonides. I would be interested in a great enterprise of the kind I have outlined, which I think in the present state of the world might be carried through more successfully than was the one for Saadia's Millennium.[4] . . . [W]

1. Max Meyerhof (1874–1945), German-born physician and medical historian living in Egypt; translated and published Maimonides' glossary of drugs, *L'explication des noms de drogues* (1940).
2. Solomon Leon Skoss (1884–1953), professor of Arabic at Dropsie College, 1924–53.
3. George Sarton (1884–1956), historian of science; professor at Harvard University, 1916–18, 1920–56.
4. A project to publish the complete works of Saadia Gaon on the millennium of his birth was left uncompleted after five volumes were published. Dérenbourg, Joseph, Hartwig et al., *Ouevres complètes de R. Saadia* (Paris, 1893–99).

TO LOUIS MARSHALL, NEW YORK CITY

August 21, 1928

I have been very much interested in your exchange of correspondence with [Bernard] Louis Levinthal and thank you for letting me see it. I disclaim knowledge of law—Jewish or otherwise, but in thinking of the entire matter of marriage and divorce during the past few years, certain general ideas have taken lodgement in my otherwise vacuous brain.

The lack of uniformity in our various states has had a considerable share in the unsettlement of the family, which I regard as the basic unit of our society. About this you know better than I. A few instances have recently come to my attention to show how lightly the marriage ceremony is treated. First cousins are not permitted to marry in the State of Pennsylvania. They are permitted to marry in the State of New Jersey. Two first cousins sent out invitations to a wedding to be held in Philadelphia and their guests assembled there. The two people concerned and their witnesses went over to Camden, were married in Camden, and immediately returned on the ferry and had their wedding party in Philadelphia.

This is the way our state laws are dealt with. With regard to the matter of the Agunah,[1] I think I told you that I discussed this matter with great earnestness with Israel Levi and [Joseph H.] Hertz and one of the leading Rabbis of Wilna in Paris a few years ago.[2] Israel Levi is very favorable to the issuance of a Takkanah[3] which allows the presumption that a man who had gone into the War and not returned for ten years should be assumed to be dead, his widow to be allowed to re-marry. The Rabbi of Wilna assured us that the decree would not be recognized by the Rabbis of Poland and Lithuania, whereupon the suggestion was dropped. Our own Rabbinical Assembly, to whom I submitted the question for an opinion, was also opposed to the Takkanah, [Max] Drob telling me that their attitude was that since it was not provided for in the contract, its application would tend to weaken the force and sanctity of the Ketubah.[4] He did, however, express the opinion that it might be advisable, in view of wars or other great emergencies, to insert a clause in the Ketubah that if either party disappeared and was absent for a definite term of years they should be presumed to be dead. However, I think nothing was done in this direction.

As I understand it, however, the matter is quite different in the case of an annulment for reasons sanctioned in the Jewish law. If a man is found to have had a loathsome disease or if there were any fraud or misrepresentation of his status: if he said he was a painter and he turned out to be a cobbler, then the Rabbinical court could annul the marriage and the man was obliged to appear and give his assent.

In general, I am in agreement with you that if marriage contracts provided in advance for divorce the number of the latter will only be increased.

As for the recognition of the laws of the state, of course they must be recognized, but if a person wants the sanction of the synagogue, then he must recognize the laws of the synagogue. Two Jews can go and have a civil marriage and they can have a civil divorce and nobody will intervene. But if they want a Rabbinical marriage or a Jewish marriage, then it seems to me that they must comply with the Jewish law. The Jewish law, as a matter of fact, makes marriage easier than divorce because any two people who desire to marry and have the necessary writing prepared and make this statement before two witnesses, neither of whom is a blood relation, are legally married, but the divorce must be participated in by a Rabbi or an ecclesiastical tribunal. As a matter of fact, the laws of nearly all of the states of the union do require a magistrate or a religious functionary and the Jews, therefore, comply with this and have a Rabbi, but their laws do not require it.

All of this is, I am sure, known to you and I am just talking by the way. [W]

1. A married woman separated from her husband who cannot remarry either because he has refused her a divorce or because it is not known whether he is alive. The problem of the agunah is one of the knottiest in Jewish religious law.
2. Isaac Rubinstein became joint chief rabbi of Vilna in 1928. See letter to Felix M. Warburg, August 12, 1926.
3. A directive enacted by halakhic scholars, or other competent body, enjoying the force of law.
4. Marriage contract.

TO FRANKLIN D. ROOSEVELT,[1] NEW YORK CITY

Philadelphia, October 16, 1928

Your letter of October 13 telling me that you have not heard what decision I have made about the two Presidential candidates leads me to say that this must be due to the fact that my voice has not been loud enough. I unhesitatingly declared for Governor Smith[2] as far back as the beginning of September in a letter to Mr. Frank Polk,[3] and this statement has been given out by the National Democratic Committee in brief form in some of its publications, and was carried in more detail in the *Philadelphia Record,* the only Democratic paper in Philadelphia.

At that time, since I was asked to state my reasons, I stated them briefly, to the effect that I favored Governor Smith because I thought his stand upon the Prohibition question would put an end to the shameful hypocrisy which is afflicting the people of the United States on that subject, and that it was about time that the American people should show that they are willing to put their professions of religious liberty in practice.

The issue that you discuss with regard to the decline in eight years of our country from the high ideals of Woodrow Wilson has been very deep-seated with me. I was in Paris all through the Peace Conference; I know that Mr.

Wilson labored for an improved world, and though I was a personal friend of his, even the tragedy of his illness and death was a minor thing compared to the tragedy of the world, which resulted from blind partisanship in the United States Senate, which resulted in our declining to adhere to the League of Nations.

The first important act of the new Republican Administration, that of making a separate Treaty with Germany, in which we claimed all the benefits that would have accrued to us under the Versailles Treaty and refused to accept any of its obligations, was to me the most unmoral act of which the United States has ever been guilty in its international relations. And in various subsequent journeys to Europe I realized that in spite of the really great acts of kindness which our people had done for Europe we were despised in 1924, as greatly as we had been loved in 1919.

In foreign affairs both Republican Administrations had acted just as they did in the Prohibition question for every one knows that Geneva is over-run with American unofficial observers; that there is hardly a single subject of any importance in connection with the League of Nations that goes on in which we do not stick a finger in the pie, and that thus again we say one thing in public and do another in private.

I should be the last in the world to criticize any movement toward World Peace, and if the recently signed Kellogg Treaty[4] will help toward that end, like every other decent man, I should rejoice, but I cannot refrain from thinking that this is not so very different from the old Bryan Treaties and I cannot understand why it took seven years of a Republican Administration to work out this simple formula, with all the "best minds" present, unless it was carefully timed before a Presidential election.

I have met Governor Smith only once. I have met Mr. [Herbert] Hoover frequently and like him, and I am not going to say a word against Mr. Hoover, but I thought it was rather a painful thing that at the Republican Convention, in all the speeches of the nomination that were made—and Mr. Hoover's work during the War was properly lauded—there was not a single man who had the decency to remember that it was Woodrow Wilson who gave Mr. Hoover the great opportunity to do this work which thousands of other men would have coveted.

I am sure I could write a much longer letter than you would be willing to read. Maybe you will not even have the time to read this, but I do want to say a personal word to you. I think that your action in accepting the nomination for Governor of New York—and I have written in the same sense to Colonel [Herbert H.] Lehman so far as his acceptance is concerned—seems to me one of the finest acts of friendship that I have known in my time, and that if

Governor Smith needed any testimonial—which he does not—the finest testimonial that could be written in his behalf is the act of yourself and Colonel Lehman in undertaking a public duty, which I know both of you would have been glad to avoid, and which I feel sure you did out of affection for the Governor.

As I am a citizen of Pennsylvania, I cannot cast a vote for you in New York. I would if I could. But I shall be voting on the right side in Pennsylvania. [W]

1. Franklin Delano Roosevelt (1882–1945), governor of New York, 1928–32; thirty-second president of the United States, 1933–45.
2. Alfred Smith (1873–1944), governor of New York, 1918–20, 1922–28; Democratic candidate for president, 1928.
3. Frank Lyon Polk (1871–1943), lawyer and Democratic politician; led the American delegation to the Versailles Peace Conference.
4. Kellogg-Briand Pact (1928), an international agreement renouncing war as an instrument of national policy. Ultimately 62 nations signed it.

TO HENRY S. MORAIS, NEW YORK CITY

November 15, 1928

I have been giving a good deal of consideration the last week or so to your recent letter. I shall not discuss our previous correspondence nor go over the reasons which impelled me to return to you the papers of your Father[1] and suggest that you place the writing of his biography in other hands. Let me say, however, at once that this action has nothing to do with the Biography of Jacob H. Schiff. The manuscript of that work was finished in January 1928 and all the subsequent work was simply revision or proof reading. It remains to be seen whether I am a successful writer of biography or not. That I presume the public and the critics will determine.

I thought that you would be able to place this work in other and younger and better hands. I am not a professional writer for my life has not permitted me to be. Moreover, the trail, so to speak, was no longer fresh, and there are gaps in materials which make a real biography, in my opinion, difficult. However, I confess that none of these were the actuating cause of my returning the papers to you, but they were those which I gave you at the time. Since now you have asked me again to undertake the biography, I am willing to undertake it on the following conditions:

I shall be the final and sole person to determine what goes in the biography. I shall be willing and even glad to submit a copy of the manuscript to you and to consider every criticism that you may make, but as I shall have to accept final responsibility of the book I am to determine finally what goes in it. I cannot make this point too clear because I think upon it depends my peace of mind in the undertaking, and if you do not trust me with this then you cannot trust me with the book.

I think you will find that my point of view in undertaking the work affects not only the content but also the style. I am not given to verbiage or extravagances, nor to praise or blame. My purpose would be to have the subject of the biography speak out for himself so far as his writings and letters permit, and only to weave a narrative together. I do not accept the new school of biography which seeks to estimate the subject or the mind of the author, nor the previous school of biography which undertook to extravagantly praise or sometimes to just as extravagantly dispraise.

There is another matter in which I should wish to have a free hand and that is the publisher. In my conversations with you a number of years ago there had been an understanding that any works issued were to be issued by the Seminary. From the point of view of the dignity of the [Jewish Theological] Seminary this of course is very pleasing to me as I like to see its imprint upon good books. I would have a certain hesitation, however, in asking the Seminary to publish a book by myself because the authorities would be put in the position of being virtually forced to accept the proposal or offend me. I would not think of the Jewish Publication Society either at the moment but maybe even of an independent publisher. It may be that the book will come around to the Seminary, but on this point too I want a free hand.

The third point is one which I do not know much can be done about now but you might be able to do something—maybe a good deal. The materials for your Father's life, outside of my recollections, which, after the lapse of thirty years must have many holes in them, are not as full as they ought to be from the point of view of his own correspondence. Among the latter there are a good many letters to him which are of interest, but not so many letters of his own. I am wondering whether there might not be correspondence, or a correspondent even, whom you know—whether in America or in Europe—whose family might have preserved his letters. I am saying this because in preparing the Biography of Mr. Schiff I got some of the most remarkable things in this way, through his son, who knew his old friends and it happened that two or three of these old friends had preserved letters from his boyhood concerning which nobody here knew anything, which gave me an idea of the beginnings of his career. Now if there are any such people whom you can think of, whether in Italy, or in England, or anywhere else, it would be most desirable to secure a few such letters.

I have also been thinking whether some public notice to the effect that his letters were desired for purposes of his biography spread in the press of the United States, and maybe other countries, might not bring a few that would be significant. You see your Father, while he occasionally made a copy of a letter on an important matter, did not in the main keep copies of his letters, and letters to him very often do not reveal much of a point in his own biography.

This was the conclusion that I had reached after two examinations of the material in hand. I do not say that it is impossible to prepare a biography on the basis of it, but I do think that a more interesting one can be prepared if some of his more intimate letters, and especially of his earlier years, can be found.

Now I want you to think this over carefully, and again I say that if some younger and better hand can be found to do this work he shall have my assistance. If, on the other hand, you still want me to do it and accept the conditions that I have stated above, if you will kindly return to me the material that I sent back to you and anything else that you may have found in the meantime, if you have found anything else, I will set about the work. [W]

1. Sabato Morais. See Moshe Davis, "Sabato Morais: A Selected and Annotated Bibliography of His Writings," *PAJHS* 37 (1947): 55–93.

TO LOUIS MARSHALL, NEW YORK CITY

December 31, 1928

Admiration from Sir Hubert Stanley[1] is praise indeed and while I shall make due allowance for your affection for Mr. [Jacob H.] Schiff and for my own person, I am very greatly pleased and encouraged by what you write me of the Schiff Biography. I must admit that there came a time when the work was finished and the wearisome business of proofreading was on that I had great misgivings as to whether it was at all well done or whether anyone would ever read the book through. That in the great pressure on your time you have done so is in itself a high compliment.

Big as the book is it could have been twice the size if I had thought that people would read it, for after all I made only a selection of his interesting letters and then too much had to be omitted because of the frankness with which he dealt with people still living.

It seems to me rather a pity that there has been so little of biography of American Jews for while few if any have played the role of Mr. Schiff there are a number who should not be allowed to have passed away with a mere biographical sketch. Judah Touro's life is being written for the biographical series of the Jewish Publication Society by Leon Huhner.[2] Isaac Leeser could have been done by Mayer Sulzberger but he never found the time. Judge Sulzberger himself should have a volume and so should Dr. [Sabato] Morais.

We have so few men with the interest, the patience and the opportunity to do this work. . . . [W]

1. Possibly Sir Herbert Stanley (1872–1955), British colonial administrator.
2. *The Life of Judah Touro* (Philadelphia, 1946).

TO MOSES SCHORR,[1] WARSAW, POLAND

January 9, 1929

I am afraid that I have been very derelict in not replying sooner to a letter which you sent me during the summer with reference to the suggestions made at the meeting of the Committee on the Institute of Jewish Studies of the Hebrew University in Jerusalem regarding the calling of a world Congress on Jewish science[2] and furnishing also a general program for the Congress, and asking my opinion about it.

I must say that I do not find myself very much in sympathy with this idea. In general I do not believe that there is any particular value in these international scientific Congresses, although in years past I aided the Congress of Orientalists somewhat. But to our regret, I think we have to admit that these international gatherings have not made for peace or friendship and that they have also not brought out notable or important discoveries. They are largely taken up in the reading of general papers, in entertainment, they are expensive, they are troublesome and I do not believe, in the present condition of the Jews and of Jewish scholarship such a Congress would repay either the energy or the expenditure of money. Moreover, these International Congresses get a good deal of their standing through Government patronage and official delegates which we could not expect or even want.

What I have urged for a number of years is the formation in each country, where there is a group of Jewish scholars of a local academy and when these academies become strong enough then I think there should be an Association of Academies. It is in these academies that work can be planned out, projects made and plans formed to carry out the projects. I do not think that by getting together in a Congress the things that you hope for will be accomplished. With so many different sections, with so many different interests, with so many different plans, each one pushing itself forward as the most important, I believe that the one would destroy the other.

There are probably certain fundamental things upon which we could all agree without the necessity of our spending large sums of money in travelling to one central point for a meeting, and this too is not an inconsiderable matter because the men engaged in Jewish science are not men of wealth and the travel item is an important one.

I presume that nobody would doubt that there ought to be edited and published under Jewish auspices a new edition of the Masoretic Bible. There are manuscripts in existence which have never been used by any scholar. Ginsburg's Bible[3] is not a final edition.

I would assume that it would be agreed that a critical edition of the entire Talmud is desirable. Such a text as that of the Tractate Taanit was, as you know, published by the late Professor [Henry] Malter in the Jewish Classics Series and the justification for this, with all the apparatus, is now in press and will be issued by the American Academy for Jewish Research.[4] It seems to me that scholars ought to study this text and Doctor Malter's method, criticize it, and if his method and the plan seem upon the whole feasible an effort be made to produce such a critical text. I believe that that would reasonably occupy the time of the Jewish scholars of the world for a generation.

I have another project in mind which I have been considering for some time, and which I mean pretty soon to propose publicly, and that is that in celebration of the eight hundredth anniversary of the birth of Maimonides there should be launched an undertaking, first to publish his unpublished manuscripts, and second to publish a critical edition of all his works. In other words, a definitive edition of Maimonides.[5]

While I recognize the great importance of a Thesaurus, I do not think we are ripe for it yet and at all events we might as well concentrate upon seeing [Eliezer] Ben Yehuda's Thesaurus[6] out before a new project is started.

There is a plan which has been under consideration in this country for a number of years and for which we have never found the means, and that is an Index to all of the Responsa literature. I am sure you know as well as I do that whether it has the means or not the Jewish world does not seem disposed to give us the means for these purposes at the present time, and if we concentrated upon one effort and tried to see it through that is the most that we may expect.

I hope you will not mind my disagreeing with you or writing to you in this frank and informal way. [D]

1. Moses Schorr (1874–1941), Polish rabbi, scholar, and political leader.
2. The first World Congress of Jewish Studies was to be held in 1947 in Jerusalem.
3. Christian David Ginsburg (1831–1914), biblical scholar; edited two standard editions of the Hebrew Bible (1894, 1911).
4. See letter to Felix M. Warburg, December 1, 1924.
5. See letter to Louis Ginzberg, July 17, 1928.
6. Ben Yehuda's *Thesaurus of Ancient and Modern Hebrew,* 17 vols. (Jerusalem, 1910–59).

TO FELIX M. WARBURG, NEW YORK CITY

February 8, 1929

. . . The whole question of the publication of the works of scholars is a tragedy. As you know, in our own Seminary group when a man gets a piece of work done I come to the Board of Trustees and beg from you or Mr. [Louis] Marshall. The splendid *Thesaurus of Hebrew Poetry,* which the Seminary is publishing, edited by Doctor [Israel] Davidson, was paid for by the late Nathan J. Miller,[1] and I may say, for your information, that Doctor Davidson got this money through the good offices of Doctor [Hyman G.] Enelow.

Only this morning Professor [Max L.] Margolis came to my office and told me of the difficulties that he was having in connection with the publication of his scientific work. He had worked for years on a critical edition of the Book of Joshua in Greek, which was accepted four years ago by the Harvard Press, but which has not yet appeared, probably owing to lack of funds.[2] And another book which George Kohut undertook to publish from the Kohut Foundation,[3] which is being printed in Vienna for the sake of cheapness and he gets eight pages at a time, being sent back and forth across the Ocean. He calculated that it will be five years before the book can be published on this basis.

I am telling you this because the situation is now simply that if a man works ten or fifteen years on a book, unless he has a personal friend, or I have a personal friend for him, there is no way of printing the book. I did not mean to tell you such a long story, but in effect, any support of the [American] Academy [for Jewish Research] would be toward the publication of the work of these men. These Societies are purely voluntary Societies, they have no expenses except a few dollars a year for postage; there are no salaries; there are no paid collectors and they have to depend upon the good will of those who have an interest and an understanding. [D]

1. See letter to Louis Marshall, January 2, 1925.
2. Margolis's study was published in four volumes (Paris, 1931–38).
3. Established in 1895 by George Alexander Kohut to sponsor the publication of works of Jewish scholarship.

TO FELIX M. WARBURG, NEW YORK CITY

February 12, 1929

I read with care and interest the educational part of the Jewish Communal Survey.[1] As an abstract of course it means that only high lights are picked out and I suppose it is not fair to form an opinion of the survey. Nevertheless, since you may place some slight value upon my remarks and as I am outside of New York I will give them to you for what they are worth.

The report in the main seems to me to be directed toward supervision, administration, and experimentation. In these fields one gets a fair idea of what is being done in New York and what is not being done in New York. I have an idea that it does not sufficiently cover the experimental work carried on in several of the Teachers Institutes because in these alert faculties men are experimenting with methods through the supervision of the practice of their own teachers, and also in the reform of syllabi which are intended as experimental text books.

Then too something that I miss is some idea of the actual meat of the Jewish education. What I mean is this: We get no picture at all, at least in this brief report, of the actual education that is being given in the large number of Synagogue schools—which after all constitute the greatest part of Jewish education in New York—except as they themselves are organized into groups. Thus for instance, I note particularly the statements about the United Synagogue on pages 11 to 12 where I know the conditions. There are said to be fifty-three congregations affiliated with it in New York and with one exception they all maintain schools. There is no idea given at all of the number of pupils in these schools, nor of the kind of education given. As a matter of fact, while it is not universal, the Congregations connected with the United Synagogue, nearly all of which are ministered to by the graduates of the Seminary, have adopted the middle policy with regard to Jewish education, one that I have strongly advocated for twenty years, which I think is calculated to meet many of the difficulties that are set forth in these reports. The Sunday school meets one session a week on Sunday morning, which is inadequate in the course of a few years to give a fair idea of the Jewish religion, its history, etc. The Talmud Torahs meeting five times a week, Monday, Tuesday, Wednesday, Thursday and Sunday morning, present a program which will not be accepted by the great majority of Jewish families in America, even if their children were willing to do it, as the general theory of some time for play, or for extra things like music, has to be given to the child. Hence the theory that we have evolved is to have three sessions a week and by this arrangement each school building can be used for a double shift, and therefore do double service, say Sunday morning, Tuesday and Thursday for one group of children; Sunday afternoon, Monday and Wednesday for another group. This too makes it possible for such schools to employ teachers on full time basis.

Now I am personally convinced that it is not necessary to spend $65,000 or $85,000 a year to find this out because I believe it has been found out.

I very strongly approve of the idea of forming an educational council because this will bring the people with different ideas together and if they are not too set in their ways they may learn something from each other.

What I would, however, warn the leaders in New York against is to accept too great a burden in connection with Jewish education. The Synagogue or Temple is the first proper Center. It ought to maintain a good school; the schools of the various types ought to have uniform curricula so that if a family migrates from one congregation to another the child has a proper place in the new school. The future of Judaism in my opinion depends upon the growing attachment to the Synagogue. A detached communal school which has no relationship to a Synagogue or Congregation and whereby the child forms no Jewish social contacts is in the last analysis a purely cultural undertaking, and while undoubtedly it has value it is not the kind of value which justifies the sacrifices that parents, and for that matter children, are called upon to maintain.

I seem to have got in the habit of writing you long letters in these days and I hope you will forgive me. [W]

1. A survey of the Jews of greater New York taken in the years 1927–29.

TO LOUIS MARSHALL, NEW YORK CITY

April 18, 1929

I want to return to the subject of the Yemenites about which I wrote a letter to Mr. [Harry] Schneiderman some days ago. Since that time I have met Mr. R. D. Kesselman,[1] of Jerusalem, a certified accountant who has been spending nearly three months in Aden in order to straighten out some business affairs there. A good number of Yemenite Jews have trickled into Aden, and moreover he had many opportunities of getting information as to conditions in Yemen. He confirmed the statement made to me by Mr. Jack Mosseri[2] of Cairo that the only European power that would have any influence with Iman[3] [*sic*] was Italy, and that he did not think that the Soviet arrangement was a real thing. He told me furthermore that Iman would not permit European or American businessmen, or railroad people, or even scientific people to come in as he was very suspicious and believed his own independence depended upon keeping the world at arm's length. Mr. Kesselman suggested that the only way to get into Yemen would be through a medical mission. Tuberculosis and trachoma were the scourges of the country and he thought that Iman would not only receive but welcome a medical mission of three men who should preferably be Americans, and who might quite well be Jews, and that this would form the opening wedge for a better treatment of the Jews in Aden. Of course it is a question whether such men can be found, and I fear that it would be necessary that they should be able to speak Arabic.

I have discussed this with Mr. [Felix M.] Warburg and Dr. [Judah L.] Magnes and they both think that it is a good idea. No one seems to think here that Iman would be moved by any political pressure. There has been talk among sympathizers of the Yemenites of bringing the matter before the League of Nations, but the Iman is not a member of the League of Nations, and I do not think anything would be accomplished in that way.

As for the treatment and conditions of the Yemenites, it does not seem to be exaggerated, and in addition to the degradations which they constantly have to endure it has become a custom to seize the orphan boys and girls and forcibly convert them to Islam.

Mr. Kesselman tells me that the number of Jews in Yemen does not exceed 25,000 of whom the majority, about 15,000 are in the City of Sannaa, and the rest scattered in about six or seven places. There are about thirty merchants among the Jews of Yemen. The richest of them is worth about £7,000. They are particularly in need of this medical help of which I spoke and of a trade school. The Jews in Aden number about 5,000 and one of them, a certain Menachem, has a business valued at about £2,000,000. It was the books of this business that Kesselman went down to straighten out. He further tells me that he is the only man of considerable means and does all the Jewish charity that is done in Aden and for the Yemenites. . . . [W]

1. Robert D. Kesselman (1862–1942), accountant and American Zionist leader; in 1920 moved to Jerusalem and set up an accounting firm there.
2. Jack Mosseri (1884–1939), Jewish communal leader in Egypt.
3. The imam of Yemen, Mahmud Yahya b. Hamid al-Din (1863–1948), ruled from 1904 to 1948. During that time, the conditions under which Yemenite Jews lived grew harsher as the imam strictly enforced the onerous regulations for religious minorities in a Muslim state contained in the so-called Pact of Omar.

In 1929, Adler returned to Palestine and toured the country, experiencing first hand the progress attained by the Yishuv *in the period of the Mandate. He had little inkling of the troubles which were to come and which were to involve him greatly.*

TO JAMES A. MONTGOMERY,[1] PHILADELPHIA

June 7, 1929

I returned two days ago and am very anxious to have a talk with you about my experiences in Palestine,[2] but in these busy times at the end of the term it may be a week or ten days before we can meet and so I want to let you have my first impression of the School in Jerusalem. The building is a good and substantial one and the grounds are very charming. The fact that Professor Albright[3] was taking his students off on his annual archaeological trip and his willingness to let the Warburg families and ourselves take over the house added immeasurably to the pleasure of our stay in Jerusalem. Incidentally it made us feel at home because the ladies had all the pleasures of housekeeping and we reaped the advantage.

I think more than ever of Albright and believe that he is going to be a great force at Johns Hopkins and will add to our group of oriental students in this country. No one of us has had his experience of the Orient, both for the life there and as an archaeologist and I think that he will vivify us whenever we meet.

Moreover, Dr. Albright has made for himself an exceptional position in Jerusalem. He is respected and beloved by all classes and kinds of people, and even from the political point of view adds immeasurably to American prestige in the Holy Land. Many people came to me and deplored the fact that he was leaving but I explained to them that it was part of our policy not to keep a man there permanently, and I may say to you privately that I think the double task of scientific work and administration has weighed very heavily upon Doctor Albright and that it is necessary even for his health that he should now withdraw into more or less academic seclusion. This does not mean that we should give him up as a working archaeologist and I hope that when the time comes the Johns Hopkins authorities will enable him from time to time to go back to Palestine and continue work there.

Now I am going to make a complaint and I do not want you to think that it is in any way personal with me because we lived in comparative luxury, but I feel that we ought never again permit a director to work under the handicaps which Albright has suffered. There is one male servant about the house, an

Arab, Shukri by name. He is also the messenger and general factotum. If he happens to be absent and big bales or trunks are delivered the director hustles them about. He is his own typewriter and secretary and he is also the librarian. In other words, we have permitted the Institution, or let us say the American public has permitted the Institution, to go along in something that almost approaches penury. I believe in economy but there it is carried too far. A comparatively small sum of money would at least put the director beyond menial work. His wife is the working housekeeper. I do not know whether we have the right to demand that either. I want to assure you that they did not make complaints but it was very patent to my eye during the few days that I came there before the others came and while the students were still there how much of the time of these two good people went into the merest housekeeping.

The allowance for the library is so small that they cannot afford to subscribe regularly for the magazines in the oriental field and they get the exchanges of the Journal of the American Oriental Society and I believe the Society of Biblical Literature. The editors of these two journals in America no doubt peruse these journals and send them at their convenience and in several cases I found that the magazines were nine months back. Surely this ought not to be permitted especially as it involves all the students who come there eager for work.

The field for archaeological work in Palestine, as you know, is almost immeasurable and the American School hardly gets a look-in for lack of funds. Of the advantages of the School to a professor or to an advanced student I need not tell you. He can learn Arabic and Hebrew at first hand. He will understand his Bible as he never understood it before. The opportunity to study the mixture of languages and peoples in Palestine surpasses in advantage all the best books on ethnology. We have not enough fellowships. As you know we have no funds for the publications of any monumental research. Altogether I almost felt, while I was there, that we never had a right to put up this School unless we had within us the power to get the means adequately to support it.

You probably know these things because you were there in 1914 but then the situation was not as difficult as now because there was not the building to keep up and there was not such keen competition in the matter of archaeological work.

Many things interested me in Palestine and I am afraid that my visit there has brought me to many new obligations, but I should not rest content if I did not say this to you and urge that new steps be taken to secure a respectable endowment or fund for up-keep and to assure you that I will second your efforts in any way in my power. [W]

1. James Alan Montgomery (1866–1949), professor of Semitic languages at the University of Pennsylvania.
2. See *IHCD*, pp. 360ff.
3. William Foxwell Albright (1891–1971), biblical archaeologist; professor of Semitics at Johns Hopkins University; director of the American School of Oriental Research in Jerusalem, 1920–29, 1933–36.

TO ALEXANDER MARX

Philadelphia, June 10, 1929

For quite a number of years there have been missing from the library of Dropsie College the Geniza fragments of which I enclose you a list. The numbers on this list are, of course, the numbers in Halper's Catalog.[1] I would be very much obliged to you if you would ransack your memory or have someone examine the manuscript collection of the Seminary library, if possible, to determine whether any or all of these had been loaned to any member of the staff of the Seminary for their work on Geniza fragments. I am prompted to do this as I have recently received a request for photostats from these missing numbers and could neither find them nor find any record of the year. My dear friend, Dr. Halper, who was in charge of the manuscripts, was not accustomed to keep records, as far as Dr. Reider[2] knows, and I am quite sure that if any of these things turn up in your collection you will let me have them.

I am moved to this suggestion because there was a manuscript of the Pentateuch with Haftaroth which was the gift to the Dropsie College of Judge [Mayer] Sulzberger. Dr. [Max L.] Margolis has several times called for this, but it could not be found. Dr. Reider tells me that at a recent visit to the manuscripts of the collection of the Seminary he saw this copy marked with the label of the Dropsie College. Do, please, good Professor Marx, let us have our manuscripts back unless they are in actual use by some student at the moment and even then do not keep them too long. You have so many and we have so few. [JTS]

1. Benzion Halper (1884–1924), Semitic scholar; taught at the Jewish Theological Seminary and Dropsie College; editor of the Jewish Publication Society, 1916–24; published the *Descriptive Catalogue of Geniza Fragments in Philadelphia* (1924).
2. Joseph Reider (1884–1960), librarian and professor of biblical philology at Dropsie College.

In the autumn of 1929 civil disorder spread throughout Palestine, preceded by several months of disputes between Jews and Arabs over the Jewish right to pray at the Western Wall. Beyond the immediate consequences of the disorders, Jewish leaders had to reassess the situation of the Jewish community in Palestine.

TO FELIX M. WARBURG, NEW YORK CITY

September 3, 1929

I just sent you a wire as follows, which I hope reached you:

WELCOME TO YOU AND CAROLA   AM WRITING YOU ABOUT CORRESPOND-
ENCE WITH WASHINGTON   FAIRLY BUT NOT OVERLY SATISFACTORY   IF YOU
CALLING MEETING THURSDAY OR FRIDAY AND NEED ME WILL COME OVER

There has been a good deal of division of counsels here as you may imagine. When we returned on Tuesday night we found that there had been an excited meeting the previous Thursday night and a Committee, of which Jonah Goldstein[1] was a member, took a night train and went down and saw Mr. Stimson[2] and the President.[3] They both expressed sympathy and said they could not do anything by way of a warship. As you know from radio messages, I had a meeting of the Executive Committee of the American Jewish Committee on Wednesday morning, August 28, and I still felt that for moral effect we ought to make another effort with the President, but my colleagues were only willing to do this if you approved as they thought you, having been in London, would know the situation best. Your reply, which was transmitted through Lewis Strauss, came at a time when the situation seemed better in hand and Lewis thought, and I agreed with him, that nothing would be gained at the moment by pressing the matter.

. . . The Emergency Fund seems to be meeting a ready response. Of course there is difficulty in our not being able to indicate the amount required because you know how people are. Jimmy Becker called me up from Chicago yesterday and wanted my own view as to what people should be asked to give. [David] Brown has given out a statement that for five days we will send $50,000 a day and I suppose this will be made good. It seems to me, if he seeks your counsel, it would be advisable that those remittances should stop until we get word from [Frederick H.] Kisch as to further news. I do not think it is easy to spend that much in a few days in Palestine.

As to the general situation, it requires thought and not hysterical action. I saw [Chaim] Weizmann's defiance that every ship should carry our pioneers, and Lord Melchett's action through Frieda. Whether this is sound does, it seems to me, require a little thought. If one can forget the brutalities and bloodshed, one must admit that the Arabs have been entirely consistent in their opposition to the Balfour Declaration ever since it was announced. The White Paper[4] was supposed to have brought the so-called "National Home" within such limits as would meet this criticism, namely, that Palestine was not to be as Jewish as England was British but that a National Home for the Jewish people must be built up in Palestine. The Grand Mufti[5] and some of the leading families in Palestine are bad actors and have determined to get control of the country. I think that they have been emboldened by the policy of the labor Ministry in Egypt, taking the withdrawal of the regiments from Cairo and Alexandria, as a sign of weakness. It seems to me obviously impossible to establish any kind of a beautiful and peaceful national, or any other home if it has to be with British guns, and that after a commission has investigated and all that is over, somehow, somewhere the future of the Jewish settlement in Palestine depends upon an understanding with the Arabs, repugnant as this might seem at the present moment.

I have the feeling that the impartial British Commission that is being sent out will find things to criticize also in the Jewish attitude. One thing is certain—the Jewish Agency should never allow Palestine to be denuded of all its leading officials. Neither congresses nor the gathering of funds will administer a country or keep the excitable elements in check. Two or three of the executives should always be on the ground no matter what time of the year. [W]

1. Jonah Goldstein (b. 1886), New York jurist and communal leader.
2. Henry Lewis Stimson (1867–1950), U.S. secretary of state, 1929–33.
3. Herbert Hoover.
4. White Paper issued in May 1922 by Winston Spencer Churchill (1874–1965), then colonial secretary, which, while reaffirming the Balfour Declaration, assured the Arabs that Palestine would not become wholly Jewish and that Jewish immigration would be limited to the economic absorptive capacity of the country. At about the same time Churchill separated Transjordan from Palestine and gave it to Emir (later King) Abdullah (1882–1951).
5. Haj Amin al-Husseini (1893–1974), Grand Mufti (religious leader) of Jerusalem; organizer of the Palestine riots in 1929 and 1936.

Louis Marshall, leader of American Jewry, architect of the "Pact of Glory" that resulted in the enlargement of the Jewish Agency, died in Switzerland on September 11, 1929. He died of a sudden illness mere days after the establishment of the enlarged

Jewish Agency. With his death, Adler lost a close friend and his closest collaborator on the Committee. The leadership of the American Jewish Committee now passed to Adler.

TO SAMSON LACHMAN,[1] NEW YORK CITY

September 17, 1929

In the last week I have often been thinking of you. I know that there is no one to whom Mr. [Louis] Marshall's death is a greater grief or loss than to you and I extend you my heartfelt sympathy.

I know that it will be a consoling thought to you, excepting for his last brief illness, that our friend was extremely well. We sailed on the 2nd of August on the Majestic, he was in excellent spirits and health all the way over. During the formation of the Jewish Agency meeting and Zurich he was never more forceful and at the same time suave and diplomatic. It was a marvel to all the Europeans there that a man past seventy could have this wonderful vigor and clear resonant voice. He was very happy over the result. The meeting concluded on the evening of the 14th of August and on the 15th he mostly spent sitting about, resting and talking. That very night, Thursday, the 15th, he came over to a group of us at a table in the corner of the lobby of the Hotel and sat up until quarter past eleven, telling stories and enjoying stories. That night he was taken ill but we knew nothing about it. Mr. [Jacob] Billikopf, who was in the next room, was awakened by him but they both thought that it was an ordinary attack of indigestion and it was not until noon that the Doctors were summoned. There were of our party Emanuel Libman[2] of New York and Solomon Solis-Cohen of Philadelphia, probably the two most eminent diagnosticians in their respective cities. It did not take them many hours to find out that there was something very wrong and at first they suspected an abscess on the gall bladder, with possible involving of the pancreas. They at once made arrangements for an operation, got nurses and a local physician who could write prescriptions. However, in the course of a couple of days his temperature vanished and he seemed very much better. On the 19th of August, while I was at a University meeting the Doctor telephoned me that Mr. Marshall had no temperature and wanted to see me. I went over, sat at his bedside, he grumbled a bit about being kept in bed, said that it was the first time in his life that he had been bothered with nurses, and I told him that his physicians had said that while he had been a very poor lawyer he had been less a good patient, at which he laughed and quoted some of the things his Mother used to say to him in like circumstances. I left with a heavy heart but still with a sort of feeling that his vigorous constitution would somehow pull him through. Two days out on the ship Doctor Libman radioed me "marked improvement" and that gave me very great hope, but two days later there was another radio about the necessity of another operation, and the rest you know from the newspapers.

I am saying this to you because I want you to feel assured that Mr. Marshall had the best possible treatment and that nothing more could have been done for him anywhere than was done for him in Zurich. Doctor and Mrs. [Judah L.] Magnes were there, as you know, James [Marshall] sailed over, his sister, Mrs. Rosenberg, who was only four hours away, came to Zurich. Even after the first operation, as Mrs. Rosenberg wrote to his other sister, Mrs. Leopold, he was in good spirits and asked whether it was really his gall bladder. When he was told no he said "I am sorry, I should like to have given my whole gall for Palestine."

I thought you might want to know this. [W]

1. Samson Lachman (1855–1931), New York jurist and communal worker.
2. Emanuel Libman (1872–1946), New York physician; member of the Board of Governors of the Hebrew University, 1925–46.

TO FELIX M. WARBURG, NEW YORK CITY

October 15, 1929

. . . I do not like the reports of this morning in the [*New York*] *Times.* Of course I do not know the exact reason for the High Commissioner's[1] forbidding of the blowing of the Shofar to end the Yom Kippur Service at the Wall, though I can imagine that in the present nervous state he feared that it might attract a crowd and cause trouble. On the other hand, if this was the reason, as it undoubtedly was, and he considered it valid, I do not like Rabbi Kook's[2] form of protest—no doubt agreed to by all the local Jewish politicians—that they would obey but no such limitation had been put upon them even in the middle ages. If the High Commissioner is trying to prevent them from being killed it seems to be unfair that they should make faces about it. [W]

1. Sir John Herbert Chancellor (1870–1952).
2. Abraham Isaac Kook (1865–1935), Ashkenazic chief rabbi of Palestine.

TO LUCRETIA E. EVANS,[1] CHARLESTOWN, NEW HAMPSHIRE

October 22, 1929

I am wondering whether you object to hearing from me on a typewriter. I am sure you can read my typewriter better than you can read me. You wrote to Mrs. Adler in the autumn and I said that I wanted to answer you because it was such a long time since I had written to you.

I thank you for your sympathetic remarks about Palestine. I do not think that all the Arabs are bad, in fact it must be quite obvious on reflection that the uprisings were premeditated by a political leader and that only a comparatively small section of the Arabs was engaged in it. At all events I had the opportunity of seeing Mr. Ramsay MacDonald[2] while he was in this country and he gives an assurance of an impartial inquiry into the causes of the trouble and steps to prevent any outbreaks in the future. The trouble really arose because everybody was lulled into security. I have said several times that we went about the country as peacefully, as quietly as though we had been in a New England village. We had no guard. We sat down at Arab villages and ate our luncheon and altogether this is not in my opinion a rising from the people.

Otherwise we all continue about the same. Mrs. Adler, I am happy to say, is in better health than she has been for a good many years. Sarah is still a very tall, thin girl, with her ups and downs, largely I think because she is too thin and she is doing some very nice literary work for me, and altogether I consider her a satisfactory daughter.

I am busier than ever and seem to stand it pretty well. I rarely get back to Washington anymore though I am expecting to go down within a few weeks. I was there about a year ago. It was a very changed town, quite overgrown and much of the spirit of repose has gone out of it.

I hope you will be passing a comfortable autumn and winter and am, with warmest regards from all of us. [W]

1. Lucretia E. Evans (1847–1937), former housekeeper of Samuel P. Langley.
2. Ramsay MacDonald (1866–1937), British Labour Party leader; prime minister, 1924–26, 1929–31, 1931–35.

TO RACIE ADLER

October 29, 1929

Felix [M. Warburg] and I talked mostly [Jewish] "Agency"—I read dozens of telegrams and letters which arrived since last week—not all necessary. Hexter[1] does not go for a week. The Goldsteins are coming back. No news yet from [Judah L.] Magnes from Palestine. Remind me to tell you the real story of Weizmann and Brandeis. Felix and Frieda are planning their spring trip to Palestine. I do not think the pictures will go to the National Gallery. Much talk about stocks—more by the women than the men.[2] Freddie said at Lehmans everybody was saying oi, oi, oi, so he got tired of it and went over to Morgan's where young Morgan[3] and young Lamont[4] were saying the same thing with an American accent. [W]

1. Maurice B. Hexter (b. 1891), social worker; member of the Jewish Agency Executive, 1929–38.
2. The stock market had crashed on October 24.
3. John P. Morgan, Jr. (1867–1943).
4. Thomas S. Lamont (1899–1967), partner in firm of J. P. Morgan.

TO FELIX M. WARBURG, NEW YORK CITY

November 15, 1929

I have not replied sooner to your letter of the 12th, enclosing copies of your cable to Lord Melchett and of their reply because I had expected to see you.

In effect, you are told that all diplomatic matters (and probably they mean a good many others) must emanate from London and that everyone else is to keep hands off. Moreover, the sentence "Committee feels strongly that for no consideration whatsoever must fundamental on which our work is based be jeopardized" can only mean that the gentlemen in London are willing to sacrifice every Jewish life in Palestine and all the property for the Balfour Declaration. If they do not mean that then they ought study the English language.

What seems to me important both for the work and to prevent mis-understandings is an exact interpretation of the duties and limitations of the Administrative Committee. I had supposed that the Administrative Committee had full power to act for the Council between meetings and hence all acts should clear through you, as Chairman, either to the Executives in Palestine or to any standing on special Committees of the Agency. You may delegate certain matters to men in London or Jerusalem if you see fit but my theory of the working of the machinery is as I have described above.

The sooner this is settled, the better, but it ought be done when [Chaim] Weizmann is here rather than through correspondence. [W]

TO JAMES A. MONTGOMERY, PHILADELPHIA

December 2, 1929

I am in receipt of your letter of November 23rd, enclosing statement and correspondence concerning a happening in connection with the [American] School [of Oriental Research] in Jerusalem in the latter part of August, 1929. I note your statement that you "wish at once to acquaint the Jewish members of our Board of Trustees with these documents." Let me say, at the outset, that the fact that I am an adherent of Judaism has never entered into my thinking or action as a Trustee of the Schools. These I regard as scientific institutions—interesting to students of theology but equally interesting to all students of the civilizations of the Near East. May I now proceed to an analysis of the documents and maybe to some discursive remarks concerning them?

The School, as stated, is in a strongly Arab neighborhood. Most, if not all of the neighboring Arab houses, belong to wealthy and cultivated people who freely intermingle with Jews and Christians. In all likelihood, no danger was to be apprehended from them, though possibly from their servants. The neighboring hospital was not a public institution, but the private hospital of a Jewish physician, Doctor Danziger. The statement that shots had been fired from it or that reports had been heard that shots had been fired from it do not tally with my information that before the happenings on August 23 or thereabouts several Arabs had removed their wives who were patients in the hospital and that this led to a justifiable apprehension that the hospital was to be attacked. Let me add parenthetically that Doctor Danziger has sent his family to Hamburg and has himself removed to Tel-Aviv. He was a highly scientific and cultured gentleman. His removal is a distinct loss to Jerusalem.

There is one phrase in Director McCown's[1] letter which I wish to call to your notice: "Indeed it seems to me that, in view of our request for tax exemption, we must beware of appearing to become a boarding-house open to all comers."

This strikes me as a very cold blooded statement to have been written on August 29th. When people are being killed and maimed and one or two in their fright seek shelter, one would imagine that questions of tax exemption would not come into consideration. Director McCown then proceeds: "The more important consideration, of course, was that the School cannot afford to be thought a Jewish institution, as might have been the case should it become known that all the people staying here were Jews. For Dr. and Mrs. Rothman I felt that everything should be risked, since they were here by right, but I did not feel like adding to the danger to them and to the School by admitting others who had no claim upon the institution." That is a valid consideration to a man who felt that way in an emergency. One can hardly suppose, however, that there was any danger of the School being considered a Jewish institution. Its Director for the past ten years was a Christian, its name is well known and the American flag would have advertised its character had the national emblem been flown. Mr. Levy[2] did not, I believe, cable the story to the *New York Times,* nor has any newspaper carried it to my knowledge.

Director McCown concludes his statement: "In any case it seems to me that I took the right course" and in this you and Doctor Barton[3] concur. If by right is meant that he believed that he was acting in defense of the property of the School, of himself and his family and of the people who were already there, then I agree, but I express the opinion he acted in fright just as Mr. Brawley acted in fright in seeking admission for his family to the School.

Let me say that I do not follow the reasoning of Professor Barton and yourself: "inasmuch as there was no immediate danger." This you can say after the event—but if there was no immediate danger to the Brawley family there was no immediate danger to the School either. You further say that the persons seeking refuge "had no claim upon our hospitality." Does one speak of hospitality when people consider their lives in danger?

Let me now come to Director McCown's letter to you of November 2nd. I think Doctor [Judah L.] Magnes might very well have abstained from taking any hand in the matter. It was over, the Brawleys' lives were saved, the McCowns were saved, the Rothmans were saved and the School was saved. Certainly as Chancellor of the [Hebrew] University, Doctor Magnes had no concern with the matter, although his note of October 25th is not included in the correspondence.

Director McCown, in the course of his letter of November 2nd, writes speaking of Doctor Magnes: "His letters suggest that he thinks the School is a subsidiary of the Jewish University." Certainly there is nothing in the letter of Doctor Magnes which is quoted which lends color to such a suggestion.

There is yet one other statement in Doctor McCown's letter of November 2nd upon which I would like to comment: After speaking of the Rothmans (Doctor Rothman, I believe, is a member of the Faculty of the Hebrew Union College), he says: "Not being Zionists, they can make few Jewish friends." A statement like this certainly shows lack of understanding of the situation. Doctor Magnes is not a Zionist, as his statement at the opening of the Hebrew University showed; moreover, he is a graduate of this same Hebrew Union College and was once in charge of its Library. I am not a Zionist and I had no difficulty in meeting all the people I wanted to. Moreover, many of the Orthodox Jews in Jerusalem are not Zionists.

All this, by the way, to indicate that Doctor McCown has not yet got hold of the situation.

Possibly Doctor Magnes' interference was dictated by other considerations. He is an American, a Californian by birth. Doctor McCown is also, I believe, from California. Maybe Doctor Magnes was shocked that a man from his native state was not willing to take a risk to shelter fellow-beings— some of them Americans—who believed their lives in imminent danger.

Let me now conclude my discussion of this painful subject: I think the Trustees of the School should lay down definite regulations with regard to its use for dormitory purposes—first, for Director and staff; second, for students; third, the Trustees of the School when visiting Jerusalem; fourth, for Faculty and Trustees of affiliated institutions when visiting Jerusalem, always in the order mentioned. If this is followed and no deviations permitted, the Director will have a definite rule. It is true that in the past it was most desirable to fill up the building as the revenues were imperatively needed, but if the Rockefeller money comes, that source of income will obviate the necessity of renting out rooms as has been done occasionally—and I believe quite infrequently in the past. No rules, however, made 4000 miles away can take the place of the judgment of the Director on the spot in the case of an emergency or catastrophe. So much must always be left to the discretion and humanity of the officer in charge.

It is my opinion that the Trustees should take no action in the matter and unless it is brought up again the papers should be filed. I have no objection to your sending a copy of this letter to Doctor McCown if you see fit or to Doctor Magnes if he brings the matter to your attention. I am not aware of his intention to come to America soon. [W]

1. Chester Charlton McCown (1877–1958), biblical scholar; director of the Palestine Institute, Pacific School of Religion.
2. Joseph M. Levy (1901–65), *New York Times* correspondent in Palestine.
3. George A. Barton (1859–1942), professor of Semitics at the University of Pennsylvania.

TO NORMAN BENTWICH, JERUSALEM

January 7, 1930

. . . I have refrained so far from comment on the situation in Palestine, partly because I thought there was too much comment and partly because having been one of the Committee that met the Prime Minister[1] when he was in America, he indicated that in all fairness since the situation in Palestine was in the hands of a Commission of Inquiry and therefore subjudice, that the report of the Commission should be awaited. I have always believed that the way could be found if the way were earnestly sought and on the Jewish side it seemed to me that there was some provocation—I have never quite been able to reconcile myself to the conditions involved in the attitude toward the exclusion of Arab labor, which naturally is bound to bring about reprisals, and in addition there has been a certain amount of Jewish swagger which ought to be eliminated.

On the other hand, I naturally do not agree with the Arab attitude as expressed by the Moslem Consul [sic], with, I fear, the Christian Arabs in the background willing to egg on their Moslem friends but not brave enough to come out in the open. . . . [D]

1. Ramsay MacDonald.

One of the main areas of contention between Jews and Arabs in Palestine in 1929 concerned the right of Jews to pray at the Western ("Wailing") Wall of the Temple Mount in Jerusalem. Adler was called upon to present the Jewish Agency's case before a commission of the League of Nations.

TO LOUIS B. NAMIER,[1] LONDON

January 30, 1930

I am in receipt of your letter of January 21 concerning the question of representing the [Jewish] Agency before the Commission[2] to decide the question of the Wailing Wall. The request, originally conveyed by Doctor [Chaim] Weizmann through Mr. [Felix M.] Warburg, places upon me a great responsibility which I am far from anxious to have, but which I do not feel that I have a right to shirk if it is the deliberate judgment of everybody concerned that I am the person to undertake the task.

The question of time has something to do with it. I could not very well leave America until after the 17th of March without interfering with very important public obligations which I have taken upon myself and which are already arranged for. The longer the time for gathering and digesting material the better, but if the arrangement, which I understand is now under consideration, of a meeting of the Administration Committee in London toward the end of March goes through and the hearings with regard to the Wailing Wall could follow thereon that would be the most convenient for me. I am quite aware that you cannot arrange such things and if the hearings on the Wailing Wall were much later in the year then I could not attend the meeting of the Administration Committee, much as I should like to do so.

However, recognizing the urgency of the matter I am proceeding day by day in the gathering of material. Of the memoranda of which you speak I have but numbers 1 and 2, the latter from the file of the Zionist Organization in New York which has been furnished to me. It will therefore be necessary for me to have the following:

3. The Kotel Maaravi [Western Wall] question from the British Occupation till 1928 (L. J. Stein,[3] 21.9.29).

4. The Kotel Maaravi Question, 1928–1929 (L. J. Stein, 22.9.29).

5. Notes on the Buraq Legend[4] prepared by members of the staff of the Hebrew University (19.11.29).

and I am asking Mr. Warburg's Office to cable somewhat as follows:

SEND ADLER NUMBERS THREE FOUR FIVE

I have other material beside that of which you speak—the article of Doctor Luncz[5] which appeared in *Yerushelaim,* volume 10, 1913, copiously cited by Doctor [Adolph] Büchler, a much longer article in Hebrew in *Zion,* volume 3, Jerusalem, 1929,[6] and a pamphlet which I have just received from Doctor Alfred Wiener,[7] of Berlin, *Juden Und Araber in Palestine* [sic], containing a chapter on the Wailing Wall.

In the meantime, and while Mr. Warburg was away on a short vacation, his office, at my request, undertook certain steps, cabling to Jerusalem for any exact drawings of the Wall and its surroundings in existence, and these I understand were mailed several days ago. Also, the enclosed cable was sent to London on January 21 and later a cable to Doctor Weizmann requesting that inquiry be made of Doctor Gotthold Weil,[8] of Berlin, whether he could furnish material from Turkish or Arabic sources. Possibly, therefore, all these matters are being attended to. I hope they are.

May I suggest that if you come across material which you think will be helpful it will be worth while to have copies made and forwarded to me at once (even at the risk of duplicating material in my hands) so that ten days or so would not be lost in getting the material in my hands through cable requests.

I judge from correspondence and memoranda that your office has in its possession certain photographs indicating the usage at the Wall and as these might prove very valuable I would ask that you have copies of these photographs made and sent to me, retaining the originals yourselves.

It would, of course, be important to ascertain at as early a date as possible in what language or languages the material must be presented to the Commission. I assume that coming as it would from the Agency the original should be in English, but if it were possible for me to know whether a French copy were required I might have that prepared almost concurrently with the English to avoid any waste of time at the meeting of the Commission itself.

I have written this letter in Philadelphia and am forwarding it to Mr. Warburg to New York so that if it comes to you you will know that he is apprised of the correspondence and that it goes forward with his approval. [W]

1. Sir Louis B. Namier (1888–1960), English Zionist; an organizer of the Jewish Agency.
2. The outcome of Adler's effort was the *Memorandum on the Western Wall, Prepared for the Special Commission of the League of Nations on Behalf of the Jewish Agency for Palestine* (Philadelphia, 1930), which outlined the argument for Jewish rights at the Wall. A League commission was never sent to Palestine. Instead, the League's Permanent Mandates Commission held an extraordinary session at which the Mandatory Power's handling of the disturbances was examined and criticized.
3. Leonard Jacques Stein (1887–1973), British lawyer and Zionist historian; political secretary of the Zionist Organization, 1920–29.
4. According to Muslim tradition, based on the chapter "Night Journey" in the Koran, when Muhammad journeyed from the mosque of Mecca to the "farther temple" (the al-Aska mosque in Jerusalem) he rode on his winged steed al-Burak ("Lightning"). He left his horse in the narrow street of the Western Wall, which thereby got its Arabic name, *Hosh al-Burak,* Courtyard of al-Burak. The steps leading to the Dome of the Rock from the eastern side are called *Daraj al-Burak,* Stairs of al-Burak. The words of the chapter "Night Journey" are inscribed on the exterior of the Dome of the Rock.
5. Abraham Moses Luncz (1854–1918), author and editor of works on the geography and history of Palestine.
6. Isaac Ezekiel Yahuda, "The Kotel Maaravi," *Zion* o.s. 3 (1929).
7. Alfred Wiener (1885–1964), secretary-general of the German-Jewish Centralverein. His book was published in Berlin in 1929.
8. Gotthold Weil (1882–1960), Arabist; subsequently became professor of Turkish studies at the Hebrew University, 1935–52, and head of the National and University Library, 1935–46.

TO CHAIM WEIZMANN, LONDON

February 12, 1930

I am enclosing you copy of a cable which I have just forwarded. I have already got together a great body of material with regard to the Western Wall. The Zionist Organization of America has placed their file at my disposal and I have received all the memoranda requested by cable from the office in London. I have also studied all the existing memoranda and have had many books searched. I hope within a short time, maybe a week or ten days at most, to sit down and digest it and form a conclusion as to what I think can and cannot be claimed.

I am expecting to come over to the meeting of the Administrative

Committee with Mr. [Felix M.] Warburg and by that time will use every endeavor to have this material in reasonable shape, though possibly it will not be ready for final presentation, unless I get an urgent cable that it must be.

What seems to me necessary is that whatever conclusions I come to should be laid before some Committee and approved as the claim to be made on behalf of the Agency. I say this because in the letter of Colonel [Frederick H.] Kisch of January 21, addressed to the Executive in London, copy of which was forwarded to me through Mr. Warburg's office, it would appear that it is the expectation that this Commission of Three of the League of Nations will sit in Jerusalem and that various groups, the Vaadleumi,[1] the Rabbinate, etc. are to appear before them. Now I think you know that I do not want too much responsibility and that I am a democrat to the bone, but if a Commission of the League of Nations is expected to hear testimony of various bodies and claims based upon this testimony which may vary we may get no report or a hung jury.

Then while it is a minor matter, still I hope you will not mind my calling your attention to the fact that as late as January 21 the Executives in Jerusalem stated that they would like to see Doctor [Adolph] Büchler's memorandum. It is rather astonishing to me that they did not have this memorandum long ago. It was prepared in April, 1929 and we have had copies here at least since November.

Even before I made up my mind whether I could undertake the responsibility of representing the Agency before this Commission I commenced to gather the material and instead of appointing Committees, as Colonel Kisch suggests, I discussed the matter with both Faculties of the Dropsie College and the Jewish Theological Seminary, and requested each man to take up a certain line. I did not get much material from this but did get some.

Colonel Kisch also asks that I transmit the material I have collected to Jerusalem. This is not what I understood when I received the request to undertake to represent the Agency before the Commission.

I assumed that I was to gather material, prepare a memorandum, draw some conclusions and then submit them to whatever was the authorized body of the Agency to determine whether this was the claim which the Agency would finally put forward. I did not expect that either I or any other one person should determine this but I felt that it was my duty to make an impartial study of everything that I could get hold of and then draw a conclusion which seemed to me sound and justifiable.

As for the portion of the letter in which he suggests that someone should undertake research in the British Museum, etc., that I presume is being attended to or has been attended to in London.

What I particularly would like to know about is the statement number 4:

It is also worth mentioning that Government circles here have been very greatly impressed by the fact, only recently disclosed to them, that the authenticated record left by "saint" Jerome[2] included a reference to Jewish observances at the Western Wall.

Jerome has been quoted by travellers and writers on Palestine for upwards of fifty or sixty years. In a Hebrew article published in Jerusalem about six or seven months ago, and recently reprinted, there is a reference to Jerome which says that Jerome refers to the Temple Mount. Colonel Kisch, you see, says that he refers to the Western Wall. There is a very great collection of the Church Fathers edited by Migne,[3] Paris, 1884, and I have diligently examined the reference to Jerome on page 1354, line 14, which is the commentary Zephaniah-15, and I see no statement either about the Western Wall or the Temple Mount, but simply the indication that the Jews used to have to purchase the privilege to come to Jerusalem and pray there on the 9th of Ab.

Now I am very fearful that if I am right about Jerome and the Government in Palestine has been definitely told that Jerome mentions the Wailing Wall, and then some good Christian scholar points out that he does not, there will be an unpleasant repercussion. I am sure I do not have to labor this point.

In fine I would hope that Jerusalem, London and New York should each be knowing what the other is doing or saying and that we should not increase our difficulties on this difficult enough subject by making or supporting statements which we cannot maintain. [W]

1. Vaad Leumi—the executive branch of the elected assembly (*Assefat ha-Nivharim*) of the Palestinian Yishuv, founded in 1920 and formally recognized by the British in 1928.
2. St. Jerome (c.345–419/20), Church father; author of the Latin translation of the Hebrew Bible (Vulgate).
3. J. P. Migne (1800–75) published the texts of the major Christian writers between the years 200 and 1438 in both Greek and Latin.

Achieving peaceful relations between Jews and Arabs in Palestine was a goal shared by both Adler and Magnes. This goal, while officially adopted by the Zionists, nonetheless served to set them apart from the mainstream of opinion in an era of increasing hostility between Jews and Arabs.

TO JUDAH L. MAGNES, JERUSALEM

Philadelphia, March 5, 1930

I had been intending, ever since the middle of January when you sent me the memorandum of the Brith Shalom Society,[1] and later your pamphlet "Like all the Nations?,"[2] to write to you but I put it off when I heard about your Diary[3] which I thought would shed light on the whole situation, and this Diary I received about a week ago and have now read. I do not know that I have anything very illuminating to say to you and it would have been so much better if we could have sat far into the night months ago and had a talk. Still, for the sake of satisfying my own mind and before I go to London,[4] where I shall probably hear more or less of politics, I do feel that I owe it to you to acknowledge your goodness in letting me see all these various documents, and since you have often told me that you value my opinion let me give it to you.

I am not going to answer letters or documents or anything of the sort seriatim, but tell you how the thing shapes itself in my mind, and in doing so I am not trying to sit in judgment on you or anybody else, but maybe what I tell you will at least give you an outside and detached view.

You and I had a good many talks in years past and last year in Palestine, and I think there was one point upon which we definitely agreed, and that was that within any time that we could foresee the idea of securing a Jewish majority in Palestine was a chimera and that if a national home meant that, the idea might as well be given up. In all probability a large proportion of the leaders of the Zionist Movement recognize the fact too but, having through a long period of years deluded their followers with the expectation of another result, were unwilling to acknowledge publicly what they admitted privately.

Now let me jump to an entirely different angle. I am not a pacifist, but I am a peace-loving man and for many years I hesitated about the whole Palestinian matter because I feared that a conflict was inevitable. There was nothing tangible; it was just the sort of unconscious judgment that one probably forms from a lifetime of study and observation. However, I agreed some years ago to join the [Jewish] Agency if it could be formed and in spite of the perfectly delightful impression that I got when I was in Palestine last year, and the apparent peace that prevailed throughout the country, I came away with a very uneasy feeling as to a sort of latent hostility, which at the time seemed to me to be based more upon the labor problem than anything else. I even think I recall that you, peace-loving gentleman that you are, told me that because a certain company that received the concession to lay the electric lights in Jerusalem was employing only Arab labor and no Jewish labor you, along with other Jews in Jerusalem, would boycott the company and not use their electric light. Well, a boycott is of course a preparation for war.

Early in last July, long before these troubles arose, I gave a private talk before the Rabbinical Assembly at Long Branch, of which there was a stenographic copy made, and in which these misgivings were expressed (of course I did not make any allusion to you and the boycott of the electric light).

Now let me jump and come to quite another angle. In the talks that we had in Jerusalem, after Felix [M. Warburg] had strongly urged you to come into the Agency, and even be his partner as it were, resident in Jerusalem, you gave many reasons for not coming in but the one that seemed to determine you was that you were the head of the [Hebrew] University, that it had been your constant fight to keep the University out of politics and if you went into the Agency you, as head of the University, would be in politics. Upon the whole I thought that was sound, although at least in America our great University heads do not seem to scruple on that point. But still the Hebrew University was a young and tender plant and you were not in an easy position.

Now the criticism which you have evoked has been to a considerable extent based upon this one point of having constantly and steadily refused to have anything to do with political Zionism since you have been in Palestine, and having declined to go into the Agency because of the University you nevertheless did go in, and to that extent did not stay upon the course that you had marked out for yourself. I know, and I see from the Diary, that you were under great stress and that in a way the thing was forced upon you, and yet whatever the surrounding circumstances, the very fact that you have laid great stress upon the extreme privacy of this Diary shows that you will not be in position to justify yourself against this criticism.

Let me take up another thing. I want you to feel that I am not one of those who criticize the speech that you made at the opening of the University.[5] This you were entitled to do and I think that if you had not done it people would have said that you were cowardly. No head of the University could have opened it after what had taken place in the preceding months with an address on biblical archaeology or Hebrew poetry. After all, a University is not a dead thing and it must have some relation to the living people, and I, who have claimed so much of academic freedom for Professors, have sometimes been obliged to claim academic freedom for Presidents and even for Chancellors. But I must say that I think that the criticism was not based upon the speech but upon the negotiations which, in spite of your having carried them on privately did become known to quite a number of people in Palestine and elsewhere before they became public. Now I really think that these negotiations you should not have had in view of your whole attitude against engaging in politics and that you ought to have been strong enough to resist it even when it was in a measure thrust upon you.

As to the thing itself, I think that the Brith Shalom are on the right track. Naturally there must be something more than mere expression of the desire to have peace with the Arabs. The Jews in Palestine and elsewhere do not all seem to have been able to make peace with each other, but the thing that impressed me mostly in Palestine was the fact that, in my opinion, the Jews underrated the Arabs too much and that is an error, whether the man be a friend or a foe, because he unconsciously recognizes that he is being considered an inferior and resents it. More important I think than any detail is the creation of a state of mind by which people of different religions and different geographical origins can work side by side and respect each other without necessarily giving up their own views or ways of life. And this is an idealistic situation which, if created, could have many practical results.

Excepting a few fanatics on either side I do not suppose that anybody would differ with these general propositions nor would they question that after the riots it was necessary that such a state of mind should be created.

As far as I am able to read between the lines and in spite of all the statements that have been made the thing narrows itself down to a question of method, whether the approach should be made by the Jews to the Arabs, or by the Arabs to the Jews, or to both by the Government. I think that probably the difference between yourself and the Agency people in London was on this matter of method, and that your approach was held to weaken the Jewish position from the strategic point of view—but there was a little more than that in it because Ramsay MacDonald in the interview that he had with us in America distinctly insisted that things should stay as they were until the Shaw Commission[6] reported, and having gone into consultation with him the Jewish Agency I think was bound to remain by that. I believe myself that whenever it is possible to establish a representative Government this ought to be done. The British Government did propose this as you may recall as early as 1922 when an Order of Council was promulgated establishing a Constitution and providing for a Legislative Council of twenty-two members, twelve of whom were to be unofficial and not less than two Christians and two Jews, and there was all kinds of provision for primary and secondary elections, etc. An election was ordered, the majority of the Arab population boycotted it and in May, 1923, the High Commissioner decided to suspend the establishment of a Legislative Council. In October of the same year he made an offer to representative Arabs for the establishment of an Arab Agency similar to the Jewish Agency; this was rejected by the Arabs within twenty-four hours. And so the situation of being a sort of Crown Colony was one for which neither the English nor the Jews were responsible and the Arabs entirely responsible. How can one assume, in spite of the many talks that you had with Mr. Philby,[7] that they really changed their mind?

I suppose I have talked to you enough through the medium of my faithful secretary, and I hope you won't feel that I am trying to pass judgment upon you or doing anything more than I would do if we sat down and talked together.

I have always felt very strongly a sense of corporate responsibility to men with whom I am engaged in an enterprise and I think in the long run if we Jews are going to accomplish anything important we must all get this point of view. Self-expression is a wonderful thing. It relieves the man who gives expression to himself, but it does not always clear the surrounding atmosphere.

I suppose the people in London—in fact I know that the people in London—hold that some of us in America have been playing a double game, part and parcel of the Agency, and yet encouraging your independent action which of course you know not to be the case.

Well good-by, dear man. As I indicated above I think I have talked too much today even across this big span. . . . [M]

1. Covenant of Peace, a society founded in 1925 to encourage harmonious relations between Jews and Arabs in Palestine.
2. Published in Jerusalem, 1930.
3. See Norman Bentwich, *For Zion's Sake, a Biography of Judah L. Magnes* (Philadelphia, 1954), p. 179; Arthur A. Goren, ed., *Dissenter in Zion: From the Writings of Judah L. Magnes* (Cambridge, Mass., 1982).
4. Adler went abroad in the summer of 1930 to attend the meeting of the Administrative Committee of the Jewish Agency.
5. Published in Magnes's *Addresses by the Chancellor of the Hebrew University* (Jerusalem, 1936).
6. The Shaw Commission, appointed by British Colonial Secretary Lord Passfield (1859–1947) after the riots of 1929, concerned itself with Jewish rights at the Western Wall. Although it blamed the Arabs for the outbreak of the riots, it recommended a review of Jewish immigration policy.
7. Harry St. John Bridger Philby (1885–1960), formerly chief British representative in Transjordan; at the time an unofficial advisor to the Saudi Arabian government. See Magnes, *Like All the Nations*, pp. 33–41.

TO CHAIM WEIZMANN, LONDON

April 2, 1930

I have only now had an opportunity to glance at the Report of the Shaw Commission, and I see that the Commission lays a good deal of stress on the matter of the Wailing Wall, which occupies in the body of the Report pages 26 to 56; I shall study all this stuff carefully.

We have had several talks in the last ten days, and I have had a talk with Mr. [Pinhas] Rutenberg. I now think the case for the Wailing Wall is stronger than it seemed to be a few weeks ago. My interview with the Grand Rabbin and Dr. [Joseph H.] Hertz on Monday was entirely satisfactory; we agreed upon a brief declaration which they will get signed by the Rabbis of various countries and of different shades of thought, and I suggested that Israel Levi himself should present the declaration, but he seemed rather diffident on this point, and wanted a Committee.

I have already written you a note as to the place of the sittings of the Commission, but cannot too strongly express my opinion that it should be in Geneva.

There are certain other matters touched upon in our conversation the other day which were not finally decided, and I do not wish to take the responsibility alone; the British Government requests, for instance, that none of the Commissioners shall be Englishmen. Is it your thought that this should apply to the persons who appear before the Commission on behalf of the Jews? As I indicated to you the other day, I should like to have the assistance of a barrister and a good Arabic scholar. One of the two men I talked to you about was Dr. Billig[1] of the University. On the other hand, when the Arabic Faculty of the University submitted a memorandum with regard to the Buraq, I was told that "for obvious reasons" they had not signed the memorandum. It is therefore a question whether the University would be mixed up in this matter.

Mr. [Menahem] Ussishkin, at the meeting of the Political Commission, strongly urged that I should take David Yellin as the Arabic expert. This would satisfy the Yishub,[2] as he is the Chairman of the Committee investigating the subject in Jerusalem. This suggestion to my mind has many advantages and some difficulties. I do not know Dr. Billig himself. On the other hand, Mr. Yellin I know well. When I discussed this subject the other day with Israel Levi, he said that he thought Dr. Billig would be more desirable because he would approach any question put to him from a scientific point of view, and this, he thought, might be more useful. Mr. Rutenberg, on the other hand, strongly urges Yellin.

I assume that Dr. Jacobson[3] will be present at the hearings of the Commission if it is held in Geneva.

I find among the papers handed to me a reference to Lord Reading's[4] having addressed, on the basis of a memorandum submitted to him by Mr. Rutenberg, a communication on the subject of the Wailing Wall to the Prime Minister in 1929, but neither this Office nor Mr. Rutenberg has a copy of this communication. It is possible that he simply transmitted Mr. Rutenberg's statement, but it is also quite possible that he may have given some general advice on the subject. At all events, if Lord Reading were to give an opinion as to the presentation of the case, it would be of enormous value.

I think it is agreed that this case should not be presented as a lawyer's case; in other words I am to endeavor to establish the historical basis for the Jewish claim that for at least one thousand years they have had free access to the Wall for the purpose of prayer, but nevertheless, I should like to have legal assistance, not so much in the actual preparation of the brief, as to have someone present at the hearings to aid me in any legal points which may arise. I believe the man who would be most helpful in this matter is Mr. Sacher.[5] I have not spoken to him about it, or even intimated anything to him, but perhaps, if you approve, you would ask him to read this letter. [W]

1. Levi Billig (1897–1936), Arabist.
2. The Zionist settlement in Palestine was known as the Yishuv.
3. Victor Jacobson (1869–1935), Zionist leader; lobbyist for the Jewish Agency at the League of Nations.
4. Rufus Daniel Isaacs, Lord Reading (1860–1935), former lord chief justice, 1913–21, and viceroy of India, 1921–26.
5. Harry Sacher (1881–1971), lawyer and British Zionist leader.

TO CHAIM WEIZMANN, LONDON

May 29, 1930

I am sending you to-day, via the Europa, the Memorandum on the Wailing Wall. I have been obliged to have this put in type and printed without the opportunity for the criticism which I had hoped to get. Everything seemed to be moving so leisurely. I was waiting for more information and of course I had no idea until I received a cable on the 27th of May that the Commission was expecting to sit in Palestine, or that it was expected to sit as early as June 15th.

I ought to explain that I have been under rather severe handicaps for the last three weeks or so, because I had sinus trouble which also affected my throat so that only yesterday for the first time was I able to speak on the telephone, and I have had other ailments which prevented me from walking. Hence I have been virtually a prisoner.

As soon as the cable came announcing the meeting in Jerusalem on June 15th, I had a consultation with several physicians, who told me that it would be absolutely impossible for me to start for Europe or Palestine or anywhere else for the present time. I thus have no recourse but to send in the Memorandum. I am sending several copies to Mr. [Louis B.] Namier and I think he may want to show it to Doctor [Selig] Brodetsky and also to Doctor Cecil Roth, who has been most helpful.

I am well aware of the shortcomings of the Memorandum and I anticipate criticism, but that is not what disturbs me. I believe that I have made out a good case and I believe that I have made the strongest claim that it is possible for the Jewish Agency to make. Some may think it is too strong, but since I have not used demands and words of that kind, it may help.

Of course, I had expected to appear and have many supporting papers, some of which I have sent in duplicate to Jerusalem.

You will recall that in a letter I handed you on April 2nd, I suggested as my associates, assuming that the meeting would take place at Geneva, Mr. [Harry] Sacher, for legal assistance, and Mr. [David] Yellin as an Arabic specialist.

Now if the plan holds to have the meeting in Jerusalem, I would suggest that the Memorandum be presented and defended by Doctor [Judah L.] Magnes, provided Doctor Magnes agrees with the Memorandum.

I would think it most inadvisable that anyone connected with the Executive in Jerusalem should handle this matter. In a sense, Doctor Magnes probably represents the same attitudes of mind which caused you to choose me to prepare this Memorandum. I am the head of several important Jewish religious institutions of learning and I represent a definite Jewish religious sentiment. Doctor Magnes does the same.

Moreover, the best chance in my opinion of winning our cause before this special Commission of the League of Nations is not through militancy but through the stressing of the religious attitude and of our peaceful purposes. Of course the final decision rests with you, but, in sitting by myself for many hours of the day and awake many hours of the night, I have thought this matter over carefully and this is the best advice I can give.

It is more than likely that within the next few days I shall have an opportunity to talk with Felix [M. Warburg] and you may have some cable communications from us.

P.S. As I am not equal to dictating many long letters, I have thought that I would make the matter plain to the people concerned by sending a copy of my letter to you to Colonel [Frederick H.] Kisch, with five copies of the Memorandum, and a copy of my letter to you to Doctor Magnes, to whom I am also sending a copy of the Memorandum. This will probably make it simpler for you to communicate with these gentlemen. [W]

At the dedication of the Free Library of Philadelphia, June 1927

Racie Adler, 1928

Committee of the American Philosophical Society to Present a Congratulatory Address to President-Elect Herbert Hoover, January 1929. LEFT TO RIGHT: *Albert P. Brubaker, Whitman Cross, Arthur W. Goodspeed, J. Bertram Lippincott, Francis X. Dercum, Charles Greeley Abbot, John A. Miller, Adler, Arthur L. Day, Leo S. Rowe*

In Jerusalem, April 1929. LEFT TO RIGHT: *Rabbi H. Pereira Mendes, Adler, Max Warburg, Felix Warburg*

Adler and family
on board the S.S. Espenia
in Naples, May 1929

In Baden-Baden, July 1931

Adler in California, 1933

In Woods Hole, July 1936

*At the celebration of
the Fiftieth Anniversary of
the Jewish Theological
Seminary,
January 1937*

The Jewish Theological Seminary faculty and class of 1939

TO ISAK UNNA,[1] MANNHEIM, GERMANY

June 10, 1930

I am in receipt of your letter of May 21st. The Constitution of the Jewish Agency contains the following statement:

> The activities of the Jewish Agency shall include within their scope provision for meeting Jewish religious needs, it being clearly understood that individual freedom of conscience shall remain safeguarded and assured.

I was not a member of the Constitution Committee and I think Mr. [Louis] Marshall sat up a good part of the night trying to get this much.

Of course, it is known to you what the general attitudes in Palestine have been. Ever since the considerable migrations, there are three attitudes; the definitely religious attitude, which is held by the Agudah,[2] the Mizrachi,[3] and quite a number of the older Jewish settlers who are not allied with either party; the center attitude, which declared neutrality toward religion, this representing the Zionist party; and the workingmen's attitude, which includes both socialists and communists, who regard Jewish literature as a part of world literature.

I think the Mizrachi have accomplished more than you think. They have in at least thirteen colonies placed shohatim and their schools are growing in numbers. In other words, there is a drifting from the neutral attitude toward their attitude.

I have done what I could to help bring about the appointment of a Committee of the Administrative Committee to meet a Committee of the Agudah, but from the point of view of religious life, the Agency, I think, is weakening its possibility of effecting something through the Agency by insisting that the Agency should have nothing to do with education.

You cite the fact that people in Emek eat hometz[4] during Pesach. Of course, it was always hoped that the soil of Palestine would make religious men of all Jews. I never expected this, because I witnessed with my own eyes the attitude here in America of the radicals who came from Russia thirty and more years ago, who used to give a ball every year on Kol Nidre[5] night and offer ham sandwiches to the people as they came out of the Synagogue. Their actions even provoked riots in several of our large American cities, but I am happy to say that at least this situation has entirely disappeared in America.

When I was in Palestine last year, of course I sensed all of these difficulties, but this much at least I can say to you; that there is much less public desecration of the Sabbath than there used to be. Thus there was an exhibition at Tel-Aviv and the Manager of the Jerusalem–Tel-Aviv Railway, a Christian, thought that instead of running trains two or three times a week he should run trains every day. He ran a train from Jerusalem to Tel-Aviv on Friday afternoon and confessed to Mr. [Felix M.] Warburg that he did not have a single passenger.

I am not certain whether there will be a meeting of the Administrative Committee this summer in Europe or whether I can come to it, although I believe one is planned for the end of August, but I shall bring this subject up, because I am sure you know that I feel it as deeply as you do. [W]

1. Isak Unna (b. 1872), German rabbi and author.
2. Agudat Israel—world Jewish movement and political party, founded in 1912, seeking to preserve Orthodoxy by adherence to Jewish religious law as the principle governing Jewish life and society.
3. The religious wing of the Zionist movement.
4. Leaven—forbidden during Passover.
5. The prayer which prefaces the Yom Kippur evening service.

TO JUDAH L. MAGNES, JERUSALEM

June 16, 1930

I have to-day received your cable and have replied to you as follows:
THANKS YOUR KIND CABLE. HAVE SENT LENGTHY CABLE KISCH REQUESTING HIM TO SHOW YOU IT. PRACTICALLY RECOVERED. WILL BE IN GENEVA ABOUT END JULY. LOVE.

I want to thank you very much for your kind words about the Memorandum. I struggled with it under great difficulties.

I am also enclosing for your personal information copy of a cable which I sent to-day to Colonel [Frederick H.] Kisch. I have asked that you see it, but I sent it to you nevertheless. As the cable indicates, we are going to Europe this summer, as I feel it my duty to attend the meeting of the Administrative Committee of the Jewish Agency in Berlin on August 29th. Of course, I am interested, but I do this largely for Felix [M. Warburg]'s sake, because these meetings are very difficult for him. He is carrying a very heavy burden and I want to lighten it where I can.

I am also hoping that I may have a chance, before the report on the Wailing Wall is written, to see the Commissioners. My cable to Kisch is very full.

Of course, I would not have brought you into this thing at all, but for reasons which I indicated to Doctor [Chaim] Weizmann and I sent you a copy of the letter I wrote him.[1]

I do not fully accept your advice for this reason. In some way or other, some how or other, some sort of order must be put into this thing. I did not ask for this task. It was given me by the Agency. I hesitated for a week or ten days before I accepted. There were, of course, a good many materials in existence, but you would be astonished at the inaccuracy of the compilations. [Isaac E.] Yahuda was the best, but he added words to the people from whom he quotes, he gave incorrect references, and as far as I could get hold of the books, everything had to be proved. I had no mandate from the Vaad Leumi nor from the Rabbinate in Palestine and I am quite certain that if six months from now either body found one sentence that they did not like that they would disavow the statement that I was acting on their behalf.

My suggestion that they should associate themselves with the Memorandum if they approve and make reservations if they desire seems to me essentially a fair one.

I know I am wandering in dictating this letter, but to get back, I was asked by the President of the Agency to take this when I was in London; I took all my papers with me; I gladly submitted them to the Political Commission of the Administrative Committee, which consisted of I think eighteen people; they appointed a subcommittee consisting of I think seven, who spent hours going over the subject with me. The whole matter and the course of the argument was presented to a full sitting of the Administrative Committee; I spent several hours alone with [Pinhas] Rutenberg going over certain ideas and plans that he had and the only one which was my own that I have introduced into this Memorandum was that instead of endeavoring to get rid of the Wakf [Muslim religious endowment] back of the Wall by purchase and for like purchase in the City for the Wakf by the Government through the Agency that I would present the idea of a rental or lease for a long term of years, whether ninety-nine years or otherwise, I did not care, and I was moved to this in a sense of fairness in the idea of easing Moslem law, if such exists, for I could not forget that even though the National Fund is not a Wakf, every piece of ground purchased in Palestine by the National Fund is inalienable that they cannot give it over to the Governors of the University and so it seemed to me that what was sauce for the goose was sauce for the gander. I had a real desire to win the cause which had been entrusted me and not to play politics with it. [W]

1. See letter to Chaim Weizmann, May 29, 1930.

TO ABRAHAM S. E. YAHUDA, LONDON

June 26, 1930

. . . I do not know that there is much use in our writing at arm's length about the situation in Palestine and about the official situation. Although everything was apparently peaceful when I was there, I sensed the trouble, for which I think there is blame on both sides. Naturally I had no idea that it would take the dreadful form that it did.

I have my own theories that I gave to some friends in London, but they do not agree with me. A great many people claim to know the psychology of the Arabs and many explanations are being offered by magazine writers and other people for the present situation. I am not going back to the remote causes of the difficulties, but I personally believe that the immediate cause was the withdrawal of the British troops from Cairo and Alexandria and the general weakening of British influence in Egypt. This emboldened the Mufti and his friends in Palestine, who, in spite of the Scotch verdict in the Shaw Report, I believe regularly organized the rioting and pillage of August 1929.

I can understand your feeling about the bureaucracy which grew up in the Zionist Organization, which the Agency has inherited, and which, of course, it will try to improve if it is given time. Of all the men about 77 Great Russell Street,[1] I thought [Louis B.] Namier was the most active and intelligent, but of course, as you say, he is rather new to the business.

There is one thing, however, that cannot be denied or overlooked. From the day of the Armistice until the present, the British officials in Palestine have been in an overwhelming percentage anti-Jewish and I think that they have done much to breed the difficulties between the Jews and the Arabs, both of whom have groups among them that are amply capable of making mischief.

However, let us hope that the question of the Western Wall will be settled and will be settled justly and properly and that at least one cause of strife in Palestine will have been removed.

As for withdrawing from Palestinian work or any other work because people are difficult to work with, if I had taken that attitude, I would have withdrawn from Jewish work long ago. I remember years ago, when I refused to go into the Zionist movement, [Israel] Zangwill wrote me a letter and told me that he hoped I would be happy in my academic seclusion. I have not been able to enjoy much of it. [W-JTS]

1. The address of the Jewish Agency in London.

TO CHAIM WEIZMANN, LONDON

July 1, 1930

I want to acknowledge with thanks your cable of June 25th. I did not cable a reply because there seemed to be no need of it and I presume I have sent and maybe received enough cables.

I do not want you to be under any misapprehension with regard to my attitude of mind in the matter, because I like to have the people with whom I deal at least understand me, even if they do not agree with me.

I was not at any time, nor am I now, in the least concerned about the question of my authorship of the Memorandum or my name appearing or my having charge of the presentation. I got the impression very definitely, when you made the initial request of me in January, that you thought that quite aside from my being able to prepare a document, which I suppose a good many other people could have done, there would be an advantage to the cause in my appearing on its behalf. It was for this reason that I put my name on it and did what I have never done before; indicated certain official connections and titles, which I thought might be useful.

I had constantly in mind the three gentlemen, who happen to be from Holland, Sweden and Switzerland, who will have to render final judgment on this subject. At best, it is difficult to rationalize in agreeing to establish the holiness of a place, a wall, a pavement, or anything of that sort, and my real reason for doing what I did was to just leave a faint suggestion in their minds that the argument was not being presented by a mediaeval fanatic, but by a more or less modern person. That was all there was to it as far as I am concerned. I did not have in mind the Yishub or the Vaad Leumi or anybody else, but was trying to direct my remarks straight to these three men. I purposely chose French and English sources for descriptions when I could have had at least as good descriptions from Jewish sources—maybe better.

I realize the difficulty of cabling from Jerusalem, but there are codes between Jerusalem and Felix Warburg; one can telephone to Cairo and all that I asked was a brief statement as to what was being taken out and why it was being taken out and as to what was being added. In the last analysis, the only thing was a message saying that Sir Patrick Geddes'[1] letter was being removed. Well, that was an appendix. It was sent to me, and even here it was sent to me from Colonel [Frederick H.] Kisch, through Mr. [Louis B.] Namier, and again it is possible that the effect of the letter upon the minds of the three commissioners would be that here is an eminent English architect and city zoning planner, who, from his point of view, makes recommendations very much like the Jews made. You see, I too have my theory of the art of persuasion.

Of course, there was an initial error in my undertaking the work at all. Philadelphia or New York was no place to write this Memorandum. It should have been written or at least the materials for it should have been gathered in Jerusalem any time within the past five years. Had the detached judgment of someone in London, or myself, or several people been wanted as to the form of presenting the material after it had been got together and the language in which the document should be put or action requested, that might have been something that we in the West could have helped along in.

I sensed in the whole incident, as I have sensed in other things, the extreme difficulty even of carrying on the work in Palestine between Jerusalem and London and almost a sort of despair when it begins to come across the Ocean.

I am planning to sail with my family on the 16th of July and I am going to Geneva. If the Commissioners come to Geneva and you desire me to see them and they desire to see me before they have made their decision, I should be glad to meet them. The Shaw Commission, I believe, heard Mr. Jabotinsky[2] in London and maybe the Wailing Wall Commission might hear me in Geneva, although I do not know at all that I have anything to add to what will have been settled in Jerusalem. You will doubtless have been in touch and will let me know. I am at present not decided as to where I shall put up in Geneva. My address in Europe will be in care of The Frank Tourist Company, 10 Rue Edouard VII, Paris.

Not knowing whether you will be in London when this letter reaches there, I am sending a copy of it to Mr. Namier, who I presume is thoroughly apprised of what is going on, although he might not feel at liberty to open a letter addressed directly to you. [WA]

1. Sir Patrick Geddes (1854–1932), British biologist, sociologist, and town planner.
2. Vladimir Jabotinsky (1880–1940), Zionist leader, soldier, and writer; founder of the Jewish Legion in World War I and of the Revisionist movement in Zionism.

TO JUDAH L. MAGNES, JERUSALEM

Geneva, July 27, 1930

I received in Paris the copy of the letter which you had written to Felix [Warburg] to New York. As we sailed together the original had not reached him in New York so I gave him the copy. I do not know whether he will be writing you soon as he is engaged in a [————].[1] There were several matters in the letter which seemed so important to me that even though it wasn't addressed to me I shall venture to give you the dis-advantage of my views.

I am sorry that you found the phrase "no domination of Arabs over Jews or of Jews over Arabs," so senseless, because I spent a lot of time over that phrase in London. If you will think it over you will see that it corresponds to a series of facts which it was intended to merit. However why bother about phrases when there are more important things in the world.

I cannot follow you in your plan of a Palestinian parliament based, I presume, on universal male [suffrage] and the qualifications for voters to be bona fide residents, not subjects or citizens of any other country, and literate. I prefer as a beginning the comparatively small council proposed by Sir Herbert Samuel with the important modification that the members representing the country should be elected—not appointed. [Pinhas] Rutenberg's plan has in my opinion less merit except that it would give more chance for more people to talk. Your plan, I think, would break up the whole show. You may be quite sure, aside from any other disadvantages that the reservations with regard to immigration and land purchase would not be kept—next would go the language rights and the whole painfully built up structure would disappear.

Moreover—and on this point I think—I can speak with certainty—the Jews of the world will not support such an attenuated program.

This matter, moreover, will in the last analysis be settled between Jerusalem, Geneva and London and for the time being London has the casting vote. In these circumstances contradictory efforts can only nullify each other. Let me say therefore with brutal frankness that since you have declined to associate yourself with the rest of us who, for better or for worse, have taken what is called "political" responsibility, expressly because you were through with "politics" you ought abide by that decision of your own. I wrote you in this sense last March before I left America for London and I feel it even more keenly now.

Another day I shall write you about the Kotel Maarabi[2] affair. I hope I did not embarrass you by bringing in your name. This was—or at least should have been—distinctly not a political matter nor treated as a legal one. However, more there is nothing to do but await the Decision. [M]

1. Word illegible.
2. Western Wall.

Despite the recommendations of the Passfield White Paper, issued in October 1930, which recommended severe restrictions on Jewish immigration and land purchase in Palestine, Adler, like many others, retained his faith that England as a mandatory power would keep its promises to the Jews.

Doctor Adler's Statement to the Jewish Daily Bulletin

October 23, 1930

It is a heartening thing to find that the leaders of a great political party in England, Stanley Baldwin,[1] Sir Austen Chamberlain,[2] and Mr. Amery,[3] the three responsible officials in the last Conservative Government, have completely dissociated themselves from the attitude of Lord Passfield and the present British Government with regard to the Palestinian policy. In effect, their letter in the *London Times* of Thursday, republished in the American papers of the same date takes the same ground as Mr. Felix M. Warburg in his letter of resignation which is a coincidence so remarkable as to indicate that Mr. Warburg's view was not simply the view of the Jew or member of the Jewish Agency, but the view of a fair man.[4]

It is more than likely that the chiefs of the Liberal Party will take the same view, but whether they do or not, it is plain that the best sentiment of the English people will not tolerate a breach of trust, whether it be with a great nation or with a small people whose weight cannot be made felt by navies or armies. I still repose confidence in the honor and good faith of the English people. For this reason I deeply deplore hasty and ill considered statements which tend toward an anti-British agitation in this country or in any other country. The English people do not merit this at our hands and any attempt to foster it would react not only upon the speakers who desire a little applause in a moment of excitement, but even more heavily upon the Jewish people themselves and particularly upon Palestine. The feeling of anger and despair was natural, but no Jew has the right to give vent to his own feelings in a way that will ultimately harm his own people. [W]

1. Stanley Baldwin (1867–1947), leader of the Conservative Party; prime minister in 1923, 1924–29, 1935–37.
2. Sir Austen Chamberlain (1863–1937), Conservative Party leader; foreign secretary, 1924–29.
3. Leopold Amery (1873–1955), colonial secretary, 1924–29.
4. Warburg had resigned his position on the Jewish Agency Board in protest against the British policy of restricting immigration to Palestine.

The rise of Adolf Hitler's anti-Semitic Nazi party in German politics had been accelerated by the Depression. By 1930, Nazism was a growing threat to the wellbeing of German Jewry.

TO MORTIMER L. SCHIFF, NEW YORK CITY

November 3, 1930

. . . You may be sure that we all understand that it would unfavorably affect the position of the Jews in Germany if it were known that there is any interference from America, nor have we thought of such interference.

You also know that I spent a month in Germany this summer and that, although I left three or four days before the elections, the German Jews seemed to know pretty well the strength that the Hitler movement was gaining, although they did not estimate that it would have more than 80 seats in the Parliament. . . . The only thing that I have in mind that could be accomplished to this end is that we should aid the Jews in Germany to meet the highbrow scientific agitation which is being carried out against them. It comes from professors of theology. It also comes from anthropologists and biologists who claim to have discovered by microscopic investigation a totally different blood as between Jews and Teutons and so on. There was a congress of anthropologists in Hamburg the first week in September and I understand that Professor Boas,[1] of Columbia who is an anthropologist and not too much of a Jew, was made aware of this pseudo-scientific attack upon the Jews in Germany.

At all events, I felt it would be wrong if we did not talk together, face the situation, and at least see what can be done, especially in view of the fact that a number of direct appeals have been made to me to this end. [AJC]

1. Franz Boas (1858–1942), American anthropologist.

TO FELIX FRANKFURTER, CAMBRIDGE, MASSACHUSETTS

December 16, 1930

Within the past week or so Mr. [Felix M.] Warburg, Mr. Szold,[1] Mr. [Bernard] Flexner and I have been having a good many talks and reading a good many cables, and on one occasion Mr. Flexner and I sat down with a section of the Administrative Committee of the Zionist Organization of America, Mr. Tulin,[2] Mr. Rosensohn,[3] Mr. Neuman[4] and others. I have seen the recent exchange of telegrams, letters between yourself and Mr. Warburg. As a result of all these talks and of my own reflection, I have come to the conclusion that we have reached a point in our discussions with our friends in London where it is either essential that you should go over or that we should refrain from giving them any further advice.

I know from your last letter to Mr. Warburg that your judgment does not accord with that of the rest of us and that you are moved by a very deep conviction of your own. But may I point out to you that the question of your presence or your absence is not a matter of principle and therefore not one to affect your conscience?

I could understand your point of view before the election in Houndsditch. You may have thought—your friend Flexner I think did—that the British Government was trying to rush these matters in order to influence that election and that they were endeavoring to use you and him as pawns. That election is now over.

Moreover, when we met at Washington at the home of Mr. Justice [Louis D.] Brandeis there was a pretty general conviction that the present British Government will shortly fall. Now, so far as one can judge, the political situation in Great Britain has changed. Mr. [David] Lloyd George prefers to be the makeweight of the Labor government rather than risk the certainty of a Conservative government and is giving his own party a year or two for recruiting its strength. Hence the tentative conclusion which we reached in Washington based on the theory of a change in Government in Great Britain no longer controls.

Moreover, from the point of view of the World Zionist Organization, and certainly from the point of view of the Jewish Agency, the present state of affairs should be terminated, because I believe that if this does not take place there will shortly be a complete collapse. You know that I am not very strong on business affairs; but, with all these rumors going about of the difference between the Jews in America and England, with the dissatisfaction and almost despair which has seized upon many warm friends of Palestine, with the fact that the Palestine Executive has been paying its employees in notes which are at a thirty per cent discount, that the banks are getting nervous about their credits—there is a grave danger that the whole movement will be put into actual bankruptcy, and I need not tell you what the moral effect of that will be.

Now I firmly believe—and I would not say it to you if I did not believe it—that in some intangible and maybe almost mystical way your going over at this time will greatly help to restore confidence and be the additional driving force that will overcome the dead point of the Palestine machine. So much has been said about your coming over ever since last July—so much has been published—your not going over has been so generally construed as due to wide divergence of opinion between us in America and the representatives of the Agency in London—that if only as a symbol I consider your making this journey of paramount importance. I am sure you realize that an act of this kind to restore confidence is the highest kind of diplomacy.

But you will be able to do much beyond that—you will give assurance here that a new and courageous head is in the business; you will stiffen the backbone of the people over there. You will come to direct grips with Laski[5] and get all kinds of inner information which the many cables and even telephone talks do not give. In general, you will derive all the advantages to the cause of a general in the field, rather than occupying a position, three thouand miles back of the line, in your library.

We have been discussing this up and down and I see no recourse but the one that I have outlined at the beginning—namely, either that you should go, or that we should give the people in London a free hand and accept responsibility for what they do.

I am saying all this to you not as an individual, as you know. What I said in Washington is quite true. I had, from the very beginning of the Zionist Movement, the gravest misgiving as to the possibilities of the whole thing. It was not till the War and after and the fact that it appeared that Great Britain's political necessities were bound up with the age-long desire of Israel for "next year in Jerusalem," that I thought there was any possibility of a practical substance to the thing at all. I am sure you know that I did not lack appeals to my heart strings or to my Jewish pride in the meantime.

By the accident of the new White Paper and the fact that I did not resign because I thought that someone should stay in office and provisionally carry on, I have been put into a position of responsibility which I am sure I did not want. Had I taken the individualistic point of view, either now or years ago, I could have readily said that my own personal judgment was against my having anything to do with the whole Palestine matter; that I was devoting my entire life to Jewish work anyhow and doing my share; that I had left Washington twenty odd years ago for the purpose of doing it; and could readily refuse to follow any path which my private judgment did not commend.

But whether we Jews like it or not we are held responsible the one for the other. We are assumed to possess a solidarity. If that solidarity fails us at a critical moment because on a matter, not of principle, not of conscience, but of practice of technique, the key man does not see his way to fit himself into the hole (and just at the moment it is a very big hole) in which his friends believe he is the only one that fits—then we are in the same position as we were when the Romans were attacking the walls of Jerusalem and the Jews on the inside were cutting each others' throats. And Palestine will fall again. [W]

1. Robert Szold (1889–1977), lawyer and American Zionist leader.
2. Abraham Tulin (1883–1973), American Zionist leader.
3. Samuel J. Rosensohn (1879–1939), lawyer and American Zionist leader.
4. Emmanuel Neuman (b. 1896), American Zionist leader.
5. Harold Joseph Laski (1893–1950), British socialist and political theorist; a proponent of the Zionist cause within the Labour Party.

The Depression was causing a drastic decrease in the amount of money raised for Jewish causes. This was taking its toll on all Jewish institutions, the Jewish Agency no less than the others. At a critical period for the Yishuv, the Jewish Agency was facing bankruptcy. How to prevent this bankruptcy and its catastrophic results was the concern of Adler and his colleagues.

TO FELIX M. WARBURG, NEW YORK CITY

December 18, 1930

I have read with great care your letter of December 12th to Mr. [Bernard] Flexner and that of the previous date to Doctor Wasserman[1] and the memorandum of Mr. Joseph C. Hyman[2] of December 17th on the status of the Jewish Agency and have had the advantage of conversation with you and Mr. Flexner in the meanwhile.

One important consideration in my mind, so far as your financial plan is concerned, is the element of time and I will explain what I mean by this. Your own letters and Mr. Hyman's analysis show the great difficulties of the unwieldy administrative and financial machine that has been set up for what is a comparatively small task, though beset with great difficulties. I agree with everything that you say on this point, but I cannot separate in my mind the situation from the present political situation.

Whether we like it or not, our representatives are now in constant discussions with the British Government. Aside from their own political needs, the only hold that we have on the British Government is the theory of a solidarity of front and of financial contribution in the upbuilding of Palestine.

You know as well as I do how little real solidarity there is in the front and at least if the front line is permitted to look solid there are plenty of people in the second and third lines who are pulling at their coat tails, not to speak of an occasional missile. If the action that you propose were taken, say within the next thirty days, I think that the World Zionist body would be thrown into the hands of the Revisionists, the straight out demand be made that the White Paper should be withdrawn prior to any real discussion, that the British Government would be thrown more than ever into the arms of the Arabs and the whole enterprise would blow up. If you think I am wrong in this, tell me, and if I am wrong, what I am going to say next will be of no value.

As I understand, there are two urgent situations to meet. One is to satisfy the pressure of creditors and, as I am sure you know, the pressure will become strong and urgent as soon as there is any hint of a break. The second is to at least secure money for the treasury as to enable the machine to work without the incurring of new debts.

Now these two are intimately bound up and the suggestion that I made to you informally, about taking care of the first by a mortgage or some other form of refunding, was one which you characterized as making a new debt to pay old ones. Of course that is true, but the difference is that a bank loan is for a short period and a mortgage which gives definite security can be got for a longer time and is usually subject to payment by gradual reductions. I have never mortgaged anything myself and I have never made a bank loan, so that both of the things are theoretical with me, but at least I know the difference.

For the working out of this transfer of debts in the form of a mortgage, every one of our organizations which has real property in Palestine should be called on to participate and here I would include the Keren Hayesod, PEC [Palestine Economic Corporation], anything that has property. Put it at its worst and I still think that the Jewish world could for the period of a couple of years be counted upon to meet the interest on such a mortgage.

In the time of a crisis, moreover, we are entitled at least to call in those organizations which have so far stayed outside of the Agency, such as PICA [Palestine Jewish Colonization Association] and ICA [Jewish Colonization Association]. They may refuse, but we have a duty, I think, to approach them.

Hand in hand with this must go a complete change in the current expenditures, and this may mean and probably will mean a lowering of standards and a slowing up of tempo. There is every reason in the world why Palestine should have excellent health conditions. Palestine is overhospitalized and too much there is free. The same is true of the educational system, which was speeded up to top-notch. In 1920 and 1921, the ravages of the War had to be repaired. Now the Jewish settlement in Palestine is entitled to as good a school system as it and the Government will support and the hospitals and health centers such maintenance as the people can pay for.

Then there is another point which you and Mr. Hyman bring out most clearly. There was great insistence for the Keren Hayesod as the fiscal agent of the Jewish Agency, but apparently the Keren Hayesod had loaded itself up so much with debts that very little filtered through to the treasury of the Agency and the cost of campaigns, of collection, of administration must run into a figure which would probably be scandalous if it were known—at least so I surmise, but we do not know it.

Beside cutting down the number of persons employed by the Agency to a minimum in the rank and file, serious consideration ought to be given to those in the upper ranks. I think you know that I am a friend of education, but when I was in Palestine I felt that there were enough inspectors to cover a school population of 200,000 instead of a school population of 20,000. There are too many people in the Executive. I do not know how high their salaries are, but I imagine that in the days of inflation they were put upon a very generous basis. No system of reform in the finances would be justified when it involves dismissals if the higher paid people were not themselves willing to accept reductions.

I have no ideas—maybe you have—who pays for all of the cables that are passing, and that have been since I have known the work, between New York, London and Jerusalem, but the item must be a frightful one. I think we shall all have to get our nerves a little more under control and be satisfied, except in the greatest emergencies, with the mails. Ships come very fast now from England; there is an airplane service between London and Palestine and there ought to be an agreement that this item should be very greatly curtailed.

Then there is another thing which ought to be taken more firmly in hand. I know the proper affection which you and other men have for the Hadassah organization and its work, but my experience now of a year and a half or so indicates to me that they do not play the game. They are in and they are out. They have their own special campaigns and they have super campaigns and even in these difficult times are draining the goodwill of the public for funds, not one penny of which goes to the general coffers. The same thing is true to a lesser extent of the Mizrachi, who have a knack of demanding their pound of flesh when they know it will hurt the most.

Now the net result of my cogitations is something like this: I think that your plan for putting the finances in order through somebody in England taking some step which will act as a lever to bring the budget of the Agency into some reasonable shape is sound—that is to say, you are using force where persuasion has failed, but it is sound not only for Palestine but for the Jewish people everywhere, if that force is applied from within and not from without, in other words, that it does not become public property.

I shudder to think of the effect upon the Jews of the entire world if the Jewish Agency or, not to be technical, the entire Palestine movement should be put into bankruptcy. I believe that it would be the greatest blow that we have ever inflicted upon ourselves and would make us the laughing stock, of course, of those men who predicted failure, but also of the entire world.

With the situation such as it now exists in Germany, with the position in Roumania, in Poland—I need not give you a list of the countries—the power of resistance and the morale of the Jews would be so weakened that we would bring upon ourselves a catastrophe infinitely worse than a massacre. This is the situation as I see it, which makes me think that the bankruptcy of the movement in Palestine would be taken as equivalent to the bankruptcy of the Jewish people and this situation entitles us to call upon any and every force within the Palestine movement itself and upon such forces without as have not hitherto joined themselves with us to present to them the gravity of the situation before your final step is resorted to.

You must remember that the best face has always been put upon everything, that all the damaging things have been secret and confidential and that the situation is really unknown to most, even of our Jewish people.

I am very much afraid that this letter has not helped. If it is even of a little assistance or gives a single new lead, that is all I can hope. I expect to see you next week, when we can have a further talk. [W]

1. Oskar Wasserman (1869–1934), German banker and communal leader; a founder of the Jewish Agency.
2. Joseph C. Hyman (1899–1949), a leader of the Joint Distribution Committee; close associate of Felix Warburg.

TO MORRIS S. LAZARON,[1] BALTIMORE

Philadelphia, January 7, 1931
. . . Would it not be better if we could all come to an understanding that what we were trying to do was to restore to such of the Jewish people who desired to go to Palestine an opportunity to build up their homes, to cultivate the Hebrew language, to practice Judaism, to produce art, literature and music in a Jewish environment, and in general to do certain things; and not concern ourselves so much about the words, or even theory, underlying them? This is the case where schoolmen, in order to be useful, must translate themselves into action.

I can understand the difficulties which Reform Jews of, say, the third generation have in meeting the whole Palestinian situation. When a man is a Reformer of the third generation he ceases to be a Reformer and becomes a Traditionalist; he feels himself bound to the tradition of the founders of this movement, so that it is just as difficult for him to adjust himself to new conditions as it is for a member of the Agudat Yisrael. You may think this whimsical, but I believe there is more in it than meets the eye. . . . [W]

1. Morris S. Lazaron (1888–1976), rabbi of Baltimore Hebrew Congregation; a founder of the anti-Zionist American Council for Judaism.

TO SAMUEL SCHULMAN, NEW YORK CITY

January 13, 1931

. . . I have in the past year or so seen many people in Europe, and a good many in America to whom the question of Palestine is a real anxiety, and many who are not interested overmuch but who, since the uprisings of 1929, the Shaw Report and the [Passfield] White Paper, feel deeply that the honor of all Jews is involved.

I am not very much of a nationalist anywhere. I love America but I can see its faults and criticize it. I am a subscriber to that extraordinary statement which Woodrow Wilson spoke on the 4th of July in Independence Hall in Philadelphia during the War, praying for a new patriotism. "Not my country right or wrong, my country. But, my country, may she always be right." This I think is the note that teachers of morality should sound whether it be for America or Palestine.

To come down to the meat of the business at the moment, the situation is about as I stated it. The economic depression and the lack of confidence which has been engendered in the Palestine administration and to an extent in the British government, has stopped the support for Palestine. Great commitments have been made, tracts of land purchased with only 20 percent paid down and 80 percent mortgages, which commitments have to be met or the land will be lost and with it the monies put in, to a very considerable amount. Other projects of all kinds have been started, worthy enough in themselves, most of them, but without any real appreciation of what was involved. This is the legacy that the [Jewish] Agency inherited. There are only three men in the world who are giving any considerable support. The old Baron Edmund de Rothschild is manfully upholding his splendid undertakings quite independently. The other two men who stepped into the breach are Felix Warburg and Oscar Wasserman of Berlin. I believe that these two men have given, or obligated themselves for, something over one million dollars in the last year and a half. And of course no one or two men can or should be expected to give more. In the last year, we have cut and pruned and lopped off excrescenses in jobholders so that whereas in previous years the Zionist Organization of America or the United Palestine Appeal was expected to raise $3,500,000 with what seems certain from Europe, the machine can be kept going with $1,250,000 from America for the year 1931. That does not mean expansion, as you can readily realize. To get back to the entire theory, although this is hardly the moment for philosophic calm, I think in many aspects—though not in all—you and I are not in agreement. I believe that the dispersion saved Judaism. To me Judaism is the important thing, the Jewish people important because they are its vehicle. Judaism has grown greatly by its contact with the large world. Indeed, it was not without this contact in ancient times and in Palestine. I do believe that there is an opportunity for it to flourish again in Palestine, and if the Jewish people are, as indeed they ought to be, the vehicle of Judaism, then those that can be taken out of East European countries where they can hardly breathe, are just that much to the good. . . . If one views the matter purely as a humanitarian, it is worthwhile, but I think there is a little more than that.

Recently, a very distinguished Christian talked for three hours on the subject with a friend of mine, endeavoring to find out how real the aspiration of the Jewish people toward Palestine was. Just by the way, he told him about the Seder Service, of the fact that toward the end of it year after year, some millions of Jews had been saying "Next year in Jerusalem" and that seemed to impress him more as indicating the long continued earnestness of the Jewish people on this point than any practical statement that had been made to him. Farms and industries and schools and universities left him cold, but that phrase he took as the evidence of a hope which pressed through the ages.

You see, my dear Schulman, the real fact is that there is something mystical about the whole business, and when we go into the realm of logic and philosophy we are just as apt to go astray as by following our own intuitions. [W]

In a reflection on the situation in Palestine, Adler warned the Zionists emphatically against underestimating the Palestinian Arabs, who, Adler felt, were being treated by the Jews as inferiors.

TO CHAIM WEIZMANN, LONDON

January 19, 1931

I have read again your notes on the attitude of the British administration in Palestine toward the Jewish National Home.[1] I myself raised the question when I was in London last March with various people and even at one of the sessions, why Englishmen, who were in many ways more friendly to their Jewish fellow-citizens than people in most countries were, should unfortunately have adopted an unfriendly attitude in Palestine from the very beginning, indeed as soon as the military occupation began. I am in agreement with you that the British are not anti-Semitic and think you are right in dismissing anti-Semitism as the underlying cause of the difficulty in Palestine.

Let me say parenthetically that what is meant by the Jewish National Home is not always expressed with clearness by its proponents and it is certainly not clear in the minds of many Jews and so leaves room for a reasonable amount of misunderstanding on the part of non-Jews, whether they be British officials or otherwise.

Your analysis of the motives which caused England to offer the Balfour Declaration is, I think, also fair. In other words, the motives were mixed: they were partly utilitarian but they were partly sentimental, but the fact cannot be overlooked that in the long run nations are moved by motives of self-interest and if the utilitarian motive to continue the policy laid down in the Balfour Declaration is not strong enough, the likelihood is that the nation will not persevere in it. It is therefore strongly to the interest of the Jews that the continuance of Britain as the Mandatory Power shall be to the interest of that Power.

I do not view as a very strong argument the offer of any country which contains a considerable number of Jews to find a territory to which these Jews could migrate. That might equally represent a willingness to get rid of them and of course the idea that anything like a preponderating section of the Jews in the world could actually settle in Palestine has always been a fantasy. In other words Palestine will not settle the Jewish question. Years and years ago it might have been within the realm of possibility that this question should be solved in the Near East. If the great migration which came to North America and other countries could have flowed into Palestine, Syria and Mesopotamia, there might have been a possibility of the greatest Jewish community the world has ever seen growing up within those three countries of the Near East, but nobody was ready for it and certainly in any distance of time that we can see in the future nothing of that sort will be possible.

Your underlying idea of the dream of an Arab-Moslem Empire in the Near East to insure Moslem friendship and support for the British Empire I think presupposes in your mind, or at least in the minds of the people who are directing the policies of the British Empire, a form of Moslem unity which, in my opinion, does not exist. There has been no such unity for a very long time. Persia with its Shiite heresy[2] has always been out of the fold and this Persian influence is not without force in India and Turkey. The orthodox Moslems of Egypt, of Morocco, of India and of other sections gave only a tacit allegiance to the one great Moslem power, Turkey, and I need not tell you that during the last half of the nineteenth century there were many Moslems who were disposed to dispute the Caliphate of the Sultan of Turkey. There is at the present time no Moslem unity even among those who follow the same tradition. I have believed and I still believe that much of the unrest in Iraq and in Palestine and in Egypt is based upon a desire of various Moslem leaders to get the power which they think the Caliphate might bring again.

I have reason to believe, and I have had the information directly from India within the last few weeks which confirms the belief, that, excepting for the baseless rumor that the Jews had seized the Mosque of Omar, the Moslems of India are not interested in Palestine at all. If they have used this supposed interest with the British Government, I believe it has been for trading purposes.

I think your argument in paragraph 15 is entirely sound. Without a Jewish National policy, there would have been no Mandate.

I think you are entirely sound in raising the Bolshevist question. There is no use in trying to conceal this. And I, on the other hand, have always felt it unwise for the Jewish Agency to encourage the Kevuzot [collective agricultural settlements] because nothing should be permitted that would lend color to this very charge. Your concluding argument seems to me very strong.

There are some things that I want to jot down here which do not necessarily affect this paper, but they keep floating in my mind and I may have said them to you on other occasions. It has been my opinion, in the first place, that in the course of the development of the Zionist movement there has been a good deal of unfairness to the Turks. In spite of their many faults, they are the only Moslem people that have shown a capacity to maintain a state for the last three or four hundred years, and although originally and during the War it was part of the policy of the European powers that no matter what else happened, the Turks were to go, they have emerged infinitely stronger than they entered it. To my eye the only power that benefited by the War was Turkey. They cannot be left out of reckoning in the Near East.

I believe that it is the settled policy of the Arabs to get rid of the English if they can and, from this point of view, the riots of 1929 can hardly be omitted from your discussion, because I believe that they were really an attack upon the British Government. The course of reasoning is extremely simple. A Mandate was granted to Britain in order to carry out the Jewish National Home policy. "If we show that we will not live with the Jews, if we show a continued refusal to accept the Mandate," say the Arabs, "the English have no place here." There is a great deal to be said, maybe too much cannot be said in praise of the Yishub and of the Jews who have settled in Palestine in the past ten years, but they have faults and their principal fault, in my opinion, is the fact that they have underestimated the Arab, both intellectually and culturally. They came with the arrogance of the European and the arrogance of the Jew, with a long history in both cultures, to deal with a people whom they looked upon with the same amount of respect that a Southern planter did on a Negro. Whereas they were really mistaken in this people, who had themselves great pride of race, traditions of culture and a combination of fear and suspicion against the intruder. Fear, because in a dim way they knew that he was superior; suspicion, because they believed that it was the purpose of the new man who came ultimately to drive them out. No amount of reasoning, of expression of goodwill, will overcome the result of incivility or contempt, and I know that both of these were practiced in Palestine. We must drill our people to avoid these, if a harmonious relation is to be cultivated.

We are still undisciplined—I need not tell you that. There comes to my mind the fact that when the Nebi Musa procession was taking place, in the early days of Pesach, 1929, and the Zionist Executive had sent word to the different sections of the community to be good enough not to make pilgrimages to the Wailing Wall that day; I was in the Synagogue and at the conclusion of the service, somebody arose and said: "We will now go to the Kotel Maaravi." I saw the crowd of Jews press on and through the procession and I thought it was a miracle that the trouble which broke out in August did not take place in the April before.

However, I am not going on with this discussion, which will probably only weary you. There is no need for you to trouble yourself to reply to this letter which is merely an answer to you. [W]

1. At this point Weizmann was attempting to convince the British government to change its position on Palestine as enunciated in the White Paper. On February 13, 1931, Ramsay MacDonald, in a letter to Weizmann, reversed the policy.

2. Shi'a—a sect recognizing Ali as the legitimate successor of Muhammad; the dominant Muslim sect in Iran.

TO FELIX M. WARBURG, NEW YORK CITY

March 24, 1931

I have read [Maurice B.] Hexter's letter of March 11th to you. The questions that you marked are:

1) With regard to the combination of the Haifa Technicum and the Biram School.[1] I think we agreed when we were in Palestine that the Technicum was scaled too high and that instead of producing architects and engineers it should produce foremen and good hand workers. Whether this can best be carried out through Doctor Biram or someone else, I am not in position to state, nor do I know what, if any, conflicting interests are in Germany, because I do not know which particular groups are interested in which particular schools. It seems to me that as this matter is really between Germany and Palestine, Doctor [Bernard] Kahn ought to be entrusted with its working out. I may say parenthetically that a couple of weeks ago, when I was walking with Morti [Schiff], he asked me about the Technicum and very strongly expressed the opinion which we have as to altering the character of the Technicum. You know he was once really interested in it.

I am very much pleased with the part of Hexter's letter relating to an understanding with the ICA [Jewish Colonization Association]. I hope he is not too sanguine. Certainly it would be a great thing to bring them in.

With regard to Geneva, I do not think that Hexter correctly understood me. I did not suggest that we should not have an office in Geneva. I did say that I thought the present one was highly unsatisfactory. Even if [Victor] Jacobson were the man, this thing of flitting between Geneva and Paris, having an office closed and the box stuffed with mail did not seem to me advisable. I think that when we were in Berlin last year, I pointed out the inefficiency of our office in Geneva and the comparative inefficiency of the Jewish Telegraphic Agency representative, Doctor Weinberg, I believe his name is, a very good scholar, a man interested in scientific research and without any journalistic sense at all, as far as I could see.

You will recall that when every effort was being made to get a copy of the Permanent Mandates Commission document in Berlin, the first copy that arrived was the one that was sent to me by Clarence K. Streit,[2] a representative of the *New York Times*.

Jacobson is an oldish man, which, of course, is not against him. He flits in and out of offices, he devotes a good part of his time to semi-mysterious intrigue, to attendance at communal meetings, youth societies and things of that sort. In all probability, his best outfit is linguistic, as he speaks French, German and English with great ease. He was of extremely moderate service to me.

I have a recollection that there was another man in Geneva. I thought his name was Kahn or Cohen, who seemed to me abler than Jacobson, but he labored under the disadvantage of knowing no English, which is a genuine disadvantage in view of the fact that so many of the important people in the League [of Nations] are Englishmen and even Americans.

My conclusion, finally, is that we ought to have an office in Geneva and that it ought to be a good one.

I do not think that Doctor Hexter is right that matters there can be left to the occasional visits of Doctor [Chaim] Weizmann. It is the keeping in constant touch with a body of that kind that at least helps to prepare the way and what is of equal importance provides necessary information. Moreover, it is entirely unsound to put everything on one man's shoulders. There I believe in your favored idea of understudies, even if I do not always follow it.

Of course, if there were a correspondent who could also act as a representative of the Agency, that would be of great help, as I think, other things being equal, a good correspondent can get more news than the representative of any organization, but the correspondent would have to be a very good one. [W]

1. The Reali high school, Haifa, whose principal was the noted educator Arthur (Yitzhak) Biram (1878–1967).
2. Clarence Kirshman Streit (b. 1896), journalist and author.

TO FELIX M. WARBURG, NEW YORK CITY

March 31, 1931

I have your personal and your quasi-official letters of March 30th. Mr. [Joseph C.] Hyman talked to me last evening for a few minutes in between Magnesian functions, and again this morning. My natural disposition would have been to give time for reflection in view of the seriousness of the subject, but since Mr. Hyman has indicated that they wanted my views soon and as there are three days this week which the good Jewish law provides as a complete rest, I shall have to give you the first product of my immature thought.

First and foremost, I am concerned about you. I want you to get well. I want you to do everything that you should do and stop doing everything you should not do for the purpose of getting well. In this last category, there are no doubt many things from which you can and ought to give yourself a rest. This is the purely personal side and on this side I mean every word I write—there is no need of my protesting that I say it out of sheer affection. . . .

Now to the business of the letter about which you must have some misgivings, since you say that you will probably destroy it or change it. I am not so sure about destroying it, but changed it should be.

In the very beginning you address me as "Chairman of the Provisional Committee of the Jewish Agency." This I am not. I am only—alas for my sins—the Chairman of the Provisional Committee of the American members of the Jewish Agency—a small, extra-legal body to carry on the work that you had done as Chairman of the Administrative Committee.

As I read your letters, the two straws which have (nearly) broken the camel's back are the cables of Doctor Senator[1] and Doctor [Chaim] Weizmann. Let me deal with Senator's first, with due consideration of the fact that his English is not to the manor born and some of the nuances may escape him. He uses the phrases "unable to accept suggestions," "cruel cuts in budget" and "unable to agree reduction."

These phrases indicate that although Senator was our own choice, and never held such language when he was with the Joint Distribution Committee, the wine of Palestine has got into his blood and as Treasurer and member of the Executive he gives orders and does not take them; in other words, he has become a "member of the Cabinet," Chancellor of the Exchequer and First Lord of the Treasury. The exaltation of Palestine shows itself in more ways than one. To be offset against all this are two considerations: Senator is quite obviously a man of nerves, and he is the hardest pressed man in Jewish Palestine. When people are desperate and hungry and that too on the basis of money due them for work actually done, they are apt to make a treasurer's life miserable. He, in turn, has the tendency to take it out by making the life of other people miserable.

As for the last cable of Doctor Weizmann, in the welter of papers I do not happen to have it before me. His previous cable, in which he said that your attitude is not justified, I have. As I remember the last cable, and it may be that I have no copy of it and that it was simply read to me by Mr. Hyman, he says in effect that in addition to coming over to stimulate the Campaign, he wants to devote himself especially to the debt-funding proposition to which we were pledged and which he is convinced is necessary if the work in Palestine is to proceed.

Thus shorn of any unpleasantness in expression, I want to bring to your mind the fact that as recently as last November or December, you and Mr. Rosenberg,[2] and possibly even Mr. [Bernard] Flexner, though I am not sure of this, were almost on the point of admitting that through some friendly proceeding it might be necessary to put the Agency into bankruptcy. I combatted this because I thought that not only would the moral and political effect be disastrous on Palestine, but the moral effect on the Jewry of the entire world would be disastrous and I suggested a long-term loan put out upon a business basis, resting upon properties which belong to the Agency.[3] I was told that due to the complications of the Keren Kayemeth and the Keren Hayesod that the Agency itself had no such properties and at that meeting Mr. Flexner stated, having been won over to the thought of no bankruptcy, that the PEC [Palestine Economic Corporation] would do everything in its power and use its resources to prevent the then threatened financial collapse.

In a way, my dear Felix, you laid yourself open to some expectations, because, if I recall, you made a proposal that the elder statesmen, among whom you reckoned yourself, should withdraw from the active work and give themselves over to the payment of the obligations which the Zionist Organization and the Agency had incurred, meeting these obligations over a period of ten years. Not, it is true, directly to meet the deficit, but rather for the purchase of land which was to be sold to individual holders and the money so derived to be turned over to the banks to which the Agency was indebted.

Then, it is a fact, as you point out, that many things intervened. The principal one was the White Paper and the Hope-Simpson Report,[4] which we all took to mean rendered the purchase of land on any kind of scale impossible and therefore destroyed the main foundation of your plan; no doubt you were further disappointed by the declination of [Osmond] d'Avigdor Goldsmid to accept the chairmanship of a committee charged to execute this plan and that you had probably expected Lord Melchett to participate. The large sums of money which you had already advanced or made yourself responsible for were apparently forgotten. I knew of the advance of I believe $200,000. which you made in Zurich in 1929. I never knew until long afterwards of the $500,000. which you and Doctor [Oskar] Wasserman had made yourselves responsible for and had you consulted me I should certainly have advised you against the second advance, because dealing as you were with eager and impecunious people and being considered as you were an inexhaustible gold mine, it is not entirely to be wondered at that these men think that by using a little sharper machinery more and more nuggets will be forthcoming. I am not much of a mine expert and maybe my figures of speech are wrong.

I deplore, as much as you do, the difficulty and confusion to which we have been put by the breaking up of the Allied Jewish Campaign, but we have to be fair enough to admit that the move for this severance was not wholly on the Zionist side. Both Doctor Wasserman and your brother Max, if my memory serves me correctly, strongly advised this severance and to them, as to the Zionists, the name Keren Hayesod seemed to be a magic slogan.

The blame for the White Paper could not be laid wholly on the shoulders of Weizmann. It is true that there was an impasse and maybe somewhat of his making, but during those summer months, with his approval and with your approval, I think, [Pinhas] Rutenberg who was in London and who was the deus ex machina, was to rescue us from all of our troubles and certainly Passfield's interview with you, which he requested, left no reason to suppose that the White Paper was to follow. There are remarks upon page 1 and half of page 2 of your letter.

The paragraph beginning "I fully appreciate" is one which I think could stand in any letter that you finally decide to write, though I do not think I should be put in the forefront of the effort on behalf of the Campaign, but that Mr. Rothenberg[5] and his colleagues should be given the credit that is due to them.

Your paragraph 4 on page 3 is justified and I think you have a right to feel discouraged, even pained, at the lack of appreciation of your generosity and your efforts and they should recognize, as I do, the effect which this whole situation is having upon your health. This, as I have said, is to me the primary consideration.

There is, however, one point in your tendering your resignation as a member of the Council of the Agency. Membership in this Council, as I understand, expires by limitation. Those who were members of the Council in 1929 have to be re-elected or re-appointed for membership in the Council of 1931 and if you decide upon this course finally, it would simply be by a notification to the Nominating Committee or in whatever method these elections take place, that you decline to stand for another term.

What the effect of this will be, I do not want to present to you now because that might look as though I were more interested in the cause than I am in your health. Every cause can get along without any man and some-times must, whereas if one man loses his health, as Cyrus Sulzberger said in another connection, he loses it 100%.

If your entire attempt to secure peace of mind and leisure were limited to your retirement as a member of the Jewish Agency, I very much fear that this would cause a grave misunderstanding, even though unjustified. In spite of minor differences, you have strongly supported Weizmann. You have let it be understood, certainly among non-Zionists and I think to a great extent among Zionists in this country and that has its reflection abroad, that he was the man whom you considered indispensable to the whole movement. While for a time you backed the other tendency of the Zionist Organization in America, from this you have certainly derived little satisfaction. Now, your leaving the Agency will be construed to be a withdrawal of that support and as far as you know with no one to take his place. You heard, as did the others, what Professor Laski[6] said about him so far as dealing with the British Government was concerned.

Now the purport of this homily is as follows: I think you once told me that you were a member of either 53 or 54 boards or committees. If you would withdraw from half of them for the purpose of securing rest nobody would have a right to draw any inferences from it as against any one cause, but if you do not and only withdraw from one, then I think and this may sound hard to you, that such withdrawal will do more harm to Palestine than the good that you have done in all these years. Forgive me if this sounds hard, but between us there is no need for compliments and I hope none for apologies.

And then I come to your last paragraph. I remember quite a number of years ago, before the first steps were taken toward the formation of the enlarged Jewish Agency and before the Survey Commission was planned, that I went to see Bernard Flexner and made the suggestion to him that we Jews in America should, with the then PEC and any other forces that he could draw into it and without Zionism or non-Zionism, or the Agency, or politics, devote ourselves in America to one or two particular things which we would take up as the American contribution to the upbuilding of Palestine. I thought that was sound then. It may be sound now, but I doubt it. We have mingled political and economic affairs too much to be able to divorce them. If you want to build houses, you must have security. If you want to manufacture goods, you must have tariffs, or at least Palestine thinks it must have tariffs. The possibility of making people self-supporting depends upon their taxes. If not too heavy a burden is to be laid upon the PEC, there must be influence brought to bear to see that the Government does not neglect to do those things connected with the economic life of a people which a government ought to do.

I am sure that you would be doing a great deal if you continued your interest in the land that you got and are working, in the PEC, in the Dead Sea concession, which I believe you are in, maybe in the Rutenberg plant, if you are in that, and certainly not withdraw your interest in the University. Those would satisfy any reasonable expectation that the Jewish people might have on any one man who has done and who is doing so much in other directions.

If you withdraw, it will involve the withdrawal of many other non-Zionists in the Agency in this country and possibly some abroad. One has to contemplate what the final effect will be. Of course, I cannot predict the coming elections to the Zionist Congress, but with the announcement of your withdrawal I imagine a considerable part of the support of Weizmann would fall. The Revisionists, joined by the Mizrachi, would I think probably control the Congress. A man like Deputy Gruenbaum[7] might become the leader. He is frankly for a Jewish State and Jewish majority. That these results are unattainable in any span of life that we understand, I think you and I agree. We would probably, therefore, witness of necessity the complete yielding of the British Government to Arab demands and a minority status of the Jews in Palestine, possibly less favorable than the minority status which they suffer or enjoy in some states of Eastern Europe and so the bubble will be pricked and all the fine hopes and all the great aspirations will go aglimmering as have the hopes of the Jewish people in the past.

No one word of this is written for the purpose of altering your determination, but only to put the picture before you as I see it, I admit rather dimly and hastily. I conclude my letter as you conclude your personal note to me with certainty this letter ought to be changed and probably it ought to be destroyed.

You talk about the worm turning. I think too much is said about and sometimes against the worm. It is a long time since I read the works of Charles Darwin,[8] but I recollect one of his most fascinating books to have been on the earth worm and if my memory is not wrong this very humble creature by his turning succeeded in raising the level of the earth by an inch in a year or maybe in a century or whatever it is. But, at all events, the worm does something very important to the earth and we worms of the Jewish people who one time or another have thought that we could move our Jewish world and move the whole world by leaps and bounds, probably have to be satisfied with the thought that if we move it by inches in years or decades we have done about all we can do. [W]

1. David Werner Senator (1876–1953), Zionist leader; a member of the Jewish Agency Executive, 1930–35.
2. James Rosenberg (1874–1970), lawyer and philanthropist; a former chairman of the Joint Distribution Committee.
3. See letter to Felix M. Warburg, December 18, 1930.
4. The report of Sir John Hope Simpson supported that of the Shaw Commission and

recommended curtailment of Jewish immigration to Palestine. It was issued simultaneously with the Passfield White Paper.

5. Morris Rothenberg (1885–1950), jurist and civic leader; president of the Zionist Organization of America, 1932–35.

6. Neville Laski (1890–1969), English lawyer and communal leader; president of the Board of Deputies of British Jews; brother of Harold Laski.

7. Yitzhak Gruenbaum (1879–1970), Polish Zionist leader; representative in the Sejm, 1919–32.

8. Charles Darwin (1809–82), English naturalist who developed the theory of the organic evolution of living creatures. The book referred to is *The Formation of Vegetable Mould Through the Action of Worms* (London, 1881).

TO FELIX M. WARBURG

May 25, 1931

I am returning to you herewith the papers which Miss Emanuel sent me and on which you wanted my comment.

Doctor [Maurice B.] Hexter's letter to you of May 11th:—I think it was wise that such a meeting as that presided over by Doctor Ruppin[1] should have been held. It seems to me that the question of leadership in the Agency revolves about the question of leadership in the World Zionist Organization. The Agency as such has not, to my knowledge, evinced any desire for a change in leadership. I assume this to be true for America, England and Germany—at least. For the other countries I cannot speak. This, of course, depends upon Doctor [Chaim] Weizmann's willingness to retain such leadership.[2] It is his own right to determine whether for reasons of health or his own private concerns, or both, he cannot retain the leadership. Every movement that is worth while must be stronger than any one man, and hence the situation of an alternate must be faced. In any event, and for reasons of ordinary prudence, there should be a Vice-President of the Agency. Both of these officials should reside in Europe in my opinion. . . .

As for the Zionist Organization itself, the whole tone of the discussion leaves on my mind an impression of bewilderment. "Center," "Labor," "Mizrachi," "Revisionist" and what not, all mean a continental parliament and its numerous blocs. The tone that should be adopted at the Zionist Congress—and this irrespective of person—is that Palestine in the present juncture cannot afford this luxury of individualisms and that, unless these are sunk, the effort and hope of years is certain to end in disaster.

The question as to whether a strong American Section of the Agency can be established does not rest with one man, but rather with a question of discipline, in the first place among American Zionists. If they view the

Agency as a body to which Zionists as such owe no particular adhesion except in Campaigns and hold the right to have parallel bodies and committees and issue separate pronounciamentoes, the Angel Gabriel himself could not create a real unity. The task of winning the mass of non-Zionists is not an easy one. So far there has not been much help for it. We have had many reproaches for our tardiness and little help by way of consideration. The slowness of non-Zionists to come in has been more than matched by the desertion or separatism of many Zionists.

The [London] *Jewish Chronicle* has been an enemy of the Agency from its inception and the American correspondent of the *Chronicle* has systematically misrepresented and belittled the movement in this country. In this effort Jacob de Haas, who is considered by many—without reason, I hope—to be the mouthpiece of Mr. Justice [Louis D.] Brandeis, has been the leading spirit. . . . [W]

1. Arthur Ruppin (1876–1943), sociologist and Zionist leader.
2. In protest against Weizmann's policy of cooperation with the British, the Revisionists and other Zionist factions at the 1931 Zionist Congress at Basle demanded that the creation of a Jewish State be declared the official goal of Zionism. The motion did not carry and Jabotinsky stormed out of the Congress with his followers. Weizmann, nonetheless, resigned and Nahum Sokolow succeeded him to the presidency of the Zionist organization.

TO FELIX M. WARBURG, NEW YORK CITY

June 29, 1931

I had your letter of June 26th. I am glad to hear that Sir Leonard Cohn[1] has been brought around. I am afraid there are real difficulties ahead about the [Hebrew] University, although, as I understand, [Albert] Einstein says he does not consider the question of an academic head immediately urgent. He wants a University, but he does not want the creation of a learned proletariat and so long as the University is not made a real university, the young men of Palestine will continue to migrate elsewhere.

To return to [Chaim] Weizmann, whether Einstein is right in saying that Weizmann's taking over the academic headship will renew confidence in the development of the University that was lost, I do not know. Weizmann is a man of science, whereas [Judah L.] Magnes is devoted to the humanities. Whatever Magnes knows of science he has learned mostly in the last four years. On the other hand, Weizmann has neither knowledge nor experience which would bear upon either the Institute of Jewish Studies or the Oriental Department of the University.

With regard to [Arthur] Biram,[2] while no doubt I shall see him, so far as I am concerned I do not mean to take any part in developing his school and the Haifa Technicum. As you know, I have tried several times. There seems to be no support for it but only talk in America. Moreover, I think that our experience dictates that we should not overburden ourselves in this country. As about 80% of the support for the University comes from America and we have concerned ourselves a great deal about the affairs of the University, I think the group in Germany might take over the leadership of these two schools. . . .

Of course, Baron Edmund [de Rothschild] is sound in the theory that elementary education comes before and is basic to higher education, but I think that the local people ought to support elementary education themselves—certainly to a much greater extent than they have. I do not, of course, blame him for not aiding the development of the University at this time.

I am simply writing these down for you as a last bit of chat and do not expect an answer.

There is one point in Baron Edmund's letter which leads me to this thought. He is undoubtedly right in saying that your influence is very great. I do not know what arrangements you have made with Mr. [Joseph C.] Hyman about keeping informed, but I do think that you might be able to render very great service if you were willing, upon information received either during the sitting of the Administrative Committee or the Council, to give your full advice by cable.

I am not returning the letters to you but am taking them as a sort of memorandum.

I am not mailing this letter but carrying it to New York and assume that I shall be able to get it into your hands by some discreet messenger.

We shall miss you very much. [W]

1. Sir Leonard Lionel Cohen (1858–1938), British banker and railway magnate; president of the Jewish Colonization Association, 1929–34.
2. See letter to Felix M. Warburg, March 24, 1931.

TO FELIX M. WARBURG, NEW YORK CITY

September 9, 1931
The first thing I am going to trouble you about is maybe not of the highest importance to you but urgent in the matter of time. I am sure you know all about this effort of calendar reform[1] which is being promoted by

Mr. Eastman[2] and the objection of the Jews to it because it would make a floating Sabbath. While we were at Basle Doctor [Joseph H.] Hertz turned up and told us that Rabbis had done all they could in the matter and that moreover it was necessary to have some influential laymen to indicate that this was not purely a stand of reactionary Rabbis. Accordingly, [Osmond] d'Avigdor Goldsmid and I called a meeting of about twenty men in Basle and we agreed to submit a petition. I understand that this petition will be presented in person by D'Avigdor Goldsmid and, if they can secure his presence, Baron Edmund [de Rothschild]. They are very anxious to have your consent to have your name signed to it and if you will write or telegraph me to that effect, I will notify them by cable. I shall be greatly obliged, too, if you will return this draft to me.

I would like very much to have Herbert Lehman permit his name to go on and then I shall try for another man—maybe Judge Cardozo.[3] [D]

1. The reform of the Gregorian calendar would have a year of 364 days with a "blank" day (two in leap years), which would not be reckoned part of any week. This would cause the Sabbath to come out on a different day each year, with resulting hardship to Jewish Sabbath-observers.
2. George Eastman (1854–1932), American industrialist; popularizer of photography.
3. Benjamin Nathan Cardozo (1870–1938), associate justice of the United States Supreme Court, 1932–38.

A Museum of Jewish Ceremonial Objects, ancestor of the present-day Jewish Museum in New York City, was established as an adjunct to the Jewish Theological Seminary Library in 1929.

TO ALEXANDER MARX, NEW YORK CITY

Philadelphia, September 25, 1931
. . . Theoretically speaking if it is possible I should like to have the museum open every day, let us say from 10 to 5. A museum that is only open on certain days is no use, and nothing is so exasperating as to find a museum closed, and the museum to be open requires an attendant be present all the time. The grade of attendant we can discuss. I think as everybody requires relief we could enter into an arrangement with the [American Jewish] Historical Society whose collections could also be open with ours, that their curator should be on duty on certain days during the week for certain hours to relieve the other person.

I should also strongly favor keeping the library open in the evening and that, again, is a question of money. We must see whether we have it, but this fine big place ought to be available in my opinion, every week day from 9 to 9 or from 10 to 9 and even on Sunday morning. I do not feel that we have a moral right to have assembled the greatest collection in the world and then deal with it as if it were only available to a privileged class. [JTS]

On October 12, 1931, the New York Times *published Adler's letter on the worldwide economic and social chaos.*

TO THE EDITOR OF THE NEW YORK TIMES

Philadelphia, October 7, 1931

My life has been spent in teaching, scientific work and administration of religious, scientific and educational institutions. In this work I have been outside of the current activities of the age—industrial, political and researches in the natural and physical sciences, which in their turn have led up to the great inventions which have promoted industrial life.

I shall not try to appraise the cause or the effect of the great war but consider only the period since its ending. Within that time the world has been led by statesmen, politicians, captains of industry, bankers, journalists and professors of political economy and social science. I think that it does not require much frankness on their part to admit that they have failed and that the world is in a mess.

The need is very great, and it has occurred to me that since all these great minds have failed it might be in order for a devotee of the older learning—which takes into account not only today and tomorrow but also the entire experience of the race—to contribute something which would help to diagnose the present situation and, maybe, point the way to a remedy.

The present generation has lost faith in God. They transferred that faith to man. Then they lost faith in men. Now each man has lost faith in himself. This is the major cause of the present situation of the world. There is more food in the world than people can eat, and yet there is starvation. There are more articles manufactured in the world than people can buy, and yet there is deprivation; there are hoards of gold and money, in some parts of the world, at least, but banks are breaking. Educated and trained people are draining gold from banks and putting it in safe-deposit boxes and the economic arteries of the world are rapidly approaching a state of paralysis.

We have been living under the general direction of physical science and the mechanical industry which grew therefrom. The Western world created as their god something they called Progress. Progress essentially meant machinery. Work was to be taken off men's backs and out of their hands. A tractor and a mowing machine could do the work of ten men on a farm. A steam shovel could do the work of fifty men. This process has gone so far that everything that the world can absorb is being produced, there is an overplusage, and twenty million people in the Western world are out of work.

What is the remedy? I would say, in the first place, a return to the belief in God. I would add a return of confidence of men in each other and of each individual in himself. Our whole modern economic life has been built upon confidence, sometimes called credit, in itself a form of faith; once that is lost, the economic structure is destroyed.

Men used to work twelve hours a day for $1 a day; on farms for 75 cents a day. Today they work eight hours a day for $6 a day. They must work six hours a day for five days in the week and for less money. We have been obfuscated in America by slogans like "Do not lower the standard of living." What sense is there in a proposal that maintains the standard of 85 per cent of the population and throws the other 15 per cent on charity?

Another aspect of the situation must be faced frankly, and that is women's work. Formerly they were homemakers and regarded it as an honorable pursuit. With the "emancipation" of women they came into many new fields of endeavor. They were capable, efficient, interesting and accepted lower wages than men. They have displaced large numbers of men who may never get a job again. If the woman supports a family there is no criticism. But if it is a question of a fur coat, some extra frocks or cosmetics—to that extent the economic situation is disturbed.

There is so much work to do in the world; there are so many people to do it. Hence it must be divided in such a way that every one shall have a share of the work. The old talk used to be of a division of wealth; today the demand is a division of work. Let our "best minds" set themselves to this task.

What, for example, could the Federal Government undertake? It expends $26,000,000 per annum on rented buildings. It could without greater ultimate cost create a great building program of $525,000,000, which would put many men in employment. The interest on money borrowed for such a purpose would be less than the rent paid.

The city of New York expends per annum on rents for buildings occupied for public purposes $2,500,000, which it could, with a saving to the public, put into a building program of $50,000,000. The people who rent buildings to the city of New York earn at least 5 per cent on their capital, which the city could borrow at a lesser rate. The city of Philadelphia pays at least $450,000 annually for rented buildings. It could readily put $9,000,000 to work upon buildings.

People of means should try to rid themselves of the fear that they will end their days in the poorhouse. They should buy and build and carry on to the extent of their means. The idea of not giving out work to save money to give to charity is wholly mistaken. Most people do not want charity—they want work.

I hesitate to touch upon the question of money standards, and yet this, too, must be considered. Gradually the two metals used for coinage—gold and silver— gave way to gold. Without taking into consideration the recent disturbances, the depreciation in the value of silver has almost destroyed, or at least greatly lessened, the purchasing power of China and India, holding over 700,000,000 people.

Finally, the politicians must take a hand. They must realize that in the modern world isolation is impossible, and war, or the threat of war, a crime. If they can be brought to realize this before it is too late, the faith and the confidence of men will be restored and we shall witness the beginning of the end of a hysteria which seems to have bereft mankind of sanity.

TO ARTHUR HAYS SULZBERGER,[1] NEW YORK CITY

October 14, 1931

I have your letter of October 12th and thank you for sending me the clipping of the publication of a part of my article in the *New York Times.*[2] I think it hangs together pretty well, although, of course, in one or two places it seems to me a little jumpy. Your editorial department improved the article much in many ways. It removed what was too much of my personality and of my humility in approaching this great subject, though I think that any one person must be rather humble in approaching so great a subject as the present situation of the world. Men who have not the privilege of the pulpit, or the editorial page, or the college chair are not apt to be dogmatic.

There were, however, some real thoughts which I was not allowed to get across but which I would be glad if the eminent men who sit around the *Times* luncheon table would think of anyhow. I am well aware of the fact that the dole which has brought England to a bad financial crisis, but maybe saved it from a revolution, is a sort of continuing promise and has many abuses, but all of our states and municipalities have been for the last two years making annual appropriations out of public funds to create employment and to give actual relief, and I think we are not facing the situation frankly, as indeed we have not faced many situations. We must recognize the fact, too, that large numbers of people are acting in the most disgraceful fashion both as to the hoarding of gold and the whispering of lack of soundness in bank A or B. Maybe I was more impressed than you have been in New York because we have been enormously unfortunate in Philadelphia on just that point.

I am also convinced that one of the important ideas which you would not allow me to put forward was the necessity for the return to handicrafts and the halting of the creation of labor-saving machinery. We are in such a machine age in this country that people are no longer learning to work with their hands and I am going to give you a curious incident. A number of years ago, I had purchased a barometer and clock, which I brought from Paris, for my mother on her eightieth birthday. The figures were bold and the dials luminous. There was nothing very recondite about it. It would have been twenty-five years ago a very simple piece of instrument making. A few years after that, a friend of mine, a lady, reached the age of seventy-five years and I was trying to think of something that I could give her and finally thought I would get one of these barometers duplicated. I had the first one made in Paris by Hasbrook, on the Rue de la Paix. I went to every instrument maker in Philadelphia to find out whether they had such a thing or would make it. They all said no—they could not. I then spent some time in New York and finally, after failing everywhere, decided to go to Meyerowitz in New York, who have two distinguished places in Paris and one in London. They had not the article and when I saw the manager and asked him whether they would make one for me, he told me that there were no workmen in America who would undertake it and that he would have to have it made abroad. I am sure that this statement can be duplicated in hundreds of ways by other people. . . . [W]

1. Arthur Hays Sulzberger (1896–1968), son-in-law of publisher Adolph Ochs; publisher of the *New York Times*, 1935–61; Cyrus Adler's cousin.
2. See letter to the editor of the *New York Times*, October 7, 1931.

TO GEORGE ALEXANDER KOHUT, NEW YORK CITY

November 19, 1931

I have your letter of November 16th and I shall make it a point, sometime when I can do so, to telephone you when I am in New York so that we can talk about the Kohut Foundation, though heavens knows I have enough problems to solve as it is.

The American Jewish Historical Society meeting was a disappointment in one way and a great satisfaction in another.

The satisfaction arose from the fact that we are vastly increasing our collections and that we are commencing to get them in order, and I am very happy that I have been able, through the Seminary, to place proper accommodations at the disposal of the Society. Probably the minds of everybody concerned this year were on the collections and on getting them in order and the details of the meeting were left to go by the board.

As was pointed out, many of the officers of the Society are getting older and they are less likely to be as active as they have been. I had nothing to do with the arrangements for the meeting, but I think the meeting was badly staged. The room chosen was much too large. For such a society, an attendance of fifty to sixty people is very fair and that many I think we had on Saturday night, but we were in a room that holds over two hundred and so it looked rather sparse.

I had the impression that emphasis would be laid for the rest of the papers on Sunday afternoon and that most of the Sunday morning session would be devoted to the meeting of the Council, and indeed I understand that there were both papers and visitors who came for the Sunday afternoon meeting.

I think that papers ought to be scheduled for definite sessions: A, B and C being put down for the evening session, D, E and F for the morning session, and so and so many people for the afternoon session. I think that every person should be allowed twenty minutes for a paper and nobody should present more than one paper at a given meeting until every other person has had an opportunity. A person who has more than one paper and there is no time, the second paper and the third paper should be read by title.

Of course, our great lack is and always has been that we are virtually without trained historians who will devote themselves to American Jewish history. The young historians whom we train in this country—and they are not so many—prefer to go off to Rome or Posen and edit their work over there. We shall never get a trained body of men in this country until we can offer a fellowship or two in American Jewish history to a graduate student of one of our institutions. That seems to me to be the real thing to undertake.

. . . I shall have a talk with Doctor [A. S. W.] Rosenbach sometime in the near future about the mechanics of our meetings. I can remember the time when the most eminent members of the community, wherever we were, deemed it a privilege to attend our meetings.

I was impressed by the activity of some of the people in the Shearith Israel Congregation, even though it runs almost entirely in the direction of genealogy.

Finally, I have come to the conclusion that Saturday night and Sunday are about the worst days for a meeting. I recently tried an experiment at the opening of the Seminary. We have always had our openings on Sunday night on the theory that that was the time that there were no theaters and no other attractions to keep people away from these occasions. This year, without any added attraction, we had our opening on a Monday night and twice as many people came as on any previous occasion.

All of this is more or less gossip and you need not trouble yourself to reply to it. [W]

For the Jews of Germany, the news continued to worsen. Anti-Semitism was increasing apace and the methods used by the German Jewish community to combat it seemed to be doing little good.

TO FELIX M. WARBURG, NEW YORK CITY

November 30, 1931

. . . I think the expenditure of any considerable sum of money to study the subject of anti-Semitism in Germany or anywhere else would be a waste of time and a waste of money. As you know, the American Jewish Committee had such a study made for Germany not so very long ago, at a cost of $7,500. We studied the report carefully and we got certain information, including the fact that there was an international organization with headquarters in Switzerland. As you know, the Jews of Germany have spent hundreds of thousands of dollars in the publication of books, scientific and popular, in the effort to counteract the anti-Semitic movement. I need not tell you either that the anti-Semitic movement in Germany is not, by any means, solely due to the War. Anti-Semitism, as a movement, was created in Germany. I have always believed that it was deliberately fostered by Prince [Otto von] Bismarck to distract the minds of the German people from some of the things that he was doing. The highly cultural position of Germany resulted in the anti-Semitic movement being carried to other neighboring countries: Russia, France, Austria, etc., but, beyond that, anti-Jewish hatred has been strong in Germany for hundreds of years and is one of the real reasons why there is so large a population of Jews in Poland who speak Yiddish. These Jews in Poland came from Germany.

Now this idea of stressing the contributions of German Jews, or Austrian Jews, to cultural civilization, etc., in the hope that it might offset this anti-Semitic agitation seems to me to promise no result at all. The more you stress what Jews have done, the more hatred and envy you will arouse. We are not dealing with rational beings in Germany just now. I was told by one of my colleagues, who was present at the International Congress of Orientalism in Leiden last September, that a German professor from one of the large universities—I do not happen to remember his name—read a paper protesting against the phrase "New Testament" on the ground that this implied and gave authority to the Old Testament and hence indicated the beginning of Christianity from Judaism. Now when a professor of a university can think that by changing the name of the New Testament he could obliterate references in the Gospels and in the Epistles to the Hebrew Bible, I think we are dealing with madmen. . . .

You may recall that a number of years ago . . . the Jewish Publication Society invited the late Doctor Joseph Jacobs to write a book entitled "Jewish Contributions to Civilization."[1] He did not quite finish the book at the time of his death, but a committee of us went over it very carefully and came to the conclusion that there was so much meat in it that we would publish it. In other words, I am rambling along. But there have been many studies and a great deal of literature on it. The literature of anti-Semitism and the studies about it would make quite a little library.

What is really needed is to put some decency into the hearts and souls of men. The really sad part of the whole business is that whereas in the Middle Ages or later hatred of Jews—I am not interested in the euphemism "anti-Semitism"—came from the ignorant classes and in the main was due to superstitions and distorted teachings of the Church, to-day it is in the main an intellectual cult of professors and university students. I feel a little defiant in the matter. I myself almost never pay attention to anything that is called anti-Semitism. I try to live a decent life and do my work and if anybody hates me for it, I hope he will go to Hell, if there is such a place. . . . [AJC]

1. See letter to Joseph Jacobs, July 6, 1916.

TO FELIX M. WARBURG, NEW YORK CITY

December 17, 1931

. . . I am afraid you are right that we have to keep on the map because I am getting more and more bad news from Poland. These latest troubles are an excuse for a further boycott.

I think I am rested but I am not well. I have a combination of a few minor complaints all of which keep me rather below par. I was in New York yesterday and the day before; I did not call you up because you were busy and I had nothing to bother you with. Tuesday evening I went into my little room and spent the entire evening by myself and went to bed. That is also a way of resting. Last evening I had Mr. Stroock,[1] Rabbi [Max] Drob and Mr. Oppenheimer[2] to a little dinner meeting before some of them went to a meeting at Morrison's[3] house. I spent several hours with the Faculty in the afternoon. I am oppressed in every quarter with the terrible business of money and reducing salaries, and maybe even discharging people.

Somehow or other I cannot quite get it into my head how this country ever expects to restore business. We say that business depends upon the purchasing power. If people can purchase the factories can run; if factories can run then the railroads will have goods to carry. But we are doing the whole thing the other way. We have inaugurated economy; we are throwing people out of work; we are cutting their salaries and reducing purchasing power, and then on the other hand we are collecting great funds to help the unemployed. Certainly this dog has his tail in his mouth. I hope you won't mind the little homily on economics.

Here in Philadelphia in our Library I shall be forced to a decision as between discharging one-third of the employees or reducing all the salaries by one-third. I have decided that if the City Government decides on discharging one-third of the force, I shall resign, as I am not willing to do that.[4]

I am writing you this not because I want to turn my troubles to you but because I think that men in your position in the business world ought to think out some plan other than the appointment of a Commission by the White House, or the getting up of a pool to support banks. Those two methods are not going to get anybody any work. [W]

1. Solomon Marcuse Stroock (1873–1941), corporation lawyer; active in the Jewish Theological Seminary and in the American Jewish Committee; succeeded Adler to the presidency of the Committee.
2. Arthur Oppenheimer (1895–1959), partner at Kuhn Loeb; director of the Seminary, 1926–59.

3. Isidore D. Morrison (1872–1938), lawyer and communal leader; director of the Seminary, 1931–38.

4. Adler was a member of the Board of Trustees of the Free Library of Philadelphia from 1913 on and served as president, 1925–39.

TO BRUNO BLOCH,[1] ZURICH, SWITZERLAND

January 20, 1932

. . . It is well for a Jew not to be too much concerned about the everyday life of the Jews in the world, because it is far from pleasant. Certainly the situation in Germany, in Poland and in Roumania give cause for anxiety, and in Russia, while the Jews live, Judaism may die. The hope in Palestine too is beset with enough difficulties to cause one anxiety and yet I find that there the people still have enthusiasm. Here in America, and I am not speaking of Jews now only, there is a great deal of concern. Unemployment is common; people who were once rich have become poor and men seem to think that the ground is crumbling under their feet. I doubt very much whether there is a general physical reason for all of this despondency, but it is as though the nerves of our people here had failed them. I may be misjudging it, but so it seems to me.

For myself, I still cannot report complete return to health. My skin is not yet normal, the disturbance being, however, confined mostly to my hands, ankles and the left shoulder, and it is not of a nature to distress me but only to annoy me. Following your advice, I have kept to your remedies and have not visited any other dermatologist, though if I do not clear up entirely during the winter, I shall be looking forward to the warm season of the spring and summer with a little misgiving. I have had other disturbances: an attack of ptomaine poisoning and a bad cold, so that I cannot report myself being in excellent physical condition. However, I too put in a great many hours of work every day and everybody seems to bring their burdens to me as of yore.

You may be interested to know that my daughter, our only child, is going to be married on Thursday of this week. She is marrying a musician,[2] a rather nice boy, a good violinist and a member of a quartet who are accustomed to do their practicing each year for several months at Lausanne, so that she is more likely to be getting to Switzerland than I am. . . . [W]

1. Bruno Bloch (b. 1878), dermatologist. He had treated Adler in Gstaad in 1931.
2. Wolfe Wolfinsohn (1899–   ), first violinist of the Stradivarius Quartet.

TO JOSEPH T. ROBINSON,[1] WASHINGTON, D.C.

January 28, 1932

I suppose you will wonder why a resident of the State of Pennsylvania is addressing you rather than addressing the Senator of his own State. I should like to say in my own defense that in the first place I am a native of Arkansas and, though living away from there for many years, have always felt a strong affection for the State; and secondly, I think that you would more likely be interested in what I have to say to you than would the Senator from Pennsylvania who is [not] a member of the Committee on Foreign Relations.

I should like to urge with all the force at my command that the Senate Foreign Relations Committee report the World Court protocols[2] to the Senate now. I am of the opinion that the present important economic reconstruction legislation, which is being enacted by Congress in the hope of bringing our country out of the despondency in which so many of our citizens find themselves, will not be effective unless and until the United States takes some definite step toward stabilizing the peace of the world.

I am not now proposing that we enter the League of Nations, which under the present administration I presume to be impossible. President [Woodrow] Wilson never somehow entered into an alliance with the powers of Europe, on whose side we were engaged in War, but always insisted upon the word "associated" instead of "allied"; and our American traditions might be satisfied if we became associated with the League of Nations instead of a member of the League of Nations. I myself would not be afraid of direct membership, but that is not the point at the moment.

I believe that the major unsettlement of the world is not due wholly to the destruction of property in the last war, but to a constant fear of the next war, and the aloofness of the United States, in spite of all of our observers at Geneva, is a major factor in contributing to this uneasiness. We are the only people who are really considered disinterested because we have enough land, we have plenty of coast-line and we have enough mineral wealth and everybody knows that we have no designs upon the property of another nation.

Failing our entry into the League, the next best thing that we can do is to enter the Court, and I believe it is the only thing that we can do to help along our own stability and that of the world in the present crisis. If the Committee on Foreign Relations would only report the World Court protocols to the Senate they could then be put upon the Senate's calendar and have a chance, and I hope a good chance, before the Senate itself. This would be our real present contribution toward stabilization.

I hope you will not mind my writing to you in this way, and am, with great respect. . . . [W]

1. Joseph T. Robinson (1872–1937), U.S. senator from Arkansas, 1913–37.
2. The United States never joined the court because the Senate refused to ratify its statute without reservations.

According to the constitution of the enlarged Jewish Agency, Zionists and non-Zionists were to have parity. In practice, the Zionists managed to maintain an effective control over the organization, owing to the fact that they were organized and the non-Zionists represented no organization. Mutual recriminations between Zionists and non-Zionists were a perennial feature of Jewish Agency politics.

TO MOSES A. LEAVITT,[1] NEW YORK CITY

February 11, 1932

I received your letter of February 1, together with the verbatim Minutes of the meeting held on January 16, 1932. A good portion of the discussion took place after I had been obliged to leave, and so I read that part through more carefully, and I must say with a certain disgust. I do not expect to attend any more meetings with the representatives of the Jewish Agency if the non-Zionists are to be made the target of constant reproach. If these gentlemen cannot keep a civil tongue in their heads, as far as I am concerned, they can talk to blank walls. Since 1929, outside of the Emergency Fund, about 40 per cent of those who contributed to Palestine in the United States were non-Zionists. Of the Emergency Fund, the greater part was contributed by non-Zionists. It was my observation that from this Emergency Fund the Zionists held off and thought this was the non-Zionists' job.

Considering the fact that the Zionists have had since the Summer of 1898 to organize, it does not seem to me that their showing for Palestine has been so strong. As you know, a very considerable part of the financial burden of the enlarged agency was due to the miserable failure of the American Zionist Commonwealth,[2] as that was the name of that splendid organization.

The constant use of the word "facade" is distinctly insulting. Mr. [Louis] Lipsky was the gentleman who started it. What did he leave behind by way of a real organization when he was retired from the presidency of the Zionist Organization? What is the real size of the present Zionist Organization? It seems to me for all its noise it is a "facade." The majority of its members are women of the Hadassah organization and a good many women join Hadassah on the plea of the work.

Mr. [Felix M.] Warburg and I have been reproached for not continuing to take responsibility. Well, during the troubled times after the White Paper when I did take some responsibility, whenever they chose, the Zionists did a little sniping in the back. I would sit around with the others at meetings; we would agree upon the cables, and then separate cables would be sent, differing from the ones the Committee had decided upon.

There is a great deal said about organizing a non-Zionist constituency. I feel sure that it cannot be done. Among the Jews of America, only a handful are members of the Zionist organization and the others are potentially interested in Palestine. It is impossible to organize 95 per cent of the Jews of America just for Palestine. As far as I can see, the only feasible suggestion is that presented by Judge Horace Stern, in which every congregation would have, among other things, a committee that would interest itself in Palestine. Moreover, I do not believe in making a fetish of organization. I am interested in the result and the result is the upbuilding of Jewish life in Palestine. . . . [JTS]

1. Moses A. Leavitt (1894–1965), assistant secretary of the Joint Distribution Committee.
2. American Zion Commonwealth, company founded in 1914; affiliated with the Zionist Organization of America, for the purchase and development of land in Palestine. It was dissolved in 1931.

TO FELIX M. WARBURG, NEW YORK CITY

February 22, 1932

I am having difficulties with the American Jewish Congress because they want to insist on proposing an early conference "in a country contiguous to Germany" and I see in the press that they have voted for a world conference next summer.[1] I am resolutely determined not to agree to this and if necessary shall break off relations with them. It is my present idea to cable Sylvain Levi[2] suggesting that he and our English friends should meet together, which they can readily do without any publicity, and after they have a programme to inform us of it by cable and if the matter is very urgent we can telephone to them. I really do not see what we can do, but if we can do something we must. . . . [W]

1. The World Jewish Congress first met at Geneva in 1936.
2. Sylvain Levi (1863–1935), French orientalist; president of the Central Committee of the Alliance Israélite Universelle, 1920–35.

TO NAHUM SOKOLOW, NEW YORK CITY

March 10, 1932

. . . May I remind you of the history so far as this past year is concerned. I virtually gave a promise, when I was in Basle, promptly upon my return to undertake movements to strengthen the Jewish Agency in America. I made frequent approaches to this subject, but owing to the divergencies that had been created in the Zionist Organization itself, the Zionist Organization did not know who was going to be in charge and I was requested to postpone any call toward establishing an American Section of the Agency until the Zionist Organization of America had settled its own difficulties. After these difficulties had been settled, I was again requested to postpone until you came over so that the establishment of the American Section of the Agency might coincide with the presence of the President of the Agency in America. You will recall this meeting; you were present at it. It was not a haphazard meeting. It had been preceded by at least two lengthy conferences and I had understood that there was an agreement that the persons who were called together should be organized as the American Section of the Jewish Agency. You will also recall the opposition, all of which came from the Zionist side, and the whole matter was referred to a Committee. The Committee was appointed. They seem to have come to the conclusion to organize the Section upon the basis that I proposed last January, when almost two months had been lost, but the Secretary said that each member was asked to give his comments before another meeting was called. I have given my comments;[1] I have heard nothing more. So far as I am concerned at the present time I am simply one member of the Council of the Agency.

I believe that if you will address an urgent suggestion particularly to Mr. [Robert] Szold and Mr. [Louis] Lipsky, and if they agree, there will come into being an American Section of the Agency and then somebody will be authorized to approach all these other communities. At present the situation is simply chaotic and certainly the fault is not to be laid at the non-Zionist door.

I have used, as you see, very direct language, because the situation calls for direct language.

I may add that within the past few days there was a conference held in my office in Philadelphia with regard to the launching of a campaign in Philadelphia for the Agency during the month of May.

Let me add one word to this. One could hardly expect that the general tone of the Zionist Congress at Basle would not have repercussion which would alienate non-Zionists. There was a general feeling among them (and I am not speaking of myself now) that the academic discussions which took place, added to the violent explosions between the different parties, could only mean that there was no hope of a united Israel for Palestine, or anything else; that if the Zionists themselves could engage in the sort of discussion and charges that were rife, there was no hope. I know that it is sometimes difficult to get Zionists to see this. They seem to glory in discussions; they seem to think that it shows that they are alive and that they are members of a real continental parliament, but the Congress of last summer certainly did alienate a percentage of non-Zionists' support, and you know it is much easier to alienate support than to secure it.

Let me say in conclusion to this rather rambling letter that I strongly urge the formation of this American branch so that some people, whoever they are, could speak in its name to our different communities.[2] [W]

1. See letter to Moses A. Leavitt, February 11, 1932.
2. The American section was never formed.

The German elections of 1932 meant increased Nazi activity and increased fears for the safety of the German Jewish community. By now, American Jewish leaders had begun to wake up to the danger and to explore avenues of action in support of German Jewry.

TO FELIX M. WARBURG, NEW YORK CITY

March 10, 1932

. . . I thought that I would have a reasonably quiet time in Washington, but there broke loose a cable through the Jewish Telegraphic Agency, part of which was published in the [*Jewish Daily*] *Bulletin,* which purported to send a request to the American Jewish Committee and the American Jewish Congress to see Mr. [Herbert] Hoover and get him to make a statement against Hitler, [William E.] Borah, etc., etc. Stephen Wise came to Washington, Alfred Cohen, of the Bnai Brith, was there and I was completely taken with conferences and telephone calls and telegrams.

As the charge was made that the *New York Times* correspondent in Berlin was minimizing the Hitler situation and especially with regard to the Jews,[1] I called up Adolph Ochs on the telephone getting him at his house rather late in the evening and he said that the *Times* was holding nothing which its correspondent told them but that he would send a special cable indicating that there were rumors that the *Times* was not getting the news.

The cable which appeared in the *Times* this morning, March 10th, was an answer to that.

I flatly refused to see the President, because I thought it was ridiculous to ask Mr. Hoover to take action with regard to the German elections on any ground, but I said to Wise, who had seen Borah and said that he had received the offer of Borah to go with me to Hoover, that since Mr. Borah made statements on all subjects, why not let him make a statement on this subject. Borah, however, replied that, in view of my conversation with Mr. Ochs, he would await a statement in the *New York Times*. Now the *New York Times* this morning said that Borah was being quoted by all the German parties.

Then came a telegram from James Waterman Wise[2] addressed to three Chairmen of the Goodwill Committee—Newton D. Baker, Roger W. Straus[3] and Professor Hayes,[4] respectively Protestant, Jewish and Catholic— urging that this Goodwill Association put itself on record against the Nazis. We had a long conference on the subject and there was a general agreement that if this Association did make such a statement that it would be said in Germany that the Jews in the Conference had incited the Christians to do it. However, there was a very strong feeling that they should not shirk and so one of the officials, who is also Secretary of the Federal Council of Churches of Christ in America,[5] got up on the floor and on his own individual responsibility made a statement which will, of course, be carried to the press. Just as I was starting to write to you, Roger Straus called me up on the telephone from New York and told me that Doctor Cadman,[6] who is connected with some international fellowship of Protestant churches, would adopt this statement as his own, cable it to the Lutheran churches in Germany and give it out here.

I also saw Mr. Simms,[7] of the Scripps-Howard newspapers, laid all the facts before him and by Friday, I think that all of their papers will carry a column on the subject. My object has been, as you see, to get this statement of American opinion without our appearing in it ourselves; but [Jacob] Landau has made a fuss about it and James Waterman Wise has made a fuss about it and of course I suppose all of the Yiddish papers have.

A number of the Christians who were attending this Goodwill Conference in Washington were very much concerned and two men came to me and said to me that if Hitler won and if it were a fact that the first attack upon the Jews would be toward expelling the one hundred thousand Jews now there that they would like to be considered as taking part in a general movement in this country for funds to help the people so expelled to settle in another country. I am writing this to you to-day. To-morrow, Friday, is probably the last day that any voice can come out of America that would have any effect on the elections. If, after you read this, you think that there is anything further that I can do or that anybody else can do, will you not call me up on the telephone? I have a feeling that in view of what Wise said that Borah said to him, Borah ought to give one of his blasts to-morrow morning, if you think that would help. [AJA]

1. The report from Berlin emphasized that the anti-Semitic element in the Nazi election campaign was negligible and made oblique reference to "sources outside of Germany" to the contrary.

2. James Waterman Wise (b. 1901), journalist and author; son of Stephen S. Wise.

3. Roger W. Straus (1871–1957), cochairman with Carelton Hayes of the National Conference of Christians and Jews; son of Oscar Straus.

4. Carelton J. H. Hayes (1882–1964), historian and diplomat; cochairman of the National Conference of Christians and Jews, 1928–45.

5. S. M. Cavert, general secretary.

6. Samuel P. Cadman (1864–1936), former president of the Federal Council of Churches of Christ in America, 1924–28.

7. William Phillip Simms (1881–1957), foreign editor for the Scripps-Howard newspapers.

TO HENRY S. MORAIS, NEW YORK CITY

March 24, 1932

. . . What I think you ought to feel is that the work that your father did is being carried on. He feared, at one time, that the Mikveh Israel Congregation would not continue after him. The seed that he planted for the [Jewish Theological] Seminary has grown and blossomed. I have repeated to you time and again that I have tried to keep his name living at the Seminary and his name, his portrait and his memory do continue there.

As for the biography,[1] I shall do it if I live. I presume you know the Jewish press sufficiently well to realize that aside from the field of education and religious work, intolerable burdens have been put upon me. I doubt whether there is another man of my age anywhere who is working harder than I am day and night. If I found other men to take this work and could give it all up and finish in a year your father's biography, it would be the happiest thing for me. Endeavor as I will, I cannot get this relief. I, too, have been, beside all these labors, not in good health and so I think you must accept the statement that I am giving everything that I humanly can to it.

It would have been so much better if you, with the help of some of the rest of us, or if we, with your help, when we were younger and we were in good health, could have taken up the preparation of a worthy literary memorial of your father. Now of necessity it drags. But his name and his memory are enshrined in the life of American Judaism and of Jewish learning and I do not think you should feel so badly about it as you seem to in the letter that you have written to me. [W]

1. See letter to Henry S. Morais, November 15, 1928.

TO FELIX M. WARBURG, NEW YORK CITY

May 31, 1932

I had your letter of May 26 enclosing the correspondence with Mr. Waldman.[1] I have tried to put myself in your place to begin with. The clause to which you object was one that I have examined pretty carefully. It is not well phrased but I do not think it was intended to bear the interpretation which you have put upon it. You interpret that you are asked to deflect or "switch" as you put it, your interest in helping the Jews of Germany to the meeting of the current needs of the American Jewish Committee.

My own reading of the words would be that since no requests have been made to the American Jewish Committee this year for financial aid by the German Jews for any of their quasi political purposes Mr. Waldman assumes that we will receive no such requests. Then his line of thought is that since for two years you have contributed the sum of $5,000 to the Committee for this purpose and since there is no demand for it this year, and since the Committee's back is to the wall you might be willing to give at least a part of what you had been giving through the Committee to Germany for the direct purposes of the Committee. As an exegete that would be my interpretation and not the one that you put upon it.

I myself had not seen this letter when it was sent to you by Mr. Waldman otherwise I should rather have advised that it be not sent but it is possible that he wrote to you instead of waiting for our meeting because he had understood that you were going to Chicago and might not be at the meeting of the Committee. . . .

Our position is very serious. If the American Jewish Committee should be obliged to close its doors it would injure the position of the Jews in a good many countries. It would certainly give cause for great delight to some of our unfriends in the United States. It may be that our services are not very great but at least they have the reputation of being great and an inability for us to go on would, I feel be a very great reflection upon our Jewish community and upon me personally. I do therefore hope that your resentment at the tone of Mr. Waldman's letter will not deter you from giving that aid to the Committee and to me in what is a real crisis. [W]

1. Morris David Waldman (1879–1963), social worker and rabbi; executive secretary of the American Jewish Committee, 1928–45.

During the Depression, nearly all educational institutions, the Hebrew University included, had no alternative but to tighten their belts and wait for the economic crisis to pass.

TO FELIX M. WARBURG, NEW YORK CITY

June 13, 1932

. . . Let me take his letter first. Of course I know that [Judah L.] Magnes feels badly and indeed most of us do, and he probably feels worse than many of us because he is not well and also because he has been possessed in the past of a spirit more buoyant than most people. Hence, when the spirits fall, the fall seems a little harder.

With the exception of the University of Chicago, I have never known of any University that had gone further in seven years than has the University of Jerusalem. Now it has fallen in evil times but not so evil as the rest of us. Unless I am very much mistaken the decrease of the budget of the University is not so great as the decrease of the budget of the Jewish Theological Seminary, for example, in New York. Here we have an Institution turning toward its fiftieth year, in the greatest Jewish community in the world and cut down close on to fifty percent as against 1929. Judah, I am sure, will realize that he is not the only person who has to guide an Institution through these very difficult times and try to prevent it from going under. As you know, in New York, when cuts became necessary I left it to the men themselves, and if our plan of the Teachers Institute goes through some of the men will be voluntarily reducing their income by from fifty to sixty percent just to keep the Institution afloat. Palestine has suffered less and is suffering less in its income than most other parts of the world.

Then there is another point about which I think Judah ought not feel so badly. He feels this great responsibility for these fine young men whom he has brought from Europe. Well, I think with one or two exceptions these fine young men from Europe would be much worse off if they stayed in Europe than they will be in Palestine. Certainly one cannot think that a Jewish scholar in Germany, or Hungary, or Austria would be better off in those countries now no matter how hard the situation in Palestine. I think possibly the only two men who would be better off would be the one man who came from America and the other man who came from England, I mean Roth[1] and Kligler,[2] and I think in the last analysis they could probably re-establish themselves.

Many of our people are covering up their difficulties. The University of Pennsylvania Faculty which had a ten percent cut in salaries this year faces another twenty-five percent cut next year. Even Harvard had to cut down. Columbia apparently is the only place that is really keeping itself afloat and I do not know the inside of that.

Now the moral of all this is that nobody can isolate themselves and that the University at Jerusalem has got to take its chances with the rest of the world. If Magnes can put himself in the frame of mind that he is doing better and not worse than others and that he has really done a remarkable thing and has not brought about a failure, that ought to have a psychological effect which, together with the good mountain air and rest ought to cheer him up. After all he is younger than the rest of us and ought to have better recuperative powers.

Of course there are other elements in the situation apart from the University which no doubt are weighing on his mind and these are the political and factional atmosphere among the Jews in Palestine which is sorely troubling his spirit. I wonder where these can be avoided. Certainly not in Poland, certainly not in Germany, certainly not in America. I think that the thing that ought to give Magnes the most courage is that the men in the Faculty themselves who, as he intimates, once looked upon him as a fund-raiser, now regard him as the person to hold the Institution together on the inside. Why is it not the thing to do?. . .

. . . To get back to the University, I do not see much need of bringing up any suggestions excepting that of funds. Certainly there can be no new developments at the present time, and the University, like all the rest of us, must hold on by the skin of its teeth. At the meeting of the Committee of the American Friends of the University a couple of days ago it seemed to me that upon the whole the showing for the University is better than almost for any other interest, certainly better than for any of our American interests and infinitely better than for the Keren Hayesod. I should say, roughly speaking, that the University and Hadassah are the two main interests for Palestine among the Jews of America. . . .

1. Leon Roth (1896–1963), brother of Cecil Roth; professor of philosophy at the Hebrew University, 1927–51.
2. Israel Jacob Kligler (1889–1944), chairman of the department of hygiene at Hebrew University.

TO CHAIM WEIZMANN, LONDON

New York City, June 13, 1932

It was very good of you to go to the trouble to write such a nice long letter in your own hand on the ship. I learned from the press that you have landed safely in England. I received only the other day the *Zionist Record* of May 6th and I could see that you and Mrs. Weizmann were the principal inhabitants of South Africa.

It happened that your letter came just on Shabuoth and as Sarah [Adler Wolfinsohn] and her husband were with us, I read the opening part to them. They and Mrs. Adler want me to thank you for your very kind wishes. Sarah will be living in New York. I really cannot remember whether I wrote about the young man whom she married, but he happens to be a native of South Africa and is a member of the Stradivarius Quartet. Therefore, they must live in New York. They only came back a few weeks ago from Europe and have been dancing in and out since.

I can imagine that your work in South Africa was difficult and I was very sorry to hear that both you and Mrs. Weizmann had ptomaine poisoning. At least, after all the good work that you did in South Africa, they might have treated you to better food. But seriously, undoubtedly you have proportionately done more for Palestine this year than anybody else, as indeed you had for many years past.

Here, I am not in very close touch. In the early part of the Campaign, Mr. [Louis] Lipsky used to send me a weekly statement of pledges, etc., but I have not been getting it lately and I imagine the result is not very good. In Philadelphia, we got about the same amount as last year.

When [Nahum] Sokolow came over here, largely I think under the inspiration of [Emmanuel] Neuman and [Felix] Frankfurter, his energies were bent toward the formation of a Pro-Palestine Committee of Senators, the Vice-President, etc., etc. I think weeks were expended on that. I took no part in it because I see no use in it. So long as we are not the Mandatory Power, so long as we have not a seat in the Permanent Mandate Commission of the League of Nations, it is a matter of indifference to me whether our politicians are interested or not. I am inclined to think that their principal interest is in getting a few votes from Jews. On the other hand, I am rather afraid that in some quarters this move was construed as a hint to the present Mandatory Power that American politicians were interested, which they probably are not really.

There have been numerous threats of the publication of the French report, but so far the French report has not been published. If it is reasonably unfavorable and is published with a statement of the policy of the Government which does not agree with the French report, then the evil will be a mitigated one. Maybe even the Jewish people will get used to reports.

I am going to give myself the luxury this summer of not attending any meetings. I have had a hard winter and through the loss of one of my colleagues, Professor [Max L.] Margolis, about which you may have read, I had an extra amount of work, which I must see through personally, principally in connection with the [Jewish] Quarterly Review; so it is my plan to finish out the July number, complete the October number and then go away toward the end of July and for once take an absolute vacation, a thing which I have certainly not done any summer since 1925 and, as far as I recall, never before that.

The University continues to hold a considerable interest here and I must say Doctor [A. S. W.] Rosenbach has done a good deal for it. While of course it too will not receive the funds that it ought to, proportionately it is doing better than any other of the appeals, because there is always the competition between the Keren Hayesod, the Jewish National Fund and Hadassah (all of which are said to be united, but really are not) and the numerous other things that are going on. As a matter of fact, our backs are to the wall with regard to our own institutions—certainly I can say it with regard to those over which I unhappily preside. Our big Jewish Theological Seminary in New York has to reduce its expenditures by over forty-five per cent and, in the last analysis, that means taking our flesh and blood, as you know.

Well, I really ought not to complain at all and ought to have tried to be cheerful when you have come back from such a long and hard trip, but I dare say that it is better that friends should be allowed to look into each other's minds than send each other Pollyanna stuff.

Here, the great excitement is on the part of your friend, Doctor S. S. Wise, who is now getting up a World Conference for a World Congress, which I presume means to deal with the troubles of the Jews of the world. Judge [Horace] Stern and I and the rest of the American Jewish Committee decided to take no part in it and in all probability I shall say so rather emphatically in public. As far as I can find out, although I may be doing them an injustice, that particular group has not been doing very much for Palestine.

At least, if they have, it has been *sotto voce,* which is not in accordance with their custom. [W]

The Hebrew University suffered from a crisis of identity in its early years. Should it be a degree-granting institution or simply a collection of research institutes, as Weizmann desired? In this dispute, Adler opposed Weizmann and sided with Magnes' vision of a university for the Jewish people.

TO FELIX M. WARBURG

July 15, 1932

It was good of you to send me a copy of Doctor [Chaim] Weizmann's letter of June 28th and your draft of a reply to him of July 7th.

It seemed better that I should not change your draft at all, but write you a letter which, if you wish, you can send to Doctor Weizmann to check up my memory or lack of memory.

I had been presiding over the meetings of the Council of the Jewish Agency at Zurich last summer and sitting up more than half the nights at sub-committee meetings, and I did not enter the meeting of the Board of Governors very fresh. I have no recollection at all of any discussion with regard to chemistry, but then I want to add further that I was ill at the time and did not stay out the meeting. I only attended two days.

This entire meeting, to my mind, was vitiated by politics, whatever the record, and no doubt there were quite a number of resolutions adopted. The entire time was taken up with the discussion of the election of Norman Bentwich, and not only the professors who are members of the Jewish Agency, like [Selig] Brodetsky, but even the professors who have nothing to do with it, like Hadamard,[1] for example, insisted that the political question had to be considered, and the point was not to elect Norman Bentwich to the professorship because it would give the British Government an easy way out of its dealings with Bentwich. During the course of this very long discussion, from which of course Bentwich absented himself and which went through several sessions, I went out and saw Bentwich and I asked him if he were elected whether he would accept. He said he would. Later I returned and made the argument that Bentwich was a grown man and should be able to decide for himself and I introduced the motion that he be elected, and I think I was the only person who voted for him. There may have been another. I am telling you this to show you that this meeting had a most unacademic atmosphere and I very much doubt whether other questions were likewise discussed upon their merits. It was right on top of a week's discussion of the Endziehle of Zionism.

Of course, there was a predominant feeling of having to cut down on account of budgetary difficulties and this, too, changed everything. . . .

I am going to another aspect of Doctor Weizmann's letter and since we are all writing frankly to each other about University matters, I may as well take this up too. He complains that, although President of the University, he has no place in it. He says that during the last three or four years his connection with the University has been purely nominal and that while his name figures in the Year Book as "President," he cannot influence the University nor has he attempted to influence it.

One of the ways in which the President not only can but ought to influence the University is to exercise his functions as President, whatever these functions may be. I have not the Constitution before me, but certainly one of the duties of a President is to preside at the meeting of the Governors. I, who am not a founder of the University and who came to be interested in it maybe in 1924, have attended all the meetings since 1926 and I do not remember ever to have seen Doctor Weizmann there. In 1929, when the meeting of the Governors took place immediately after the formation of the Agency, I was called to preside over the Governors in place of Doctor Weizmann and to preside over the Academic Council in place of Professor [Albert] Einstein. I think I presided over meetings of the following year. Last year, I insisted upon the election of somebody who could do the things that were necessary after meetings and it was at my proposal that Professor Ornstein[2] was elected Chairman of the Board of Governors and of the Academic Council.

I know that Doctor Weizmann was tired after the formation of the Jewish Agency. So was I. And he was tired last year, and so was I. For a President to stay away from meetings of consequence which can only be assembled once a year when he is in the immediate neighborhood, argues in the minds of his colleagues a lack of interest. It may be unjust, but it undoubtedly was there. If Doctor Weizmann is going to be President of the University on the sphinx plan, as Mr. [Louis D.] Brandeis is the leader of Zionism in America, it is no wonder that his influence is not felt in the Councils of the Governors. I am putting this with brutal frankness because I think it is essential that somebody should make it clear.

Doctor Weizmann has said some very important things in his letter to you and I think, considering the fact that he was the founder of the University and I believe intensely interested in it, that he has been remarkably objective, but being objective does not necessarily mean that one is correct. Cuts in budget and the crippling of the scientific staff of the Hebrew University or of any other university are a great misfortune, but they have gone on in many directions. I should not be surprised if they have gone on even in England. Certainly I need not tell you that instructors' salaries have been cut and instructors have been dropped from many of our institutions in America.

However, that is not the point. What I mean to say is that any temporary crippling of an institution of learning is not "beyond repair." I believe that when money begins to come in and funds are available, it will always be possible to restore an old faculty or recruit a new one. . . .

Doctor Weizmann next takes up the founding of the University and his desire to have scientific institutes. His objection to giving degrees is one that we have discussed before. He and I discussed it, and you and I have discussed it, and I have discussed it with Professor Einstein, and I have the temerity to differ with Einstein and Weizmann.

If it had been Doctor Weizmann's intention to establish a series of scientific institutes at Mount Scopus, in which physics, chemistry and mathematics should be studied, and of course Jewish studies in a separate institute, then he had no right to throw out to the Jewish people and to the world the idea that he was establishing a University, because calling such a series of institutes a university is a pure piece of bluff. This would have been an academy, a place for research, a place where no students are taken or even wanted. I do not have to labor the point. Doctor Weizmann knows the difference between the Sorbonne and the Institute of France with its Academies; he knows the difference between Oxford and Cambridge and the group of Royal Societies. Why on earth must we Jews, especially when we consider Palestinian matters, always be eccentric? Why should we have in mind the establishment of a few Institutes and call it a University? When I heard about a University, I took it in good faith. I assumed that it was the desire and intention that the Jewish people, who have studied in all the universities of the world, give back one University to the world. I assumed that they would establish in Palestine a higher seat of learning which would initially serve the country, not as the second-class institutions of higher learning established by the English in various parts of the East produced second-rate men for the civil service, but to give particular attention to those scientific problems which were important to the development of Palestine. I suppose I do not have to labor the point with regard to agricultural chemistry or things of that sort.

Then, too, there was another problem and that was the Numerus Clausus against Jewish students in various countries of Europe. This hungry Jewish youth was clamoring for a place to study. They were largely Zionist.

The announcement of a University made them believe that they would have such a place. These are the reasons that have impelled me, not because [Judah L.] Magnes approved it, nor because Jones approved it, but because I believe it to be fundamentally right to favor as soon as was humanly possible the establishment of regular courses of instruction for the giving of degrees. I do not in the slightest regret my part in this. I also, of course, had your thought in mind, because each year we were getting an increased number of Palestinian young men in America who came here to study because there is no place for them in Palestine to study. The inauguration of a University by Doctor Weizmann and whoever joined him in it was no doubt a bold project, with the aeroplanes buzzing overhead, but it had the same statesmanlike view which impelled George Washington during the Revolutionary War, and when the fate of the Colonies was trembling in the balance, to advise his fellow-countrymen to establish institutions of higher learning and for the general diffusion of knowledge, because he wanted to make it unnecessary to expose the American youth to the wiles of the European institutions and wanted them trained at home. . . .

Now to get back to the University on Mt. Scopus. The laying of its cornerstone was a magnificent gesture, based upon a shoe-string. When Lord Balfour was invited to Jerusalem to open it and the universities and learned societies of the world to attend, it was necessary not simply because of Doctor Weizmann or anybody else, but because of the honor of the Jewish people, that it in some way resemble what the world understood by the word "University." The merit of Magnes was that here he threw himself into the breach. It was my sense of obligation much more than my sense of the wisdom of the establishment of the University which awoke my interest at that time. I want to remind you that the institutions with which I am connected in this country, first the Dropsie College and afterwards the Jewish Theological Seminary, contributed within the first year and a half to the actual service of the University three of their most distinguished scholars, whom we could ill afford to spare.

I must come to an end with this long letter and I realize that it is far from satisfactory. Maybe being in bed on a hot day puts me in a bad temper and maybe when we lose our suavity we are more likely to speak in naked terms.

And now I am going to say a final word. I believe that the present organization of the University is wrong. I think the Board of Governors should be entirely reconstructed and that every professor on the Board of Governors should be asked to resign and the Board of Governors should frankly become a fund-raising Board. I believe that the Academic Council should be the one that gives advice on academic subjects to the University, although it should receive proposals from the University as it does now.

I think the President of the University should assume his duties and obligations, whatever they are, under the Constitution. Certainly he should attend the meetings of the Board and preside over them and do whatever else that he can that is necessary. In this, as in all other things, persons are much less important than the whole establishment. If Weizmann and Magnes cannot sit down and talk to each other about matters in which they both have a profound interest and in which neither is self-seeking, then I think neither of them is useful to the University. They surely have no such personal antipathy towards each other that they cannot meet. They both are rather charming men. But, alas, grown up men still remain children and maybe this is what makes them so delightful.

This may sound like a rather foolish ending to a very unwise letter, and if you want to throw it away or destroy it, you can do so, or, if you want to extract anything that you consider sensible, you might do so, but in the last analysis what I mean is that this project, unwisely conceived by Weizmann, impulsively taken up by Magnes, having as I consider a rather remarkable development for a short period of years, suffering now as everything else suffers, should not be allowed to go to smash because of two egocentric individuals who cannot get into each other's orbits. [W]

1. Jacques Salomon Hadamard (1865–1963), French mathematician; member of the Administrative Board of the Hebrew University.
2. Leonard Salomon Ornstein (1880–1941), Dutch physicist and Zionist leader; member of the Hebrew University Board of Governors, 1925–40.

Despite his preoccupation with Jewish concerns, Adler found time to be active in the leadership of the American Philosophical Society.

TO CAROLINE F. SKINKER,[1] PHILADELPHIA

Philadelphia, December 1, 1932

I regret that it will not be possible for me to attend the meeting of the Committee on Policy on Saturday, January 14th.

About a year ago, on January 15, 1932, in response to a letter from Professors Scott,[2] Goodspeed[3] and Miller,[4] I addressed a letter to Professor Goodspeed with regard to the general question of the future policy of the

[American Philosophical] Society. I wish this letter cancelled because a new situation has arisen which makes that letter rather obsolete.

First I think ought to be considered as part of the policy of the Society its present and future home. The discussion about this has been drawn out over a long period of years and should in my opinion be settled as promptly as may be. At recent meetings I have noticed that our present quarters even from the point of view of space for the transaction of necessary business are quite inadequate. I should therefore recommend that until a new building can be erected, if any leases in our present building should expire they be not renewed and the Society should secure more space for its actual work.

I think all efforts should be bent toward having the new building built if, as I believe we are all decided, this should be done. First of course the title to the ground should be made absolutely clear. Second, funds should be made liquid so that payments upon the building operations can be made when due. I believe that all funds for the building purpose should be held either in cash or in Government Bonds which might be expected to be realizable at par, but I am even in doubt as to whether they should be in anything but cash. With minor exceptions, we cannot greatly enlarge the work of the Society until we get this matter of the building settled. However, looking to the future I would like to make the following suggestion:—

That in any annual budget prepared as a minimum ten per cent of the income should be set aside to be added to the capital; this in the natural expectation of the falling of rates in interest.

That provision should be made for an increase in the staff of the library so that our books should be readily available and there would be sufficient intelligent help for anyone who wished to engage in research work. In general, there should be a larger sum allotted to the library, not necessarily for purchase, but for service and for binding.

I am inclined to think that when the new building shall have been completed a reserve of $50,000. per annum may have to be put aside for its up-keep. I am assuming a building which will be open much longer hours than our present building is open; if we have a proper museum, maybe at night which means light and an additional number of attendants.

I believe that one of the great needs of scientific men at the present time is increased opportunities for adequate publication. I believe that the publications of the Society should be increased in number and improved in form, both as to paper and illustration, &c., and that above and beyond any sums now allotted for the purpose, $25,000 per annum should be set aside for publication.

I think that there should be two secretaries, or maybe under-secretaries, if the present form of voluntary office is to be continued, who should be charged with promoting the work of the Society respectively in the fields of the natural and physical sciences and in the field of the humanities. These men might themselves engage in research. They could stimulate and advise other people in research and could act as advisors to the Publication Committee with regard to papers submitted in their respective fields and possibly aid in editing and publishing these papers.

I think it is understood that in view of the large bequest of the American Genealogical Society the likelihood of there being adequate funds for research in that department would relieve the Philosophical Society of expenditure in that direction. If at all possible I should think that the fixed charges of all kinds and the appropriation for publications &c. and salaries should not at the maximum exceed 65% of the total income, and 10%, as I have said above, should be appropriated to the capital plus any balance out of the 65%. There would then be left 25% of the total income of the Society to be utilized in the promotion of direct research work.

I should be very much inclined to recommend that this be the direct research work sponsored by the Society or by its members and not any cooperative efforts and that wherever such work is provided for the Society would have the first claim for publication, if it desires to exercise that claim.

If, as has been proposed, the Society is to be broken up into groups for the nomination of members these same groups might also function as bodies of reference either with regard to projects proposed by members of the Society, or might themselves be invited to initiate such projects.

Another and minor matter of policy but yet having some importance is entitled to consideration. It is generally agreed that our annual meetings are among the most distinguished in kind known anywhere. We might add to their distinction by setting aside a definite sum to enable the Society to pay the travelling expenses of men who are invited to read papers if they desire to be reimbursed for their outlay. I think this point is quite obvious. Many men would hesitate to come from Berkeley or Pasadena, California, or even from Hanover, New Hampshire if they had to be out of pocket for the journey. The members of Philadelphia and the vicinity already have a great advantage of being near to the Hall and those from out of the city should not be financially penalized when they are asked to present papers.

I realize that this is all rather rough and disjointed and it is written without the advantage of suggestions from my colleagues. [W]

1. Caroline French Skinker, assistant secretary of the American Philosophical Society. Adler was a member of the society's council.
2. William Berryman Scott (b. 1858), paleontologist.
3. Edgar J. Goodspeed (1871–1962), New Testament scholar.
4. John Anthony Miller (1859–1946), astronomer.

PART SEVEN
1933-1940

The years 1933–1940 saw a drastic deterioration in the situation of European Jewry as a result of Hitler's rise to power. Palestine was the scene of increasing hostility between Jews and Arabs. America, still reeling from the effects of the Depression, saw a rise in anti-Semitism, while American Jewry's political and economic fortunes were on the decline. This was the situation which Adler, in failing health himself, was to face.

TO HENRY PEREIRA MENDES, ATLANTIC CITY

January 11, 1933

. . . We seem to have very little sense of proportion. When, in the United States, the two largest States in the Union elect Jews as Governors, when all over the country in various cities Mayors are elected, when we have several smaller States elect Jews as Governors, who profess to be Jews, even if they are not of our stripe, all of this talk about anti-Semitism makes me a little tired. Columbia [University] is simply stocked with Jews.

I know it is a sad reflection but we must remember that in spite of all of our good societies and resolutions, etc., we are living in a period of hate, rather than of love. Do the Frenchmen love the Germans? Is America falling upon the neck of Russia?

I think that this movement for the promotion of Good-Will between Jews and Christians is a useful movement. It is productive of understanding not only between Jews and Christians, but what from the point of view of America is even more important, namely, between Catholics and Protestants, because for the last ten or fifteen years I believe that the prejudice on the part of Protestants against Catholics was much stronger than their prejudice against the Jews. It is therefore a welcome sign to me when I read in the newspapers this morning that Catholics and Protestant Episcopal educators were meeting together in Atlantic City.

At bottom, my dear Doctor Mendes, many of our difficulties come from ourselves. If every individual Jew was one hundred percent honest and upright, and had good manners, I think we would be immensely better off.

Maybe we would have to be one hundred and fifty percent in order to carry our way through the world. But unfortunately we are not.

You may have noticed in the report of President [Herbert] Hoover's Commission recently that the two institutions which according to this survey had suffered the greatest decline in America were the Church and the Home. What applies to the whole of America I am afraid applies to the Jews in America and our whole effort must be in the direction of the restoration of the Synagogue and the restoration of the Home. We have lived through a wild generation and maybe the misfortunes of the last few years have had a chastening and sobering effect. I have noticed in the papers that there is a decline in the number of divorces in Reno.

I could run on for an hour but I have not the time and I dare-say you have not the time to read. [D]

TO HENRY PEREIRA MENDES, ATLANTIC CITY

January 27, 1933

. . . Of course, it is a fact that virtually all Reform Rabbis, with the exception of the few old die-hards, with whom Reform has already become a tradition, are introducing ceremonials into their congregations, but I am not so sure that this is a trend of theirs as it is a demand of their congregations. You see the matter is quite simple. The Reform congregations now have a large percentage of their membership—certainly in the east—from among the first generation of the Russian-Jewish migration, who joined these congregations, I am sorry to say, for social reasons, because they think their children will get into better society; but they cannot quite give up all their old customs and so they want Hebrew in the school and a little more of the flavor of the old religion.

To give you just an idea of a single instance of how people's minds work: Mr. Abrahams,[1] the Secretary of the [Jewish Theological] Seminary, the last time I was there, told me that the day before a woman came to see him and told him that her brother had died during the month; that she was a member of a Reform congregation, but she would like a prayer said in his memory in the Seminary Synagogue because it was Orthodox and she left a contribution of $100 in his memory. You see, my dear Doctor, very few people are loyal in these days.

One other point in your letter that I take up, which is of considerable importance, is that something is being done. Several years ago, the American

Jewish Committee came into possession of certain very crude Sunday School cards which were being used by the Lutheran Church in the Middle West, such as "Who killed our Savior—the Jews." A conference was held at the Seminary between myself and various Christian clergymen and one or two representatives of the American Jewish Committee and we pointed out that as long as this sort of thing went on in the education of children the efforts at goodwill at the top would not be very availing. The Federal Council of Churches and an organization known as the National Education Association undertook to make a comprehensive study of Christian pedagogical literature. Through our influence, an outside organization has appropriated $5,000. for this purpose—I mean that it does not come directly from the American Jewish Committee, because we thought that this study should be made by Christians themselves. When they get their material together, wherever there is literature which would result in inciting Christians against Jews, the Federal Council itself would bring the matter to the attention of the individual church. This, I think, is a good plan and I want to say that this statement ought to be kept confidential because the less we have to do with it the better for us. . . . [D]

1. Joseph B. Abrahams (1884–1969), secretary of the Jewish Theological Seminary, 1901–41.

TO JESSE ISIDOR STRAUS, NEW YORK CITY

March 15, 1933

As an ordinary citizen I have differed a good deal with my fellow-countrymen in recent years concerning their attitude toward France. I believe that the French have been the only realists in Europe. I think that when America made its separate treaty with Germany, and when the English were falling all over themselves about Germany, and we commenced to criticize the little failings of the French—their thrift and their parsimony—that we were following a very wrong track. France is the great free country of the world. It had a bit of hysteria back in 1896–97 with regard to [Alfred] Dreyfus, but I think no country is more liberal in the true sense of the word than France and I do hope that you will be able to inspire friendlier sentiments in America for France than we have had heretofore.[1]

I do not know whether the thought entered Mr. [Franklin D.] Roosevelt's mind or yours, but if America had wanted to give a demonstration to this terrible barbarian Germany of to-day that it does not agree with their barbarous sentiments against the Jews—for that matter they are evincing reasonably barbarous sentiments against the Catholics—no better attitude could have been taken than your appointment as Ambassador to France.

I hope you will permit me to hail your appointment not only as a great personal satisfaction and as a friend of yours and of your family but also as a Jew. . . . [W]

1. Straus had just been nominated as United States ambassador to France.

When the Nazis took power in Germany on April 1, 1933, all Jewish-owned shops and the offices of Jewish professionals were boycotted, with S.A. guards posted to assure the observance of the boycott. Though presented as a spontaneous demonstration by the German people, the action was clearly organized by the Nazis.

TO LOUIS GINZBERG, NEW YORK CITY

April 7, 1933

. . . What you sent me from your friend is not only true, but far below the truth. The situation in Germany is indescribably bad and the shifting of the policies from day to day almost makes one think that the country is a madhouse—I am afraid it is. The situation is absolutely unparalleled in modern times. I am receiving cables along the same line from German friends who are now in France and we have much correspondence from those who have gone to Switzerland, indicating that the situation is about as bad as it can be.

Great pressure has been brought to bear from this country, from London and from Rome; and, with pressure from the inside, they have stopped the formal boycott. [AJC]

TO HORACE STERN, PHILADELPHIA

April 7, 1933

. . . I think it is quite obvious that we are in for a long campaign. The Nazis have got a complete grip upon Germany now that they have taken over the business as well as the Government. Their determination to regulate the

Protestant and Catholic Churches would, one might suppose and under normal conditions of the world, prove their undoing, but so many astonishing things have happened that this may happen also for a time. The Soviets have held out pretty long in their campaign against all religion—why should not the Nazis regulate religion? In effect they are really veering away from Christianity to Paganism because the substitution of German sagas for the Old Testament removes the foundation and basis for Christianity. Without the prophecies cited in the New Testament there can be no Jesus and without Jesus there can be no Christianity. Altogether, it is a very far reaching thing that they are engaged in which may break them—but it may not. We shall have to fight on many fronts and I am suggesting an entirely different one.

The Swastika, which is the symbol of this Aryan Heathen movement, and which by some strange fantasy has been adopted in Germany, is, as I recall, not a specific Aryan symbol at all. Someone, for instance, ought to bring out this aspect. Mr. Thomas Wilson, Curator of Prehistoric Anthropology in the United States National Museum, published in the report of the Museum, the year ending June 30, 1894, issued at the Government Printing Office in 1896, a paper of three or four hundred pages on the Swastika in which it would appear that there is no certainty at all that this is Aryan or Indo-European, that the Swastika was extensively used by the Chinese and indeed by all nations and is found all over in prehistoric Europe. In other words, the Swastika is not a symbol of Christianity, it is not a symbol of pure Aryanism, and the Nazis' theory on this subject is just as wrong-headed as their theory on all other subjects.

Then too his [Hitler's] comparison with the Chinese and his action on the Jews is entirely untrue. America, whether we liked it or not, was faced with a Chinese population of some four hundred million of whom twenty or thirty million of the Chinese coolies would have moved into the United States if there had been no restrictive legislation on that ground. As I recall it we did not drive out those who were here. We put up bars against more coming in. That Hitler should use this as a basis for driving out or ruining the population that has been settled in Germany for fifteen or sixteen hundred years is the height of illogicality.

I hardly assume that our Government or some of its officers would permit a statement like that to stand and if they do permit it to stand we ought to see that it does not stand.

Then his [Hitler's] statement that America is not ready now to open its doors to Jews from Germany is one which of course he had no authority to make. I wonder whether it was provocative. That part of his statement should be studied very carefully.

This whole question of Aryan civilization ought to be studied. I am not going to write a dissertation to you on the subject now. There have been some strange things happening in scientific minds in the last twenty-five or more years, but we ought to settle certain problems and we ought to draw within our circle a number of professors in both our theological seminaries and various of our universities who would undertake to prepare memoranda or statements upon subjects that we think require a statement. Most of the pronouncements of Hitler on these scientific subjects could easily be knocked into a cocked hat, and they must be.

The Jews of the world and maybe other people of the world have made the mistake of rather underrating this enemy. Everyone thought he was a fool and shrugged his shoulder—well, the fool has got into the saddle.

These are some of the things I would have said at the meeting, maybe with more restraint though I doubt it, if I had been able to come and I would like you particularly to express to all of my colleagues my very great regret and indeed sorrow at this critical time that it is physically impossible for me to appear with them. I have, during this past week, though in bed, given every minute of the day to the Jewish situation in Germany.

I presume that there will be some practical men who will say, "Well, what can we do for the Jews in Germany—this apparently will go on for some time?" My answer would be first that we will continue to endeavor to see whether our Government can do anything. Then I think that our people ought to be urged to support the Joint Distribution Committee in its effort for funds, a considerable portion of which would be used to alleviate the situation of those Jews who have already fled from Germany and are in neighboring countries where they are without means of support and where they cannot get jobs. I think the fact ought to be mentioned that the French have already organized such a Committee.

My private advice to any Jew in America who has relatives in Germany would be, if at all possible, for him to arrange to get them out. They need not be brought to America necessarily. Many of them probably could not or would not wish to come to America. There are neighboring countries—Switzerland, Holland—where they would be welcome, as I am sure they will be welcome in France and Italy. I believe the best thing that can happen for the Jews of Germany if at all possible would be to take every last one of them out. I know this is not possible but I am saying it in order to indicate my judgment as to what would be their interest because let it not be forgot that this is not a new phenomenon in Germany, that it cannot be excused by the War, it cannot be excused by the misery of the German people, that such agitations have taken place before—took place about 1848—and it was really that agitation which brought most of the German Jews to America that came here. Such an agitation was inspired by [Otto von] Bismarck himself in the Court Circle and you can go all the way back to the Middle Ages; the Jews of the world should not deceive themselves about Germany. [AJC]

The quandary facing American Jews was how best to respond to Nazi anti-Semitism. There were those who advocated a policy of boycott and public demonstration. Adler felt it was best to rely on diplomatic action. Demonstrations, he felt, were certainly satisfying to the demonstrators, but did they do any good? Did they not merely make the situation of the Jews they were designed to help even more precarious?

TO MORRIS S. LAZARON, BALTIMORE

April 13, 1933

. . . Now as to the general subject of asking me whether I would be willing to attend an intimate conference at which there were representatives of the American Jewish Committee, the B'nai B'rith and the American Jewish Congress; I do not know whether you are aware of the fact that over the course of years quite a number of efforts of this sort have been made. The last one was taken up at the invitation of Mr. Alfred M. Cohen, of the B'nai B'rith, and each one of the three organizations mentioned named five persons who met together on the 22nd of February. After a conference lasting a good many hours and recognizing the seriousness of the situation, it was agreed that a sub-committee of six should be appointed of persons all resident in New York who would meet together every day from day to day and pass upon current matters, only calling the larger body together where there was difference of opinion or where the emergency was great. A good many useful suggestions were made by this larger committee of fifteen and by the smaller committee, and definite tasks were assigned to particular persons and organizations and were carried out.

Then, all of a sudden and without consultation, the American Jewish Congress decided upon a policy of large public demonstrations and calmly invited the other two organizations to come along. The other two organizations deemed these mass demonstrations unwise and dangerous, basing this opinion not only upon their own judgement but upon telephonic communications which were had with representative German Jews who were in Paris and who advised against these as being likely to bring harmful repercussions to them. This information was communicated to the Honorary President of the American Jewish Congress [Stephen S. Wise] prior to the Sunday night meeting at the Hotel Astor at which all kinds of things broke loose and the police had to be called in to keep order.

Every kind of effort was brought to bear, not only from Germany where of course opinion was constrained but also from Paris and London, to prevent the mass demonstrations which were organized in this country, but to no avail. The American Jewish Congress had to have its little mass meetings in New York, Philadelphia, Baltimore, probably Cincinnati and everywhere else; I do not know. And then they were called down by the Department of State.

Now I am telling you this story and I would tell you much more if we had a chance to meet, because I believe that your proposition for another conference is an absolute waste of time. I see no use in trying to deal with people who break agreements.

The American Jewish Committee, which, by the way, has some twenty or more affiliated organizations, including a very large following, assembled delegates of these constituent organizations some weeks ago and with the exception of the one or two representatives of the Order of Roumanian Jews there was complete unanimity in supporting the policy which the American Jewish Committee had followed out. There is also complete agreement with the B'nai B'rith. All of the three large synagogue organizations are represented in the American Jewish Committee as are indeed the three large rabbinical organizations.

Your letter is all couched with the idea that you are making a perfectly new proposition on which I have not endeavored to do anything. I believe that I have done more toward bringing about unity in American Israel than most people—certainly I have striven for it, but this particular American Jewish Congress is an organization which was created for the purpose of disunion. It was created with the intention of destroying the American Jewish Committee. It was a wartime organization. It made a public agreement, in order to bring about unity during the wartime, that at the end of the Peace Conference it would go out of existence. It adjourned at twelve o'clock one night and re-organized in two minutes. It never drew an honest breath and to me it has been almost a matter of besmirching myself even to have to sit down with those gentlemen, which I have done many more times than you have any idea.

Let me say another thing to you, my dear Doctor Lazaron. Just at the moment I am not concerned about the Jews of America; I am concerned about the Jews of Germany. If the Jews of America want to make faces at each other, let them do that; they always have. What I object to is to have men get up in New York or Baltimore, where their skin is safe, and make a noise which is going to bring about stripes on the Jews of Germany. [AJC]

When Hitler gained control of Germany, a wave of refugees crossed the German frontier. With nearly all countries in the world closed to immigration, finding a place for these refugees to go was an uphill struggle, a struggle that had only just begun.

TO MORRIS D. WALDMAN, NEW YORK CITY

April 19, 1933

. . . I am inclined to feel that the situation is not one which is being approached with any sense of the magnitude of the problem involved, with the possible exception of our friends in England and France who are discussing the opening up of great new sections in South America or great projects in Palestine or Trans-Jordania or things of that sort. I believe that here in America we are subconsciously acting on the theory that this insanity cannot last and will soon disappear. I have just been writing a letter to Mr. Vogelstein[1] and have sent a copy of it to Mr. [Paul] Baerwald in which I point out a specific problem that is commencing to come to me and I know to others. It is the problem of the Jewish professor who wants a position in the Dropsie College or the Jewish Theological Seminary or any other institution; people who have already been deprived of their livelihood. A thing of this sort is a matter for real large thinking. I understand that Dr. [Simon] Flexner has received scores of applications from scientific medical men. This is bound to happen even if the situation improves. . . . I do not think that this will be a good time to see the Polish ambassador. For the present I want to keep my mind on the German situation. I am returning to you the first draft of the statement to be left with or sent to the Polish ambassador. I am afraid that it is too historical. I see no reason why we should go into ancient history to begin with. A definite recital in perfectly cold-blooded memorandum of the wrongs under which the Jewish population in Poland suffers is in my opinion the thing to do, if we are to prepare a memorandum at all. I can hardly think that any ambassador will forward a memorandum like this to his government. [AJC]

1. Ludwig Vogelstein (1871–1939), American business executive, philanthropist, and communal leader; chairman of the Union of American Hebrew Congregations; brother of Hermann Vogelstein (1870–1942), German rabbi and scholar.

TO FELIX M. WARBURG, NEW YORK CITY

April 25, 1933

. . . I am glad that you have arrived at the idea that there must be two kinds of Joint Distribution Committee work. In fact yesterday [Morris D.] Waldman was over here in Philadelphia and I asked him to give a message to [Paul] Baerwald with the following suggestion: Just as we aided in the establishment of the fund called the Ezras Torah Fund for the support of Rabbis—this was not administered directly by the Joint Distribution Committee and the recipients were not known to us—so I think we may have to do the same sort of thing for professors and scholars. Since I talked to you on the telephone on the subject, I think I have received four more requests from people who need to be helped.

I also have an idea which may sound strange, but I think it might be worth thinking about and that is that we should approach the Guggenheim Foundation and ask them whether they would change their statutes for the time being and instead of giving scholarships to Americans to go abroad to enable German scholars who are thrown out of their positions to carry on research work either in Germany or elsewhere. That sounds like a bold step, but after all we have to face something that may continue for some years and cannot be provided for by constant collections. There might be some other foundations which could be approached in the same way. I thought that in the first instance the matter should be brought to the attention of Roger Straus who, I believe, is Vice President of the Board of Trustees of the Guggenheim Foundation.

I am very glad that you wrote the letter to the Red Cross that you did.

I have read with interest Otto Schiff's[1] letter, which confirms his cable. Of course it is very easy to criticize [Ramsay] MacDonald or the head of any other state, but I am afraid we Jews must maintain our perspective and, important as we are to ourselves, the whole world cannot be allowed to go to smash on our account. Besides, the Jews have caused MacDonald a good deal of trouble in connection with Palestine and maybe he is a little tired of us. If you get a chance to talk to him, of course I know that you will. I have done the only thing I could do. . . . [W]

1. Otto Moritz Schiff (1876–1952), English communal worker; active in refugee work; a nephew of Jacob Schiff.

TO CORDELL HULL,[1] WASHINGTON, D.C.

May 3, 1933

I was unable to make earlier reply to your very kind letter of April 28 because I had been ordered out of the city by my physician for a complete rest for five days so that no mail was forwarded to me. While I have not seen in the press the statement that you were good enough to enclose I assume that it was generally published.

May I inquire whether you have had the time to explore the exchange of cables, communications and telephone messages between the Department and Germany either through our Embassy or direct with German officials since March 4, 1933? I know that you have been, and still are, extremely occupied with great matters of State but my associates, both in the B'nai B'rith and in the American Jewish Committee still have the feeling that in spite of your own energetic and successful labors and those of your Department so far as the public knows our Government has not come out in the way that the British Government did through its parliamentary debates, the French Government did, or even Australia.

Now I am not at all certain in my own mind that the introduction of a resolution such as I suggested would be useful unless it would have the concurrence in advance of the Committee on Foreign Affairs and Foreign Relations of the two Houses respectively, but there are many people who think that some expression of feeling—and I use the word "feeling" advisedly—ought to come from a great and liberal Government like the United States. . . .

There seems to be no hesitation on the part of German representatives in expressing themselves most freely. The German Ambassador[2] in his speech delivered before the Academy of Political Science, I believe on April 28, stated most explicitly that Germany had a revolution within the forms of law, and he used the phrase to the Academy "in a group like yours, thoroughly averse to slogans, disfiguring of the truth is clearly perceived, and distinction readily drawn between the policy and volition of a government and the occasional effervescence of the youthful vigor and enthusiasm which have ever accompanied revolutions." Now this is a highly disingenuous statement. The internment of thousands of people—their own German citizens—in concentration camps; the "coordination" of business enterprises, built up by Jews by the forced retirement of Jews from their direction and control; the expulsion of university professors of liberal tendencies from their chairs; the introduction of a numerus clausus for Jews at universities—these and other measures, which have been responsible for the self-exile of many liberals and for a startling increase in suicides, were made possible almost solely by government connivance; and the continued reports that I get, from reliable private sources, of actual brutality going on within the past week or ten days certainly do not justify the Ambassador's statement.

On the same page of the *New York Times,* strangely enough, the new German Consul General in New York, Doctor Johannes Borchers, does not quite agree with his Ambassador. He is quoted as saying "Please remember in discussing what has transpired in Germany that it was not an election but a revolution; and, as in a revolution, some suffer."

I wonder what the Consul General means by saying that there was not an election. There was an election on March 5th at which thirty-nine million people voted and in this election the National Socialist Party, in spite of it having complete control of the press and of the radio for several weeks before the election, received only a minority of the Reichstag and then by combination with the Nationalist Party got a majority of fifty-two percent of the votes.

The Ambassador says in his speech that everything was done within the forms of law and that the necessary two-thirds of the Reichstag voted to suspend the Constitution, but he failed to say that this two-thirds vote was secured by putting in prison some seventy-eight or eighty men who were elected to the Reichstag on the Communist ticket. So Ambassadors and Consuls of Germany seem to be indulging in a propaganda in America with statements that are wide of the facts, and their reliability in private may be somewhat judged by their reliability in public. But probably I have no right to discuss this matter in such detail. I know that you can give but a very small portion of your time to the subject whereas it fills my days and nights to the exclusion of all other matters.

I can best give you an instance of how people feel about it when I tell you that one of the most distinguished Jews in America, one of our very greatest minds, has said that he regrets that he lived to see these days.

I have not tried in speech to be eloquent to you, dear Mr. Secretary, but I think you realize that this is not and should not be treated as an internal German question. If Germany says in effect that the Jews are not fit to be members in good standing of a modern State, that is an attack upon every Jew throughout the world and the longer Germany maintains that position the more intense will the feeling on the part of the Jews grow.

I solemnly believe that the present action of Germany with regard to a section of its citizens is a challenge to the economic security of the world and through that a challenge to the peace of the world. It obviously is a matter of international concern. If fifteen or twenty thousand Jews from Germany make their way for their very safety into neighboring countries, such as

Holland, Switzerland, France, England, Czechoslovakia, where there is already unemployment, it does become a matter of international concern for those countries. Unless I am very much mistaken Chancellor Hitler, in an address some weeks ago, taunted the American Government with the statement that we would not receive any of these refugees and that we had closed the doors to immigration.

Dear Mr. Secretary, the executive order forbidding Consuls to visa passports has, as I mentioned to you at our last interview, resulted in the fact that, within the past three years, on the average, America has received twenty thousand persons a year less than granted in the German quota.

I believe that this matter lies between yourself and the Secretary of Labor, no doubt with the approval of the President, but no action which America could take at the present time would be more heartening to the Jewish people in this country than a rescinding of that executive order so far as Germany is concerned. I am quite sure that it would not result in any disturbance of the labor market. The usual conditions of guaranteeing a person against becoming a public charge could of course be enforced, but I repeat that it would be a fine and generous thing for America to do and one which would not only earn the gratitude of the four million and a quarter Jews of America but I believe the respect and admiration of the entire world.

I am afraid I am trespassing upon your patience but I should like to revert to the memorandum of Max J. Kohler, Esq., which Mr. Alfred M. Cohen and I sent to you and about which we had only a few words at our last meeting. In these days of new and broad thought in our Government I earnestly hope that the Department of State will not be bound by the traditions of the past twelve years when we were only concerned with American citizens, but that we shall revert to our earlier and more liberal traditions that what is human concerns us and that we shall dare to do as the mightiest country in the world what we freely did when the Republic was young and feeble.

I am writing this to you from Philadelphia, Mr. Secretary, but I shall be going to New York in the course of a few days and if you find the time or care to reply to this letter, I should be glad if you would send it to the office of the American Jewish Committee, 171 Madison Avenue, or, if you prefer to discuss it with me, I shall hold myself at your disposal any time after the tenth of May. . . .

I am writing this letter without consulting with the officers of the cooperating Institutions of the B'nai B'rith, and more especially without consulting with the President of that body, Mr. Alfred M. Cohen, who, as you know, lives in Cincinnati, but I am quite sure from letters that I have received from him that he would be willing if he were here to sign this letter with me and I shall send him a copy at once so that if he dissent to it in any way either in general or in particular he will make known his dissent either to you or to me.

I have written this letter because I felt it urgent, out of the depth of my heart, and I trust that if I have gone beyond the limits of the usage of letters addressed to the Department you will lay it to my inexperience.

May I conclude, Mr. Secretary, with a word of gratitude to you for the very great consideration that you have given both my colleagues and myself and for the earnest efforts that you put forth amidst a multitude of labors so exacting that they are hardly to be measured. [AJC]

1. Cordell Hull (1871–1955), U.S. secretary of state, 1933–44.
2. Hans Luther (1879–1962), German ambassador to the United States, 1933–37.

TO WILBUR K. THOMAS,[1] PHILADELPHIA

June 15, 1933

I want to thank you for your courtesy in sending me copy of the Third Annual Report of the Carl Schurz Memorial Foundation[2] and for your letter in which you express the hope that I am in sympathy with the efforts of the Foundation to contribute to the efforts of goodwill between Germany and the United States.

I think you know from the various contacts we have had that I would like to see the furtherance of such goodwill; but I confess personally at the present time that I find myself far from believing that such goodwill is desired by the ruling classes in Germany, except upon the basis of advantage to themselves. The present government in Germany, and at least a majority of the people of Germany, in my opinion are in a frame of mind and conduct which is more nearly that of the barbarism of the Middle Ages than that of a civilized society in the twentieth century. A country which will drive from its universities, schools, medical profession, legal profession and civil service those people who committed no other offence than that of not being members of the dominant party or not belonging to what is fancifully called the "Aryan group," is not one with which good understanding may be cultivated.

You are doubtless aware of the creation of a movement in New York by Mr. Johnson[3] entitled the University in Exile. In the long run it may be that the support of such an Institution would be the best way of bringing about an understanding because it may bring the people of Germany to their senses.

I myself do not at all feel that America is at fault in its dealings with Germany. We kept out of the War as long as we could and until it was discovered that there was an intrigue on the part of Germany in regard to Mexico and Japan, in which they were promised certain advantages if they would join Germany against us.

We did not sign the treaty of Versailles, but we made direct treaties with Germany of peace and friendship. We helped to feed them; we have loaned them huge sums of money by which they might recuperate. The two international meetings held under the chairmanships respectively of Dawes[4] and Young[5] scaled down their debts almost to a vanishing point. And if there is to be any real move for goodwill, it ought to come from their side.

Present day Germany, or at least its government, is engaged in a relentless war against everybody who differs from the majority in race, language or religion. It is endeavoring to destroy the Jews who have been there for two thousand years, to make of the Protestant Church an annex of the government, and to lessen the freedom of the Catholic Church in every way that it dares.

I would be quite recreant to my own opinions if I merely wrote you a polite letter instead of this rather unpleasant one. [AJC]

1. Wilbur K. Thomas (1882–1953), formerly executive director of the American Friends Service Committee, 1918–28; executive director of the Carl Schurz Memorial Foundation, 1930–46.
2. The Carl Schurz Memorial Foundation was established in 1930 in memory of Carl Schurz (1829–1906), a German-American political leader, to promote the understanding and appreciation of the role of the German people in the United States and the world. After the Nazi takeover, the foundation persisted in its attempt to foster understanding and good will between the United States and Germany.
3. Alvin Saunders Johnson (1874–1971), founder and president of the New School for Social Research, New York City.
4. Charles Gates Dawes (1865–1951), financier and diplomat; vice-president of the United States, 1925–29; author of the Dawes Plan, 1924, to solve the problem of German reparations.
5. Owen D. Young (1874–1962), co-author of the Dawes Plan.

TO WILBUR K. THOMAS, PHILADELPHIA

June 20, 1933

. . . You speak, and I am afraid it is true, of the increasing spirit of anti-Semitism in the United States. I think I can tell you how some of it is being brought about. There is a definite organization of the Nazi party in the

United States and has been for several years, even before Hitler became Chancellor. Poor Germany, which finds it so hard to support its own people and cannot pay its debts is nevertheless finding it easy to get money to conduct a very active and expensive propaganda in the United States against the Jews. There is a Doctor Vollbehr,[1] a book collector and bookseller, who in 1930 succeeded in having an appropriation bill passed in the Congress of the United States to purchase for the Library of Congress a collection of his for the sum of one and one-half million dollars. This Doctor Vollbehr lives apparently in affluence in the Hay Adams House in Washington. He has recently sent out a statement covering about five or six pages, as I recall, beautifully printed, attacking the Jews in Germany, which is a combination of ignorance and falsehood such as I think I have never seen equalled. He sent it to all of the college presidents in the United States and that is how a copy happened to come to my hands.

There is another propagandist, a former American Consul. This gentleman is Irish by birth, naturalized in the United States and was a Consul in Germany at the outbreak of the War. His name is St. John Gaffney.[2] It is his function, on the basis of his having been formerly a Consul in Germany, to circulate anti-Jewish material among members of Congress and other officials in Washington.

There is a leaflet printed in English, but published in Hamburg, which is being thrown around in the subways in New York.

Anti-Jewish propaganda is appearing in Mexico and the articles are obviously translations into Spanish from German sources.

I have myself tried to prevent public demonstrations, parades and announced boycotts, but without success. People who are not so calm maybe as you and I cannot be repressed and, while I deplore the fact, it is hardly to be wondered at.

1. Otto Heinrich Friederich Vollbehr (1872–1946), bibliophile. In the 1930s he issued a publication entitled *Memorandum; a German view of the present world condition and its possible solution.* He sold the Gutenberg Bible to the Library of Congress.
2. Thomas St. John Gaffney (1864–1944), U.S. consul in Dresden and Munich, 1905–13.

TO IRVING LEHMAN, NEW YORK CITY

July 3, 1933

It was very good of you on such a warm day as June 29 to sit down and dictate a letter to me giving your impressions of the conferences that you held with the representatives of the Jewish Congress.

To begin at the beginning, however, I am going around by water to California to get a sixteen-day sea trip, rather from compulsion than by choice. I have been told that if I did not take a long rest I would probably be of no use next winter. I feel very much of a slacker because in spite of all the advice I have hesitated almost to the last day about doing this and thinking of going to England instead. Not that I think any of us can be of any use on the political side but the relief problems are growing so heavy in London that they are almost imploring us to send some of our people over.

You know of course that there is a sort of a Committee sitting in London and [Osmond] d'Avigdor Goldsmid is very anxious, and indeed insistent, that they should have American wisdom in their consultations, if such a thing exists.

Through copies of cables which Mr. [Paul] Baerwald has sent me, received the end of last week, it appears that the situation in Germany is growing more serious every day—indeed critical and they are imploring us for help and by that I do not mean money help. I think you know that the Jews in England have already subscribed to help in the German situation in the amount of £150,000, more I believe than has been subscribed in the whole of the United States as yet. However, I am getting off my subject and off your subject too, but what I want to tell you is this:

I asked Mr. [Morris D.] Waldman a few days ago to consider with the Joint Distribution Committee whether it would be possible to have two of our men go over one specifically to advise in relief problems, and Bressler[1] I thought would be the best man for that; and not thinking that you could go over I suggested of our Committee either [Solomon M.] Stroock or Roger Straus. I thought Roger would be more likely to be able to go because a business man can get an understudy better than a lawyer. You can judge from this how urgent I think the situation is. I further think that in this crisis we ought to have several people who would be able to go and stay in Europe, a matter of six months or so and not simply flit back and forth as vacationists. We are at the greatest crisis in our history since the Middle Ages and ought to act in some way to indicate that we are willing to take our share.

I understand that you are of the mind not to alter our form of the American Jewish Committee nor to go into a world congress. Both of these I consider quite sound. I also agree with you that unnecessary dissension should be avoided.

You will, however, find that what these conferences really mean is that gentlemen will be bound by them and those who are not gentlemen will not be bound by them. I noticed this morning in the *New York Times* the violent attack by [Stephen S.] Wise upon Brainin[2] and also a violent attack by him upon the Central Conference of American Rabbis.

There is of course one thing very strongly in favor of a better result with the Congress from the representatives of the American Committee than heretofore. You gentlemen were willing to go to Doctor Wise's study, which I would not have been. I have met him in some public room. You have either an affection or at least a regard for him which I do not possess. In other words you and Judge Proskauer[3] and Mr. Stroock approached these interviews with much greater sympathy than I could.

I think our real difficulty is that nothing that has been done or is being done is of avail; the strong representations in the British Parliament, the cold shoulder in Italy, the representation of Mussolini's Ambassador at Berlin, the direct speech of the President and Mr. [Cordell] Hull to Schacht[4] and [Hans] Luther, the protests—the chorus of the press have produced, as far as I can see, just nothing. Parades and demonstrations have produced something—a strengthening of the Nazi propaganda in America and the creation of a sort of counter-offensive in this country against the Jews.

I know that I will be charged with a spirit of defeatism—maybe I have it—but at this moment I cannot think of anything that can be done which will curb the Nazi Government. I have no regret as to the methods we followed and the efforts we put forth because I believe that they were the soundest that could be used. The only thing I see is the keeping alive of public opinion by the actual spread of the happenings that are taking place in Germany so that they are damned out of their own mouths.

We are getting through the press much less than the truth. I give you an example: The other day an American woman who is married to a German came over here with her children. She is a connection of a relative of mine. Her husband stayed back in Germany because he has not yet been thrown out of his position. He holds an important office with the Shell Company. This woman, with her children, have not ventured on the streets of Berlin for over two months, not that they feared bodily harm but such insults were hurled at her and the children that they were not willing to face them. She was only allowed to use her telephone to order food. She further says that many people have disappeared and I have heard this from other sources also. This woman is not a hysterical woman.

The other day Professor Oualid[5] of the University of France was in to see me. He was on his way to Chicago. He is a member of the Central Committee of the Alliance and also of the Committee for the Relief of German Refugees in France. He told me that there were twenty-five thousand German refugees in Paris, six thousand of whom were Jews; that the problem of dealing with them is growing very difficult, and he said that so far as the Jews were concerned, the difficulty is enhanced by the fact that they are immensely patriotic Germans and want to stay Germans, that they have no desire to merge themselves with the French. Is not that pathetic?

I do not know whether you have seen or heard from Henry Moskowitz who came back only recently. From him I learn that the American Jewish Congress has a representative in London who has been having conferences with Mr. [Neville] Laski and Norman Bentwich, all with a view to the international congress. Mr. Goldberg[6] insisted upon some form of public appearance to indicate unity but to this Laski declined, thinking that this international conference would be bad and saying that the English Jews might call a conference of their own. He emphasizes the fact too that a central clearing house in London for emigrants, for the use of funds, etc. is of extreme importance.

The Jewish War Veterans have "demanded" an equal representation of three with the Consultative Committee holding that they are the real defenders of Jewish rights and that they are entitled to sit with the American Jewish Committee, the American Jewish Congress and the B'nai B'rith in equal proportion. They are holding a conference in Atlantic City at which Mr. [Samuel] Untermyer is to be the star and no doubt there will be more boycott resolutions. . . . [AJC]

1. David Maurice Bressler (1879–1942), social worker; connected with the Joint Distribution Committee.
2. Joseph Brainin (1875–1970), journalist; member of the Committee on Minority Jewish Rights of the American Jewish Committee; had written that "revisionism is Jewish Hitlerism," a position Wise denounced vehemently.
3. Joseph Meyer Proskauer (1877–1971), jurist and communal leader; became president of the American Jewish Committee in 1943.
4. Hjalmar Horace Greeley Schacht (1877–1970), German finance official.
5. William Oualid (1880–1943), French jurist and economist; vice-president of the Alliance Israélite Universelle.
6. Abraham Goldberg (1883–1942), journalist and Zionist leader; vice-president of the American Jewish Congress.

TO LEWIS L. STRAUSS, NEW YORK CITY

October 19, 1933

. . . The political situation is so shifting that there is nothing that I could say to you that might hold a week or ten days hence. What this new appeal of Hitler means to the German nation, that if they will all get behind him in foreign affairs, he will forgive and forget domestic differences, may put an entirely different face on the situation by the time you get over. Let me analyze for a moment. His appeal may mean that the opposition in Germany to the Nazis is growing stronger and that in order to unite the nation he brings about a foreign issue. You know how this united Russia. I can imagine, maybe in my optimism, that if the Communists and the Marxists and the Jews and the other people would in this plebiscite of November 12 indicate that they were one hundred per cent back of his demand for equality, he would, on their agreement not to try to overthrow his Government by force, retract a large percentage of the things that he has done, maybe even including the concentration camps. If this were the case then our American attitude would be that we were concerned about relief, care of refugees, support of the High Commissioner of the League,[1] etc. and the question as to whether the German Jews would accept such a proposition from Hitler is their affair.

In speaking of the High Commissioner, I want to repeat what I said to you that a great figure like Lord Robert Cecil[2] might be able to accomplish more even though he be less practical than would a lesser figure, and I am not at all minimizing Mr. James McDonald when I say this.

I believe that you would be fully representing the minds of our Committee in saying that at no time would our Committee proclaim a boycott. We think that the whole agitation was harmful and believe that the boycott was taking place long before anybody commenced to shout about it. By proclaiming a boycott we would only be giving a weapon to the Hitler Government against the German Jews.

The American Jewish Committee is also opposed to a World Jewish Congress and will not take part in it. We are of the opinion that the Jews of each country have a right to organize themselves in the way they see best fitted for their needs and that these things differ in different countries. We have no objection to their conferring together from time to time as they are doing in London on October 29[3] and we would have no objection either, if it were feasible, to setting up a sort of Committee of Conferences which would sit continuously for the purpose of meeting day to day problems, but we believe that the separatism involved in a World Jewish Congress based upon a plebiscite, marking Jews off from the citizens of their own country in separate voting groups and with all the implications of a Parliament which would claim the right to legislate for the Jews of the world, holds within itself a program which we believe would be suicidal.

The English Jews have experienced and wise statesmen among them. Mr. [Neville] Laski I do not know; [Osmond] d'Avigdor-Goldsmid I know very well and as soon as you shall have gone I shall cable him of your coming. Lord Reading is, as it were, the Dean.

I have indicated to you the major matters that may come up, not because I believe that you are not able to meet them fully yourself and without any advice from me, but because you indicated that you wanted some advice.

We are all in a very momentous time in our history and I pray to God that you and your colleagues will be given to see the way to lighten the burdens of our brethren in Central and even in Eastern Europe. [AJA]

1. James Grover McDonald (1886–1964), League of Nations High Commissioner for Refugees, 1933–35.
2. Edgar Algernon Robert, Viscount Cecil of Chelwood (1864–1958), president of the League of Nations Union; winner of the Nobel Peace Prize, 1937.
3. On that date, representatives of forty-five Jewish organizations met to study ways of aiding the German-Jewish refugees.

TO DAVID PHILIPSON, CINCINNATI

November 9, 1933

. . . I, too, often think of old times—in fact I wish I could give more time to thinking of them because they are pleasanter than our own days. Did we ever think when we were young men or even twenty years ago, of which you speak, that the world would be in the position that it is today or that the Jewish people would be in the position that they are in today?

I have not had much correspondence with you of late and I do not know whether you and I are still of the same mind upon a good many subjects, but I feel that in America the Jews are doing themselves enormous harm by the stridency of their voices and their constant publicity. In my mind, if Samuel Untermyer lived another seventy-five years he could not repair the damage he has done in the last six months, and those who thought they could have saved the Jews of Germany by demonstrations and parades have not even the frankness to admit that their demonstrations and parades were without avail.

I wonder whether you hear, as I heard in communities in California last summer, and as I hear in the East, a sort of growing dread on the part of the Jewish people of the United States that something may happen to them like that which happened to the Jews of Germany. If there is any sentiment of this sort in Cincinnati, I should like to know about it. I myself have no such feeling, but when I say that the answer is: "Well, that is the way the German Jews felt." [D]

TO NEVILLE LASKI, LONDON

December 27, 1933

. . . I think that what you in England and we in America, and Jews in other countries should endeavor to determine, if possible, is what are the grounds of the attacks that are being made upon the Jews—the ostensible grounds and the real grounds.

At the present time in Germany the ostensible ground is that of race and incidentally of culture. The theory is that the Jews as a race are separate and apart from the race which predominates in Germany, namely the Aryans; that because of this difference of race they are not properly a part of the German civilization and therefore must be removed or put in such a position in the life of the nation as to prevent them from exercising any influence upon the national culture. Now whether this be the true reason or only an ostensible reason, it ought to be met. This question of the differences of race is a scientific question. It is a question to be dealt with by biologists, anthropologists and ethnologists, first whether it is true that within the framework, let us say, of the white race there are these profound differences, and second, whether it is true that any race as such is superior to any other race; and also whether the differences which the Germans are endeavoring to stress go back to differences of language or biological differences.

Then there is the question to be studied as to whether, assuming that white people of different stocks migrate from one country and settle in another, the climate, food and environment in general does not so alter the mental and even to a certain extent the physical structure of these migrants as to constitute them part of the nation to which they have migrated.

If it be true that Fascism in England is definitely taking an anti-Semitic turn this cannot be charged against Fascism in Italy which at no time took on such a coloration.

I assume that the modern man cannot get away from the thought that the peace and welfare of the world depends upon its economic situation and by peace and welfare of the world I mean the peace and welfare of all those inhabitants, including Jews. To the extent that Jews are in any way disturbers of the economic situation, or to the extent to which they take advantage of the difficult economic situation of their neighbors, if they do, they are their own worst enemies and in every community I think there ought to be wise advice circulated among our people both as to their ambitions and their avocations. There must be some vocational guidance for our young people. It will probably not be permitted in any country that one or two percent or even four percent of a certain group should have an over-whelming percentage of judges, lawyers, doctors or even professors. In other words, we must be a little sensible about ourselves, and as I sometimes say to some of my friends here, we must try to be 101 percent righteous. If other people do not like us for that then at least we will have the satisfaction of knowing that we are not to blame.

I am afraid that I have wandered from the point but I shall leave this stand nevertheless. Here we are of course watching the press—but I am beginning to feel that the forces which have been unleashed in Germany and the direct propaganda from that country here in America does make the situation in our own country one of great concern. While we must do everything we can to help the German refugees and if possible to alleviate the situation in Germany we must also consider the situation of the large populations in our own countries. [AJC]

On January 9, 1934, a resolution was introduced into the Senate calling upon the President to express to the German government the "surprise" and "pain" felt by the American people upon learning of the oppression of the Jews of Germany. This and a similar House resolution were never released from committee.

TO KEY PITTMAN,[1] WASHINGTON, D.C.

January 31, 1934

On behalf of the American Jewish Committee, I desire to urge favorable consideration by the Committee on Foreign Relations of Senate Resolution 154, introduced by Senator Tydings[2] of Maryland on January 24th. For nearly a century the Congress of the United States or the Executive Branch of our Government have in one form or another expressed their sympathy with people who are victims of discrimination and injustice, and in some cases have by resolution in the Senate or the House of Representatives, or both, placed their views upon record. At no time since the origin of our Republic has there been a more righteous occasion for sympathy and indignation than the present treatment of the Jews in Germany and of the many hundreds of thousands of Christians of more or less remote Jewish origin and of hosts of others who still believe in freedom of learning, freedom of speech, and freedom of conscience.

Unless my memory is at fault, the first occasion when such a question was raised in the United States Senate was in 1824 by Daniel Webster on behalf of the Greeks who were then endeavoring to free themselves from the

Turks and there has been an unbroken line of precedent of similar action ever since 1840. It is interesting to note that when Daniel Webster raised his voice in the Senate, one hundred and ten years ago, we were a small country in numbers as compared with today.

My colleagues and I, who represent the members of an organization whose object is to prevent the infraction of the civil and religious rights of Jews in any part of the world, feel it a solemn duty to urge upon the Senate the adoption of this resolution. Our Government has already recognized in various ways this great injustice in Germany and the suffering resulting from it, but more particularly I call your attention to the fact that the Secretary of State, in accepting membership in the Commission authorized by the League of Nations to aid the refugees from Germany, indicated this acceptance in the following terms: The United States has always "regarded with a sympathetic interest all efforts to alleviate the plight of unfortunate peoples who find themselves in destitute circumstances, beyond their control." The President appointed as a member of this Commission Professor Chamberlain.[3] An American, Mr. James G. McDonald, has been appointed by the League, High Commissioner for the refugees.

What will strike a responsive chord I think, not only in the hearts of the Jews of the United States but also in the hearts of many millions of Christian men and women, will be that the Senate of the United States should express itself in the terms of the resolution of Senator Tydings in order to give notice to Germany and to the world that humanity still exists and that democracy is not dead. [AJA]

1. Key Pittman (1872–1940), U.S. senator from Nevada, 1913–40; chairman of the Senate Foreign Relations Committee, 1933–40.
2. Millard E. Tydings (1890–1961), U.S. senator from Maryland, 1927–51.
3. Joseph Perkins Chamberlain (1873–1951), professor of public law at Columbia University.

TO JAMES G. McDONALD, NEW YORK CITY

March 21, 1934

When I had the pleasure of seeing you last Sunday, I told you that owing to certain fixed engagements in Philadelphia I could not come to the meeting on Thursday evening, March 22nd. I am sure you know the effort that is being made by the Joint Distribution Committee and the American Palestine

Campaign for their own current needs, but more largely for the purpose of aiding German-Jewish refugees for settlement in Palestine and in other lands, will have my undivided support.

I feel that the appointment of yourself for this purpose by the Council of the League of Nations and the setting up of a special Commission composed of representatives of some fourteen or fifteen states with the very distinguished Lord Robert Cecil at their head is an act of high statesmanship which puts the dictates of humanity above all other considerations. In choosing you to direct this effort, I feel that a wise and sound selection was made and I wish to express my gratitude to you for having taken upon yourself this very onerous and difficult task. Men freely unite in good works in the face of earthquake or famine when the forces of nature, usually beneficient, cause destruction and misery. It seems to me that it is even a higher purpose to aid human beings who for whatever reason are minorities in a State and become the object of violent hatred and oppression. This is what has happened in Germany. To you has been confided the very great task of binding up some of the wounds inflicted and if, as I pray God, you succeed, the effort will result not only in saving a number of broken lives and helping them to reconstitute themselves, but may result in drawing together the hearts and minds of all good and right-thinking people throughout the world. [W]

TO FELIX M. WARBURG, NEW YORK CITY

May 9, 1934

I have your letter of May 8th, enclosing [Chaim] Weizmann's letter to you. In the meantime we have talked together.

I am sorry that I could not arrange to be with you tomorrow but I am sure you will do very well without me, nor will I be able to read the report through unless I sit up the better part of the night, and I want to write to you so that you receive this letter tomorrow morning, since you tell me that Doctor [Albert] Einstein is coming to your house for lunch.

This much I have gathered from the report by turning the pages and reading sections that attracted my attention:

In effect, I think the Survey Committee[1] went far beyond the letter of reference and in certain cases usurped both the functions of the Academic Council. I particularly note in the case of the Institute of Jewish Studies, in which I have a special interest, that here is what is recognized as the only autonomous Institute within the University where recommendations are made with regard to the most important department of the Institute, namely the Bible, even by name, and whereas at no time has the Board of Governors exercised the right to pass upon appointments in this particular Institute. In passing, I want to say that I think the theory that is held that there should be no major subject unless there is a full professorship is an absurd technicality. If there are six assistant Professors in one department and no one is given rank of full professor, it is not the subject that is secondary, and whereas in another department through one full professorship it might be considered a major subject.

I am not able to read sufficiently between the lines to note what is in the minds of the Survey Committee but the rather strange plan of abolishing the office of Chancellor and creating the office of Provost apparently in its stead seems to me one that is designed to offer an occasion for [Judah L.] Magnes' resignation by reason of the minimizing of his office. . . .

I have never quite understood the mystery about Sukenik.[2] He has recently written me about his anomalous position. As a matter of fact, Palestinian archaeology is the one thing that can be better carried on in Palestinian soil than any other subject, and Sukenik is a well-trained man who has acquired a world-wide reputation.

In reading over that portion of the report in which Magnes made his own statement, I think he did it with singular indiscretion. He accepts full responsibility for everything that was good and for everything that was bad, which of course no one man can do, including the fact as to whether money was got in the United States and whether the Board of Governors met, and all that sort of thing, and apparently left the impression on the minds of his Committee that he thought he was a Dictator and accepted the responsibility of Dictatorship. Coming from an old line Democrat as he used to be, he placed himself in a position in which he should not have done.

I will probably understand the whole picture better after I have read the report, including the small type.

There are one or two things, however, that I want to say about the Board of Governors, as I have seen them. I have attended at least two meetings of the Board of Governors in Europe—I think three. At one of the meetings of the Board I presided for nearly three days and nights. I was told that it was the only meeting of the Board which covered its agenda. At neither of these meetings did Doctor Weizmann appear. At the second meeting I did not preside but asked Doctor [Leonard S.] Ornstein to preside, although of course I held no position, but the fact was that the President of the Board of Governors himself never really organized the Board. . . .

Finally, and again without having read the report through, but only skimmed it I would say this:

The Hebrew University in Jerusalem has grown very considerably and I believe very well. It has too many people on its Faculty, too poorly paid. They are mostly dissatisfied. I notice, for example, that in a particular case it is recommended by this Committee that Doctor Sperber[3] be employed at a salary of £120 per annum. I am expecting to be able to offer him $4,000 in this country through the Committee on Exile and the Rockefeller Foundation. If a man—call him President, Chancellor, Dean, anything you please—has a Faculty, a large proportion of whom are receiving incomes which are not equal to that of a first rate mechanic, I can well imagine him seeking to avoid interviews because all of his time would be expended in listening to perfectly true and heart-rendering narratives which he is in no way able to alleviate.

The complaint of the Survey Committee in the main is too great centralization of power or to use their word, Dictatorship. My own experience with the University has been somewhat to the contrary. Within a few months I was asked in the name of the Chancellor, and I presume with full authority, to discuss with a German Professor, now in America, the acceptance of the Chair of Psychology. He is one of the men mentioned. When I took it up with him, however, in this formal way, I found that the subject was nothing new to him, that individual members of the Board of Governors had either written to him or spoken to him on the subject. So you see the people are talking all over the lot.

However, if I do not stop this long letter you will not have time to read it. [W]

1. The Survey Committee—consisting of Sir Philip Joseph Hartog (1864–1947), vice-chancellor of the University of Dacca; Redcliffe Nathan Salaman (1874–1955), director of the Botanical Research Institute at the University of Cambridge; and Louis Ginzberg—was appointed by the Board of Governors of the Hebrew University to formulate plans for the reform and development of the university and to aid in the absorption of German Jewish scholars in the faculty. Its recommendations were adopted by the Board of Governors in 1935.
2. Eliezer Lipa Sukenik (1887–1953), archaeologist; Dropsie College graduate; professor at the Hebrew University.
3. Alexander Sperber (1897–1970), biblical scholar.

TO SOLOMON M. STROOCK, NEW YORK CITY

May 18, 1934

. . . I have never agreed thoroughly that we should do certain things which we were not willing to do ourselves in a Christian "front." I too believe in fighting in the open and have time and time again been restrained from directness by my more cautious colleagues. The Christian "front" idea was really based upon an earnest recommendation from Sir Osmond D'Avigdor Goldsmid a little over a year ago, which did not result as was expected. . . .

I have never believed and never shall be converted, no matter how great the weight of the names of the people on the other side, as to the idea that the publicly declared boycott on the part of Jewish organizations has been a useful thing. It has injured Germany's trade, but it has vastly injured the Jews in Germany. When I hear about our sacrificing the small percentage of Jews in Germany for the benefit of the whole it reminds me of Artemus Ward's[1] statement during the Civil War that he was going to see this war through if it cost him all his wife's relations. . . . [AJC]

1. Pen name of Charles Farrar Browne (1834–67), American humorist.

TO FELIX M. WARBURG, NEW YORK CITY

June 29, 1934

I could not go away without saying a word to you at least in a letter. I want in the first place to mix into something which is none of my business, namely your business, and to express my gratification at the fact that your firm has been the first really to resume private financing. It was necessary for somebody to have the courage to break the dead-lock and I am glad to see that you have done it. I hope much good will come from it. . . .

Our friends in Baltimore have got worked up again and this due to a reported conversation of Rabbi [Morris S.] Lazaron with yourself and [James G.] McDonald to the effect that pogroms against the Jews were imminent in Germany. I have just been talking to Mr. [Harry] Schneiderman on the telephone about it and told him that if there were such rumors either the Joint Council, or the AJC, if the Joint Council did not agree, at least had the duty of laying such a statement before the Secretary of State, not ascribing it to anybody but saying that there had been reports to the effect that such troubles were imminent and have the Secretary of State, through our Ambassador, express the feeling of this country. I note from the statement of Mr. [Cordell] Hull published in this morning's paper that he is not feeling any too amiable toward Germany anyhow. Upon the whole I believe that the way he phrased this statement is much better than if he had made a statement directly about the Jews. . . .

. . . I thought you might be interested in the letter which I wrote to Mr.

[Morris] Rothenberg, copy of which I enclose you. He wanted me to come down and make a speech which I decided not to do (I think you are a perfect angel to go down in this hot weather) but then when he asked for a message I sent him this one. Since that time I have had a long talk with Locker.[1] Locker is opposed to a meeting of the Administrative Committee of the Jewish Agency because he says that if only two or three come from America and three or four from Europe of the non-Zionist group it will deepen the idea on the part of the Zionists that the Agency is falling apart. What he proposes is that there should be an informal conference of a few people in order to talk out the situation fairly. I told him, as I told Sprinzak,[2] that the fact that there was no organization of non-Zionists in America of the Agency went straight up to the Zionist organization itself; that every time I proposed steps for a membership campaign, and you know I have steadily proposed them, I was met by a request not to do it at that time because it would always interfere with some Zionist Drive or Appeal. . . . [W]

1. Berl Locker (1887–1972), Labor Zionist leader; member of the Zionist and Jewish Agency executives.
2. Joseph Sprinzak (1885–1957), Labor Zionist leader; became the first speaker of the Israel Knesset.

TO FELIX M. WARBURG, NEW YORK CITY

July 2, 1934

. . . With regard to Otto Schiff's letter I had the impression that I had seen in one of the newspapers that Professor Hermann Zondek[1] did have some kind of a place offered him in this country but that may not be true. I believe that such a man could get into one of our larger Jewish hospitals, if not in New York then elsewhere. . . .

With regard to the young golf professional I should think that with all the sentiment aroused in the Jewish golf clubs something might be done there too. Our largest Golf Club here is the Philmont Country Club of which Mr. Ellis A. Gimbel[2] is President. There are several other clubs, the Ashbourne Country Club and the Green Valley, but I have not the time to look up their Presidents. I think that any one of these clubs which is not absolutely flat on its back would make a little effort to help take care of such a boy.

With regard to Doctor [David Werner] Senator's letter I think he is right about the Arlosoroff trial.[3] We have already talked about this.

I think also it is right that the labor party in Palestine is in many ways the most reasonable and progressive party but they are extremely partisan and, to my mind at least, their two political representatives in the Executive of the Agency who are dealing with the High Commissioner are far from tactful. . . .

Finally, with regard to Judah's [Magnes] letter, there are two things that I would like to take up. One is the suggestion that Judge [Benjamin N.] Cardozo should give him, Judah, his proxy. Whether that is wise or not I do not know. Judge Cardozo spoke to me very sympathetically about Magnes also and his interests in the University and knows more about it than people think. I can understand a man of his position—indeed I can understand almost any man declining to give a proxy. I am not even sure from the point of view of Magnes whether it is advisable that he should hold proxies. That is something to be thought about. If Justice Cardozo wishes to give me his proxy I would exercise it under any restraint that he would impose upon me. Maybe Judge [Irving] Lehman would give a proxy for the Governor's meeting.

Then there is Judah's suggestion that it might be a good thing for the University if [Chaim] Weizmann would carry out his threat to resign. That is quite possible because I think that he has greatly neglected University affairs. In all this question of the revision of the Constitution I think that it might be advisable, since people are talking about the abolition of titles, if there should be a new President he should not be a President but Chairman of the Board of Governors. It is a confusing thing to have two general titles like President and Chancellor. You will have time to express your opinion about these matters through your charming son[4] whom I hope to see in London.

I trust that the day was not too hard on you and in spite of the terribly disturbing state of the world that you will take as many breathing spaces as you can this summer.

I was a little surprised to see that Judah and Beatrice were going to go to a little place in Austria for the summer. Why on earth anybody wants to go for a rest on that disturbing continent of Europe this summer I do not know. Indeed I think that the disturbed state of the Continent would even be a further argument in favor of holding the meeting of the Governors in England. If there are more of these present excitements Holland will participate in them, at least she will get the aftermath both in excitement and in refugees and to my eye the most tranquil place across the water at the present time is England. If you are intending to cable Judah at the present time I will be grateful if you will say this to him in my name. [W]

1. Hermann Zondek (b. 1887), endocrinologist; was to join the faculty of the Hebrew University.
2. Ellis A. Gimbel (1865–1950), business executive.
3. Chaim Arlosoroff (1899–1933), leader of the Labor Zionist movement in Palestine,

murdered in Tel Aviv in June 1933. Members of the opposition Revisionist party were accused of his murder and tried in 1933–34. Although the defendants were acquitted, the trial caused a great controversy that never entirely died down.

4. Edward Mortimer Morris Warburg (b. 1908), son of Felix; philanthropist and art collector.

TO FELIX M. WARBURG, NEW YORK CITY

October 3, 1934

I want to thank you for sending me copy of Sir Osmond's [d'Avigdor Goldsmid] letter of September 20 and of his cable of September 25. I never thought there was very much in the intrigue story but I think it is a fact that none of our European friends, including Doctor [Bernard] Kahn, are favorable to [James G.] McDonald.[1] This is partly due to the fact that some of them like to hold the limelight and particularly due to the fact that he is an American, and we are not popular, and partially due to the fact of his own vagueness. I believe that he has corrected these difficulties in the statements that he has made and I hope that he will be extremely definite at the meeting of the governing board. Both [James] Rosenberg and I emphasized this to him very strongly and I believe much depends upon it.

On the other hand I believe the entire question of the international refugees now depends upon McDonald. If this particular administration is not supported I do not believe the League of Nations will bother to appoint anybody else, so that I feel, as I am sure you do, that everything should be done to support him, as I know you will do.

There is one thing that I raised in our discussion the day I arrived and which I still bring back. I suppose that Mr. [Paul] Baerwald has sent you a copy of Sir Osmond's letter to him. We are trying to intimate very strongly to the ICA [Jewish Colonization Association] that they should use some emergency funds in this crisis and Mr. Baerwald is disappointed at the tone of Sir Osmond's letter. Sir Osmond on the other hand, intimates very strongly that we should do more in America and that some of the money in the new Corporation should be available for emergency purposes. Possibly both are right. I really think you ought to examine this angle of the matter very seriously. I have no voice in it myself because I do not know exactly what the statutes of the new Corporation are or whether the new Corporation has really gone into being as yet. [W]

1. See letter to James G. McDonald, March 21, 1934.

TO JOSEPH KAYE,[1] BROOKLYN

October 3, 1934

I have your letter of September 28. I have objected to taking part in symposia and most invariably refuse to do so. But the question that you put is one which seems to me to be so fundamental to the position of the Jews in the life of America that instead of answering your questions categorically I prefer to make a statement.

You ask whether I approve of Jews holding administrative governmental positions. Put in this form the question touches one side of an issue. Do you mean that Jews should not hold administrative governmental positions but might hold elective ones? In other words it is right and proper that the people of New York, or the people of Illinois, or the people of Oregon should elect one of their citizens who is a Jew to the leading position of their State, but that it is wrong for a Jew to accept appointment from the Governor of Pennsylvania or the Governor of Ohio, or above all from the President of the United States? It seems to me that the entire query is a sort of an absurdity.

Jews have been citizens in the American colonies since 1740 by an act of the British Parliament.[2] There have been here and there inhibitions but they are full citizens of the United States and they are absolutely entitled to occupy any position which they are capable of filling just as is any other citizen of the United States.

Your second query is whether I believe that Jews holding such offices arouse anti-Jewish feeling. My answer would be again that in my opinion it does not if they hold these offices worthily. Everything depends upon the good conduct and ability and honorableness of the person holding the office.

In view of the fact that your publication is issued in Brooklyn I should like to make another statement. In your section of greater New York there was formed, as I understand, some months or more ago, a Jewish Democratic party. This of course is opposed to all theories of propriety in our political system and should be discountenanced in every way, and the corollary of this is that Jews should never seek office as Jews, nor should Jews support Jews for office as Jews. We are here engaged in a Democracy in which American citizens as such should stand upon an equal plane. Any hyphenation of this citizenship, whether by Jews, Germans, Italians, or anybody else, is a distinct derogation of the high plane upon which American citizens should stand. [AJC]

1. Editor of the *Brooklyn Jewish Center Review*.
2. The Naturalization Act of 1740.

TO FELIX N. GERSON,[1] PHILADELPHIA

October 15, 1934

I have your letter of October 9th in response to my letter of October 8th. In your letter you tell me that you endeavor to maintain an attitude of fairness and non-partisanship on the editorial page, and that you refer to Jewish news of the passing hours whether the activities are those of the American Jewish Committee, the American Jewish Congress, or any Anti-Nazi movement.

In my letter to you I did not raise any question with regard to your fairness, nor did I say anything about the American Jewish Committee or the American Jewish Congress. What I questioned was the wisdom of the fact that you are supporting the assault made by Mr. [Samuel] Untermyer on the Secretary of State, and I asked whether it did not occur to you that the idea of the Jewish people in America being able to fight everybody does not represent the policy that is likely to do anything but lead to the harm of the Jewish people. This is the question that I put to you and I think it is one worthy of consideration. If you are satisfied that your comments, for which you alone are responsible, are such as to be conducive to the good of the Jewish people I have nothing further to say. I have myself never attacked any high official of my own government on my own responsibility.

I presume that an editor can do no wrong but I know some other and larger papers in which the general policy of the editorial page is discussed around the table by a Board of Editors or contributors, and in which outside people, even like myself, have occasionally been permitted to take part. While you say that you are deeply appreciative of this manifestation of my interest and comment, the general body of your letter hardly bears out that statement.

Of course I understand that the editorial page of the *Jewish Exponent* must discuss important matters in the news. I presume, however, that the ultimate end of all Jewish work and publication is the welfare of the Jewish people. You, I suppose, like the rest of us, are not engaged in the purely objective analysis of things, as though you were looking at a new bug under a microscope, and I thought it became pertinent to raise the question whether the Jewish people would with wisdom engage in battle on so many fronts; also whether it is wise to support direct and personal assaults upon our Secretary of State which, by the way, was not the first assault which has come to him from the same quarter. [D]

1. Felix N. Gerson (1862–1945), editor of the *Jewish Exponent* (Philadelphia).

Birobidzhan, a region in Soviet East Asia, was set aside by the Soviet government in 1928 for the colonization of Jews; it was named "A Jewish Autonomous Region" six years later. Many factors, not the least among them the harsh climate of the area, doomed the project. In 1929 an American scientific expedition went to the area to explore possibilities for Jewish colonization there. An American association, Ambidjan, also supported the project.

TO HENRY J. RUBIN, LOS ANGELES

November 26, 1934

I have your letter of November 9. I usually do not express my opinion in connection with debates because I get so many of them that I could easily occupy all my time in answering such letters. You, however, have raised a question which I think is premature in a material sense.

First it has to be decided whether Biro Bidjan is a section of Russia in which a large number of Jews would want to live. I recently met a man who was born in that part of the world and he described it as a dreary waste which would require enormous sums of money to render it habitable. I have seen in the newspapers reports that were made by experts who went there but these reports were very fragmentary.

I am very averse to the establishment of a Jewish State so-called because in effect it would be a Soviet State. All possibilities for maintenance of Jewish religious or cultural life would be removed and I think by promulgating the idea of having such a State we would be rendering a disservice to the Jewish people at large. If, moreover, we favored such a State it would give further credence to the statements frequently made by our enemies that we are in back of communism, whereas communism is not only not a Jewish movement—although there may have been a few Jews in it—but is entirely opposed to our whole theory of Government and property which we have developed from the time of the Bible down.

I am giving you this statement with the distinct understanding that my name is not to be used in any way in connection with it because I do not want to engage in any controversy on the subject. [D]

TO LOUIS FINKELSTEIN, NEW YORK CITY

December 27, 1934

. . . As there are constant statements, and many of them underground statements, that the Jews are responsible for communism, we may want to get up some form of statement to indicate that this is not warranted by the facts. But I would like to go a little further and even indicate what the nature of the law of the Bible is with regard to property—in other words to establish the fact that the Jewish people always believed in private property, which of course is mitigated by many humane provisions. If you will look at [Max L.] Margolis' *Micah*,[1] page 83, you will find an additional note entitled "The Rich and the Poor." As I remember very well, this note was prepared by Professor Margolis at the instance of Dr. [Solomon] Schechter, who thought it very necessary to make some such statement. . . . [AJC]

1. *Micah* (Philadelphia, 1908), the first volume in the series, *The Holy Scriptures with Commentary*. The note mentioned is found on pp. 83–86.

TO JULIAN MORGENSTERN,[1] CINCINNATI

January 31, 1935

I want to thank you for your friendly and confidential letter. I have met with Professor Julius Lewy[2] once and was very favorably impressed with him personally. I reached the conclusion to have him give a course of lectures in the [Jewish Theological] Seminary rather than in the Dropsie College because I thought that I might help him better to establish himself permanently in New York than in Philadelphia. In Philadelphia we really have no need of another Assyriologist. As a matter of fact since Doctor Hoschander[3] left here I have not had an Assyriologist on the Faculty of the Dropsie College because by an arrangement with the University of Pennsylvania those students who wish to take Assyriology can do so with Doctor Speiser[4] out there without the payment of a fee.

I know from a talk I had with Professor Lewy himself that the University of Chicago, where I thought he could be placed, is not intending to fill the place of Professor Chiera[5] because of lack of funds, and I also knew that there was no opportunity for him at Yale.

My thought was this: I would give him very little work to do in the Seminary and he would have the opportunity to become acquainted in New York. Columbia has no Assyriologist, the Union Theological Seminary has none, and as far as I know the Metropolitan Museum has none. Lewy has a good personality and I thought he might, through acquaintances, make his way there. [William F.] Albright I am sure will be glad to help him.

Since we are writing confidentially to each other I very much fear that [Richard] Gottheil would not do anything to help him get in. Gottheil has never favored having another Professor in the Semitic Department. He likes to have young instructors.

What I told Professor Lewy was that after he had been in New York a few weeks and had investigated the Assyrian collections in New York City, if they justified the appointment of a scholar to put them in order, publish them, etc., I would take that up with the Director of the Metropolitan Museum. I have known Herbert Winlock[6] since he was a child. His father was my colleague at the Smithsonian Institution and when his father died I was consulted by his mother about the boy's education, and we have kept up a friendly relation ever since. That would be the only point of approach that I would have for anyone of the Institutions in New York. I do know that strangely enough the New York Historical Society has a collection of Assyrian slabs which were presented to it many years ago by James Lenox.[7] I think they were the first that ever came to America.

It will be, of course, necessary to reach a decision about both of these men, though it may not be imminent, for another year. I received a letter the other day from the Secretary of the Committee on Exiled Professors asking me what was the likelihood of these two men being absorbed by any of the Faculties in this country and stating that their future action would somewhat depend on the answer to that question because I had made an application for both Lewy and [Alexander] Sperber for another year. The present commitment is only up to July 1.

Now as to the possibilities in the Seminary and the Dropsie College: I presume that you are better off than I am. The Dropsie College is at present very badly off and I could not dream of making any new appointments. Indeed I may have to go out for money for the Dropsie College. We have never sought any funds before. We undertook to live upon the endowment we had but you know how income from endowment is shrinking. Without having the figures before me I think our income has shrunk about 45% and at the moment one of our considerable sources of income will at least be temporarily held up, maybe for six months, because of a litigation in the United States Courts, undertaken of course not by us but by other parties. Any excuse not to pay in these days is readily grasped. If great governments can have a moratorium, so can great corporations.

Now as for Sperber, I have not made up my mind. Next week he will begin to teach in the Dropsie College[8] and I shall have a better chance to observe him. I do need someone in the Seminary where I am glad to say the finances are a little better than they are at Dropsie College. What I need most in the Seminary is a Biblical exegete. What Doctor Sperber seems to be most interested in is Targum and above all the Septuagint. Whether he could take up the whole Biblical subject as a teacher and maintain his special studies as a research man is something I will try to find out. I am sure he knows the Bible and if his mind is flexible enough to accommodate itself to what would be the regular teaching in the Jewish Theological Seminary, he would be a good man. There are three other men who are very anxious to get the post held by Doctor Hoschander.

And so I have laid before you the facts and my difficulties. I have not yet conferred with any of my colleagues at the Seminary with regard to this matter.

I shall always be glad to hear from you on this point or on any other, but as I say, if you have a definite plan for Professor Lewy on which you could help him I think you ought unquestionably go ahead. Mine, as you see, are a little vague, and were held so at his request. In fact it was I who brought up to him the subject of his getting a permanent place here rather than he did to me.

Finally, with regard to the Hebrew University, I am pretty sure that the authorities there would come back and say "we would be glad to have Lewy if you can find us the funds." I was present at the meeting of the Board of Governors last summer, as I believe you know, and the question always hinged on whether such and such a thing could be done on the budget. I personally think that the University has got along very well for its ten years but there is a very strong element now on the Board of Governors which is trying to throw the weight on the physical and natural sciences, feeling that the Institute of Jewish Studies and the Oriental Department, which got the first start, had received more than its share of attention. [D]

1. Julian Morgenstern (1881–1977), Reform rabbi and biblical scholar; president of Hebrew Union College, 1921–47.
2. Julius Lewy (1895–1963), Assyriologist; professor at the Hebrew University, 1936–63.
3. Jacob Hoschander (1874–1933), professor of Bible at Dropsie College, 1910–23, and the Jewish Theological Seminary, 1923–33.
4. Ephraim Avigdor Speiser (1902–65), orientalist and archaeologist; professor at the University of Pennsylvania.
5. Edward Chiera (1885–1933), archaeologist and Assyriologist; professor at the University of Chicago, 1927–33.
6. Herbert E. Winlock (1884–1950), archaeologist and Egyptologist; director of the Metropolitan Museum of Art, New York City, 1932–39.
7. James Lenox (1800–80), New York philanthropist.
8. Sperber lectured at Dropsie College, 1935–38, and at the Jewish Theological Seminary, 1934–70.

The problem of the German Jewish refugees caught American Jewry largely unprepared. The organizational difficulties posed by a migration of such magnitude was to tax the American Jewish leadership's ingenuity.

TO JOSEPH C. HYMAN, NEW YORK CITY

March 22, 1935

I have your letter of March 21, more particularly with regard to the German refugees in the various localities. The matter was not brought up at our meeting last week because that was a general meeting and I thought it very unwise even to discuss it there, but the matter is constantly being hammered at me in letters. I had one today again from the director of the Welfare Society. I am seeing a German refugee this afternoon.

I feel sure that for Philadelphia, whatever the size of the problem it cannot be taken care of by local charities. In all the organizations connected with the Federation, there has been this year a horizontal cut of 15% and that of course means certain restrictions in the obligations we have already assumed.

If you think from the point of view of the Joint Distribution Committee, it would be easier not to raise the subject, then we might take such action here, setting aside a small sum from our campaign, that would not require any discussion with Messrs. [Louis] Lipsky and [Morris] Rothenberg. As a matter of fact I understand that the New York chairman also did it without consultation.

On the other hand, I am anxious to hear what Professor [Joseph P.] Chamberlain tells you, because don't you see, if the National Coordinating Committee asks Philadelphia or any other city to take a certain number of refugees, then the National Coordinating Committee ought in some way or other suggest how the funds can be secured, because in New York, an allotment was made from the United Jewish Appeal.

To show you the strange ramifications of this difficulty, I had a letter today that about fourteen German-Jewish children between the ages of twelve and fourteen and I believe even sixteen, were temporarily placed in the Clara de Hirsch Home[1] because no families have been found for them. The question has arisen as to their care over Passover. The girls can be taken care of by the New York Young Women's Hebrew Association, but the Young Men's Hebrew Association closes its food service during Passover, probably to avoid expenses of getting new dishes, etc., and so I am asked, and indeed, have agreed, to take these boys in the dormitory of the Jewish Theological Seminary, by no means an appropriate place for them, because they will be mixing almost daily with quite grown up people. Still, I presume they will find enough companionship among themselves.

My dear Mr. Hyman, what I fear is that this refugee question in America, even if it is not large, has not been carefully thought through. We have too many committees and offices attending to this work and no plan. We know how to plan in Europe, but apparently we do not know how to plan in America, and that part of my thinking is due to a certain reluctance to recognize the fact that a German refugee is a refugee, whether he be in New York or Amsterdam or Prague. [AJC]

1. Named for Clara de Hirsch (1833–99), wife of Baron Maurice, who participated in her husband's philanthropies and continued them after his death.

The World Jewish Congress, which was to convene in 1936, adhered to principles entirely opposed to Adler's. The dispute between those who favored the American Jewish Committee's methods of quiet diplomacy and those who favored the public confrontation tactics of the Congress symbolizes the lack of unity in American Jewry of the 1930's.

TO SAMUEL SCHULMAN, JERUSALEM

April 3, 1935

. . . As you probably know long before this the World Jewish Congress has been postponed for at least two years and the plebiscite for the American Jewish Congress has also been called off. Meanwhile Mr. Bernard Deutsch[1] has retired as President of the Congress and Doctor Margoshes[2] has been retired as Vice-President; Doctor Stephen Wise resumes his role as active President and Mr. Louis Lipsky as Vice-President. What all this means is a matter of conjecture, but certainly the removal of Deutsch and Margoshes is a matter of advantage rather than of disadvantage because the one is a pure politician and the other a fire-brand. My own thought is that it is really Lipsky who has won because he has been steadily opposing the World Jewish Congress fearing it would swallow up the World Zionist Organization, which I think was the intention.

Just before this meeting took place, Wise, who had been favoring the revisionist cause suddenly came out against it.

You ask me whether there is to be a meeting of the World Zionist Congress this summer and the Council of the Jewish Agency. As the Actions

Committee is now meeting in Palestine and you are going there and expecting to stay two months you will probably know much more about it than I do. It is the Actions which will decide whether there shall be such a meeting.

I have, however, been informed that the Zionist members of the Executive are considering having a meeting in August, 1935, possibly at Luzerne. I say August, 1935 because no more definite date has been supplied. The thought of these gentlemen is that fourteen days should be allowed for the Congress and that after a five day interval of rest the Council should meet in the same place as the Zionist Congress. Naturally the final decision as to a meeting of the Council will reside in the hands of Sir Osmond d'Avigdor Goldsmid, President of the Council, and Mr. Neville Laski, Chairman of the Administrative Committee. Maybe if you get some more definite information in Palestine you will send it to me. When you are in Palestine you will be able to get a better view of the relations there of the Jews, Arabs and Christians. What trickles into me, outside of the press reports which are always more or less colored, is that the human relations of the Jews and Arabs are better. They all have work and they are working together and that was one of the ways of reducing animosity.

Now in the latter part of your letter you take up an entirely different subject and that is with regard to [Abraham S. E.] Yahudah and his book on the Language of the Pentateuch and its relation to Egyptian. I confess that I have not studied the book carefully though I have it before me. You seem to be very much taken with it and think that Professor Yahudah has won his case. I happened to come across, after you wrote me, a criticism of his book not by a biblical critic and not by one of the Assyrio-Babylonians but by an Egyptologist, Peet,[3] and published in the *Journal of Egyptian Archaeology* for May, 1930. Yahudah's book is not a new book. It was published in Germany in 1929 and only translated into English and published in 1933 by the Oxford University Press.

Peet argues with you in this one point; he says that if Doctor Yahudah succeeds in proving his thesis many of the results of the higher criticism may at once fall to the ground. But he does not seem to think that he has actually proved his thesis. The evidence is purely philological and the archaeologist and historian also have to be taken into account. If you go to the Hebrew University or the American School you probably can see this number of the *Journal of Egyptian Archaeology,* vol. XVI, part 2, May, 1930, and on pages 157 ff. you will find this review.

Peet does say that many of the points are open to criticism and that Yahuda does not give any definite statement as to when he thinks the Pentateuch was committed to writing.

I, as you know, have never accepted the higher criticism, but felt that it was always perfectly natural that there should be Babylonian elements in the Pentateuch and that the stories of the creation of the flood, etc. could have been brought by Abraham and his tribe from Ur into Canaan. I was for nine years exposed to Paul Haupt's intensive teachings of the higher criticism and never accepted it.

I would say this too with regard to Egyptian influence: There is no doubt that there was some Egyptian influence on the Pentateuch. That may be accepted without in any way accepting all the details which Yahudah points out, and in some of which critics think he is wrong.

But there is a very important point with regard to the whole question of Egyptian influence on early Israel which Yahudah, as far as I can see, has overlooked, and which Peet has also overlooked. You know that during the whole period of say from 1600 and 1400 B.C. or a little later even, that period covered by the Tell-el Amama [sic] letters,[4] what we now call Palestine was an Egyptian province. These letters are from the Egyptian government Viceroys in Palestine.

As excavations have been going on in Palestine many Egyptian objects and even some Egyptian Temples have been found of this very early period, so that the influence of Egyptian on Hebrew thought and even language could have been influenced not only in Egypt itself but in Palestine as well. I do not think therefore at all that Yahudah made the best of his case.

You say you do not know him at all. I do and quite between us I do not like him. Yahuda is a Palestinian by birth and you may find some of his family there. He was educated in Germany and has written quite a number of articles in German. You may remember that at one time he was called to the University of Madrid as Professor of Semitic languages but that did not last long. He is a good Arabist and up until the time that he wrote his book I have never heard that he knew anything about Egyptian. He is rather arrogant.

There is just one last point. I do not think that the Egyptologists are opposed to Yahudah.

You know that beginning with the late Professor [Aaron] Ember of Johns Hopkins University, who was unfortunately burned to death quite a number of years ago, quite a new attitude has been taken by the Egyptologists; they are constantly engaged in discovering similarities between Egyptian and the Semitic language and in fact some of them claim that Egyptian is a Semitic language.

The Pan Babylonian School as you know is a German school and had something to do with German politics.

Assuming, therefore, that there is something in Yahudah's suggestion he is not the man best qualified to make it. I think he once said in a lecture that the Pentateuch was originally written in Egyptian, which is probably nonsense and yet maybe he has started something that will prove of value.

You and Mrs. Schulman will be spending Pesach in Palestine, as Mrs. Adler and I did six years ago. I hope you enjoy it as much as we did. I am glad that you are both having good health. We too are about as well as busy working people can be.

In spite of your scientific mind there is one thing that you failed to do and that is to furnish me an address in Palestine, so I am sending this letter to you in care of Doctor [Judah L.] Magnes who I am sure will see that it is delivered to you. [D]

1. Bernard Deutsch (1884–1935), president of the American Jewish Congress.
2. Samuel Margoshes (1887–1968), Yiddish journalist; editor of *Der Tog*, 1926–42; Zionist leader.
3. Thomas Eric Peet (b. 1882), Egyptologist.
4. The Tel el Amarna Letters—a collection of cuneiform tablets containing the diplomatic correspondence of Egypt from the fourteenth century B.C.E.

TO FELIX M. WARBURG, NEW YORK CITY

April 23, 1935

Some time ago I received correspondence between the Joint Distribution Committee and the American Jewish Committee, enclosing cables from the Joint Distribution Committee and papers from HIAS [Hebrew Immigrant Aid Society], and finally the statement of a conversation with Professor John F. Coar.[1]

As you asked me my opinion about the latter statement I will take it up first. I can well imagine that his statement about the dissatisfaction of the University circles with the Aryan theory is correct. A great many Professors can be fooled but I do not think all of them can be fooled on a point like this, and the reaction against this theory has been very strong in scientific circles outside of Germany. This was particularly the case last summer at the meeting of the International Congress of Anthropologists and Ethnologists, where not a single person raised his voice in favor of the theory, although there were quite a number of Germans present, and there was much criticism against it. However, the statement that sixty percent of the German people are opposed to the Aryan business is one that cannot rest upon anything except a mere guess.

The statement that "never in the history of Germany have the Jews been held in as much respect as they are today" is one which I would also be inclined very much to doubt. I do not see how any person can prove such a thing. If it were possible to have a poll conducted by the *Literary Digest,* and people were free to express their opinions, we might get a vote, but a mere off-hand statement like that means very little to me.

I do not agree with Professor Coar concerning the election in Danzig.[2] Every kind of pressure was brought to bear from the Nazi party; all their big guns were there and they still do not carry the necessary two-thirds vote.

I would be very much interested to know what suggestion he made to the officials of the State Department which he cannot disclose, opening the way for a change in the German policy insofar as the Jews are concerned. Maybe we will get that information from the State Department.

Altogether his views do not impress me very much but then I am inclined to be skeptical in these days.

With regard to the other papers, I think that we can no longer advise repatriation of refugees to any country, whether in Germany or Poland. The situation in both countries is too difficult.

This is in brief a reply to the documents.

I am coming to New York Saturday night, April 27, and expect to be there Sunday, Monday and Tuesday, and hope that we may have a chance to talk about some of the things that you want to talk about or that we ought to talk about. [W]

1. John F. Coar (1863–1939), professor of German; had spent 1934–35 as a lecturer of the Deutsche Akademie at various German universities.
2. In the Danzig election, held April 7, 1935, the Nazis obtained 43 of 72 seats on the council. This marked the beginning of the total Nazi takeover of Danzig.

TO WILLIAM WEISS,[1] NEW YORK CITY

June 4, 1935

. . . When, under previous administrations, protests were made with regard to Roumania and Russia there was never any action taken toward breaking off diplomatic relations. I remember very well, in 1906, on the occasion when I was deputized to present a gold medal to President Theodore Roosevelt by the Committee who had organized the celebration of the 250th anniversary of the settlement of the Jews in America, I took the opportunity earnestly to discuss the situation in Russia with President Roosevelt. He threw up his hands and said, "Everything that diplomacy could do has been done. Do you want me to go to war with Russia?" I replied, as I think anyone would have replied, "No, Mr. President, great as are the sufferings of the Jewish people in Russia we would not wish to involve the United States in a war with any country."

The breaking of diplomatic relations is the first step toward war. If such diplomatic relations were entirely broken, it would mean that we would send away the ambassadors and ministers and all our consuls. The representatives of the people of the various countries in the United States will be safe enough, but in spite of the hard situation, and I must speak in particular now of Germany, the American ambassador and consuls do constitute some brake at least upon the power of the Nazi regime. . . . [AJC]

1. William Weiss (1887–1955), lawyer; president of the Union of Orthodox Jewish Congregations of America, 1933–42; member of the executive and administrative boards of the American Jewish Committee.

TO FELIX M. WARBURG, NEW YORK CITY

June 10, 1935

You send me the memorandum from Elisha Friedman, Maurice J. Karpf[1] and Edward M. Warburg, and ask me "what next."

First and foremost I would say that I do not think that any survey of the University should be undertaken this year or next year. The University had one commission go out and had one survey.[2] The results can hardly be said to have been happy. The University ought to be allowed to settle down from this last up-rooting.

There are two points, however, with regard to the University which seem to me to present major problems and which have not been mentioned in the memorandum. One is the international character of the composition of the Board of Governors. These governors, scattered all over the world, meeting at best once a year and sometimes not for several years, will always present difficulties.

The other important point to me is that the Hebrew University in Jerusalem was not established for Palestine but in Palestine. It was intended as a University which might serve the Jewish people throughout the world. It seems to me, therefore, that any restudy of it should not be bound up with a restudy of the educational system in Palestine.

Now this educational system in Palestine certainly ought to be overhauled. It is six years since I devoted a good deal of time to it and then it was far from being in a satisfactory condition, and I thought rather over-emphasizing studies that would create a white collar class. Also, there were too many normal schools. With the great influx of Jewish people in the last six years I have reason to think that the system is growing more and more inadequate for the present day needs. This system is now under the charge of the Vaad Leumi though the [Jewish] Agency I think still contributes to it and so does the government. Nobody probably contributes enough.

I would suggest that for the present the University should be let alone and that the adequacy of the educational system should be examined, if you choose, by a joint action of the Vaad Leumi and the Agency. Since the Agency shoved the education off on the Vaad Leumi I think the Vaad Leumi should be given the opportunity to take the initial step and propose such a study to the Agency.

I am not impressed with the idea of having a commission of three, consisting of an Englishman, an American and a Palestinian. I think it quite likely that there are enough people in Palestine now who represent experience and education to have a commission of their own. That would not necessarily eliminate Dushkin[3] or Berkson,[4] who are Americans and who are there, or some Englishman who is resident there. I am very much opposed to the sending of a commission of any kind to Palestine at the present time but would rather prefer that the people in Palestine should make their own studies. I am sure they know the facts and probably can state them fairly.

Now the memorandum calls attention to the lack of uniformity in the school system in Palestine. Well, I do not sorrow at that. Uniformity is not such a tremendously valuable thing. The little red school house in the rural districts is quite a different thing from the Horace Mann school and is bound to be, and so the schools in the colonies will be different in hours and curricula from the schools in Tel-Aviv.

It is quite impossible to blink the religious question. There are some people who think their religious duty is done when they learn Hebrew and settle upon the soil of Palestine, and there are others who propose to keep up the traditions of Jewish law and practice which have come down through several thousand years. Now it would be wrong to force the conscience of either group, and so I think the Mizrachi and the Agudah are just as much entitled to have schools reflecting their ideas as the Histadruth.

What I think is important, and very important, is that there be enough schools to meet this wave of migration and that the very first consideration should be that, and depending upon a possible combination of the Vaad

Leumi, the government and the Agency, if it has any money, adequate schooling facilities should be not only provided for those who are there but provided for those who are coming, if we continue to have a migration.

I think one of the most horrible things that could happen would be the growing up in Palestine of a quasi-illiterate or quasi-delinquent group of young Jewish people. This is beginning and will grow, unless early and very strong steps are not taken to prevent it [sic].

We have no time for the survey, we have no time for the theoretic examination which is here proposed. All that, it seems to me, is a matter to be done at our leisure.

The problem of giving schooling to every Jewish child, in proper surroundings, without over-crowding classes and seeing that they have recreational facilities, and in general do not go to the dogs, is the educational problem that I consider "next," to answer your question. [W]

1. Maurice J. Karpf (1891–1964), director of the Graduate School of Jewish Social Work, 1924–42; non-Zionist member of the Jewish Agency Executive, 1930–45.
2. See letter to Felix M. Warburg, May 9, 1934.
3. Alexander Dushkin (1890–1976), head of the department of education at the Hebrew University.
4. Isaac Baer Berkson (1891–1975), superintendent of the Jewish school system in Palestine, 1928–35.

TO NEVILLE LASKI, LONDON

July 8, 1935

Your letter of June 17 and mine of June 26 crossed, and apparently we discussed the same subjects. In the meantime you have received word through my secretary that my plans for going away on June 27 had to be altered by reason of an indisposition which has kept me in the house and mostly in bed for about ten days. This is the first day that I am dictating a letter. I am now better and Mrs. Adler and I look forward to resuming our proposed summer vacation some time next week.

I was glad that you liked Doctor Margolin.[1] I felt sure that you would.

I think that you and your colleagues did absolutely the right thing by not commenting upon the speech of the Prince of Wales[2] in any way. There would be nothing to be gained by the comment and possibly something to have been lost. I looked at the last number of the *Jewish Chronicle* that has arrived over here but it did not contain anything about this incident; the only thing I saw was a very handsome picture of yourself.

I am, of course, aware, and have been for some time, of the very strong sentiment that has grown up in England against war, and indeed a very proper sentiment, and you will recall that I told you when you were in this country in January that Lord Lothian[3] had talked at great length with me in that strain the previous November. The plebiscite which Viscount [Robert] Cecil organized is of course a very powerful argument for people who want war because it emboldens them to think that England will not fight until the enemy is on her soil, which I am quite sure is not true.[4]

When Sir Osmond [d'Avigdor Goldsmid] was over here some of your news came just before he left. He was not feeling very well and looked very grave about the whole situation and he told me that he thought it would be necessary to take up some definite propaganda steps in England.

I have a suggestion to make to you which I am also making, through this letter, to my own associates on the American Jewish Committee. I think we ought definitely to keep up the propaganda and that it ought to be done upon two lines:

First and foremost, we should concentrate upon attacking the race theory. After all, the disqualification of Jews in Germany and the attacks made upon them are apparently put upon the ground of this theory. It is constantly being put forward. Therefore, that theory is the one that we must combat and we must not allow the word "Aryan" even in quotation marks to sink into our own thinking and talking. I believe the Jewish people made a great mistake when they adopted the term "anti-Semitism" which first originated in Germany in the Bismarck regime. It should be combated both by scientific work and by popular work. I may or may not have called your attention to an article by Julian Huxley[5] which appeared in the *Yale Review* for June which, in my opinion, is the best popular article that I have read on the subject. It should be hammered at week in and week out.

My other suggestion of a form of propaganda is to attack Germany as a bully and a coward, whose sixty-five million people, or at least their rulers, are afraid of one half million. I would consider this as an evidence of their inferiority complex, and this inferiority complex of the Germans could be shown in many ways to exist. No German ever considers himself a well dressed gentleman unless he tries to imitate an Englishman, which he never could. At a previous time no German considered himself a civilized man unless he could speak French well, and imitated the French. This was true of Princes, Dukes, etc. I am not in position to elaborate on the plan of the propaganda but I am throwing it out to you, and these are two lines upon which joint action could be taken. You can prove a scientific people to be unscientific, and you can prove a boastful people to be cowards.

Now to continue with the rest of your letter rather briefly. I am sorry that the separate Polish appeal was not more successful. I know that you never favored it particularly. There has been a good deal of talk about a separate Polish appeal in this country by the Federation of Polish Jews but I doubt very much whether it will come off.

I do hope that you will succeed in getting a good secretary and assistant secretary for your Board and Joint Foreign Committee because it would not do to let all the work fall upon you and Mr. Leonard Montefiore.[6] Of course I know that the matter of financing is difficult, as indeed it was with us until within the past two years, but after all, the work of organizations like yours and ours are preventive work. If we can even hope to take steps that would prevent discrimination and persecution we would not have to expend large sums of money for the relief of those who have been persecuted. This, I believe, is a perfectly sound argument to be made to a small group of men. It is not something that could be made to the public.

In my letter of June 26 I discussed with you the new world situation which was created by the separate naval treaty of Great Britain with Germany.[7] This, in the intervening weeks, has grown more acute.

Meanwhile there has come the appeal from Abyssinia[8] to the United States to take the initiative under the Kellogg-Briand pact, and our flat refusal, which I can understand but with which I do not at all sympathize. I was very greatly disappointed at the fact that our President and Secretary of State did not take this up as a purely moral question, but—alas—it seems that nations have become amoral and that a treaty or a pact has little value. We seem to be getting back to the days of 1914. If this sounds unduly pessimistic put it down to the fact that I have not been well.

As soon as our trip is settled I will send you another itinerary but my face is set toward the West and I am not coming to Europe this year. My brief illness has been a very severe warning to me that I must stop work for a time. [AJA]

1. Arnold Margolin (1877–1956), Russian lawyer who defended Mendel Beilis. (See letter to Louis Marshall, December 10, 1913.) He emigrated to the United States in 1922 and became a journalist and lecturer as well as a lawyer.
2. Edward Albert (1894–1972), the future Edward VIII, and subsequently Duke of Windsor.
3. Philip Henry Kerr, Lord Lothian (1882–1940), British journalist and statesman.
4. The "Peace Ballot" was a referendum organized by Cecil in England on disarmament, armament manufacture, etc. These issues received a vast majority vote in the affirmative.
5. Julian Sorell Huxley (1887–1975). The article referred to is "Scientific Pitfals of Racialism," *Yale Review*, n.s. 24 (1935), pp. 668–82.
6. Leonard Nathaniel Goldsmid Montefiore (1889–1961), English communal leader and philanthropist; president of the Anglo-Jewish Association, 1926–39.

7. The Anglo–German naval treaty under which Germany's navy was allowed 35 percent of the strength of the British fleet.

8. Italy, bent on colonial expansion, would attack Ethiopia in October 1935, and annex it to the Italian Empire.

TO FELIX M. WARBURG, NEW YORK CITY

July 12, 1935

I fear the Russians' bringing presents. I doubt the sincerity of the statement that they have great pride in the Ginzburg Library[1] and insist upon keeping it as though it were a national monument. How can anybody explain their willingness to sell the Sinaiticus to the British Museum for $500,000 and get so terribly excited about the Hebrew manuscripts and books of Baron Ginzburg, most of which of course are in the Hebrew language, which is banned in Russia. I should have to have much more concrete evidence of good faith on their part before taking up either with the Academy of Sciences at Moscow or at Leningrad the question of appointing a research man, etc. etc. . . .

I remember very well Doctor [Boris D.] Bogen telling me that the Library was badly off, that the books were pilfered, and that he had endeavored to put a stop to this. Also, I have been told that the Library was divided, some being in Moscow and some in the Hebrew Department of the University of Kiev. So much for [Joseph] Rosen's proposition.

Now so far as [Judah L.] Magnes is concerned on this point, and I am not taking up anything else, the collection belongs to the Hebrew University. It was bought for the University and paid for, and was seized by the Soviet Government. It ought to be released by the Soviet Government to the University. It is in no sense a Russian national monument. The Soviet Government, in taking this step, has done what no other government, civilized or uncivilized, has ever done to my knowledge, namely, to take a private collection which had no relationship to the country in which it was, consisting of books and manuscripts entirely from other places, and seized in my opinion merely as a matter of loot, and possibly because of the early Soviet rage against the nationalism in Palestine. . . .

The manuscript about the discovery of America and about Cortez in Hebrew in the Ginzburg Library sounds interesting. I have no time to look at it. He does not give the date of this manuscript and therefore cannot be certain whether it is the first reference to Columbus in Hebrew literature. I have been under the impression so far that the first reference to Columbus in Hebrew literature was in the foot-note, I think, of a Psalm in the Mantua Psalter, 1516.

This is probably my last letter. We shall be starting off on Monday. I am returning to you all the papers. If you want this matter taken up seriously, at least so far as the Russian notations are concerned, and I could have these papers back in the Autumn, I can get perfectly independent opinions from men who know Russian Libraries and Russian scholars. [W]

1. See letter to Jacob H. Schiff, September 9, 1919.

TO JUDAH L. MAGNES, JERUSALEM

October 14, 1935

I received your letter from Switzerland.

With regard to the reports you have heard concerning the possibility of massacres in Germany, we communicated with Neville Laski by telephone, asking him to get the best information he could from their own sources— from France, from Holland, from Belgium and from Switzerland. The result of this inquiry was that the policy seemed to be that, added to cultural degradation, there was spiritual degradation, but that there were no massacres. Of course I thought that Hitler's address of September 15th contained a very sinister suggestion of such things. I have asked your correspondents in various European countries around Germany to consider the possibility of action in case such a terrible situation arose. I am awaiting their information. None of us here thought that the suggestion about having the Consuls of the Norwegian Governments take over the protection of the Jews in Germany feasible. While not citizens of Germany, Germany would certainly not surrender them to another country for protection. The League of Nations is of course familiar with the situation, but their whole minds are now apparently being turned to the matter of Italy and Ethiopia and, rightly or wrongly, they have a single track mind.

You ask me whether I would be interested in the plan of Taübler[1] for an exact day by day, month by month study of what is going on in Jewry. Of course I would be interested. But such studies are being made by an international Bureau in Amsterdam and, naturally, in London and in New York, where we have rather extensive machinery keeping track of what is going on. Our material is not particularly statistical, but is just the day by day covering of information which we get. The real center, of course, is Amsterdam and the Bureau in Amsterdam has both the support of London and of New York.

Since you wrote your letter—or maybe after you wrote it—there has been a great deal of talk about Zionists and non-Zionists and pro-Palestinians—the latter having always been my idea. Since I have returned I have had very little time to meet with the people who have been at Switzerland and so am not brought up to date. I hope to meet with these people in the near future.

We had a fine time in Honolulu and, strangely enough, I spent a good deal of it with a small Jewish community there—four hundred or more Jewish boys of the Army and Navy. I also saw something of our work in San Francisco and the vicinity. During the one night that I was in Panama I addressed a Jewish congregation there that had a very fine synagogue and two community houses. They were one hundred families, of which one was Ashkenazic and the other ninety-nine, Sephardic. Mostly people from Cristobal had been attracted to Panama by the opening of the Canal and they are largely engaged in trade with South America. They are a fine looking and very resourceful lot.

I am dictating this long letter on erev Sukkot. We had a letter from Benedict,[2] but I have not seen him yet. He saw Sarah and Wolfe [Wolfinsohn] at Woods Hole and I expect to see him at the Seminary next week. Our New York family were with us for Rosh ha-Shanah and Yom Kippur and the Baby[3] is getting to be a talkative youngster. [D]

1. Eugen Taübler (1879–1953), historian, classical and biblical scholar.
2. Benedict Magnes; youngest son of Judah Magnes.
3. Judith Wolfinsohn [Parker] (1933–   ), Adler's granddaughter.

TO A. S. W. ROSENBACH, PHILADELPHIA

November 1, 1935

I want to thank you for your letter of October 31, in which you tell me about the meeting of the American Jewish Historical Society. I am sorry that I could not attend.

I never see you any more—you will notice I say this rather pathetically.

I still think that the American Jewish Historical Society can be and ought to be made, after the forty odd years of its existence, a more important institution than it is now, and I think we ought to consider ways and means of doing this. I was told the other day, I am not sure whether it is true, that the Teachers School in New York of the Hebrew Union College, had instituted for this year a course of lectures on American Jewish history and that this was the first course of such lectures ever given in any institution. Now if that is true it ought to be remedied. I never thought of the Historical Society as an instrument for propaganda but I did think of it as an instrument for education, and our impact is much too limited. We have made a great collection and we are taking good care of it now, but excepting through the visits to the collections at the Seminary we are not doing anything to spread the knowledge that we are getting except to our very limited number of members. . . . [D]

TO JAMES A. MONTGOMERY, PHILADELPHIA

November 5, 1935

You may be interested to know of a recent occurrence, unless you have heard of it already. Professor Burrows[1] asked me to arrange for an interview with Mr. Felix M. Warburg in connection with the funds for the [American] School [of Oriental Research]. When I spoke to Mr. Warburg, he said to me: "Where is Professor Montgomery?" and I then told him that you had given up the presidency. I advised Professor Burrows to bring Professor Nelson Glueck[2] along and we had a very nice talk. I hope that it will result in something useful. You ought to know, however, that Mr. Warburg is commencing to take an attitude against endowment. His feeling is that ultimately safe securities will only yield about 2% and he prefers to see work done now than to have money stored away and so he made a proposition on behalf of Mrs. Warburg and himself to give a definite sum each year for five years, and Professor Burrows was going to see whether the Rockefeller Foundation would agree to match that.

If you have not heard about this from either Burrows or Glueck, keep it private until they can tell you officially. [D]

1. Millar Burrows (1889–1980), biblical scholar; professor at Yale University.
2. Nelson Glueck (1900–1971), archaeologist and biblical scholar; later became president of Hebrew Union College, 1947–71.

TO FELIX M. WARBURG, NEW YORK CITY

December 27, 1935

. . . I am not sure whether the Zionists, or let us say, the [Jewish] Agency Executive had any option in the matter of the Legislative Council.[1] It is my impression in the first place that the last World Zionist Congress passed a resolution which made it mandatory upon the Executives to oppose the Council. I have the impression too, although I do not know this, that the Council of the Jewish Agency affirmed the action of the World Zionist Congress. These are matters which can easily be obtained from the records, or if the records have not been published sufficiently then Doctor [Maurice J.] Karpf would know about them. If I am right in this surmise then of course the Executives are not to be held to blame. What can be criticized is the action taken this summer.

I noticed a telegram in the *New York Times* of this morning in which [Chaim] Weizmann calls upon all Jews everywhere to take united action and call mass meetings, etc., etc., against the Nuremberg Laws,[2] and against the Legislative Council. In other words, now that he is at the supreme head of the Jewish world he couples the two as of equal importance and endeavors in this rather shrewd way to avoid any criticism.

The same point of view of the Zionists ought to be that having always claimed to be a Democratic institution themselves they should not endeavor to prevent some form of Democratic government from growing up in Palestine. Their retort would be that the contract involved in the mandate was not made with the Jews who live in Palestine but with the Jews of the whole world. It may be possible to maintain such a thesis but so far as the government of Palestine is concerned it is sheer nonsense. One cannot suppose for a moment that in arranging the Legislative Council the Jews of Poland or the Jews of America should have a vote in a Palestinian election.

Then there is another aspect to the matter. I think that the Jewish world has been so thoroughly propagandized on this subject that even if it were in the power of the Executives, who in this particular case, mean Weizmann, Shertok[3] and Ben-Gurion,[4] to take a more conciliatory action toward the Legislative Council the Jews of Palestine would refuse to participate in the election. So that this dilemma has more than two horns.

My personal view is that negotiations should have proceeded somewhat along the following lines—for all I know they may have: The mandatory government notifies both parties, or they really deal with three parties, Jews, Moslems and Christians, that under promise to the League of Nations they were to set up a Legislative Council and that they proposed such and such proportions. They might very well too have made the condition that all parties in the first place accepted the terms of the mandate. They could then have stated that they were dividing the representation upon the basis of ascertained population of local male residents of twenty-five years of age and upwards who were citizens of Palestine, or at least did not owe allegiance to any other power. The Arabs might then have stated that they declined to recognize the terms of the Mandate which would have put an end to the negotiations. The Jews objected to the attitude of the British government with regard to permitting voting only by males and so on.

You see what I mean is this: Had the Zionists and the Agency taken an attitude from the beginning which would have made real discussion possible things might not have come to the pass as they are now. And indeed I do not know the exact position because whereas the Legislative Council has been proclaimed, according to dispatches nothing has been done to put into effect pending negotiations in London.

In view of what I have said above, therefore, it seems to me that someone with inside knowledge might try to bring all the facts out much more clearly than I have brought them out here and state them. Out of all this there may grow a discussion and clarification.

Of course you know that I am by nature opposed to the idea of non-cooperation and if in the last analysis we decline in Palestine to cooperate with the British government, I wonder who in the world there will be left to us to cooperate with.

P.S. Since dictating the above I have just read in the issue of today's Jewish Telegraphic Agency a quotation from Great Britain and the Near East which gives a point of view that is also well worthy of consideration. As a matter of fact I have the further feeling that if the Jewish people steadily refuse to have. . . [anything] to do with the Legislative Council this action will in the last analysis throw the mandatory government more and more into the hands of the Arabs. [W]

1. The Mandatory Government of Palestine had proposed the formation of a Palestinian Legislative Council. The Jewish Agency, fearing that acceptance of the Council would condemn the Jewish community of Palestine to permanent minority status, opposed its implementation. The proposal, rejected by both Arabs and Jews, was dropped after the 1936 riots.

2. Anti-Jewish laws promulgated at the Nazi party convention at Nuremberg, September 15, 1935, depriving Jews and other non-Aryans of German citizenship and forbidding marriage between Jews and Germans. This was the beginning of a series of anti-Jewish laws.

3. Moshe Shertok (Sharett) (1894–1965), Zionist leader and Israeli statesman; became first foreign minister of Israel, 1948–56, and its second prime minister, 1954–55.

4. David Ben-Gurion (1886–1973), Labor Zionist leader and Israeli statesman; became first prime minister and defense minister of Israel.

Despite the hopes and the often conflicting plans for the relief of the German Jewish refugees, the rush of events made the reality faced by the refugees a grim one.

TO HENRY PEREIRA MENDES, MORRISTOWN, NEW JERSEY

January 13, 1936

. . . I do not think there is much in the idea that many of the German Jews can or will come to the United States. That is not at all the purpose of the visit of the three English Jews to this country.[1] In fact you will recall that in the *Times* statement the idea was that they should all go to some portions of the British Empire, of course including Palestine. I do not think this statement is correct either because I believe that these unfortunate people must go where they can go and as long as there is unemployment in so many countries no doors are going to be very wide open. At present and until these gentlemen come over no one of the older organization has anything to do with this plan at all. While I have known in a vague way about it for several months, it is not an American Jewish Committee plan, nor is it a Board of Deputies[2] plan in London, nor is it even a Joint Distribution Committee plan, though a number of gentlemen connected with the Joint Distribution Committee as far back as nearly a year ago, realizing that some such eventuality might require immediate help, did subscribe quite among themselves the sum of One Million and a Quarter Dollars to help the German Jews in any emergency that might arise. This was quite outside of the regular contributions either to the Palestine Fund or to the Joint Distribution Committee.

The Nuremberg Laws have created such an emergency and the question really is whether there shall be an orderly exodus or a flight such as took place when Hitler first came in.

I do not know whether I shall be invited to sit in this conference in New York when it takes place, or indeed that I shall be able to, but since you have written to Mr. [Felix M.] Warburg I am sure you have embodied your very interesting suggestions to him. The one thing I am certain of is that there is little thought of having any considerable number of these refugees come to the United States at the present time. We have now received rather quietly, in the course of the last two years and a half, about six thousand German Jews. Most of these were people who came to families who were prepared to take care of them until such time as they could be absorbed in some walk of life here. Any attempt on our part at the present time to loosen up the immigration laws so as to permit a large number of Jewish people to come in within a short time would immediately be opposed by the labor unions, by all kinds of public opinion and by many members of Congress. We are still supposed to have ten million people unemployed in the United States. [D]

1. Sir Herbert Samuel; Simon Marks (1888–1964), industrialist and Zionist leader; and Walter Horace Samuel, second viscount Bearstead (1882–1948), British oil executive and active in Jewish affairs. They came to the United States on behalf of the German-Jewish refugees.
2. Board of Deputies of British Jews, founded in 1760, the representative body of British Jewry.

TO NEVILLE LASKI, LONDON

January 23, 1936

It was very kind of you to send me a copy of your letter to Mr. [Felix M.] Warburg with regard to the Legislative Council. I have been very strongly urged to come to a meeting which is going to be held on January 26 in New York at the Hotel Astor to protest against the Legislative Council. I said I could not attend the meeting as I have not been out at night yet[1] and have not been in New York since the beginning of December.

Then Mr. [Morris] Rothenberg asked me if I would send them a message. I thereupon wrote him an explicit letter to the effect that since the Council of the Agency has authorized the Executive to take the action they were taking I would not make any public statement against their action, but I certainly would not make any public statement supporting it.

My own view of the matter is this: As far as we can see in the future Palestine will probably be safest as a British Crown Colony. On the other hand as it is a mandate and the mandatory power had agreed or was indeed even required to set up some form of self-governing institutions, as the permanent mandates commission of the League of Nations are holding them to this and as they promised to do it, I can well understand that at a certain point they feel under obligation to carry out their promise.

To me, the argument set up by the Zionist Organization and the Executive, namely, that the mandate is a contract with sixteen million Jews throughout the world and not solely with the Jews who happen to be living in Palestine is ridiculous. Has it ever been supposed that in matters of local self-government sixteen million Jews throughout the world including the "infants-in-arms" should be given a vote?

It seems to me that the sensible ground upon which to have approached this matter or negotiated with the government was this: That the proportions in the Legislative Council should be subject to revision every ten years upon the basis of a census. In other words the number should not be fixed or crystalized; and the other important provision, that only those who accepted the mandate should be qualified to sit in the Council. As a pure matter of justice I would go even further and say that only those who accept the mandate should be qualified voters but that I know would raise such a storm that it might even provoke serious disturbances in Palestine, but it would be a very simple provision that no Moslem or Christian or Jew should sit in the Council unless he accepted explicitly the terms of the mandate.

In another letter which I have from you you ask about my health. It is very much better. I have been twice in my office in Philadelphia for a short time and happen not to have gone out today because the weather is exactly zero and I think cold winds start me coughing again. I would be physically able to go to New York but I am having daily treatments which I do not want to suspend until I am entirely cleared up. Unless there is some sudden thing happen to me you would find me almost as good as usual. . . . [W]

1. Due to illness. See letter to Max Adler, March 18, 1936.

TO MAURICE WILLIAM,[1] NEW YORK CITY

February 24, 1936

. . . No one person can know or do everything, and I am frankly a person whose training and knowledge does not qualify him to speak with authority as to where the German Jews should go or should not go. My attitude as to the places to which the German Jews should migrate is largely one of self-determination on their part.[2] Those who want to go to Palestine should be aided to go there. Those who want to go to South America should be aided to go there. There are probably at the present time more opportunities in Central America than in South America, but of that I am not certain. Some of them come here to the United States, probably a larger number than is known.

I did discuss with some of my colleagues the question of advising some German Jews to go to China, and I was asked the question as to whether if I had a cousin would I send him to China, which is constantly disturbed by Japan, etc. My answer was I would rather have him go to China than stay in Germany. It is not really possible to force human beings to do what they do not wish to do. One can only draw their attention to the possibilities.

You probably know that there has been a new high commissioner appointed, an English army officer, and that Mr. [Norman] Bentwich is going to continue to assist him, but the League of Nations will look to the private organizations to furnish the actual funds to render possible these migrations. It may be known to you that some German Jews have of their volition gone to Africa; some to South Africa, and some in the neighborhood of Zanzibar.

The recent visit of the three English gentlemen to this country has crystallized what may come to be an important aid to the gradual exodus of 25,000 German Jews a year for the next four years. This I think will largely be directed from London.

I myself have looked with favor upon a real study of the possibilities in China just because of the reasons you give, that there is bound to be a reawakening there and there will no doubt be many opportunities. [JTS]

1. Maurice William (1881–1973), author of works on international affairs and the Far East.
2. See letter to Henry Pereira Mendes, January 13, 1936.

TO MAX ADLER,[1] BEVERLY HILLS, CALIFORNIA

March 18, 1936

I was very glad to hear from you out at the Pacific Coast and hope you are well and have had a comfortable winter. You are certainly fortunate to be away from the cold in Chicago and the cold in the East. We have to call Chicago "east" now because you have gone on Western Standard Time.

With regard to Huberman's[2] Symphony Orchestra in Palestine, I noticed something about it in the papers and have been told something about it by my son-in-law, Wolfe Wolfinsohn. He tells me that the orchestra season is guaranteed for one year. I think all told they have $25,000 as a nest-egg. £2000 came from Simon Marks of London and I do not know where the rest of the money came from. The idea is to have a reduced orchestra of 65 pieces, and as you no doubt know, Toscanini[3] has agreed to go to Palestine and lead the orchestra for the first year. The American Jewish Committee naturally had nothing to do with this because it is our business to defend Jews but we do not furnish them music.

Whether it is impractical or not remains to be seen. Tel Aviv now has a population of 150,000, all Jews. At the University it is always possible to assemble an audience of 1000 people in the beautiful open-air stadium where concerts can be heard beautifully. I have heard it myself there. During recent years, quite a number of well-to-do Jews have come to Palestine and they count many music lovers. Also, it is to be remembered, in Jerusalem at least, a very considerable body of consuls, staff, etc. reside. So that it is not impossible that such an orchestra may live.

Most orchestras, as you know, travel, and Egypt might furnish a very good place for concerts of the same orchestra especially in the tourist season. It is only a night trip from Jerusalem to Cairo. This is about all I can tell you about the subject.

I hope you will be coming East as I am not likely to come to Chicago this season. It is good of you to inquire about my health. It has been rather poor this winter and I was locked up in my room for two months in Philadelphia. It is only since February that I have been able to resume my work. The rest of the family have fortunately been well. [D]

1. Max Adler (1866–1952), Adler's cousin; a Chicago business executive, active in Jewish and civic affairs.
2. Bronislaw Huberman (1882–1947), violinist; founder of the Palestine Symphony Orchestra.
3. Arturo Toscanini (1867–1957), Italian conductor; conducted the first concerts given by the Palestine Symphony.

TO LORD BEARSTED,[1] LONDON

May 12, 1936

. . . With regard to what you write about the general attitude of the American Jewish community towards the German-Jewish Appeal. As you know, during the greater part of the visit of yourself, Sir Herbert [Samuel] and Mr. [Simon] Marks to America, I was ill. I saw Sir Herbert once in Philadelphia and then at dinner in Mr. [Felix M.] Warburg's house at which time I also had the pleasure of meeting you. While there are personal differences in the Jewish community in America, as I presume there are elsewhere, I do not think this is the determining factor. Mr. Warburg and I for a number of years, against odds all around, were able to keep our two major appeals together. But this year, before your visit here, there was a split and then there was a further split through the fact that the Polish Jews felt they were not fairly treated by the Joint Distribution Committee and they organized a special Polish Appeal. To such an appeal your own community was virtually made to submit last year. I do not think the difference is going to interfere with the matter of getting money because I believe both appeals up to this time have received more money than they did at the same date in 1935. The more serious thing is the fact that there has been a failure so far actually to constitute the committee or council which was to have been constituted, and this is not a matter of vanities or personalities but principle.

The Joint Distribution Committee has felt a sort of trusteeship to the givers in America and to the Jews all over the world who need help. I attended a meeting only the other day where I heard the view expressed that the men who were chosen as the American representatives, at least those from the Joint Distribution Committee, do not feel that this can be accomplished with a committee that is overladen with Zionists, and that they would thus step in as a minority in advance and could have little hope of having their views even seriously considered. I know there has been some correspondence between Mr. Warburg and Sir Osmond [d'Avigdor Goldsmid] on that point. I have heard the view expressed that at a meeting they would face a fait accompli, that the greater part of your present funds are already committed to the emigration of 3500 Jews from Germany to Palestine, and that upon the basis of number and the amount you have so generously placed at their disposal, the plan would fall far short of the expectations of emigrating 2500 Jews from Germany per annum for the next four years.

Take this as my own personal statement and remember that I have had no direct part in any of the negotiations. I do again want to assure you, however, that from the calibre of the men, I am satisfied that at least on the part of the Joint Distribution Committee there is no personal or private question involved. It is only a matter of principle. [D]

1. See letter to Henry Pereira Mendes, January 13, 1936.

TO LOUIS FINKELSTEIN, NEW YORK CITY

May 20, 1936
With regard to the matter of the College Entrance Examination Board, I would say that I think it is probably impossible to change the date at this time. You will be told that these examinations are fixed, not only in New York, but all over the country and even in other parts of the world, and that it is too late to change them; moreover the examination papers have to be uniform.

I think an interview would be better than a letter if you really want to accomplish something, and I would suggest that you might be able to arrange for some sort of an examination on the following basis. I am assuming, of course, that they will say it is impossible and that the examinations are definitely fixed for Saturday on such-and-such a date. You might point out that Saturday lasts until 12 o'clock midnight and that the students could be ready at 8:30 or maybe 9:00 to take such examinations on Saturday night, thus complying with the conditions of the uniformity of the day.

I am making these suggestions because I once succeeded in making an arrangement here in Pennsylvania for the State Teachers' examinations. I was told by the Examiners that they could not change, and I reported that they said Saturday and that Saturday lasted until midnight. They had to agree with that. It was, by the way, an examination in which Mr. David Hoffman was involved and which finally won for him the position of professor in one of our high schools.

It is too bad that these things always come to our attention so late. As a matter of fact, some responsible body ought to watch these things a year in advance, whether it is to be the Rabbinical Assembly or what not.

When you receive this letter I advise that you call up Mr. [Harry] Schneiderman of the American Jewish Committee and find out whether they have any knowledge of this and whether the Committee itself has made any representations. You might possibly get Mr. [Solomon M.] Stroock and Mr. [Felix M.] Warburg to join you in such a matter.

I am very much afraid, however, that our real weakness will prove to be that most of the Jews will take the examination without question.

Finally, and after you have done these things, I think an interview would be better, but you ought to have the letter that you have written left as a memorandum. [JTS]

In April 1936 Arab-fomented riots broke out in Jaffa, directed at the Jewish community in Palestine and the British mandatory power. The riots were followed by an Arab general strike and involved Arab attacks on Jews and on British soldiers.

TO MAX WARBURG, AMSTERDAM

June 1, 1936

. . . Racie and I have decided to join forces this summer with Sarah, Wolfe and little Judith and have taken a house in Wood's Hole, Mass. It is, as you know, upon Cape Cod and said to be very pleasant and cool. It has for a long time been a sort of scientific, literary and musical colony, and is very informal.

Since you wrote things have been getting steadily worse in Palestine. There was a tendency at the beginning for the [Jewish Agency] Executive to soft-pedal the news and charge the Jewish Telegraphic Agency and other news agencies with exaggeration, but now it is not possible any longer to make this charge.

I am very much concerned about the World Jewish Congress which I think will not only have repercussions in Palestine but in other parts of the world and cannot accomplish anything useful. I have cabled these views to [Chaim] Weizmann today, and have made them known through such of my friends in Europe as I could reach. Unfortunately Weizmann sort of committed himself to Stephen Wise last summer and when Weizmann commits himself I presume he commits the whole Jewish Agency.

Some of my friends here are getting very restive about staying in the Agency, with virtually no voice and yet being responsible for all of its acts. I think this is also true in England. I am advising people not to resign at present as this would be considered withdrawing when things are difficult. But the policy for years now seems to be to have been wrong. This is not to say that I blame the Jewish Agency or the Jews for the present disturbances. The Arabs can make enough mischief themselves and I think they have been somewhat incited to it from outside. I have not the slightest doubts myself but that during the Italo-Ethiopian conflict Arab Sheiks were being bribed with Italian money, just as I am sure that Ethiopian Chieftains were. However, there is no use of crying over spilt milk. . . . [W]

Promotion of the observance of the Sabbath was always one of Adler's priorities. It was for him a matter of self-respect that Jewish communal institutions observe the Sabbath.

TO JEREMIAH J. BERMAN,[1] ROCHESTER, NEW YORK

July 16, 1936

I have your letter of July 8, and am profoundly distressed to hear of the attempt, which you describe, to open your new Jewish Young Men's and Women's Association building on the Sabbath day for athletic activities. If your report accurately represents the views of the proponents of the movement, I can only express my sorrow at their inability to realize the full significance of the action they are planning to take. Nothing can be better calculated to undermine the sense of Jewish self-respect which we are laboring to build up in this country than such an open and flagrant violation of the Jewish day of rest by a Jewish institution. There are many Jews in this country, of course, who in their private lives do not observe the Sabbath. But even among these, a vast majority of those who have studied Jewish life agree in the need for maintaining the morale of the Jewish youth, and its reverence for the traditions of our people. How can this be done, when the erection of a new community structure is taken as the opportunity for an anti-religious innovation? It must be remembered that most of the boys and girls who use the buildings of Young Men's and Young Women's Hebrew Associations come from orthodox Jewish homes. It is difficult for their parents to exert any positive influence on their lives under any circumstances. Indeed, one of the main purposes of YMHA buildings is to help bridge the difference between these older people and the younger generation. But that purpose is entirely frustrated, if the YMHA definitely associates itself with those who oppose Jewish tradition.

I cannot believe that loyal Reform Jews will support such a movement. I have worked all my life with loyal Jews, both Reform and traditional, and have always found that the most far-sighted among them were agreed in their reverence for the public observance of the Sabbath. You may be interested to know that the late Jacob H. Schiff never attended a meeting on the Sabbath. When once he was called to such a meeting he protested, and came only on condition that it was understood that no record would be kept of the proceedings, and that the discussions would be entirely informal. Mr. Louis Marshall, who was for many years President of Temple Emanuel, took the same view.

I do not hesitate to say that if the erection of a new and most costly building involves the violation of the Sabbath, it would have been far better for your community to have remained satisfied with the humbler building it had previously. The Jewish problem in this country is not one created by our enemies. They can do us little harm. It is one which we are creating for ourselves, through our disrespect for our ancestral teachings. What I once called the "ghetto crouch" is the main danger which faces us. No one will ever respect a person or a people who fail to respect themselves. And how can our children develop this essential reverence for Israel and its past, if our own institutions help to break down the religious morale of even a part of them.

We sternly object when Universities of whose student body the Jews form only a small percentage arrange for examinations on the Sabbath, on the ground that this helps to undermine the religious loyalties of those Jews who do observe the holy day. We rightly maintain that it is the concern of all good Americans that every young man should remain loyal to the religion in which he was reared. But how can we make such demands on the institutions maintained by private corporations or the government, if we ourselves fail to recognize the Sabbath in our institutions?

I earnestly hope that on reconsideration the proponents of the plan will realize the grave dangers it involves to the spirit and morale of the young people the institution is intended to serve, and will of their own accord withdraw the proposal. [AJHS]

1. Jeremiah J. Berman (1903–55), rabbi of Temple Beth El, Rochester, New York, 1928–39.

TO FELIX M. WARBURG, NEW YORK CITY

Woods Hole, Massachusetts, August 24, 1936

I have been thinking very carefully over your letter of August 18 and your exchange of telegrams with [Chaim] Weizmann. Technically you are entirely correct. You should not make yourself responsible for a war. But actually where does it leave us? You and I have a great responsibility for the Yishub. Our names and our acts encouraged many people to think that the situation was safe. Moreover we backed up Weizmann. You more than I. Now I am not thinking of the politics of the thing in which we may have been mistaken but I am thinking of the people themselves. Consider this poor [Levi] Billig of the University who was murdered at his work or those. . . who never did anything but good. You no doubt have seen the editorial attitude of the *London Times*. Have you read the enclosed letter of Smuts'[1] (which I shall be glad to have returned). I do feel that our alternates to the administration committee—[Maurice J.] Karpf and [Morris D.] Waldman—should be given a hint that while we are not for war, peace at any price would also be disastrous. I write this to you with great hesitation but the whole situation has made me very unhappy. In my opinion we should have yielded in the Legislative Council. I am also of the opinion that the tempo of immigration was too rapid but actual suspension of all Jewish immigration for any period would, I think, be fatal. Remember not a word has been said about suspension of immigration of Arabs.

Forgive me for this scrawl. I had to say it to you. [AJA]

1. Jan Christian Smuts (1870–1950), South African soldier and statesman.

In August 1936, a Royal Commission was appointed to investigate the disturbances in Palestine and to make a recommendation concerning the operation of the Mandate. It concluded that the Mandate was unworkable and should be terminated and that Palestine should be partitioned into Arab and Jewish states with the British retaining Jerusalem and certain other areas.

TO FELIX M. WARBURG, NEW YORK CITY

Woods Hole, Massachusetts, August 25, 1936

. . . Sitting here alone some matters become clear to me. The Palestine Government has not been able under civil government to maintain law and order. I think that we ought send cable instructions to our alternates in the Administrative Council to propose a resolution that we favor the adoption of martial law in Palestine until the end of the present emergency.

Next I think that we should propose a resolution that the Executive of the Jewish Agency be instructed fully to cooperate with the royal commission. If you are willing to join me in these ideas I shall be glad. If not I would wish to communicate them by cable to whoever is my alternate.

The proposed meeting of the Zionists if it is ordered by [Stephen S.] Wise will probably follow his orders. Judge Lewis[1] is a weak sister who plays on both sides. While there may be no love lost between [Morris] Rothenberg and Wise, the former sold out at Providence after he had encouraged his supporters to make a fight for him.[2]

With regard to the statement which James Rosenberg proposed I think there is much merit in the idea. I am returning his letter to you. The only thing to which I take objection is the cousinship of the Arabs. That has been tried ad nauseam and has not worked. Beside, most of the Moslem inhabitants of Palestine are really not Arabs.

What I think ought be done is this. You and I and other American members of the Administrative Committee of the Jewish Agency ought to express our views to the Administrative Committee by cable. As long as we are in the Agency we must work within the framework of the Agency. If as a result of the meeting on September 2 we are absolutely counted out, then we might become public dissidents, which in the end would result in our resignation from the Agency. I know all this is very drastic but I think it is the only way in which we can really help the Yishub and the Jewish world at large. If we could agree on this cable and while sending it to our own representatives let them have it leak out to the Actions Committee which is now sitting it would be all to the good. . . .

. . . The American Jewish Committee will, I am convinced, continue to hold its own as long as we keep a stiff upper lip. Wise is a blackguard and all this talk of unity has held me back from saying so. Sooner or later he and his history will have to be exposed; until that is done we shall have to suffer him. . . . [AJA]

1. William M. Lewis (1884–1939), Philadelphia jurist; active in Zionist affairs, the United Palestine Appeal, and the Council of the Jewish Agency.
2. At the convention of the Zionist Organization of America in July 1936, in Providence, Rhode Island, Wise became president of the organization and Rothenberg, in a compromise move, became chairman of its administrative committee.

TO JULIAN MORGENSTERN, CINCINNATI

Philadelphia, October 23, 1936

I have your letter of October 16th, which I have delayed answering owing to the fact that I was laid up with a cold.

Professor Julius Lewy came to see me in New York after the death of Professor [Richard] Gottheil and I gave him advice to try to make himself acquainted with the situation there, and I think I gave him a letter to Professor [John Dynely] Prince, who I thought would know. Naturally, there has been a good deal of conversation in the East concerning the post. The American Oriental Society is hesitating as to whether it should not definitely approach President Butler.[1] Doctor [William F.] Albright and I agreed that it might be unwise for us to make any suggestion, though we would be glad to if we were asked for advice. Meanwhile, a few weeks ago, I learned in New York that apparently without even consulting anybody on the Faculty, President Butler had offered the post for one year to a certain George Antonius.[2] From all I can learn about him, and that was true of [James A.] Montgomery and Albright, he is a Christian Arab who was a propagandist for the Mufti. Mrs. Gottheil,[3] when she heard of it, wrote a letter of protest to President Butler. Butler replied with a kind note that he was sure she had been misinformed. It was just, I think, the day before Yom Kippur that the matter seemed to get to an urgent point and my advice was asked. I suggested that it should be taken up as a Columbia matter and that some of the Ph.D.'s from the Semitic Department and several prominent graduates of Columbia should wait on President Butler and give him the information that we had secured. Louis Newman,[4] who seemed to have had his ear to the ground and was very much excited, arranged for an interview with President Butler to which Mr. Sol. M. Stroock and Judge [Joseph Meyer] Proskauer went. They are both prominent graduates of Columbia and Mr. Stroock is a Trustee of Teachers College Columbia. At this meeting President Butler agreed not to confirm the appointment but stated that he was writing to the British Foreign Office and to Sir Herbert Samuel to secure information. There the matter stands. . . . [AJA]

1. Nicholas Murray Butler (1862–1947), president of Columbia University, 1901–45.
2. George Antonius (1892–1942), Palestinian Arab nationalist, known for his book, *The Arab Awakening* (London, 1938).
3. Emma Leon Gottheil (1862–1947).
4. Louis Newman (1903–72), Reform rabbi and author; a student of Gottheil; leader of the Zionist Revisionist party in the United States.

TO FELIX M. WARBURG, NEW YORK CITY

November 11, 1936

It is a couple of weeks since you gave me the clippings concerning the trip which Senator [Royal Samuel] Copeland and Senator Austin[1] took to Palestine as an unofficial commission sent out by Mr. Hearst.[2] You say that you cannot quite make out what Hearst's object was in sending these people to Palestine. It is very difficult for anybody on the outside to evaluate that inscrutable mind but I am going to make a rough guess.

For reasons which I do not know the circulation of the Hearst papers at least in New York City, and possibly elsewhere, fell off very sharply within the past five or six months. There were some approaches made by representatives of Hearst to the American Jewish Committee, and I think to the Anti-Defamation League, etc., to see if this tendency could not be corrected. Some of the young men in the American Jewish Committee office thought that we ought to approach this proposed meeting in a friendly spirit owing to the great influence that the Hearst papers have. Mr. [Solomon M.] Stroock and I, when we were asked advice, made objection. It was our point of view that it was none of our business whether the circulation of the Hearst papers fell off or not. Moreover, this request from the Hearst representatives was coupled with a further request that we should throw open all our files to the Hearst papers. The point then of course was that they wanted to show that the Jewish connection with communism was very strong. That I refused to do. I said that if the Hearst papers or any other chain of papers wished information from the American Jewish Committee on any point we would give them that information but we would not throw our files open. The Anti-Defamation League did throw its files open. I am writing this from memory without looking at any documents, but that is the story.

Now getting down to the clippings:

Article I, by Senator Austin, contains a statement which I do not think is correct. He says "The Government of the United States became a party to the Mandate by virtue of the 'American-British Palestine Mandate Convention of December 3, 1924,' signed by Frank B. Kellogg."[3] There is a good deal of misunderstanding about the Mandate. Even so careful a paper as the *Near East and Great Britain,* formerly *The Near East and India,* published an editorial the other day in which it said that the Mandate was an award to Great Britain by the League of Nations and that the League was now in a very low ebb, etc. The Mandate to Great Britain was awarded by the principal Allied and Associated Powers in which America had a part, but when the Senate refused to ratify the Treaty of Versailles our connection with the Mandate ceased. However, by a resolution, which I think originated in the Senate, and was introduced by Senator Henry Cabot Lodge, and which also passed the House, we affirmed our interest in the Palestine and Balfour Declaration, etc. This Treaty of 1924 was simply that our commercial rights should not be lost in a country which was a Mandate of Great Britain. As you know Great Britain accepted the Mandate only after the Zionists accepted the Churchill Paper[4] and when that was done Trans-Jordan was a part of the British Mandate; but under a special Government with a legislature, Mohammedanism was the established religion of the country. I cannot see at all that America has any legal standing in such a matter.

Article 2. Senator Austin says "Eighty percent of the blood that was in Palestine on the promulgation of the Mandate had been there since long before Moses was put in the bulrushes, we are informed" and then he says that they were Canaanites, etc. I have always believed myself that a very considerable proportion of the fellahin represented an older population than the Arab population but nobody has ever studied it really or proved it. At present a Palestinian who is a student at Dropsie College, whose name is Vilnay,[5] a rather mature man, published some excellent works. He studied in England for many years. I am advising him to consider the question of an ethnological survey of Palestine in order just to consider that point. I believe that Austin's statement is correct but exaggerated. However, if people have been speaking Arabic let us say for eight centuries they reasonably consider themselves Arabs. As you know, the best ethonologists and even anthropologists think that most of our so-called racial classifications are linguistic classifications. I know this is a point in which you do not entirely agree with me but still I am stating it to you again.

Article 3. This relates largely to finance. I do not know whether the statement that the Jews have brought $450,000,000 worth of capital into

Palestine in recent years is correct. It sounds like a large sum of money but it may be true. I have very little doubt myself that a great many, if not most of the Jews in Palestine who have settled there do dream, as he says of a Jewish State, although it has not been officially avowed either by the World Zionist Organization nor by the Agency. The likelihood of it is enormously remote in my opinion. . . .

Article 5. There is a misstatement about the Jewish Agency. Senator Austin writes of the Agency "This body is recognized under the Mandate as a governmental instrument for the establishment of the Jewish National Home." My recollection is that it was recognized as an instrument to advise the Palestine government. I think it is true, as [Moshe] Shertok says, that when the Balfour Declaration was declared it was in the minds of everybody that Trans-Jordan was included in Palestine, but you know this was a declaration made while the War was still on and a good many things were said during that anxious period. When Mr. [Louis] Lipsky and I went down to see President [Franklin D.] Roosevelt some six months or more ago at his request to discuss with him or rather give him information concerning Palestine he specifically asked me a question about Trans-Jordan and I told him that I presumed that the British Government, which keeps the Mandate over Trans-Jordan nevertheless really signed it over to the Arabs in the hope that if they had a part of Palestine to themselves it would bring peace. He then asked me about conditions there and I told him that Trans-Jordan was larger than Palestine and that it was a fertile country but that the British were not allowing any Jewish settlement there until they felt that they were secure. He looked up at me and said, "It will be settled by peaceful filtration; this is probably much easier to bring about than a formal agreement."

. . . Article 7. It contains an interview with a man whom he calls an intelligent Arab. This furnishes a little food for thought. I am not sure that it is all true. He says, for instance that the Rutenberg Electrical Works have some eight hundred employees but only five Arabs among them. I had the impression that [Pinhas] Rutenberg had a much larger number of Arabs than that. I also agree that the Jews should include the teaching of Arabic in their schools and I think they ought to teach English also. On the other hand, it is an unfair statement that thirty percent of the Jews do not speak Hebrew. That is due largely to the very large migration in the last few years. It takes a little time to learn the language. . . .

Article 11, and the last, really deals with the British Government. Of course many have expressed the opinion that the leniency at the beginning of the strike encouraged the Arabs but it is very difficult for people not on the ground to decide such a question. We have strikes in this country and very violent strikes such as in the shipping industry on both coasts but while the Government makes an attempt to mediate through the Department of Labor, but for the Government of either the State of New York or the State of San Francisco to call out the National Guards, would be a drastic step and the Federal Government would never send troops in unless the Governments of these two States said they could not keep order. Now I know that the situation is not the same but it is very difficult to blame Sir Arthur Wauchaupe[6] for not having started in at once. My own feeling is that if after one month the police could not keep order then the troops should have been used.

I am sure you know that I have been of the opinion for some time that certain foreign influences helped to foment these troubles and that particularly Italy after it embarked on its Ethiopian adventure, became angered at Great Britain and endeavored to strike Great Britain through Palestine, which it did by helping the Arab Sheikhs with money and used other forms of propaganda. Mussolini has had his eye on everything around the Red Sea for a long while and Italy is the only European Power that has a Treaty with the Iman Yahya of Yemen, who is probably the most retrogressive ruler in the world.

I now come to the articles of Senator Copeland. The first article, 9/27/36 is fair and descriptive.

The second article again is descriptive of the situation during the strike and notes particularly the fact that they had to travel around the country under an escort of soldiers. . . .

Article ten is devoted to the prosperity brought by the Jews to the Arabs. I think this is undoubtedly true but apparently it has not pleased the Arabs enough to keep them quiet or make them behave themselves. There is a head-line in this last paragraph which says Palestine has room for millions, but there is nothing in the article which seems to justify that. I believe that in present-day Palestine, without considering Trans-Jordan, there could be settled two million people without the country being crowded from their point of view. It would be over-crowded from the American point of view.

Article eleven was really written with the Hearst papers specifically in mind. It charges that the events in Moscow had a great hand in creating the troubles and that Palestinian Jews are engaged in fighting communism. I am afraid there are also some Palestinian Jews who are communists.

Article twelve is devoted to the Huleh Concession and Senator Copeland says that the Zionist Organization paid $1,000,000 for the Huleh concession[7] and agreed to spend another $5,000,000 for the reclamation. You will know better than I whether that was true or not.

Article thirteen refers to the differences among the Arabs which Senator Copeland says was exploited by Great Britain. That is not at all impossible. The divide and rule theory has been used by many Empires.

Article fourteen, I think is really not a correct reading of history. Senator Copeland says that, speaking of the Mandate, "But the doubtful gift of fifteen years ago has now become a coveted prize, thanks to the astonishing transformation of the land by the Jews." I do not believe a word of this. I am satisfied that the idea of acquiring Palestine for Britain under a Mandate was political just as the Balfour Declaration was political, and the desire to keep Palestine was also political. The trade of Palestine is not worth a row with all the Arab nations.

Altogether the articles of Senator Copeland strike me as being in the main anti-British and possibly that is another thing that Mr. Hearst wanted. . . . [W]

1. Warren Robinson Austin (1877–1962), U.S. senator from Vermont, 1931–46.
2. William Randolph Hearst (1863–1951), American newspaper and magazine publisher whose publications were noted for their sensationalism.
3. Frank B. Kellogg (1856–1937), U.S. secretary of state under Calvin Coolidge; coauthor of the Kellogg-Briand pact to outlaw war, for which he received the Nobel Peace Prize in 1929.
4. See letter to Felix M. Warburg, September 3, 1929.
5. Zev Vilnay (b. 1900), Israeli geographer and author.
6. Sir Arthur Wauchaupe (1874–1947), British high commissioner for Palestine, 1931–38.
7. In 1934 the Jewish National Fund acquired most of the land of the Huleh valley in Upper Galilee.

TO FELIX M. WARBURG, NEW YORK CITY

November 20, 1936

. . . I do not know the attitude of the Palestine Economic Corporation but I think that they rigidly abstain from politics and I doubt very much whether they would want to be a body to speak before the Royal Commission as representing the economic life of Palestine. Quite often, although he objects to mysticism, [Maurice B.] Hexter gets a little mystic himself and he uses forms of statements in arguing which instead of clarifying issues with his colleagues are apt to confuse them.

I am in agreement that we ought to be more than happy to accept parity and that this is the only formula that will carry out the frequent declarations in the Zionist Congresses that we neither wish to dominate nor be dominated.

These statements I am making to you are probably purely academic, unless you think that a cable on that point, representing the views of American non-Zionists, if it does represent their views, might be sent to [Chaim] Weizmann. I am not very hopeful of any result.

[David Werner] Senator's letter is like his letters and on the point of parity he agrees with Hexter. I am rather moved by his statement that the non-Zionists should not stand by simply as passive observers.

As for immigration, I know that the phrase "economic absorptive capacity" of the country has been theoretically the basis of a policy but the government has rarely rigidly carried this out and one can see for a very good reason. The present High Commissioner has stated time and again that one must always be prepared for a possible drop in business or employment and if this took place Palestine would have a considerable number of unemployed on its hands. I suppose everything has to be done with common sense.

I have never liked the clauses in the leases of the Jewish National Fund. In fact I discussed this matter privately with a number of people in 1929 when the enlarged Agency was being formed but they told me it was hopeless to discuss it and moreover the Jewish National Fund is not officially a part of the Agency.

There is a proposition which I think would be humanly fair and that is that there should be a stop put to Arab immigration. It would be fair I say because the immigration would come from surrounding Arab countries which if properly developed could easily support all these immigrants and more, not only through Syria and Egypt but through Trans-Jordan and Iraq. If such a thing could be peaceably brought about it would solve a good many difficulties. . . . [W]

Relations between Zionists and non-Zionists on the Jewish Agency had reached the breaking point. By 1939, the non-Zionists had for all practical purposes abandoned the Jewish Agency to the Zionists.

TO FELIX M. WARBURG, NEW YORK CITY

January 4, 1937

. . . I will divide the matter in two parts. One, as to Agency organization. I think we ought to make it clear to [Chaim] Weizmann that we are not prepared to be an official minority in any Jewish organization. This of course was never intended but it is the position to which the non-Zionists have been reduced. If, therefore, it is a settled policy, even his settled policy, that this present condition should continue, I think we ought to tell him frankly that we are out of the picture altogether and that we would not go out by the side door either but by the front door.

Now with regard to the position of Palestine itself, there must be some accommodation between all the sections of the population, or, if that is not reached the Yishub will be defended either by British bayonets or else armed and have a civil war on its hands, and let it be remembered that even if the Jews in Palestine should go through a civil war such as is now going on in Spain, beat the Arabs and subdue them, they would nevertheless have to reckon with Iraq, Egypt, Syria and Trans-Jordan. In other words there can be no victory of the Jews over the Arabs in the present state of the world. It would be as bad as a defeat.

That of course brings me to the very harsh clause which I have always objected to in the Jewish National Fund leases, that no Arabs should be employed on the lands. No doubt the intention was high-minded but the result is one that leaves the impression on the mind of a fair-minded outsider as simply a piece of bigotry.

Another point which must be taken up and settled is the question of the illegal immigration. The position has been frankly taken by the responsible people in the Jewish Agency that while they are opposed to illegal immigration and warned the different communities against it, they will not aid the Government in trying to locate and deport these illegal immigrants. I am very much afraid that the Jewish population really demands such an attitude on the part of their leaders. To inform on a fellow Jew to get him out of the Holy Land is something that the Jewish population would never tolerate.

It seems to me therefore that the whole question of these immigration offices should be over-hauled to make quite sure that it is really so, that they are not in any way conniving at this and that they are issuing stern warnings to the population that any one who goes without a visa or certificate is apt to get in jail or even be deported.

I know and you know that not everything is strictly alright in these offices scattered in various parts of the world. There is a favoritism in the granting of certificates as between different parties of Zionism, and other things are done which should not be done. In other words, the Administrative machinery which is, I admit, very far-flung and difficult to control, needs a perfectly good house-cleaning.

I do not think it will be a very good time for you to discuss with Weizmann some of the larger things in Palestine because the report of the Royal Commission will hardly have been rendered and it would be a great mistake, in my opinion, to try to anticipate the Royal Commission's report. There is one thing, however, on which I would strongly advise that there be an understanding and that is the treatment which the Royal Commission's report should receive. Nobody, not even Doctor Weizmann himself, should be authorized to express the view of the Jewish Agency with regard to the Royal Commission's report. When that report comes out there should be a meeting, if at all possible, of the Administrative Committee, in order to decide—I do not simply say what action should be taken with regard to the report—but even what the attitude should be. Any attempt, in my opinion, to create public opinion throughout the world with a view to influencing Parliament in the matter of the Royal Commission's report, such as was done before with other reports, would be an error.

This is the most serious Commission that has been sent out; it has gone under the most solemn auspices and its report should be treated with the greatest care and consideration and not by hot-heads and public demonstrations.

Let me wander on. By the very methods which the Agency uses, and you know as well as I do that for all practical purposes these are the Zionists' methods, we are put at a disadvantage in Palestine. This is largely due to our method of bragging. We complain on the one hand that the Government does not do enough for Jewish education, that it does not do enough for health, that it does not do enough for social service; and on the other hand we tell people that within the last year or two Fifty Million Dollars of Jewish capital has gone in and that Two Hundred Million Dollars has been spent over a period of twenty-five years, etc., etc. In such matters which are really major from the point of view of the welfare of the community we have put ourselves at a great disadvantage and this is a policy which ought to be stopped. It has of course a great deal to do with the department of propaganda or publicity.

The idea of a permanent parity in Palestine is one which neither side would respect. We are always talking as though there were only two peoples in Palestine. We speak of Jews and Arabs, but there are Jews, there are Moslems and there are Christians. The Christian community is the smallest but it is probably not willing in the long run to be completely swallowed up by the Moslem community and being counted as part of the 50-50 arrangement, and if it formally agreed to such an arrangement it probably would not observe the arrangement.

In the method of a Legislative Council, if there must be one, I would favor a Council which is on what I would in general call the Democratic principle, which, in the last analysis means the rule of the majority. I would recognize that in this peculiar form of government, under which Palestine now rests, the government itself would have large powers of veto. I would also ascribe a literacy test for voters and there would also have to be a residence test so that the floaters from Trans-Jordan and Syria would not be coming in. But in the last analysis any other principle than the Democratic principle, subject to such checks and balances as even democracy must have—I say any other principle but the Democratic principle—I think would in the course of time be set aside. . . . [W]

TO MORRIS D. WALDMAN

April 5, 1937

. . . I was always at a loss to understand the attitude of Doctor [Chaim] Weizmann and I have cudgeled my brain to think of the possible cause. It is not unlikely that it began some years back at the time when Mr. [Neville] Laski and other members of the Board of Deputies, no doubt at the urging of their own body, went direct to the Colonial Office to ask for—I think the number was twelve hundred—additional certificates, this being done when there was great pressure both from Germany and Poland. I recall that when I was last in England and on the Continent this was a good deal talked about by members of the Agency Executive as being an infringement on their preroga-tive, and apparently both sides claimed to have received the extra certificates.

I do hope, however, that Mr. Laski will not, as he puts it, spill the beans. Certainly this is not the time for that sort of thing. The Jewish world undoubt-edly awaits the report of the Royal Commission and after that the action of Par-liament on that report. Any open breach in the meantime, or pending that report, will in the long run, in my opinion, be injurious to the Jewish cause, and that not only in Palestine but elsewhere. Certainly there are plenty of provocations all the time and if we gave way to them we should be constantly engaged in internal conflicts which we cannot very well afford. . . . [W]

As far as Adler was concerned, the precarious state of Jewish–non-Jewish relations in the late 1930s demanded that Jews not speak out publicly on controversial social issues. The penchant of rabbinical groups for going on record on these issues was something Adler could not let pass without comment.

TO SIMON GREENBERG,[1] PHILADELPHIA

June 24, 1937

. . . You tell me that there is quite a body of opinion in the Rabbinical Assembly which seems convinced that the only way to save religion is to identify it with radical movements and with all causes which in their opinion make for a more just and equitable social order. It seems to me that this sentence ought to be divided. A more just and equitable social order everybody wants. If this is to be secured through what are known as radical movements, the matter is open to grave doubt, and certainly an organization like the Synagogue ought not be swayed by every wind that blows.

But what I have in mind is that there should be more consideration of what I would call Jewish public policy. I remember that last year—and I presume without a Convention—the Chairman of the Committee on Social Justice of the Rabbinical Assembly[2] took open issue with Cardinal Hayes[3] on the question of Birth Control. If the Rabbinical Assembly believes that the modern methods of Birth Control are legitimate from the point of view of Jewish law and tradition, that is one thing. I am not so sure of it. But that the Committee should take open issue with the Catholic Cardinal on the subject, on which he was as much entitled to his opinion as the Rabbinical Assembly, seems to me to have been a public error.

More recently I understand that the Committee on Social Justice prepared and issued its report to the public before the Rabbinical Assembly had an opportunity to act upon it, thus committing the whole Assembly in advance and without their authority.

Since I wrote you I have had some communications from Cincinnati where some of the laymen there expressed their regret at the conflict which the Central Conference[4] provoked with the Catholic Church. I understand that some violent editorials have appeared in Catholic journals attacking the Central Conference.

I presume you know that some of the Protestant papers, especially the *Christian Century*, which is supposed to be a liberal paper, have been attacking the whole concept of Judaism as a civilization as far as America is concerned, and assert that there is room for only one civilization in America.

Now these are not isolated things but just happen to come to my mind and they certainly indicate that Judaism is not to be saved by the Rabbinical bodies taking what they call action on every moot question that arises.

I should say that the only way to save religion is by religion. If the Rabbinical Assembly and other Rabbinical bodies can promote a deep religious life with all that it implies among the members of the Synagogue, then our religion will be promoted.

I am sure it must be known to you, and must be known to other members of the Rabbinical Assembly, if they consider the matter carefully, that radical movements have destroyed religion and not promoted it. . . . [D]

1. Simon Greenberg (b. 1901), rabbi of Congregation Har Zion, Philadelphia, 1925–46; president of the Rabbinical Assembly, 1937–39.
2. Milton Steinberg (1903–50), New York Conservative rabbi and author.
3. Patrick Joseph Cardinal Hayes (1867–1938), archbishop of New York, 1919–38.
4. Central Conference of American Rabbis, the Reform rabbinical association.

TO FELIX M. WARBURG, NEW YORK CITY

June 24, 1937

I was very glad to see you yesterday and I hope you alleviated a little at lunch one of the heavier burdens which you have taken upon yourself.

There was a matter that I brought up at the meeting of the Seminary Board after you left.

I am enclosing you with this a little memorandum about Professor Elbogen[1] of Berlin. He is at the present time the foremost Jewish scholar in Germany. You may recall that we conferred an Honorary Degree upon him in absentia. He had written a letter saying that he had hoped to be able to come over to accept the Degree but later said that he could not.

After the Hitler regime began in 1933 I made some inquiry about him, I think through Doctor [Bernard] Kahn, but of this I am not sure. I was told that he and Mrs. Elbogen had decided to stay in Germany, that they had sent their children to Belgium and to England, but they had determined to live out their lives with the German Jews; that his income of course had been reduced, had taken a tiny apartment and was living there. I have an idea that Doctor Jonah Wise[2] knew about him and it is possible that Doctor Jonah Wise and Doctor Kahn gave me this information.

About a week ago I received a letter from Doctor William Rosenau of Baltimore in which he told me that he had been definitely told that Elbogen had come to the conclusion that life in Germany was impossible for him and he wanted to migrate to America, if there was any way of it. He is now sixty-four years of age and not in a position to be helped from the fund of the Emergency Committee of Displaced German Scholars because he was never a Professor in a German University.

He is a man who ought to be saved. I was wondering whether something might be done in the way that was done for Doctor Guido Kisch,[3] that through some funds which might be contributed he can be given a research fellowship. He surely still can do some good work.

When I told Mr. [Solomon M.] Stroock the story yesterday he told me that he thought possibly the American Jewish Committee could help him.

My reason for writing to you is that what Doctor Rosenau wrote to me may not be justified or may be only a rumor. I could not of course write directly to Elbogen about this but I thought maybe Doctor Kahn or maybe your brother Max could get some authentic information on the subject. I do not care to write directly to Germany. [D]

1. Ismar Elbogen (1874–1943), Jewish historian and German Jewish leader. In 1938 he was brought to the United States and appointed research professor by four institutions: Jewish Theological Seminary, Dropsie College, Hebrew Union College, and Jewish Institute of Religion.
2. Jonah Wise (1881–1959), Reform rabbi; son of Isaac Mayer Wise; national chairman of the Joint Distribution Committee, 1931–38.
3. Guido Kisch (b. 1889), Czech historian of German medieval law.

TO FELIX M. WARBURG, NEW YORK CITY

Woods Hole, Massachusetts, July 5, 1937

I am returning you herewith [Judah L.] Magnes's letter with regard to Oungre's[1] idea of an Institute for Jewish Sociology.

At least two years ago I pointed out in a report of the Seminary Directors that this was a new subject in which our men ought to have some instruction and training. These studies are now left mostly to social workers and result in papers which are read at their annual meetings. As I see it, it also has to do with the ever pressing subject of vocational guidance, of which we have much too little.

At the same time I suggested another new topic which Jewish scholars and men who go into the rabbinate ought to be prepared to deal with, and that is ethnology and anthropology, as applied to the Jewish people. The race question is one which they did not have to meet five or ten years ago but which they will have to meet for a good many years to come.

Now as to the suggestion that this general subject and the details of which Doctor Magnes speaks should be connected with the Hebrew University of Jerusalem, that also requires some thought as dependent upon two considerations, the first of which at least at the moment we cannot deal with. Whether Palcor's anticipation of the Royal Commission report is correct or not we will know in a few days, but it may be some time before we get the implications of it. I should therefore say that at the moment we ought to hold our hand with regard to starting new enterprises in Palestine even connected with the University. . . . [W]

1. Louis Oungre (b. 1880), director general of the Jewish Colonization Association, Paris.

The prospect of the creation of a Jewish state in Palestine, held out in the report of the Royal Commission, caused a great debate among Jews, Zionist and non-Zionist alike, concerning the implications of such a state for world Jewry.

TO FELIX M. WARBURG, NEW YORK CITY

Woods Hole, Massachusetts, July 7, 1937

If the report in the *New York Times* this morning and in other places that in the partition the Jewish State which it is expected to establish will be an entirely independent State, with its representatives in the League of Nations, and the right to send Ambassadors or Ministers to other countries is correct, then I think the Jewish Agency will die a natural death. It could no longer be maintained that the Jews of the world have a potential right and interest in Palestine. The State could only be composed of those who are residing in Palestine.

I, for one, according to my present feeling, would find it impossible to stay in the Agency even if that organization decided to continue. Here indeed would be a case of a divided nationality. I could not be represented by an Ambassador of a Jewish State at Washington, nor by the representative of a Jewish State in the League of Nations when the United States is not part of that body, and I do not think I could even if it were. This is my present state of mind and I am passing it along to you. [W]

TO FELIX M. WARBURG, WHITE PLAINS, NEW YORK

Woods Hole, Massachusetts, July 9, 1937

When Doctor [Maurice J.] Karpf spoke to me last night and told me that a galaxy of leaders were going up on Friday night to see Justice [Louis D.] Brandeis he asked if I could arrange to go over there. If it were a matter of life and death for somebody and Saturday was the only day, I would do it. The Jewish law commands that. But the Jewish law neither commands nor permits me to break the Sabbath for something that can just as well be done on Sunday or Monday for that matter, and so I cannot arrange to be there on Saturday. If Justice Brandeis wants to consult me himself I shall be very glad to go over and see him. If any of the other gentlemen want to consult me I shall be very glad to see them if they care to come to see me. . . . [W]

TO FELIX M. WARBURG, NEW YORK CITY

Woods Hole, Massachusetts, July 19, 1937

I have your letter of July 17 and copy of the enclosed cable to [Chaim] Weizmann which Miss Emanuel read to me over the telephone, and copy of his cable which you seem to think is not a reply to ours, and which I also think is not. That, however, does not alter the situation. Your cable is very much in line with [Judah L.] Magnes' letter in the [*New York*] *Times* of yesterday.[1] It certainly got prominence at least in our edition here because it was printed twice. I think upon the whole that Magnes is sound. At all events this letter should have pretty wide circulation since whatever happens Jewish public opinion as well as general public opinion should be informed.

I have read [David] Lloyd George's statement in the Sunday *Boston Advertiser* which I assume has gone through all the Hearst papers. I think Lloyd George may still be a newspaper stunt but he is without weight in England.

I want to hark back to the memorandum I wrote you about a week or ten days ago. It seems to me that it is very important, in dealing with the report of the Royal Commission before the Mandates Commission, that whoever on the Jewish side takes part in this should know the absolute truth with regard to the issuance of the Balfour Declaration. This may or may not be hard to get but at all events Asquith's[2] *Memoirs* could be looked up to see if my recollection is correct about Herbert Samuel's part in it.

To revert to Weizmann's cable, I interpret it as follows: He is doing all the negotiation through Jerusalem. His idea is to let the Mandates Commission act and then have the Arabs come and beg us for an agreement, and he warns all Americans off as any action that can be taken or anything said will interfere with his diplomacy. Well, he may be right but you at least are entitled to consultation. We apparently have a dictatorship before the state is established. . . .

P.S. I presume you have received from [Neville] Laski a note of the interview of July 8 in which Weizmann, [Selig] Brodetsky, Sir Osmond [d'Angdor Goldsmid] and Laski took part. It is not at all a reassuring document from our point of view. [W]

---

1. Magnes's letter to the *Times* was dated Paris, July 12, 1937. It disagreed with the Royal Commission's finding that partition of Palestine was necessary and called, rather, for "creating conditions leading to freely and openly negotiated agreements between Jews and Arabs." Magnes further maintained that the "Jewish people is faced with a three-fold destiny in its return to Zion. First, the forming of a living, creative center for the Jewish people and for Judaism. Second, helping to maturity the slumbering spiritual and intellectual forces of the whole Semitic world. Third, helping Jerusalem to become the true sanctuary of three great Semitic religions."

2. Herbert Henry Asquith (1852–1928), British prime minister, 1908–16.

Memorandum on Proposed Jewish State

July 22, 1937

The memorandum which I have received today from Mr. [Neville] Laski entitled: "Some Considerations arising out of the report of the Royal Commission" comes at the same time when it appears that we get a report that the House of Commons has refused to take any action on the report pending its submission to the Mandates Commission of the League of Nations, after which the House will fully debate and determine the policy of the British government, so that at least we have breathing space.

Not having the advantage of being a lawyer, international or otherwise, the matter seems rather simple to me.

If a Jewish State be established, with all the appurtenances of statehood, it will not and cannot have any legal effect upon Jews who are living in countries where they now have the full rights of citizenship. I instance Great Britain, the United States, France and even Italy.

When the Irish Free State was established it did not make Irish nationals of the millions of Irishmen who were living in the United States. In spite of all its pronouncements the 3rd Reich will not make German citizens or subjects of the twenty million odd Germans in America.

The situation, however, may become different for those individual Jews who, living in one country or another, nevertheless through the Zionist Organization or the Jewish Agency would claim to have certain governmental rights in connection with the Jewish State or that part of Palestine over which there is a British mandate.

In my opinion the moment that a Jewish State shall have been established and formally recognized by the powers, the moment that it will have an army, navy, and air fleet, and ambassadors or ministers to various countries, that moment would mean the dissolution of the Jewish Agency as a functioning body, and if the World Zionist Organization would take the same view, that organization also.

The claim that every Jew in the world would have a stake in the new Jewish State would have to be given up because that would indeed mean a divided loyalty. Let us suppose for example, in the extreme case, that the new Jewish State together with certain allies should have a war with some other country or countries in which Jews live and in which moreover there would be members of the Council of the Jewish Agency or the Administrative Committee. Or, let us assume that the Jewish State has a seat in the League of Nations. Who would the representative of the Jewish State speak for? Certainly for only those Jews who live in Palestine who are members of the

Jewish State. It could not undertake to speak for the Jews of Poland or Great Britain because those countries already have representation in the League of Nations.

As a non-Zionist I do not at all deplore, or indeed did not deplore the establishment of a Jewish commonwealth. In fact had the matter been seen clearly toward the close of the War something might have happened which would have completely altered the situation.

The term "National Home" does now and always has seemed to me a little ridiculous. It sounded like a big orphan asylum. Had the gentlemen in charge of the diplomatic negotiations of the Zionist Organization been bold enough to ask for the establishment of a Jewish commonwealth they might have got it; at least they would have openly stated their plans.

While this memorandum indicates that it has always been the hope of the Zionists to have a Jewish State in Palestine, it will take a good deal of proving to establish that. If so they certainly masked their ends.

It is quite possible that say in Poland or Roumania Jews, if they ask for their rights, may be told "Go to your own State," but that danger was inherent from the very beginning.

I remember as far back as 1919 hearing this story: There was an English clergyman who was conducting a sort of Mission School for little boys in the East End of London. During the war period, he was keeping the boys interested by following the progress of the War and particularly the progress of Allenby's[1] Army in Palestine. Finally a little boy held up his hand and asked the Clergyman, "Please, sir, if we give Palestine back to the Jews will they give Hounsditch back to us?"

Now that very simply points the real risk which the Zionists and non-Zionists alike have run in promoting the up-building of Palestine. The risk has not been very great in a few Western civilized countries; in my opinion it has been very great in Eastern Europe and the Balkans.

The German question is another matter.

The stateless question also does not seem to me to constitute a real question. No person in one country can suddenly opt for citizenship in another country. If a man has left Germany or Poland or Roumania or what not without a passport and is stateless and happens to be of Jewish birth that does not make him ipso facto a citizen of the Jewish State.

Of course the whole subject is complicated by the fact that the Zionists, in spite of a good deal of vaporizing, have never been willing to consider themselves even potentially a State, confining their activities to the building up of a political entity with a certain cultural, or maybe religious or irreligious tendencies. They have a movement. They would like to possess the souls of every Jew in every country of the world, mold his education, mold his thinking, and in fact be as it were a scattered totalitarian organism, based theoretically upon a democracy which is taxed a shekel every year or every other year and managed in fact by an oligarchy. A movement that conceives of itself in such a way is difficult to deal with either on legal or practical terms. [AJA]

1. Edward H. H. Allenby, first viscount (1861–1936), commander of British forces in the Middle East during the First World War; conquered Palestine from the Turks; subsequently served as British high commissioner in Egypt.

TO FELIX M. WARBURG, NEW YORK CITY

Woods Hole, Massachusetts, August 2, 1937

I am writing you another letter and I want to thank you for keeping me so well informed not only through this letter but also through the copies of cables.

With regard to your suggestion 3, that something should be done by which the Mandate Government, without too much loss of self-respect, can reconsider, etc., I am a little afraid of that compromise and really doubt whether it would be acceptable all around.

On Saturday night I received the Royal Commission's report which you were good enough to have Miss Emanuel send me. I have been steadily reading it. The impression it makes on me is of a document very well written, in fact painstakingly written. But it also seems to me a brief and not a judicial decision.

As far as I have read there seems to be a heaping up of statements which indicate that the Mandate is unworkable.

Now I think that some consideration has to be given to the possibilities of Great Britain itself. She can insist on having her plan of partition carried through, with possibly some modifications. She can postpone all consideration giving a reasonable time for the Jews and Arabs to come to a working arrangement. Or, she can decide to resign the Mandate, keeping Haifa and its port as a naval base. Haifa, I am almost satisfied, Great Britain will not give up. Now then, if she is sufficiently pushed and desires to give up the Mandate altogether, what will be the result? Italy no doubt wants the Mandate. That Great Britain would oppose. Poland wants the Mandate. She too is a Catholic country and would want to protect the Christian holy places, and she would use Palestine as a means of getting rid of her surplus Jewish population. These are the thoughts that come to me at the moment.

If, as I expect, I can read the whole report in a day or two I may write you another memorandum for your consideration.

As far as the memorandum I sent you is concerned I am going to modify it. The only criticism I have received so far is from Judge [Irving] Lehman with whom I had another long talk and he thinks that I ought to categorically deny that Jewry could be bribed by the Balfour Declaration. I have not had any criticism from either Doctor [Maurice J.] Karpf or Mr. [Solomon M.] Stroock, but within a day or so I will give you my revised memorandum. [W]

TO HORACE STERN, PARIS

Woods Hole, Massachusetts, August 3, 1937

. . . Apparently the world moves very fast. Today it looks as though Britain and Italy were trying to get on friendlier terms.

As for the Non-Intervention Committee, I really think it is the greatest piece of hypocrisy that has been played out in the modern world. If it prevents a general war it will have justified itself.

Of course we have been very much occupied here with the report of the Royal Commission. Felix Warburg is keeping me fully informed, through cables and the report of telephone messages which he has with Europe. I have had several long talks here with Irving Lehman, and Felix Warburg, Sol Stroock and Doctor [Maurice J.] Karpf came to Woods Hole, and they three, Lehman and myself spent four or five hours together. Warburg, Stroock and Sol Lowenstein[1] go to Europe this coming Saturday to be present at the meeting of the Council of the Agency. George Backer[2] has gone ahead to continue conversations with the Arabs, which he, Karpf and [Morris D.] Waldman had in New York before the report of the Commission came out. Waldman, at the request of both Warburg and Stroock, sailed for Europe Monday. He is going into Poland for about a week or so and then meet the other gentlemen either in Paris or in Zurich, I am not sure which.

I am preparing a memorandum to be presented at the meeting of the Council of the Agency and that main point in my memorandum is first a caveat about the statement of the Royal Commission that the Balfour Declaration was issued in order to secure the support of world Jewry during the war, just as the McMahon letter[3] had been written two years earlier to secure the support of the Arabs. I am taking the ground that in all countries the Jews were loyal to their own country and that if the English really thought it was necessary to bribe the Jews they were mistaken.

We agreed strongly to oppose the partition of Palestine. Blame for the failure so far to live together I think can be divided equally between the Jews, who have been unduly aggressive, the Arabs, who have yielded to nationalistic propaganda, and the British, who have not shown similar colonial weakness since their failure with the American colonies.

I then show the weakness and danger to peace of the Royal Commission's plan and propose instead that time be given to enable the Jews and Arabs to reach an understanding. I also propose this time to hold out for parity in the Executive. That is the gist of my memorandum.

Last Saturday night I received the report of the Royal Commission in a volume well over four hundred pages and I have read steadily and finished it last evening. It is probably the most comprehensive document on Palestine that has been issued since the British took over the Mandate and goes into historical as well as practical matters. It is extremely well written in many parts, really a literary work, and if you can get hold of a copy you may wish to read it.

My general impression of the document, however, is that it is a brief and not a judicial opinion. After the historical narrative it leaps from previous reports of previous commissions and from all kinds of incidents, a series of patent facts which they say indicate that the Jews and Arabs cannot live together, and hence the proposed partition.

American opinion, both editorially and among the Jewish people, is solidly against partition. Stephen Wise came out with the charge of betrayal but I notice in the J.T.A. [Jewish Telegraphic Agency] news this morning that under the hypnotism of [Chaim] Weizmann he has agreed not to say anything for publication as yet in Europe. Weizmann, as I learned from a report of a private conversation with Sir Osmond [d'Avigdor Goldsmid] and a few others, was disposed to accept partition, simply sparring for better boundaries. I think he himself was surprised at the outburst of opposition. What he will finally do I do not know.

Whatever the English papers may have said, the House of Commons, as you know, revolted. They refused to give a vote of confidence in the Palestine policy of the government and insisted that the report of the Commission is to go to the Mandates Commission of the League of Nations and the Council of the League, and then come back to Parliament for a final determination of the British policy. This resolution was drawn by Winston Churchill who apparently got enough conservative members to join him with [David] Lloyd George, the Liberals and the Labor Party, to make the government unwilling to have an open test in the House of Commons. The result is that the whole matter at least is shoved off until the end of October.

I do not know what [Jacob] Landau referred to but since Waldman has gone over and he is to meet Stroock in Paris, after they are through in Zurich they will probably attend to whatever American Jewish Committee affairs are to be attended to. [D]

1. Solomon Lowenstein (1877–1942), executive vice-president of the Federation of Jewish Philanthropic Societies.
2. George Backer (1902–74), publisher of the *New York Post;* active in several organizations aiding refugees.
3. Written in 1916 by Sir Henry McMahon (1862–1949), British commissioner in Egypt, to Hussein, Sherif of Mecca. McMahon promised Hussein that in return for his support against the Turks, England would support his attempt to restore the caliphate, an independent Arab state whose boundaries would not include Palestine and Transjordan.

Felix M. Warburg, Adler's close friend and active associate in many common causes, died on October 20, 1937. Adler felt the loss keenly. In a memorial tribute published in the American Jewish Year Book *(Philadelphia, 1938), he noted: "I have had, on a number of occasions, the sad duty of preparing biographical sketches of friends and associates who had passed away. They were always my elders. This is the first time I am called upon to describe the life of a friend and associate younger than myself."*

TO JUDAH L. MAGNES, JERUSALEM

November 12, 1937

. . . We all feel as you do. Felix's going has created a great void which will not be filled up for us in our lives. We saw a good deal of him after he got back from Europe. On the 10th of September we left Woods Hole and went down to White Plains and we stayed there three days. On Sunday, the 12th, Felix, Frieda, Racie and I and two German nephews of Felix's had a wonderful day on the boat and everybody seemed well and as cheerful as people can be in these days.

Then two weeks later Felix had assembled a large party of men at Briarcliffe Lodge, near his place, and several days were spent in talking about the Jewish questions and Palestine. It was not a formal meeting and there were no resolutions but it was just to see if we could arrive at an understanding. At this meeting, over most of which Felix presided, he was at his best. He seemed to think that he was bringing about a frame of mind which would result in some united action on this side.

I saw him the next week twice in New York, the last time on Thursday night when half a dozen of us had a long talk with Wickham Steed.

On the following Sunday afternoon he took one of his grandchildren to a moving picture and enjoyed it, and it was that night or rather the next morning, at 4 o'clock, that he was taken ill. On Tuesday he rallied somewhat and asked to see Otto Schiff who had just arrived, but toward the evening he fell into a coma and never became conscious again. Doctor Epstein, who was called on Sunday night, stayed in the house all the time but he had no hope from the beginning.

If Felix had rallied from this attack he would have been an invalid for the rest of his life and I am sure that he would have wished it to happen as it did happen.

Frieda has shown great composure and courage and is carrying on as the great lady that she is.

We are having a little conference at her house on Monday afternoon where we will talk over how best to carry on the things that Felix was trying to do for Palestine. While we have many other gaps to fill [Solomon M.] Stroock and I thought that this was the first to be taken up and Frieda wrote me that she felt very much honored that we wanted her in the counsels.

Otto Schiff is still here and he will be with us although he is leaving next Wednesday.

There is little else that I can say. During these past four weeks I have myself been very miserable as I had a fall, broke a rib and bruised myself very badly so I have been continuing with a good deal of physical distress, but over here old and young feel that we must all make some extra exertion to try to do part of the really stupendous labors that Felix was carrying on. . . . [D]

TO MAURICE B. HEXTER, JERUSALEM

November 12, 1937

. . . Every time an effort was made to bring about an understanding with the Arabs it failed. No matter whose effort it was it failed. Ever since the modern Zionist movement and certainly since 1920 the European Jews who came from Palestine systematically under-estimated and belittled the Arabs. They have done so consciously or unconsciously. Mr. Kalvarisky[1] and others are no doubt rare exceptions. I warned Mr. [Louis D.] Brandeis many years ago that his followers were under-estimating the Arabs, not only their importance but their intelligence, and asked him to impress this on his followers.

I do not agree at all with the solution which Mr. Kalvarisky proposes. The idea of putting the whole future on the race basis, that we are two Semitic peoples, etc., is no good. I know that this was the last game that was played at the time of the Peace Conference when [Felix] Frankfurter and [Nahum] Sokolow and others were talking about the Arabs as our cousins. The entire idea of a Semitic race is fraudulent, just as the Aryan race. There are no such races. There are possibly Aryan or Semitic languages but there is no argument to be had at all on the race side.

The Jews had plenty of time in the last ten or fifteen years to cultivate Arabic, to use it, and they have consistently and steadily refused to do so. They have shut out of their schools both Arabic and English. In other words they have acted as true chauvinists, just as have the Arabs.

The worst feature in all of the modern Zionist movement has been the Keren Kayemeth, which forbids the use of Arab labor, and whatever the intention this is an insult. We Jews protest against such discrimination against us in any part of the world and the discrimination which this implies against the Arabs is one which no people tolerate. [W]

1. Chaim A. Kalvarisky (1868–1947), Labor Zionist leader; active in the movement for Arab-Jewish cooperation in Palestine.

TO WILLIAM GUGGENHEIM,[1] NEW YORK CITY

Philadelphia, December 9, 1937

It was very good of you to send me a copy of the address you gave before the Mask and Wig Club on December 14, 1937.

I heartily subscribe to what you say about the University [of Pennsylvania] and I think your plan of an emergency revolving fund so that the meagre salaries of the faculties should not be reduced in times of depression a sound one. I have, like others, experienced the difficulties of the educational institutions with which I am connected. It was only this year that I was able to restore the salaries of both the Jewish Theological Seminary, of which I am President, and of the Dropsie College.

I do not share your fear of communism and by that I mean of course the communism in Russia. The Russians seem to be so busy in attending to their own affairs that they are no longer exporting communism, and in fact from what I hear they are becoming a semi-capitalist State. Many of the wild theories of 1917 even up to 1924 or 1925 did not work and I understand that the Soviet is now quite different.

Nazi Germany of course is the active propagandist and a great danger, and I believe that the danger to the peace of the world lies in the combination of Germany, Italy and Japan.

I do not like the dictatorship of Russia, nor Mr. Stalin, but I dislike even more the dictatorship of Germany, of Mr. Hitler, and certainly the dictatorship of Mussolini is now proving one of the larger causes of unrest in the world. . . . [W]

1. William Guggenheim (1868–1941), businessman and philanthropist; alumnus of the University of Pennsylvania.

TO MORRIS D. WALDMAN, NEW YORK CITY

December 23, 1937

. . . With regard to the various statements of Mr. [Jacob] Landau I would say that there is, of course, nothing that we can do to prevent the World Jewish Congress from having a vote in Poland, but I think it is quite certain that no one can force the Joint Distribution Committee to deal in Poland through the World Jewish Congress, or through anybody else except its own agents and committees that it has set up; and unless I am very much mistaken this would be the attitude of Mr. [Paul] Baerwald and the entire Executive Committee of the Joint Distribution Committee.

I do not share Mr. Landau's views that Partition in Palestine may be an accomplished fact in seven or nine months. It is my present opinion that the likelihood is that Partition will not take place at all.

Since these letters were written the Roumanian elections have taken place and it seems obvious to me that the liberal forces have lost out and that unless the King[1] has some way of stemming it and is willing to do it Roumania will become more anti-Semitic rather than less.

I do think well of the idea of having an economic committee in Poland, though with the exception of the ICA [Jewish Colonization Association] the Joint Distribution Committee is not inclined to make alliances; the ORT has very little power except such as the Joint Distribution Committee gives it.

I will not comment further on this information today, some of which may be correct and some may not be.

Except this: I am not at all surprised that the Institute of Sociology of England has declined to join the Scientific Congress as I pointed out to Sir

Robert Mond[2] on previous occasions. A Congress with such a form of statement is a propagandist matter and not a scientific matter. [AJA]

1. Carol II of Romania (1893–1953), reigned 1930–40.
2. Sir Robert Mond (1868–1938), archaeologist; leader of the British Empire's anti-Nazi boycott.

TO FRIEDA WARBURG

January 6, 1938

I am returning herewith Judah [Magnes]'s letter. I showed it to [Maurice B.] Hexter the other night, but brought it with me to Philadelphia because I wanted to think it over. You asked me to read it, not to advise you, so maybe I ought simply return it, but I know that that would not be very helpful.

It is not for me or, it seems to me, for anyone else to suggest to you a memorial or memorials that you should erect for Felix, but I do think the idea is a very beautiful one and full of the poetry which Judah can put into anything. I can imagine a building to be used for the ceremonial occasions of the University and of other bodies in Palestine, and maybe even of scientific congresses. It would seem to me, however, that a hall that would also be large enough for assemblies, or for a Zionist Congress, or even for a Toscanini concert, might mean an assembly room to hold 2,500 or 3,000 people, and that together with all the surrounding appurtenances of such a hall would become a stupendous thing among the University buildings, maybe even out of proportion.

What a wonderful calm Judah must have sitting in Jerusalem at the present time to be thinking of a garden of peace. I hope that there is something prophetic in the idea. [W]

TO DAVID WERNER SENATOR, JERUSALEM

February 14, 1938

. . . I am personally convinced that if the partition is carried out, and the separate states and British Mandate established that they will be a failure, and it may be that in the long run the British government will come to realize this.

I am not interested simply in the question of partition but in the whole question of the report of the Royal Commission which, in spite of its fine writing and apparent fairness, is I think grossly unfair. It was not a judicial opinion but a brief intended to establish that Jews and Arabs could not live together and that the Mandate was a failure. I do not think that the Mandate was a failure, but that it was the mandatory.

I quite agree with you that no responsible Jewish body can accept the theory of a permanent minority, and yet the impression was given that Lord Samuel and Doctor [Judah L.] Magnes, and possibly even Doctor [Maurice B.] Hexter agreed to this, whereas it was my understanding that the theory was that there should be a form of emigration law which would be on a 60-40 basis say for a period of five years.

Without undertaking to speak for any of my colleagues I would say that I am not in principle opposed to the establishment of a Jewish Commonwealth if it can be done.

You say that as far as you know Mr. Felix Warburg was not opposed in principle to a Jewish state. I do not recall ever having discussed the subject with him but I think we must be very careful in quoting anything in his name unless he has left something in writing about it.

There are many people who would be opposed in principle to a Jewish State and I am inclined to think that I can see their reasons. A state is a sovereign body which must defend itself and be prepared for aggression; that means a navy, an army and aeroplane forces, not to speak of other weapons of defence and aggression. The question of the ability through taxation and its own inner life of a Jewish state to exist is one which I think is extremely doubtful. To expect Jews who are citizens of the countries of the world to provide funds to aid in the maintenance of such a state would create problems of a divided loyalty which are pretty serious. I think in the long run at least in some of the Western countries it can hardly be expected that the Keren Hayesod would continue to get the support of a Jewish state.

As for the question of being a member of the Confederation of the Near East States related to Great Britain, you will pardon me if I say to you that I fear that that is a dream. . . . [W]

TO HARRY NEWMAN,[1] NEW YORK CITY

March 22, 1938

I have your letter of March 21 and I appreciate your courtesy in letting me see the editorial you propose to put in *The Judge* in the April number. I am sorry that neither I, nor any of the other members of this [American Jewish]

Committee could come to your office today as you indicated in your letter. Since you say the editorial *will* appear, I do not know that there is any point in making any comment, but as I assume you thought that some comment would be made, I am going to make it to you in writing.

In the first place I do not think you have fully acquainted yourself with the facts. You say that Jews should attack as well as defend. Well, I think some of us have attacked, in fact, last week I published a statement in the *New York American* which I do not think you will find either apologetic or defensive. I have not hesitated, nor have any of my associates for any time, to brand Hitler and his colleagues as barbarians, and his race theory as entirely false and unfounded. I can send you a good many documents to prove this. If you wish them, I will see that they are sent to you.

You say "too long you have left your explanations to religious men." Well, religious men are not such bad people, and I believe that in Germany it was mainly Catholic cardinals and bishops and Protestant ministers who made the attack against Nazi Germany. The intelligentsia and professors, and other people like that were ominously silent. . . . When you propose that Herbert Lehman or Henry Morgenthau should resign respectively as Governor and Secretary of the Treasury, the suggestions seem to be that no Jew should hold an important office in the United States. Would you not consider this point of view: the fact that Herbert Lehman has been three times elected by people of New York is a better answer to Hitler than any public announcement that he might make, and the same would apply to Henry Morgenthau. . . . I wish I could believe that you are right in maintaining that human voice now could stop Hitler, but I am afraid you are wrong. In the present day, in the European world, might makes right. Hitler and Mussolini were strong enough, apparently, to throw Anthony Eden[2] out of the British Cabinet. They would sneer at the people whom you would advise to attack them and put more Jews in Germany and Austria in the concentration camps. . . . [AJC]

1. Publisher and editorial director of *The Judge*, a New York magazine.
2. Sir Anthony Eden, Earl of Avon (1897–1977), British statesman; foreign secretary, 1935–38, 1940–45, 1951–55; prime minister, 1955–57.

On March 12, 1938, German troops marched into Austria and Hitler proclaimed the union of Austria with Germany. On March 16, 1938, the Polish government, taking advantage of the international situation created by the German annexation of Austria, sent an ultimatum to Lithuania demanding the settlement of many questions, outstand-

ing since the end of World War I, including a formal end to hostilities, the reopening of the frontier, and a regulation of relations between the two governments. Despite years of negotiations no progress had been made in the resolution of the old feud. Now the Lithuanian government, faced by the threat of war, capitulated at once and accepted all Polish demands. The Lithuanian government yielded on March 17, and within the month most of the problems were disposed of. Simultaneously there were anti-Jewish riots in Warsaw and throughout Poland.

TO OSMOND D'AVIGDOR GOLDSMID, LONDON

March 24, 1938

. . . Of course, all news is bad and even since you have written, it is a little worse. Just because Lithuania gave in to Poland, the Poles have started to rise and loot Jewish shops in Warsaw. It seems that Jew baiting is becoming epidemic on the continent, certainly in all of Central and Eastern Europe. I can hardly remember such a wave since the Crusades. While there is no use of us sitting around the "wailing wall," yet there seems to be so little that can be done. I told Mr. [Paul] Baerwald and some of the others a day or so ago, that the burden on J.D.C. has increased about 50%, and that we had never really measured up to full capacity since the Hitler regime came in. Your statesmen are more and more keeping their hands off the continent and may become isolationists, which would mean that the continent would be abandoned to Hitler and Mussolini.

I do not know why I should be writing you these morbid things, but the only way we can really keep in touch with one another is to tell each other what is in our minds. [W]

TO FRIEDA WARBURG, NEW YORK CITY

April 8, 1938

I am returning herewith the letter of Mr. Ralph Silverstein with regard to the collection of Hebraica for the Library of Congress.

I would advise you at the present to do nothing with it. You are not the only one that was honored with such a letter. Racie received one and so did I.

Rabbi David Fraenkel, as he calls him, of Vienna, is a man who has sold quite some collections. A number of years ago the late Mrs. Nathan J. Miller gave the Seminary $25,000 for the purchase of manuscripts which I think cost us $30,000 and we are paying off the remainder at the rate of $1,000 a year.

This Committee so-called is obviously a Committee got up by Rabbi Fraenkel to sell his collection. They have an Executive Secretary, as you see, in Brooklyn and a Treasurer, etc.

I am as you know reasonably placid as a rule but the first paragraph in this letter really angered me. That the endeavor should be made to collect money in America to buy $10,000 worth of books for the Library of Congress on the basis of the Austrian situation, when we know that the Austrian situation now requires numerous soup kitchens in order to prevent the poorer Jews or those who have been deprived of everything they had from starving until after the Plebiscite—that that should be used as the reason to buy books because the man happens to come from Vienna, I think is outrageous. [W]

Amid the growing shadows of war, Adler reaffirmed his ideals and beliefs. He chose the last two paragraphs of this letter to close his memoirs, I Have Considered the Days *(Philadelphia, 1941).*

TO IRENE WEIL, PALM BEACH, FLORIDA

April 15, 1938

. . . I want to begin at the end of your letter and thank you for your good wishes for Racie, Sarah and Judith. Sarah and Judith are very well; Racie and I are reasonably well. They are all here in Philadelphia now, ready for the great event of the Seder tonight when Judith will ask the proper questions in Hebrew, and we will have two great grand-nieces and one great grand-nephew at the table.

I am beginning in this way because perhaps it may indicate to you that severely shaken as everybody in the world must be at what is going on, the fact that I and others have certain firm beliefs and customs gives us some time at least when we can shed our anxieties, remember that we were slaves once before and became free, and believe that we will be free again.

I know that the present situation is hard for the young and it is hard for the old. I am in almost daily contact with some young refugee who is looking for hope in this country and sometimes I am able to help them. That after all is the best medicine for them and for me.

You implicitly raise the old question, although you do not say so exactly: Why are all these evil things allowed to happen in the world? I am not enough of a theologian to answer this. Some older theologians would say that we suffer for our sins, that the Jewish people have committed many sins and abominations and the old theory that they lost their land on that account; and when I say theory there were such warnings from all of our Prophets from Moses down. Of course that means a system of rewards and punishments in this world.

Then there are other people—and I think more good Christians—who believe that the rewards and punishments come in the next world and not in this, and there were Jewish thinkers who believed that the punishments that came to us in this world would save us from the punishments in the next world.

A clever woman like you can ask more questions than a somewhat bewildered old man like me can answer. I confess I have no answer for the questions that you have raised and many others.

This has been my philosophy of life and of action: To go on doing the best I can in any and every circumstance that arises, to be loyal to the traditions of my people and my family, to keep in fact so busy doing things that I have no time to be a philosopher. When I was a young man I read a great deal of philosophy; I studied a good deal of it. The more I studied the less I knew. Then it occurred to me that there was a modern philosopher, James the Pragmatist,[1] who is something like my conception of the rabbinic Jewish tradition.

Even so far back as the Bible we have that wonderful sentence, "The hidden things belong to the Lord our God, and the revealed things to us and to our children forever, to do all the words in this law." It may interest you to know that this has really been one of the things that has stabilized me as it were. When I was a young man my teacher, Doctor [Sabato] Morais sent me down to Long Branch to help dedicate a Synagogue, to which he could not go, and I was to preach the sermon—the first and possibly the last that I ever did preach. This text has remained my guiding star. [W]

1. William James (1842–1910), American philosopher and psychologist.

TO OSMOND D'AVIGDOR GOLDSMID, LONDON

June 7, 1938

. . . Somehow or other I have a feeling that the Partition plan will not go through because as far as I can see nobody stands to profit by it. The Jews will get a tiny corner, the British a corridor and a few cities, and the Arabs do not want a separate state. Moreover, it would seem to me that the British government will make itself responsible for law and order for a good many years. So it will be holding the bag without satisfying anybody.

We here are full of your troubles. Your old friend, Stephen Wise, is holding a plebiscite, or as he now calls it, a referendum some time toward the end of June, and is stirring up the whole country for democratic votes. The other night in Philadelphia he made a bitter personal attack upon me, although not more than a few months ago, when we were together at an amity conference it was decided that even if we had differences of opinion there were to be no public attacks made. I have not concerned myself very much about it but I understand that there is a deep resentment in this city at what he said. Among other charges he made against the American Jewish Committee was that none of us ever went to Europe and sacrificed ourselves as he did, but that we sent our hirelings, this being a compliment to [Morris D.] Waldman of course. However, I only want to show you that whereas you have troubles we have them also. [W]

By 1938 the refugee problem had become so serious that an international conference was held on the subject at Evian-les-Bains, Switzerland. Thirty-one countries, plus the League of Nations High Commissioner for Refugees, were represented. Few countries, however, voiced their willingness to take in more refugees and the conference provided no meaningful solution to the problem.

TO NEVILLE LASKI, LONDON

Woods Hole, Massachusetts, June 29, 1938

. . . I assume that your Council for German Jewry[1] will be represented at the Evian Conference—in fact I have been told that Doctor Norman Bentwich will be there, and possibly others. What I would like very much to have you do, and any other of your Jewish friends whom you can muster in England for the purpose, is to try to prevent the Evian conference from being a conference purely about Jewish refugees. While the original invitation extended by the United States Department of State had to do solely with refugees from Germany and Austria, the President of the United States himself is desirous of having the subject enlarged so as to refer to refugees from any country who are driven out because of political, religious or racial reasons. Naturally, the United States itself will not raise this subject but it is more than likely that some nation represented at the conference will.

Now if Jewish organizations in Europe swarm around the place with delegations and the news is colored as a result of this, I think the result will be unfortunate. As far as possible I think this should be avoided and you may have an easy means of following up this subject. [W]

1. The Central British Fund for German Jewry, founded in 1933 to aid German-Jewish refugees in Great Britain.

TO D. HAYS SOLIS-COHEN,[1] PHILADELPHIA

Woods Hole, Massachusetts, July 15, 1938

I have received a letter, dated June 6, from Kabul, very faintly written in pencil, of which the enclosed is as good a copy as my secretary can make. There was also enclosed, to my order, a check on the Punjab National Bank Limited, in the amount of 230 rupees, which the drawer of this check, David Joffo, has marked "for a Cyrus Adler fund."

This Mr. Joffo had been for a long time in the employ of the Emir of Kabul, and according to his story to me in Philadelphia he had secured or amassed, or got in trust, a large sum of money amounting, he told me, to something over Five Million Dollars. He came to consult me as to getting the money out. He said it was in gold and was buried. He showed me so much detail with regard to people that he knew, so many letters and even photographs of himself taken with distinguished personages that strange as the story sounded I was inclined, in this weird world, to give some credence to it. What he wanted to consult me about was getting the money out since Kabul is now virtually under the control of the Soviet.[2] I told him that there was no regular way in which he could get gold out of any part of the Soviet Dominions.

However, I am acknowledging this letter to him, not knowing of course whether it will ever reach him or not, and am telling him that I have caused this check to be deposited with the Funds of the Dropsie College and have asked the treasurer to designate it as "The Cyrus Adler Fund."

I may explain further that Mr. Joffo told me that if he got his money out he would place half of it at my disposal for Jewish causes.

I hope the check turns out good. [D]

1. David Hays Solis-Cohen (b. 1887), Philadelphia lawyer.
2. The Soviet Union briefly invaded Afghanistan in 1930 and exercised considerable influence in that country through trade agreements and political pressure.

TO HERMAN A. BACHRACK,[1] LOS ANGELES

Woods Hole, Massachusetts, August 19, 1938

. . . The Jews in the United States, like all other countries, are considered a separate group. We deny the racial theory and yet we continue Jews. Now if this be so it means that we have some strain in us that is based upon the fact that the Jews produced the Bible, the most extensively circulated literature in the known world, and that we had a long history and literature. If the Jewish people know nothing about this Bible and long history and literature they have no reason for a separate existence. As a matter of fact it is our greatest glory.

We did not discover America, we did not discover electricity, we did not invent the steamboat, and we did not build the first flying machine. Unless my recollection is wrong the first person who undertook motion pictures was a Californian. His name was Muybridge[2] and I think the first study of motion pictures was of horses.

Now I am saying these things to you because I want to revert back to what I consider our greatest distinction and our real contribution to civilization and that is the Bible and the literature that follows it. If people who call themselves Jews are unacquainted with that and do not even realize that it is their patent of nobility then of course they are sunk in a hopeless morass of ignorance. A very distinguished Professor in England said only the other day in an address that he considered the Jews as belonging to different stocks, but having one cult, and he preferred that word to culture or civilization and declared that prejudice was only another expression for ethnological ignorance.

Maybe I am wandering off a little in this letter but I want again to point to the fact that it is only decent that every Jew should know something of his history and literature, and personally I think it important that he should know something of the Hebrew language so that he may not only intelligently use it at religious services but also sometimes be able to refer to an original text.

As you probably know two great Universities in the United States, Harvard and Columbia, have especially endowed chairs for Jewish history and literature and there is such a chair in the School of Religion on the campus at the University of Iowa. Within a week I was consulted about the establishment of such a chair at the University of Texas. When I say Jewish history and literature I do not mean a chair in Semitic languages such as Hebrew, Arabic, Syriac, etc. because these are special studies for scholars, but I mean that these Colleges and Universities are coming to recognize that Jewish history and literature has the same place for an educated man as the knowledge of the Greek and Roman civilization. Very recently Princeton University has taken steps in this direction not only for graduate study but even to make these studies a part of undergraduate work.

I am putting these things to you rather strongly because it is a subject which I feel most deeply, and I hope that you will be able to find others in the community of Los Angeles who will join you in supporting these views. I will not mention names because you know the community much better than I do. [D]

1. Chairman of the Los Angeles Board of Jewish Education.
2. Eadweard Muybridge (1830–1904), photographer, motion-picture pioneer.

TO HUBERT J. BERNHARD,[1] NEW YORK

Woods Hole, Massachusetts, August 26, 1938

It is very good of you and your editors to want to get my views on certain important matters in view of my approaching seventy-fifth birthday, but I would remind you in the first place that prophecy has ceased and even if it still existed years do not make a man a prophet. However, here goes.

You want to know what I think will be the outcome of the latest anti-Jewish acts of the German government, prescribing the exact names which may be given to Jewish children born in Germany and restricted to 276 names for boys and girls. My opinion is that such an order is silly, and that a great government should stoop to trifles like this indicates that there is an unbalanced mentality all along the line of government officials. There is no particular hardship, except psychological, in restricting people to 276 names. For myself I think that Abraham and Sarah are better names than Fritz and Gretchen. The whole object of course is to set aside the Jews, and half and quarter Jews for that matter also, marking them distinctly off from the rest of the population, degrading them, humiliating them, depriving them of their livelihood and forcing them out of Germany.

This is a wrong to the Jews of Germany and a wrong to other nations who, moved by the humanitarian impulses which actuated the President and the Secretary of State in calling the Evian Conference, who will make efforts, in the interest of humanity, to do some justice to the Jews of Germany who are being so cruelly treated by the present authorities of the country in which Jews have lived for over a thousand years.

You ask me further whether I think there will be any other reaction. Well, throughout the world reaction in my opinion will be one of contempt.

You further ask me what I think will be the future of Germany. You must admit that that is a large order, but I firmly believe that the present system in Germany will break down. It is based upon a fraudulent racial theory, upon the principle of autarchy, the practice of bluffing in a world which desires peace. Some day the bluff of the bully will be called. Hitler will not accomplish what Napoleon failed to do.

I would much rather not speak about Palestine and add a little more confusion to the babble of opinions and advice that is going about the world. I am not in the confidence of the British government and do not know whether they willl feel themselves able or even deem it wise to carry out the plans of the Royal Commission to make a three-way division of the country. In fact until the Technical Commission[2] makes its report I think that the matter of policy of the government is really in abeyance.

Certainly the best plan for Palestine would be an agreed peace between the Arabs and the Jews and the British government; the carrying on of Palestine as a bi-national State under the continued government of Great Britain. This would probably be the most sensible thing to do. It only remains to be seen how sensible people are in this world at the present time.

You ask my opinion about the International Committee for the Settlement of Political Refugees which has now set up its headquarters in London and as to whether the various nations who took part in the Evian Conference showed a real desire to make sacrifices to relieve the refugees. I was not at the Evian Conference and have only the reports that were made available through the press. Not all the countries are equally capable of making sacrifices and I daresay there is some resentment that they should be obliged to make sacrifices because of the injustice and cruelty of Germany, but I am enough of an optimist to believe that there is still a great deal of humanity in the world, and I do think that some practical results will come from this Committee. Mr. Myron Taylor,[3] who presided over the Conference, certainly showed himself to be a splendid man and I am sure that there are many others of ability who will interest themselves in the work.

I believe it is the opinion of the American representative at least, and I daresay of the English and others, that Germany has a duty to cooperate in this work. If she makes life for people who have been her own citizens, and whom she now calls "members of the State," impossible, she has no right to send them out to nations with whom she is at peace stripped of everything they owned. A great deal will depend, in my opinion, upon whether Germany can be made to see this point. That she would do it from a sense of justice, I do not believe. That has left her, but she might do it from the point of view of self-interest in dealing with America and particularly with England.

You ask me whether I am doing any work at Woods Hole this summer. Well, the answer is my reply to your letter, and hundreds of other letters that are pouring in on me. I had planned to do a little writing of my own this summer but that has been frustrated. I had not, however, planned to write a history of the Jews in America this summer. I made such a plan many years ago but was not able to carry it out.

I am, however, revising a manuscript which is the result of a good deal of work on the part of a young friend and myself[4] but I prefer not to give the title of it until it is really finished and ready for publication.

Of course I do rest somewhat here and my rest consists of being with my family, enjoying the society of my friends, and reading mostly detective stories. [W]

1. Hubert Jay Bernhard (b. 1916), reporter for the *New York Journal and American*.
2. Partition commission, headed by Sir John Woodhead, to determine the technical details of partition.
3. Myron C. Taylor (1874–1959), lawyer, industrialist, and diplomat; U.S. delegate to the Evian Conference.
4. The young friend was Aaron M. Margalith (1902–61), who revised and enlarged Adler's monograph, "Jews in the Diplomatic Correspondence of the United States," *PAJHS* 15 (1906), to produce a volume with Adler as coauthor, entitled *American Intercession on Behalf of Jews in the Diplomatic Correspondence of the United States, 1840–1938*, published by Publications of the American Jewish Historical Society—*PAJHS* 36 (1943).

On November 10, 1938, in response to the assassination of a German official in Paris by a Jewish youth, the Nazis staged a savage anti-Jewish pogrom which became known as Kristallnacht. *In its aftermath, they imposed a fine of one billion marks ($400,000,000) on an already impoverished German Jewish community. This was to mark the beginning of the total destruction of German Jewry which was to culminate in the Holocaust. Whatever former illusions prevailed concerning Jewish survival in the Nazi state were now shattered completely.*

TO NEVILLE LASKI, LONDON

New York City, November 15, 1938
. . . I am writing today after word has come that the American Ambassador[1] has been ordered home from Berlin for the purpose of consultation and report. I am sure that at the present time, the American Government is greatly concerned with the Refugee question.

Without being able to consult with my colleagues, at the moment, I have definitely two opinions with regard to the present tragic situation in Germany. I do not think that the German Jews should recognize the fine imposed on them by the German Government because of the unfortunate death of the Third Secretary of the Reich at Paris. If they recognize the fine they accept the responsibility. I, myself, think that the German Government is responsible for this assassination because it was due to the desperation of a boy produced by a postcard which he received from his parents who were ruthlessly expelled to Poland.

Secondly, I do not think that one pound or one dollar from England or America should go to the payment of this fine, even if the German Jews do recognize it, or are forced to recognize it. If this were done we should simply be condoning kidnapping and banditry. I am writing this with the full knowledge of the fact that my friend, Fritz Warburg,[2] has been seized and taken to parts unknown. I think the time has come when a stand has to be made against these gangsters and robbers. I know this is not restrained language, but I do not propose to be very restrained.

At the present time the wave of indignation in America, and for that matter in England too, is so great that I think we Jews can very well hold our peace and for once, let the Christian world talk for us. [W]

1. Hugh Wilson (1885–1946), U.S. assistant secretary of state, 1937–38; U.S. ambassador to Germany, 1938–39.
2. Fritz Moritz Warburg (1879–1964), formerly head of the Banking House of Warburg, Hamburg.

TO NEVILLE LASKI, LONDON

Philadelphia, November 16, 1938

I want to acknowledge your kindness in sending me your letter of October 24 and the appended documents. In the situation as it existed at that time you and your friends were very restrained. The new situation in the last few days staggers all belief. I do not know that any words of mine would be useful or can give any comfort. I see no way out.

If the German government carries out its threat of collecting one billion marks from the German Jews, of forcing them to repair their own buildings, of requiring them to pay their insurance to the State, it means that the life of any Jew in Germany becomes impossible. They have all been reduced to starvation and since the Nazi government has shown a reasonable—though not too great tenderness—for human life, they may not allow them to starve but put them in forced labor, or what are politically called labor camps.

We once might have thought that the public opinion in the world might have made this impossible. There has been a great outburst here in America in the press and on the part of some public men. The leading Catholics in this country see the handwriting on the wall of the people of their own faith in Germany.

The calling back—it is not technically a recalling—of our Ambassador, Hugh Wilson, is the weightiest thing that our government could do to show its displeasure, and the words spoken by President [Franklin D.] Roosevelt yesterday at his press conference, although not an official document to Germany, have all the force of an official statement.

I know too that the American members of the Evian Conference have been called by the President and are in Washington now, and it is known to us and to you that our Ambassador and your government are seriously considering places of refuge. It is nevertheless humanly impossible in my opinion to remove five hundred thousand or more people in a few months.

Yesterday I was in New York and heard that Simon Marks was in conference with Ittleson,[1] [Solomon M.] Stroock and some others. We have had two meetings of the Joint Distribution Committee in the last few days and the endeavor will be made I think to raise One Million Dollars a month, not even that is enough.

Altogether, it seems to have taken the freshest outburst of savagery to arouse the conscience of the world.

There are two points upon which I am reasonably clear in my own mind, although I am not in position to enforce my opinion or even to offer it. I think that the Jews of Germany should refuse to pay the "fine" because the payment of that fine will be an acceptance of the responsibility for the stupid and cowardly assassination by this foolish Jewish boy of a minor German diplomat in Paris.

I also think that not one penny should be contributed by any Jew outside of Germany toward this fine or toward the release of hostages, and I say this knowing that Fritz Warburg was seized and that he was a very nice man and I like him very much. But to redeem such hostages would simply embolden these kidnappers and bandits.

Well, I suppose there is no use of my adding my indignation to yours.

I presume you are or will have been attending by this time the meeting of the Administration Committee of the Jewish Agency and that we shall hear in a more detailed way what the plans of the government are with regard to the Arab round-table conference.[2] At all events I think there has been a gain in the government for giving up the plan of partition. That plan was about the worst that could have been invented. [W]

1. Henry Ittleson (1871–1948), financier and philanthropist; member of the executive committee of the American Jewish Committee.
2. In November 1938 the Woodhead Commission advised that partition was impractical. The British then proposed convening a conference in London of Arab and Jewish leaders early in 1939. The conference, convened in February 1939, was unable to reach a satisfactory compromise.

TO SOLOMON M. STROOCK, PALM BEACH, FLORIDA

January 30, 1939

I hope that you have already commenced to feel the benefits of the sunshine and the balmy air. You are well away from New York which has been very mean for the last few days.

We had a lengthy meeting with the Executive Committee Saturday night, which was very well attended. Almost at the beginning, Jimmy Rosenberg, who said that he had not seen the report until that morning—although it had been sent ten days previously—commenced to rip it up the back and down the front and he made a lengthy statement as to its improvement. He charged it with being a defeatist document, etc. For the next hour or hour and a half, he was pretty much on his feet. He finally agreed that it was too long and took in extraneous matters with which we should not concern ourselves. So I was asked to appoint a committee of five, in view of the discussion which I say lasted an hour or an hour and a half or maybe more, to revise the report and have it ready for the next day. I did appoint such a committee and a very much better report was read the next day. The committee and the staff worked until 4:30 a.m. in order to get it done.

There was quite a discussion about the needs of the Survey Committee in which I thought Carl Austrian[1] was rather provocative, and tried to stand up Albert Lasker,[2] which Lasker did not take very well. He seemed to be tremendously interested and stayed through the meeting and all through the meeting next day. Jimmy Becker came on from Chicago also.

The Annual Meeting on Sunday lasted from 10:30 until about 4:20 in the afternoon. It was well but not overwhelmingly attended. The room that was secured was much too big. It looked to me that it would hold about eight or nine hundred people. I think it was the biggest room on the top floor, whereas the attendance was about 350 to 400. After the reports were presented, various cranks arose, but I do not think they did very much harm. They were not corporate members of the Committee but people who had been invited by someone or other. I think next year, if I live that long, I shall go over the list myself of those invited. Of course, there were complaints that the reports did not tell anything and that not sufficient detailed information was given.

In the afternoon Edward Greenebaum[3] gave a more intimate picture of the Survey Committee. There were no reporters present, and so kept out of the newspapers. He was not too intimate but people were satisfied with the information given. Our mutual friend, Doctor Samuel Schulman, made two speeches at considerable length. Toward the afternoon, I called Judge [Irving] Lehman to the Chair, not simply because I was tired but because I thought his appearance would be good and he made a very good Chairman to receive the Survey Committee report and expressed his great confidence in it and altogether held up his end.

Then the non-Zionists met, about twenty strong. Doctor [Maurice J.] Karpf got up out of a sick bed to come and he is back there today. The consensus of opinion was very strong that we should not send a representation to London. The reasoning was as follows. Among the Jews, if we did not take the extreme position of the Zionists and Jewish Agency, we would be hopelessly outnumbered. If we made moderate propositions, we would be charged with having betrayed the cause. The chances are we could not do anything, therefore, it was decided not to go. I am rather unhappy about it myself because I often think one ought to fight even in a losing cause. But opinion was against me. Karpf has cabled to the Executive and I have sent a copy to Sir Osmond [d'Avigdor Goldsmid] which I thought I owed him, copy of which I enclose you.

There is a gentleman by the name of Arthur Hale who at eleven o'clock every night brings the best news of the day, and is sponsored by the Hoffman Beverage Company. When he is finishing, he says, "Well, that's the news." So I have given it to you—that's the news! . . . [W]

1. Carl Austrian (1893–1970), lawyer; member of the executive committee of the American Jewish Committee.
2. Albert Lasker (1880–1952), advertising executive; member of the executive committee of the American Jewish Committee.
3. Edward S. Greenebaum (1890–1970), lawyer; member of the executive committee of the American Jewish Committee.

TO MAURICE B. HEXTER, NEW YORK CITY

February 3, 1939

. . . You say that you hope that I will still continue to call meetings of the non-Zionists and then add, "this is not the time for anyone to sulk in his tent." Well, I have no tent and if I had I would never sulk in it. I never have. I think that all along the attitude here has been humiliating. If I had been well and strong I should have gone over myself without asking anybody's permission or approval and with full confidence that what I did represented the bulk of the non–Zionists in the United States. . . .

I felt all the worse about the whole situation because of the part that has been taken at the meetings here concerning this conference, and a part, by the way, in which you to a certain extent put me. You made the appointments for me with [David] Ben-Gurion and were very anxious that I should see Ben-Gurion. You presided over the meeting at which Nahum Goldmann[1] discussed the situation with us. I took, and you and [Maurice J.] Karpf and [Morris D.] Waldman and others took a very decided part in that meeting and strongly objected to breaking off the negotiations in London, and then as I see it we turned tail.

You gentlemen are very skilled in dialectics. You can make good speeches and write very methodical letters, but the heart of the thing is this, that we had a duty and have shirked it. I hope that some way may be found by which we will not let Sir Osmond [d'Avigdor Goldsmid] and his friends down.

I suppose I am cross because I am still rather miserable but then maybe I may be permitted to get cross once in a while. [W]

1. Nahum Goldmann (1894–1982), Zionist leader; Jewish Agency representative at Geneva, 1935–39.

TO SOLOMON ZEITLIN, PHILADELPHIA

February 9, 1939

I have received your article on "The Book of Jubilees,"[1] and also your reviews. I have put your reviews to press.

I have read the article on the Book of Jubilees very carefully and would like to talk to you about it. If I print it in its present form I foresee the possibility of an acrimonious scholarly debate, to which I do not care to open the pages of the [*Jewish*] *Quarterly* [*Review*]. I think possibly this can be averted if I can have the opportunity of going over this article with you in detail.

On page 5, for instance, you say, "I venture to say that Shabuot in the book of Jubilees means not 'weeks' but 'oaths.'" Well, you venture to say it but as far as I can see you do not furnish any proof. But that is not so much what I mean.

I think you have been particularly severe in certain phrases with regard to Doctor [Adolph] Büchler.

There is a sort of germanic tinge to the number of foot-notes. Thus, for instance, if you say the Priest "of the Most High God" was used in connection with Melchizedek, there is no point in a note on that.

The statement that I have marked on page 8 with regard to the water libation I think absolutely inadmissible in a serious article.

On page 9, it seems to me there is no point in repeating Deuteronomy 28. There a reference would be sufficient.

On page 11, what you consider proof of the early date of Jubilee does not impress me as proof at all.

I am also concerned by these various remarks about Doctor Büchler which I find on page 14 and later on page 16. For instance you say that "Doctor Büchler's criticism was groundless." Then on page 17, "Doctor Büchler follows the erroneous assumption of all scholars, etc."

It has never been very clear to me why, if a man has a positive thesis to write, he has to dissect and try to destroy all his predecessors.

I had not meant to write you in any detail but as I have been housed for some time I did not want to hold the article too long.

On page 24, you say "we have established." That sounds a little dogmatic from a scientific point of view.

I hope you will not mind my making these notations and hope that you might be willing to reconsider this article.

I also think that the calendar part is not clear and I do not know whether it will be clear to anybody. It seems to me almost impossible that there ever was a time when the Israelites had a purely lunar calendar. They must have made some correction for the sun even if we have no record of it, otherwise Pesach would have been in mid-winter and Succoth in June or vice versa, and we have to give even ordinary people a little credit for sense, especially when the festivals were tied to seasons so they found some way of working them out, even if they did not write books about it. [D]

1. "The Book of Jubilees, Its Character and Its Significance," *JQR* 30 (1939): 1–31.

TO NEVILLE LASKI, LONDON

February 17, 1939

. . . I believe that the time has come when people should speak out because as Hitler himself has said in his book, a lie repeated often enough is accepted as a fact. I am entirely opposed to any further defense policy and I believe in taking the aggressive. This is indicated probably as well as I can indicate it in the address which I gave at the annual meeting of the American Jewish Committee this year.[1] I am having it printed and will probably have it circulated pretty widely, but as I do not wish to delay this letter I am sending you a rather imperfect manuscript copy of it. It is now in galley proof and will probably be out in a week or ten days.

You will see that I have declared, and keep on declaring, that the race theory and the bolshevist is a lie and fraudulent. I think we must keep on saying that it was the German Reich that paved the way for the Soviet and made a shameful bargain in doing so. In other words, it seems to me that we have got to begin to put these people on the defensive. I would be entirely opposed to any international manifesto.

Whether a statement in England would be useful or not of course I do not know. You must be the best judge of your own local situation. You are so much nearer to Germany than we are. It is an over-night trip by sea I believe and your political attitude is, I think, quite different.

It is my general impression that the present government, or at least the party that controls the present British government, is more fearful of the Soviet Union than it is of Nazi Germany, and that in all probability beside the natural and righteous desires for peace its policy has been dictated somewhat by that general consideration.

I want you to understand that this statement that I am sending you was a statement that I made in my individual capacity and the responsibility for it was not accepted by the Executive Committee, nor did I ask them to do so.

I think that you ought to keep on hammering at the falsity of the race theory and your best man to do that in England is Haddon.[2] I am sure you remember the book by Haddon and Huxley, "We Europeans."[3]

Just at the present time one of the Bureaus of the United States government, the Bureau of Education at Washington, is sponsoring a weekly radio program with the general title "Americans All, Immigrants All." Of course that is something that can be done in this country as every white man here is an immigrant and so are all the black men. The red men are the only natives.

The more of this sort of denial about the race theory and the communist link you can get from non-Jews the better, in my opinion.

I do not really know whether this answers your question or not. I have not submitted this to anybody. I have been here in Philadelphia and mostly in my house ever since January 30. I may be able to go to New York next week. . . . [W]

1. AJC Thirty-Second Annual Report (1939), pp. 53–62.
2. Alfred Cort Haddon (1855–1940), English ethnologist.
3. Alfred Cort Haddon and Julian S. Huxley, *We Europeans; A Survey of Racial Problems* (London, 1935).

TO HYMAN J. REIT,[1] NEW YORK CITY

Woods Hole, Massachusetts, July 6, 1939

. . . I have had read to me the almost interminable letter of Doctor [Jacques] Faitlovitch of May 9. You ask for my opinion but I really do not see that there is anything to guide me or anybody else in rendering an opinion. You had no word from Mr. Viterbo.[2] I know about Mr. Viterbo and the proposition of Doctor Faitlovitch to have him go to Addis-Ababa to take care of the School there I think is a good one provided we find the means for support. He points out that $250 to $300 a month is needed. I do not know what the finances of the [American Jewish] Committee are or whether you will raise that much money, or whether the Committee is in position to enter such an obligation. You know of course that I have always been anxious that this work should not be abandoned although it has been very poorly kept up, but I think you have to take stock of your possible resources before entering into any definite commitment with Mr. Viterbo.

Undoubtedly, what Doctor Faitlovitch says is true concerning the future of the Falashas. There is no reason to suppose that the Italian Fascists are going to treat the black Jews in Abyssinia any better than the white Jews in Italy.

I really think that this subject, which is largely a religious one, indeed almost entirely a religious one, should not be decided off-hand by our comparatively small Committee and that either some rabbinical groups or maybe the Synagogue Council should be consulted with before it is decided that nothing is possible. It seems a dreadful thing to abandon fifty thousand Jews. [D]

1. New York jurist, chairman of the American Pro-Falasha Committee.
2. Carlo Alberto Viterbo (b. 1889), leader of Italian Jewry who had made contact with the Falashas in Italian-ruled Ethiopia.

TO LOUIS FINKELSTEIN, NEW YORK CITY

Woods Hole, Massachusetts, July 21, 1939

. . . I am getting a little confused about the plans for the Institute of Interdenominational Studies[1] and the plan for a better mutual understanding. Now the Interdenominational course is something that you and Professor [Louis] Ginzberg strongly urged, and it was to be a purely academic thing, as I understood it. It is for this Interdenominational course that Mr. Littauer[2] gave $25,000 over a period of five years.

The Interdenominational course has not had a sufficient trial for anybody to speak about it. It ought to have a definite program, let us say for a period of three years, and also definite lecturers or instructors.

When you boil it down, assuming that we are limiting ourselves to Judaism and Christianity, the Interdenominational course can only consist of an exposition of the basic principles of these two great religions—where they agree and where they differ. That is not a terribly difficult thing to do if anybody can agree as to what are the fundamentals of Judaism and Christianity.

I had thought that the most useful thing would be if the courses were established, if the period in which Christianity evolved out of Judaism were set forth fairly and objectively, if the relationship of the Mishna and the rabbis to the New Testament were taught, and if on the other hand the New Testament were taught to a given number of Jewish students, showing its Jewish background, also in some cases its non-Jewish background.

I cannot see how anything else can be proposed than that, but if you have anything definite in mind, please bring it forth because if this is to be something that will be operative in the academic year 1939–40, it ought to be reasonably settled at the time when the academic year of our Seminary and the Christian seminaries in New York begin.

Now the other subject, that of improving Jewish and Christian relations. As I have told you a number of times, I think this Seminary ought to play its part, but I do not think it can play the major role. Its people will not be selected from that point of view and there are other and larger forces both for it and against it. You must remember that there are a great many people who are anti-Jewish who are not Christians, but simply heathens, and how on earth the Seminary is going to be the agency to cope with that I cannot say. [JTS]

1. The Institute, founded in the autumn of 1938 under the auspices of the Jewish Theological Seminary, was intended to provide an opportunity for ministers of different faiths to study together. It was ultimately renamed the Institute for Religious and Social Studies.
2. Lucius N. Littauer (1859–1944), industrialist and philanthropist; member of the U.S. House of Representatives from New York, 1897–1907.

TO FRIEDA WARBURG, WHITE PLAINS, NEW YORK

Woods Hole, Massachusetts, July 26, 1939

I know you commanded me not to reply to Nelson Glueck's letter to you but while reasonably obedient I still occasionally get a little rebellious, and I do not want you to go away to your favorite summer camp without a word of affection from me.

I know that you have been through many things this year and had many things to do, and I hope that you are going to revel in all the revels that were put up at Camp Lipstick.

I am not going to comment so much on Glueck's letter. I knew he was coming here in the autumn and I have tried to arrange with Professor [Millar] Burrows that he should give at least one lecture at the Seminary. It is too bad that all this fine idealistic work which the American Schools and the [Hebrew] University and everybody else has been trying to do in Palestine should have to be carried on under the threat of injury and death.

As a matter of fact, however, since we are all interested in the School I do want to say that as a matter of theory I think it advisable that after a man has been Director of the American School in Jerusalem for a number of years he should return. Men go stale even on field work. Of course that has not happened to Glueck yet but it might very well, and really if he would come home and take the time to write up the results of his work he could produce a number of most interesting books. Aqaba alone is one of the most fascinating points in our ancient biblical history, where it figures in the Bible under the name of Ezzion-Geber and from which point Solomon undertook to build up his empire.

Well, my dear, I am not having to give you a lecture but what I have in mind is this: You know [William F.] Albright was in Palestine ten years and he went stale. In fact his health gave way and he is now having a wonderful career as the head of the Semitic Department at Johns Hopkins University. [Ephraim A.] Speiser, a much younger man, was out in the field in Babylonia mostly for six or seven years and I think next year he will be head of the Semitic Department of the University of Pennsylvania. And Herbert Winlock, who spent at least fifteen or twenty years in the fields of Egypt and probably ruined his health, at least has had a glorious time as Curator of the Egyptian Department of the Metropolitan Museum and later its Director.

What I want to say is that field work is not an end in itself but is something that should be translated into scientific publications and even into the teaching of students.

It is rather a pity that Glueck is not connected with a great University. Of course the Hebrew Union College or any Jewish College could very well have a Chair in Biblical Archaeology. It would be a splendid thing to do but generally we have only one Professor of Bible and he is supposed to be an archaeologist, philologist and exegist, and everything else. After all, our Jewish institutions, fine as they are, have not grown to manhood.

You will probably want a word about myself. I am going along slowly, hardly walk and never drive. I am kept pretty comfortable by various palliatives, I have a wonderful diet which I think you would not like, and I do not, and then of course I have my devoted family and Judy. I am doing an hour and a half's work every day and trying to finish up my memoirs which I started in Switzerland nine years ago. I do not know whether they will be any good when they are through but I would like to finish them. . . . [W]

TO LOUIS FINKELSTEIN, NEW YORK CITY

Woods Hole, Massachusetts, July 31, 1939

. . . I quite agree that the courses in medieval Hebrew literature and the history of liturgy have been over-emphasized, dear Doctor [Israel] Davidson's idea being that in order to be a full professor, you must give very full courses.

With regard to the suggestion that the course in medieval Hebrew literature might be covered in one year, that is rather a jump from four years to one, nor does my mind follow along the suggestion that the course in medieval Hebrew literature should be integrated with the course in modern Hebrew literature. Modern Hebrew literature, as I understand it, is a recent thing and mostly based upon the renaissance of Hebrew in Palestine, and medieval Hebrew literature really covers everything from the close of the Talmud to modern times.

It would seem to me, therefore, that the two courses should remain separate, but that the course in modern Hebrew literature might be given by the same person who gives the course in medieval Hebrew literature.

I am very appreciative of your offer to give the course in liturgy, and I believe that you are very well qualified to do it. In fact, the knowledge of the prayer book and in general the history of our liturgy really has a close connection with Jewish theology. There ought to be a differentiation between the history of the prayer book and the Piyyut.[1] I do not think that the history of the prayer book was overdone. I think that Piyyut was.

I am very much concerned, however, about your taking on more work, and I really think that you ought to find some way of relieving yourself of some of the teaching that you are now giving.

In view of the fact that Professor [Albert M.] Hyamson is anxious to retire, provided he gets his full salary, I should be very happy if this could be arranged, but of course that is a matter of the budget for next year. He has been getting older very rapidly and we need a new man for Codes. Who that man is to be I do not know, but I am of the opinion that he ought to be not a purely theoretical man. In other words, the Professor of Codes or the man who teaches Codes, should have had practical rabbinical experience as well as being a good scholar.

I know the name of Saul Lieberman,[2] and I have seen some rather large books that he has published. In fact I think I have had some correspondence with him, but we ought to know all about not only his Talmudic knowledge, but his general training, and we ought to know something about him as a human being, what kind of a person he is, whether he is a person who could be got along with, and whether he is a person who could fit himself into American life.

I thank you for giving me the name of Bokser.[3] I have not seen Dr. [David de Sola] Pool in the meantime.

As to the Institute of Interdenominational Studies, I agree that the second commonwealth could be given either by Professor [Abraham A.] Neuman or Dr. Grayzel.[4] I think that Dr. Grayzel, being in his first year as editor of the Jewish Publication Society, will have his hands pretty full.

I like Dr. Bokser for Talmudic literature, unless you have a more impressive person to suggest.

[Milton] Steinberg, I think, would do very well for the Hellenistic literature.

I doubt very much whether you can get [Harry A.] Wolfson for Jewish philosophy in the Middle Ages, but you might try.

Professor F. C. Grant,[5] I do not know. I would like to know a little more about him.

I am not going to discuss with you the question of religion in general and democracy in this letter. We are in agreement in the main but we cannot write treatises to each other on this subject.

We will have to talk over some time whether this task which we both agree is important, can be undertaken by the Seminary. In other words, whether we are a strong enough institution and in a strong enough central position to do this.

I quite agree with you that we ought to get some more scientific lectures or at least science and religion, and I also agree that psychology and religion is something that has to be considered.

I would like very much to have this work done and possibly the interdenominational work done at a summer school. Our place in the winter is becoming a regular rabbit warren. I doubt whether people running from one crowded classroom to another through crowded halls ever settle down properly to think. If we had, say, twenty-five or thirty men of different denominations studying for six or eight weeks over the summer, maybe only six weeks, I believe it would create an entirely different impression on them than hectic lectures. The lectures of course we have to have for the purpose of interesting the public.

I think every plan ought to be thought through before it is begun, and that was the reason why I wrote to you some time ago, that for the Department of Interdenominational Studies, we should make a definite program covering three years, and by a program, I mean the studies to be given and the persons to give them. It ought to be a consistent program, and I think three years is a good time.

It seems to me not the best method in the summer just as we are doing now to get up a program for next autumn. Next autumn the program ought to be made for the next three years. I have put down three years because I thought that we could be assured from the money that Mr. [Lucius N.] Littauer gave us, that we could carry on, on a worthy basis, for at least three years.

I am sure you know that I agree with you on the power of ideas, but these ideas have to be promulgated. One way of promulgating ideas is to write books and pamphlets, but I think in the long run the best way is to train people to teach other people and when I say other people I mean finally those who teach the hundreds of thousands. . . . [JTS]

1. Hebrew liturgical poetry.
2. Saul Lieberman (1898–1983), rabbinic scholar; appointed professor of Talmud at the Jewish Theological Seminary in 1940.
3. Ben Zion Bokser (b. 1907), rabbi of the Forest Hills (N.Y.) Jewish Center.
4. Solomon Grayzel (1896–1980), Jewish historian; editor of the Jewish Publication Society, 1936–66.
5. Frederick Clifton Grant (1891–1974), Professor of New Testament, Union Theological Seminary.

TO MORRIS D. WALDMAN, NEW YORK CITY

September 25, 1939

. . . I myself am unaware of any considerable achievement of the General Jewish Council[1] in the period during which it has been in existence. I do not want to be a separatist; on the other hand, I think it highly inadvisable that any steps should be taken that could weaken or disorganize the structure of the American Jewish Committee. Whether we are wiser than the general world and plan out a rebuilding in the midst of ruins, I do not know. There are, no doubt, a few things for which we might keep ourselves in readiness. At any time it may be necessary to ward off an attack to give out publicity. We ought therefore have all of our information with regard to Hitler's statements concerning the Bolshevik Jews, the Soviet Republic, and similar things on hand. I do not know whether they will be called for but that is one form of preparation which we can consider.

Now as for the future, the most constructive suggestion that I can think of is the reiteration of the insistence that the relationship between nations depends upon international law, morality, the observance of treaties, etc. I think that some people, maybe not connected with our Committee, should seriously consider what form if any, the League of Nations, could take in the future. Certainly the purposes for which it was created are gone. The minorities have been submerged and the very act under which the League exists is torn up. Nevertheless, it might be well for a committee to study this in connection with some of our Christian friends. I am sure that James G. MacDonald and Professor [Joseph P.] Chamberlain both would stand ready to give advice and counsel.

In the meantime, we ought to exhort and keep on exhorting our Jewish people in America to do their duty as citizens and as Jews. . . . [AJC]

1. The General Jewish Council for Jewish Rights was founded on August 15, 1938, by the American Jewish Congress, the Jewish Labor Committee, the American Jewish Committee, and B'nai B'rith for the defense of the civil and religious rights of Jews, to combat anti-Semitism and to deal with events affecting Jews abroad.

TO GEORGE SARTON, CAMBRIDGE, MASSACHUSETTS

September 27, 1939

Your kind letter of September 13 should have had an answer sooner but, alas, I was not in position to make it. I am not going to complain to you but I have had a hard summer and am not yet able to leave my room.

I wish I could discuss with you some of the big things that you write about.

You ask whether mankind can learn anything *permanently*. Well, as an historian of science, with one who is obliged to take account of the whole history of the world I am afraid that you would draw the melancholy conclusion that mankind cannot learn anything permanently. And yet, we must not leave it so in our minds. I suppose that in the course of history wars have become a little less frequent and not conducted with such savagery as thousands of years ago, although I am not sure that the mechanized savagery of modern times is not worse than the battle-ax. . . . [W]

TO MORRIS D. WALDMAN, NEW YORK CITY

October 9, 1939

. . . The subject to which I think either the General Jewish Council or the American Jewish Committee should give its earnest attention is the following up of the situation in Europe, and that we can only do I presume through the censored press. If we have any other way of getting information, we should get it.

The subject which should be taken up for consideration and in my opinion taken up very promptly is Mr. Hitler's proposal to establish a Jewish state in Poland,[1] of course under his protection, and I can see with a certain amount of Russian influence thrown in because Biro-Bidjan[2] is mentioned as the model for such a state. As far as I know Biro-Bidjan is a failure and this proposed state is almost certain to be a failure too.

At this distance we probably ought not to decide for the Polish Jews. If Hitler makes a handsome offer of land, rights, etc., it may be for the Polish Jews to accept or reject it. As far as I am concerned I should be inclined to reject it because I think nothing good can come out of that source, but it is a subject which ought to be considered very carefully and as soon as possible because a policy may have to be accepted or rejected at almost any moment. [AJC]

1. After their conquest of Poland, the Nazis spread reports that they were going to set up reservations in the Lublin area for German and Polish Jews.
2. See letter to Henry J. Rubin, November 26, 1934.

Adler was at this point already gravely ill. Though he had continued to function as president of the American Jewish Committee, it was time to consider the succession.

TO SOLOMON M. STROOCK, NEW YORK CITY

December 15, 1939

I had hopes that long before this I would have been able to come to New York and you would have been able to spare the time so that we might thoroughly go into the affairs of the American Jewish Committee and conclude, at least in our own minds and with each other, the best course of policy to pursue. Unfortunately this has not been possible. I have required further treatment which kept me in bed for a time and whereas a few weeks ago I was writing to you that I was driving out and going to the Dropsie College, that has not been possible during the last week. I am hoping that I shall soon feel better again and really believe that I shall because in spite of many disappointments I think I am on the road to mending.

The annual meeting of the Committee has been fixed for January 21st, 1940. The Doctors have declined to express an opinion to me as to whether I would be well enough to attend and take charge of such a meeting but they say they will let me know in a week. This, however, I think is running things pretty close. I do not know how you feel about taking charge of and presiding over the annual meeting. I hope you are well enough and vigorous enough for it. We have Irving Lehman as a stand-by who presided over the last half of last year's meeting when you were away and I was not very well. Louis Kirstein[1] is also a Vice-President. That is a technical side.

The real point is with regard to the future officers of the Committee. I do not want to embarrass you in any way nor do I want to force a decision about the government of the Committee, but I think the time has come when a successor to myself should be seriously considered.

I do not know whether you recall that in 1933, when I was approaching the age of seventy, I stated to the Committee my intention to retire, and this I did already in the spring of 1933 so that there might be ample time for consideration. A sub-Committee was appointed to give thought to the election of a new President. That summer I went on a long trip and when I returned was met at the dock by Felix Warburg and I believe another member of the sub-Committee. The Committee had had a number of meetings during the summer and had come to the conclusion that in the then troubled state of the world it was inadvisable that we should select a new President who might chart a new course. I was a little doubtful about going on but Felix seemed to have the matter so completely in his mind and the importance of no change being made in view of the new Hitler regime and the then trouble, that I finally agreed to give up my intention of retiring.

Since then the subject has often crossed my mind, but without any result because the day to day things seemed to absorb us.

I have the impression that the President of the Committee is not elected by the Committee but is elected or at least nominated by a committee of the Executive Committee.

Now I am willing to do whatever is the best thing to do under the existing circumstances and I really would like you to decide this matter in consultation with whomever you care to meet.

As I have indicated above, I would have greatly preferred to talk to you about it but there is no probability of my being able to come to New York at least for another week and I cannot be more definite than that. I am able, without fatigue at all, to talk on the telephone and if you think the matter is one that should not be left to correspondence I can be subject to your call any morning between 10:30 and noon, or any afternoon after 4:30.

The subject of the Presidency is one that I of course do not care to direct. I have been in the Committee in various offices since the beginning and have had enough of a hand in it, but I think it has a particular importance in view of the action or at least the alleged action of the British Board of Deputies which was recorded in the Jewish Telegraphic Agency the other day, namely, to the effect that Professor Selig Brodetsky is to be the next President of their Board in place of [Neville] Laski. Whatever else this means, it means that this oldest representative body of the British Jews, which I think was established in 1760 or thereabouts, goes entirely into the hands of the Zionists, and that aspect of the subject ought to be considered. I am not saying this to suggest politics in the matter at all. Whoever would be most useful to the work is the man who ought to be chosen. The Committee is still an organization with a good deal of weight.

That reminds me, though I do not want to digress, that a day or two ago I received a letter from Mr. Arthur Lourie[2] of England who comes over to this country as a sort of advance guard to herald the advent of Doctor [Chaim] Weizmann's arrival. Mr. Lourie wanted an appointment today, this afternoon, which I could not make, but obviously the Zionist hosts from England are commencing to move upon us. I have been told, with what authority in back of it I do not know, that Weizmann is coming over here for some time to sound out the situation, and if he finds it feasible move the headquarters of the Jewish Agency from England to America. I do not know under what conditions he would consider this feasible. Some of his enthusiastic American friends may have told him that America would stand for Palestine. So long as the Mandate holds up and the League of Nations does not entirely disappear I should imagine that whatever the course of the war Britain would continue to hold the Mandate, although in this uncertain world, nothing is certain. I have had a sneaking feeling for some time that Turkey is very anxious to have the Mandate returned and what kind of bargains will be made in these deals it is impossible to foresee.

Well, this is a very long letter and it would be better if it were a short one but view it as a chat between us. I am not making copies of this for the office and am not sending it to the office. For the present it is between you and me although you are at full liberty to discuss it with any members of the Executive Committee that you consider desirable. [W]

1. Louis Kirstein (1867–1942), department-store executive; chairman of the General Committee of the American Jewish Committee.
2. Arthur Lourie (1903–1979), political secretary of the Jewish Agency for Palestine, 1933–48.

On December 23, 1939, President Roosevelt appointed Adler as the Jewish representative of an interfaith committee that was being established to advise the president on steps toward the restoration of world peace. Some weeks later, when the president summoned him to the White House for consultation on this matter, Adler summoned up his rapidly failing strength and made the journey to Washington. It was to be his last.

TO FRANKLIN D. ROOSEVELT, WASHINGTON, D.C.

December 24, 1939

I am only now able to acknowledge your telegram of December 23, owing to delay on delivery of the message which has just reached me. Your fellow countrymen and the world at large take new courage from the fact that you are again throwing your vivid and forceful leadership into the cause of peace. It is a noble deed to bring the forces of religion together. I have the confident hope that the leaders will unite the members of their churches and synagogues into unanimous support of your efforts. I gladly take the opportunity to send good wishes to His Holiness the Pope[1] and to Dr. Buttrick,[2] and feel sure that all true men of good faith will in their several ways further your inspired leadership. I shall of course convey your message to the various rabbinical associations for transmission to their congregations, but I can say without qualification that the watchword of the Jewish people is Israel's mission is peace and that this holds true for all the scattered communities to which the Jewish people have been dispersed and are now alas being further dispersed with great brutality.

I take this occasion to express to you our grateful thanks for the bringing together of the Evian Conference and the further efforts you have made in aid of the sorely tried refugees.

It will be a privilege for me to have the opportunity to visit you at the White House.

With the hope that you will have the time to spend a happy holiday with your family, I am

Faithfully yours. [JTS]

1. Pope Pius XII (1876–1958).
2. George Arthur Buttrick (1892–1980), president of the Federal Council of Churches of Christ in America, 1938–39.

TO DAVID J. GALTER, PHILADELPHIA

January 30, 1940

I am greatly flattered by your desire to write my biography. I may tell you privately that I have been engaged on an autobiography[1] for six years and the work is mostly done, so I see no reason why you should spend your valuable time in producing another one. [W]

1. Adler's autobiography, *I Have Considered the Days,* was published in 1941 by the Jewish Publication Society.

TO CORDELL HULL, WASHINGTON, D.C.

Philadelphia, February 2, 1940

I would not take up a moment of your time did I not feel that possibly the life of a very fine man may depend on it.

I received word two or three days ago that Doctor Moses Schorr,[1] formerly of Warsaw, had been placed in a Concentration Camp in Lwow (Lemberg), Russian-Poland, and that he had been sentenced to imprisonment for eight years because of the fact that in Poland, as it existed, he was opposed to the Communist idea and spoke against it.

Doctor Schorr is one of the leading Jewish personalities of Poland. Besides his regular College degree, he occupied the position of Professor of Semitic Languages and History at Lwow University and held a similar position in connection with the University of Warsaw. He was a Senator in the Polish regime. I had the pleasure of conferring an honorary degree upon him in 1937, and then hailed him not only as a great scholar but as one of the leaders of the Jewish community in Poland.

I realize the irregularity of the request, but I am wondering whether, if the case of such a man were brought to the attention of the Soviet authorities, they might not be willing to release him. Doctor Schorr had already prepared to go to Palestine and had his papers for the purpose, when he was seized and put in the Concentration Camp.

All the Jewish scholars throughout this country would be immensely gratified for anything that could be done to relieve Doctor Schorr from imprisonment and from the humiliation which he is obliged to suffer.

I believe that this is the first time in these last troubled years that I have written to you in behalf of any individual, so I am sure you realize that I do so only because I am greatly moved by the importance of the case. [D]

1. Moses Schorr (1874–1941), Polish rabbi, scholar and political leader. When Germany invaded Poland in September 1939, he fled eastward, but was arrested by the Russians, who moved on Poland from the east. Transported from prison to prison, he ended up in Uzbekistan, where he died.

CHRONOLOGY

1863   Cyrus Adler born in Van Buren, Arkansas.

1867   Death of Samuel Adler, his father.

1883   Received B.A. from the University of Pennsylvania and began doctoral studies in Semitics at Johns Hopkins University.

1886   Founding of the Jewish Theological Seminary of America.
Adler received M.A. from the University of Pennsylvania.

1887   Received Ph.D. in Semitics from Johns Hopkins University; appointed Instructor in Semitics.
Taught course in Biblical Archaeology at the Jewish Theological Seminary.
Appointed curator of the Department of Oriental Antiquities, United States National Museum (Smithsonian).

1888   Founding of the Jewish Publication Society of America. (Adler was a member of its Board of Trustees and, later, chairman of its Publications Committee.)

1889   Appointed custodian of Section of Religious Ceremonial, United States National Museum.

1890   Appointed Associate in Semitics, Johns Hopkins University.
Appointed Special Commissioner of the World's Columbian Exposition to Turkey, Persia, Egypt, Tunis, and Morocco (traveled to Europe, the Near East, and North Africa, 1890–1891).

1892   Appointed Librarian, Smithsonian Institution.
Founding of American Jewish Historical Society. (Adler was instrumental in the founding of this organization. He served as corresponding secretary and, later, as president [1898–1921].)

1893 Resigned from faculty of Johns Hopkins University.

1894 Joined editorial board of the *American Hebrew*.

1897 First Zionist Congress.

1898 Founding of Gratz College. (Adler was member of Board of Trustees.)
Adler appointed United States delegate to the conference establishing the International Catalogue of Scientific Literature.
Spanish-American War.

1899 Editor of *American Jewish Year Book* (to 1906).

1901 Joined editorial board of the *Jewish Encyclopedia* (to 1906).
Reorganization of Jewish Theological Seminary.

1902 Appointed Assistant Secretary, Smithsonian Institution.
Appointed President of the Board of Trustees, Jewish Theological Seminary (to 1905).

1903 Pogroms in Kishinev, Russia.

1905 Married Racie Friedenwald.

1906 Birth of daughter, Sarah.
Founding of American Jewish Committee (Adler was appointed member of its Executive Committee.)

1908 Appointed President, Dropsie College.
Became co-editor of the *Jewish Quarterly Review*, a new series.
Appointed chairman of editorial board, Jewish Publication Society Bible Translation.

1911 Elected president of Philadelphia Kehillah (to 1915).

1913 Founding of United Synagogue of America. (Adler served as vice president and, later, as president.)

1914 Outbreak of World War I.
Founding of American Jewish Joint Distribution Committee (Adler was member of board of directors and chairman of its committee on Cultural Institutions [to 1918]).
Adler appointed chairman, Jewish Publication Society Jewish Classics series.

1915 Appointed acting president, Jewish Theological Seminary.
Appointed chairman of Executive Board, American Jewish Committee.

1917 United States entered World War I.
Balfour Declaration.
Controversy over American Jewish Congress.
Completion of Jewish Publication Society Bible Translation.
Founding of Jewish Welfare Board. (Adler served as chairman and, later, as chairman of its Army and Navy Committee.)

1919   Appointed delegate of American Jewish Committee to Versailles Peace Conference.

1921   Appointed member of the Philadelphia Board of Education (to 1925).
Appointed member, Board of Trustees, American Schools of Oriental Research.

1924   Appointed President, Jewish Theological Seminary.

1925   Opening of the Hebrew University of Jerusalem (Adler was a member of the Board of Governors.)
Adler elected President of the Board, Free Library of Philadelphia.
Death of Sarah Adler, his mother.

1929   Elected president, American Jewish Committee.
Founding of enlarged Jewish Agency for Palestine.
Arab riots in Palestine; controversy over Jewish rights at the Wailing (Western) Wall.
Onset of the Great Depression.

1930   Elected President of the Council and Chairman of the Administrative Committee, Jewish Agency for Palestine (to 1931).

1933   Adolph Hitler came to power in Germany.

1936   Arab riots in Palestine.

1938   Elected Vice President, American Philosophical Society.
Kristallnacht.

1939   Outbreak of World War II.
British White Paper on Palestine.

1940   Death of Cyrus Adler.

INDEX

Adler, Cyrus (*Continued*)
  work of, for Hebrew University, as
      associate of Chaim Weizmann,
      2:221–222, 245–249
    as author of organization
      memorandum, 2:96–99
    for organization of Institute of Jewish
      Studies, 2:109–110
    for organization of Jewish studies
      department, 2:90–91, 110–113
    for Yiddish chair, 2:148–149
    in obtaining world Jewish scholars,
      2:95–96
    in selection of trustees, 2:95–96
    on Board of Governors, 2:130–135,
      280
    on draft of constitution, 2:127–128
    on university administration,
      2:150–151
  for Jewish Publication Society, 1:147;
    2:125–126
    for establishment of Hebrew printing
      press, 1:392–393
    on Bible translation, 1:234–236,
      250–251
    as chairman of editorial board, 1:154
  for *Jewish Quarterly Review*, 2:146, 244,
    360–361
    as facilitator of move to Philadelphia,
      1:155–157
  for Jewish Theological Seminary, 2:151
    as acting president, 1:300
    as author of memorandum on Isaac
      Elchanan Seminary, 2:123–124
    as commencement speaker, 1:113–114
    as lecturer on biblical archaeology,
      1:12–14
    as president, 2:92
    as president of Board of Trustees,
      1:86–88, 90–94
    for acquisition of Elkan Adler library,
      1:390–391; 2:55–58, 65–68
    on curriculum planning, 2:11–13,
      366–368
    on library building plans, 2:72–75, 147
    relations of, with faculty, 1:155–157;
      2:139
  for Johns Hopkins University, as
    fundraiser, 1:187–188
    as instructor in Semitics, 1:9
    resignation from, 1:61
    as student, 1:3–4, 8

Adler, Cyrus (*Continued*)
  work of, for Philadelphia Jewish
    community, 1:218–219
    for placement of German scholars, 2:264
    for Smithsonian Institution, 1:9–12
    as Assistant Secretary, 1:110–111
    as developer of Judaica collection, 1:10,
      17
    as half-time employee, 1:96–97
    as librarian, 1:61
    resignation from, 1:141–143, 145–146
    in cataloging Judaica collections, 1:8–9
    on history of shofar, 1:18–19
    on *Jewish Encyclopedia,* 1:89–90, 99–101
    as member of editorial board, 1:76–77
Adler, Elkan, letter to, 2:55–58, 67–68
  library of, transmittal of to Jewish
    Theological Seminary, 1:390–391;
    2:55–58, 67–68
Adler, Herman, letter to, 1:186–187
Adler, Max, letter to, 2:312–313
Adler, Racie (Friedenwald), letters to, 1:84,
    94, 98, 110–113, 115–116, 146–147,
    198, 225, 229, 234–236, 324–325,
    363–370; 2:19, 139
  wedding plans of, 1:110, 115–116
Adler, Sarah (Wolfinsohn), 1:324, 400;
    2:78–79, 81–82, 176, 305, 315
  marriage of, 2:232
Adler, Sarah Sulzberger, 1:3, 116
  letters to, 1:20–32, 34–35, 37–51, 52–54,
    63–69
Aeronautics, Adler's interest in, 2:149–150
Ahad Ha-Am, 1:189
Albright, William F., 2:169–171
Alliance (Jewish agricultural colony), 1:195
Alliance Israélite Universelle, Adler's attitude
    toward, 1:47; 2:6–7
  schools of, 1:44–45
America. See *United States.*
(*The*) *American* (Philadelphia weekly), 1:4
American Academy for Jewish Research,
    2:165
  fund of, for publishing scholarly works,
    2:54–55
  publication of Malter's Ta'anit Talmud
    method by, 2:106
American Hebrew, editorial policy of, 1:139
  letter to editor of, 1:70–71
American Jewish Committee, Adler as
    president of, 2:174
  successor to, 2:370–372

American Jewish Committee (*Continued*)
Adler's threatened resignation from,
1:296–297
Adler's views on, 1:299–300, 384–386,
2:368–369
and convening of American Jewish
conference, 1:267–269, 307, 310–311
as representing all American Jews,
1:267–269, 276–284
attack on, by Stephen Wise, 2:349–350
connection of, with *Der Tog*, 1:256–257
Executive Committee of, Adler as
chairman of, 1:175
financial problems of, 1:142
formation of, 1:126–127
Mayer Sulzberger's resignation as president
of, 1:216–217
meeting of, with President Taft, 2:40–41
misconception of purpose of, 1:135–136
non-observance of Sabbath by, 1:230–231
nonpartisan policy of, 1:247–248
on American Jewish Congress issue,
1:267–272, 276–284, 286–287,
290–292, 304, 331–333
opposition of, to World Jewish Congress,
2:274
plan for organization of, 1:122–124
policy of, on boycott of Germany, 2:274
political statements of, 1:272–273
reaction of, to outbreak of World War I,
1:253–254
to Palestine riots (1929), 2:172–173
reassessment of Balfour Declaration by,
1:338
Relief Committee of, distribution of funds
by, 1:325
politics in, 1:309–310
postwar work of, 1:359–360
sponsorship of Joseph Jacob's work by,
1:312
vs. anti-Semitism, in US, 1:400–401; 2:8–11
of Nazis, 2:261–262
vs. immigration bill, 1:213–215, 246–247
vs. Louis Lipsky, 1:226–227
vs. Turkish visa policy, 1:230
vs. Zionists, 1:212–213, 259–261, 267–269,
276–284
work of, at London Peace Conference
(1913), 1:219–222, 224–225
for abrogation of Russian treaties, 1:185,
192, 195–196, 198–201, 213–215, 252

American Jewish Committee (*Continued*)
work of, for Eastern European Jews,
1:384–386
for Jews in the Balkans, 1:231–232
for passage of Senate anti-German
resolution, 2:277–278
for refugee asylum, 1:133–134
for Russian Jews, 1:219–220; 2:136–137
for Yemenite Jews, 1:226–227
American Jewish conference, 1:267–269
convening of, 1:307, 310–311
first meeting of, 1:314–315
American Jewish Congress, 1:327–328
acceptance of, by American Jewish
Committee, 1:290–292
Adler's dissatisfaction with, 1:291–292,
312–314, 326
American Zionists' advancement of,
1:276–284
and public demonstrations against Nazism,
2:261–263
call for, 1:269–271
controversies involving, 1:273–274,
358–360
convocation of (1918), 1:354–356
movement toward, 1:271–272
on endangerment of Jews overseas,
1:292–293
on Polish situation at Paris Peace
Conference, 1:367–368
postponement of, 1:333–334
revival of idea of, 1:267–269
American Jewish education, 1:182, 345–346
American Jewish Historical Society, 1:13
and Lyons collection, 1:150, 177–178;
2:305–306
formation of, 1:19–20
funding for, 1:182–183
meetings of, 1:110; 2:228–229
work of, 1:153–154
American Jewish history, 1:18
need for graduate fellowship in, 2:228
need for scholarship in, 2:24–25
American Jewish Joint Distribution Committee. See *Joint Distribution Committee*.
American Jewish press, inadequacy of, 1:306
American Jewish scholarship. See also *Jewish
scholarship*.
and Adler's proposed Jewish University of
America, 1:320–323
and *Jewish Encyclopedia*, 1:76–77

American Jewish scholarship (*Continued*)
  bibliographic resource for, 1:209–212
  contribution of Solomon Schechter to,
    1:297–298
  development of, 1:182
    at Jewish Theological Seminary,
      1:113–114
  need for improvement of, 1:70–71
  pursuit of, at non-Jewish institutions,
    1:263–264
American Jewish Year Book, 1:381–382
American Jews, aid of, to European Jews,
    2:6–7
  to Falashas, 2:142–143
  to German Jews, 2:292–293
  and Allied alliance with Russia during
    World War I, 1:264–266
  and anti-Semitism, 2:8–10, 70, 329–330
    Nazi, 2:261–263
    Polish, 1:342–343
  confused state of organizations of, 2:127
  educational quotas for, 2:54
  effect of publicity on, 2:275
  establishment of parochial schools for,
    1:227
  membership of, in armed forces, 1:351
  mention of, in US government documents,
    1:85–86
  need for national assembly of, 1:126–127
  need for published biographies of, 2:162–163
  need for restoration of synagogue and home
    by, 2:255–256
  organization representing, 1:202–204
  political position of, 2:286
  relationship of, to US and to Palestine,
    2:33–34
  research on US government action on
    behalf of, 1:111–112
  resentment of, by European Jews, 2:5
  soundness of, 1:396
  suspected of Bolshevism and radicalism,
    1:386–387
  synagogue worship of, 2:89–90
  US appointment of racial advisor for, 1:356
American Journal of Theology, letter to editors
    of, 2:7–8
American Judaica, Lyons collection of,
    1:177–178
American Oriental Society, 1:14–15
American Philosophical Society, future
    development of, 2:249–251

American School of Oriental Research
    (Jerusalem), 1:154; 2:169–171
  attack near, 2:178–180
  funds for, 3:306
American Sephardic Jews, union of
    congregations of, 2:76–78
Anglo-Jewish Association, influence of, in
    Jerusalem (1891), 1:44
Anti-Semitic, use of term, 1:166
Anti-Semitism, American, 1:166; 2:16–19
    response of American Jews to, 2:261–263,
      329–330
  epidemic of, on European continent, 2:348
  German, 2:88–89
Antonius, George, 2:320–321
Arlosoroff trial, 2:283
Armed forces, moral training of, 1:393–396
Aryan race theories, 2:260
Asch, Sholem, 1:302–304
Ashkenazic Jews, influx of, to Jerusalem
    (1891), 1:35–37
Auerbach, Harry Jeremiah, 1:139–140
Austria, attitude toward Jews in (1891), 1:153

Bachrack, Herman A., letter to, 2:352–353
Balfour Declaration, 1:338–339
  Adler's views on, 2:49
Balkan Jews, 1:231–232
Balkan Wars of 1912–1913, 1:219–220
Baltimore, Russian Jews in, 1:32
Baltimore Hebrew College, 2:121–123
Basle Congress, first, 1:73–75
Basle platform, 1:339–340
Bearsted, Lord, letter to, 2:313–314
Becker, James H., at Paris Peace Conference,
    1:370
  European rehabilitation plans of, 1:29
Beilis case, 1:238–240
Bentwich, Norman, letter to, 2:180–181
Berkowitz, Henry, letters to, 1:135–136, 326
Berman, Jeremiah J., letter to, 2:316–318
Bernhard, Hubert J., letter to, 2:353–355
Bernstein, Herman, letters to, 1:216, 252,
    257–258; 2:70
Bialik, Hayyim Nahman, 2:125
Bible, reading of, in public schools, 1:139
  study of, at Dropsie College, 1:159
  translation of, by Jewish Publication
    Society, 1:154, 171–173
    meeting of Board of Editors of, 1:177,
      234–236

German Jews (*Continued*)
    boycott on Germany as harm to, 2:282
    fine imposed on, by Nazi government,
        2:355–357
    migration of, 2:311–312
    pogroms against, 2:282–283
    position of, in Nazi Germany, 2:201
    refugee problem of, 2:263, 292–293,
        308–309
Germany, 2:276–277
    and US immigration laws, 2:267
    annexation of Austria by, 2:346–347
    anti-Semitism in, 2:88–89
    attitude toward Jews in (1891), 1:53
    political situation in, 2:273–275
    possibility of massacres in, 2:304–305
    propaganda attacks on, 2:300–302
    public opinion on events in, 2:272
    US treaty with, 2:41–43
Gerson, Felix N., letter to, 2:287
Gibson, Hugh, effectiveness of, 1:373–374
    on Polish Jews, 1:370–372, 376–377
Gildersleeve, Basil, letter to, 1:86
Gilman, Daniel Coit, letters to, 1:16–17,
        50–51, 54–55, 59, 61
Ginzberg, Asher, 1:189
Ginzberg, Louis, letters to, 2:11–13, 92,
        141–142, 155–156, 258
Ginzburg Library, of Hebrew University,
        2:303–304
Glueck, Nelson, 2:364–365
Goldhizer, Ignaz, dinner in honor of, 1:15–16
Goldman, Solomon, letter to, 2:113–114
Goldsmid, Osmond D'Avigdor, letters to,
        2:136–137, 349–350
Gompers, Samuel, 1:342–343
Gottheil, Richard, letters to, 1:73, 76–77,
        153–154
    move of, to Palestine, 1:153–154
    vacant university post of, 2:320–321
Gratz College, as normal school, 1:115
    curriculum of, 1:75–76
    development of, 1:16–17
    progress of, 1:190
Greenburg, Simon, letter to, 2:329–330
Greenfield, Albert M., 2:66
Gregorian calendar reform, 2:222–223
Guggenheim, Daniel, and Jewish Theological
        Seminary, 1:91
Guggenheim, Harry F., promotion of
        aeronautics by, 2:149–150

Guggenheim, William, letters to, 2:342–343

Haifa Technikum, 1:189, 258–259
    Adler as trustee of, 1:154
    affiliation of, with Hebrew University,
        2:155
    language of instruction in, 1:243–244,
        252–253
    merger of, with Reali high school, 2:213,
        222
Haller's Army, anti-Semitism of, 1:388
Halper's Catalog, 2:171
Haluka, 1:48
Hamdi Bey, Osman, 1:50
Hapgood, Norman, 1:301–302
Harris, Bernard, letter to, 2:37
Harvard University, Jewish quota at, 2:54
Haupt, Paul, 1:55
    as Adler's teacher, 1:4
    conservatism of, 1:4–5
    interpretation of psalms by, 1:7
    letter to, 1:14–15
    plan of, for Jewish colonization in
        Mesopotamia, 1:74–75
Haym Solomon Memorial, 2:116–117
Hebraica collection, at Library of Congress,
        1:209–212
Hebrew language, 1:4–6
Hebrew printing press, in US, 1:325, 392–393
Hebrew Union College, 1:140
    contribution of, to American Judaism,
        1:360–361
    relations of, with Jewish Theological
        Seminary, 1:102
Hebrew Union College Monthly, on Wise's
        centennial, 1:360–362
Hebrew University, 2:96, 246, 249
    Adler's thoughts on, 1:330–331
    administration of, 2:221–222
        proposals for, 1:233–234; 2:150–151
    affiliation of, with Haifa Technikum, 2:155
    as degree-granting institution, 2:245–249
    Board of Governors for, 2:130–131
        character of, 2:298
        meetings of, 2:154–155, 280
    constitution for, draft of, 2:127–128
        revision of, 2:284
    establishment of, 2:58–65
    Ginzburg Library of, 2:303–304
    Institute of Jewish Studies at, 2:90–91,
        109–110

Jewish Theological Seminary (*Continued*)
    and traditional Judaism, 2:89–90
    criticism of, by Mordecai Kaplan,
        2:25–27, 79–81, 139
    as authority for conservative
        congregations, 1:167
    building plans for, 1:97–98; 2:71–74,
        151–152
    curriculum for, planning of, 2:366–368
    Deficit Fund of, 1:191
    Elkan Adler Library of, purchase of, 1:390;
        2:55–58, 67–68
    faculty salaries for, 2:92
    financial condition of, 1:383–384; 2:92–93,
        151
    future direction of, 1:397–399
    interdenominational studies at, 2:363–364,
        367–368
    Jewish architect for, 2:152
    library building for, 1:191; 2:75, 147
    merger of Seminary Association with
        Board of Trustees of, 1:90–93
    opening of, 1:7
    progress of, 1:113–114
    quality of instruction at, 2:50
    relations of, with Dropsie College,
        1:128–130
        with Hebrew Union College, 1:102
    representative body for, 1:397–399
    Society of Jewish Academicians as rival to,
        1:317–319
    theology instruction at, 2:11–13
    union of, with Isaac Elchanan Theological
        Seminary, 2:123–124
Jewish University (Jerusalem). See *Hebrew
    University*.
Jewish University of America, Adler's
    proposal for, 1:320–323
Jewish War Veterans, 2:273
Jewish Welfare Board, 1:385
Jews. See also *Judaism* and under nation or
    nationality, e.g., *American Jews*.
    as a race, 1:336–337, 356; 2:276
    Ashkenazic, influx of, to Jerusalem (1891),
        1:35–37
    from New York. See *New York Jews*.
    Sephardic. See *Sephardic Jews*.
    social history of, 1:336–337
Jews' College (London), 1:187
    Adler at Literary Society meeting of,
        1:25

Johns Hopkins University, Adler's work for,
    as fundraiser, 1:187–188
    as instructor in Semitics, 1:19
    resignation from, 1:61
    as student, 1:3–4, 8
    endowment fund of, 1:187–188
    exhibit of, at World Columbian
        Exposition, 1:59
Joint Distribution Committee, 2:271
    Emergency Fund of, and Palestine, 2:172
    emergency relief meetings of, 2:357
    foreign representatives of, 2:46–47
    fundraising of, for German Jews, 2:260
        for Palestine reconstruction, 1:391–392
        for placement of scholars, 2:264
        with Zionists, 2:117–118
    relations of, with World Jewish Congress
        (Poland), 2:343–344
        with Zionist relief workers, 1:259–261
    relief workers of, as advisors in Europe,
        2:271
    resentment of, by European Jews, 2:5
    work of, for reconstruction in postwar
        Europe, 1:352–354; 2:23
    reorganization of, 2:48–49
Judaica collection, at Library of Congress,
    1:209–212
Judaism, and "Back to the Synagogue"
    movement, 2:4
    Conservative. See under *Jewish Theological
        Seminary* and *United Synagogue of
        America*.
    in America, Jewish Theological Seminary
        serving needs of, 1:113–114
    in modern world, Adler's views on, 1:61–63
    Jewish people as vehicles of, 2:209
    neglect of, by Zionists, 1:338–341
    Orthodox, union of, in US, 1:175
    Reform, 1:217–218. See also under *Central
        Conference of American Rabbis* and
        *Union of American Hebrew
        Congregations*.

Kahn, Bernard, 2:153
Kaplan, Mordecai, 1:166, 308
    and Teachers' Institute, 1:197
    at Jewish Theological Seminary, 2:139
    controversial views of, 2:25–27, 79–81
    letters to, 2:29–31, 79–81
    paper by, on function of synagogue, 2:29–31

Kaufman, Edwin, as administrator of
Students' House (New York),
1:396–397
letter to, 2:25–27
Kaye, Joseph, letter to, 2:286
Kehillah (New York), 1:145, 256–257
Kellogg Treaty, 2:159
Ketubah, 2:157–158
Khan es-Sheik Mohammed, 1:45
Klatzkin, Jacob, letter to, 2:125–126
Klausner, Joseph, 2:93–94
Kohler, Kaufmann, 1:349–350
work of, on *Jewish Encyclopedia,* 1:99–100
Kohler, Max, letter to, 1:166
Kohut, George Alexander, 2:165
and National Jewish Welfare Board,
1:334–336
letter to, 2:228–229
Kristallnacht, 2:355–356

Lachman, Samson, letter to, 2:173–175
Lake Placid Club, 1:112
Landau, Jacob, letter to, 2:145–146
Langley, Samuel Pierpont, Adler as
biographer of, 1:237–238
airship expedition of, 1:102–103
as recipient of honorary degree, 1:63–67
death of, 1:127–128
letters to, 1:71, 78–79, 96–97
Oxford travels of, 1:63–69
Laski, Neville, letters to, 2:276–277, 300–302,
310–311, 350–351, 355–356,
357–359, 361–362
Lauterback, Edward, letter to, 1:228–229
Lazaron, Morris S., letters to, 2:207–208,
261–263
Lazarus, Josephine, 1:61–63
League of Nations, forming of organization
similar to, 2:369
importance of, in 1920 political campaigns,
2:18–19
J. G. McDonald as Relief Commissioner of,
2:278–279
joining of, by US, 2:14
need for, 2:49
Western Wall Commission of, Adler as
representative to, 2:181–183
Adler's Memorandum for, 2:197–198
Leavitt, Julian, letter to, 1:301
Lederer, Ephraim, letter to, 2:114–115
Lehman, Irving, letter to, 2:270–273

Leventhal, Bernard L., 1:175; 2:123–124
Levin, Shemaryahu, 1:189, 313
letter to, 1:258–259
Lewin, Benjamin, 2:54–55
Lewisohn, Leonard, death of, 1:97
Lewy, Julius, 2:320–321
employment of, in America, 2:289–291
Library of Congress, Judaica/Hebraica
collection of, 1:209–212
Lipsky, Louis, 1:226–227
London Peace Conference (1913), 1:219–222,
224–225
Lyons, Jacques Judah, 1:177–178

Mack, Julian W., as president of Zionist
Organization of America, 1:348–349
letters to, 1:216–217, 248–249, 263–264,
348–349; 2:33–34
Magnes, Judah L., and American Jewish
Congress policy, 1:299–300,
329–330
and Palestine politics, 2:185–187
as administrator at Hebrew University,
2:82–85, 101–102, 150–151
fundraising trip of, for Hebrew University,
2:115–116
letters to, 1:161–165, 168, 212, 232, 272,
299–300, 329–330; 2:44, 46, 82–85,
90, 101–102, 109, 126, 130, 185–189,
194, 198, 304, 340
personality of, 1:316
resignation of, from Temple Emanu-El,
1:190
Maimonides, works of, definitive text of,
2:164
publication of, 2:155–156
Malter, Henry, research method of, for
Ta'anit Talmud, 2:105–106
criticism of, 2:164
Margolis, Max L., 1:234–235; 2:165
death of, 2:244
Margulies, Samuel Hirsch, 1:206–207
Marriage, Jewish, Adler's views on, 2:156–158
Marshall, James, letter to, 2:153–154
Marshall, Louis, 1:229
address by, on Russia and American
passport, 1:192
advice of, on Adler's Palestinian
memorandum, 1:344–345
as critic of Israel Friedlaender's lectures,
1:266–267

Taft, William H. (*Continued*)
  interview of, with American Jewish
      Committee members, 2:40–41
  letter to, 2:118
Tariff bill (1909), 1:160–161
Teachers' College, establishment of,
      1:174–175
Teachers' Institute, 1:197
Technical Institute at Haifa. See *Haifa*
      Technikum.
Technikum. See *Haifa Technikum.*
Teller, Morris, letter to, 1:319
Temple Emanu-El, resignation of Judah L.
      Magnes from, 1:190
Thesaurus of Jewish Poetry, 2:107–108
Thomas, Wilbur K., letters to, 2:269–270,
      368–369
(Der) Tog, 1:256–257, 264–265
Treaty of Versailles, refusal of terms of, by
      US, 2:41–43
Tulin, Shaia D., letter to, 2:89–90
Turkey, Adler's visit to (1894), 1:67–68
  and resettlement of Jews in Palestine (1891),
      1:49–50
  issuance of visas to Jews by, 1:230, 236–237
  Jewish immigration to, 1:159–160
  Jewish refugees in (1928), 2:153
  Jews in, after Balkan Wars, 1:219–220
  Oscar Straus as ambassador to, 1:159–160
  Zionist movement as unfair to, 2:211–212
Turkish revolution (1908), effect of, on Jews
      in Palestine, 1:168–169

Union of American Hebrew Congregations,
      1:52–53
  as unrepresentative of American Jews,
      1:108–109
Union of Soviet Socialist Republics. See *Russia.*
United Kingdom. See *England.*
United States, anti-Semitism in, 2:269–270
  relations of, with Germany, 2:265–268,
      297–298, 355, 357
United States National Museum. See
      Smithsonian Institute.
United Synagogue of America, founding of,
      1:204–205, 222–224
Unna, Isak, letter to, 2:193–194

Vaad Leumi, 2:299

Versailles Peace Conference. See *Paris Peace*
      Conference.
Vollbehr, Otto, anti-Semitism of, 2:270

Wailing Wall, Adler as representative to
      League of Nations Commission on,
      2:181–183
  Adler's Memorandum on, 2:191–192,
      194–195, 197–198
Waldman, Morris D., letters to, 2:263, 329,
      343–344, 368–369, 370
Warburg, Felix M., as supporter of Chaim
      Weizmann, 2:219
  death of, 2:340–342
  letters to, 2:120, 172, 175, 177, 204–207,
      213–219, 221–223, 245–249, 264,
      279–281, 282–285, 296–300, 303,
      307, 318, 325–329, 331–334, 337
  memorial for, 2:344
  on aid to German scholars, 2:264
  on British options in Palestine, 2:337–338
  on course of action during Palestine riots
      (1929), 2:172–173
  on creation of Jewish state in Palestine,
      2:334
  on Jewish Agency finances, 2:204–207
  resignation of, from Executive Council of
      Jewish Agency, 2:214–219
Warburg, Frieda, letters to, 2:344, 347–348,
      364–366
  on career of Nelson Glueck, 2:364–366
  on memorial for Felix Warburg, 2:344
Warburg, Fritz, 2:356
Warburg, Max, letter to, 2:315–316
Weil, Irene, letter to, 2:348–349
Weiss, William, letter to, 2:297–298
Weizmann, Chaim, 2:172–173, 221, 316
  absenteeism of, as president of Hebrew
      University, 2:246, 249
  and Adler's Memorandum on Wailing
      Wall, 2:183–185, 191–192, 197–198
  Felix Warburg as supporter of, 2:219
  letters to, 2:183–185, 189–192, 197–198,
      210–213
  on Palestine situation, 2:210–213
Western Wall. See *Wailing Wall.*
William, Maurice, letter to, 2:311–312
Wise, Isaac Mayer, 1:360–362
Wise, Stephen, 1:217–218
  criticism of Adler by, 2:349–355

Temple Israel
Minneapolis, Minnesota

IN MEMORY OF
MICHAEL B. ALCH
FROM
JUDIE & STEPHEN ELSTON